Biophysical Measurement in Experimental Social Science Research

Theory and Practice

Edited By

Gigi Foster

ELSEVIER

ACADEMIC PRESS

An imprint of Elsevier

Academic Press is an imprint of Elsevier
125 London Wall, London EC2Y 5AS, United Kingdom
525 B Street, Suite 1650, San Diego, CA 92101, United States
50 Hampshire Street, 5th Floor, Cambridge, MA 02139, United States
The Boulevard, Langford Lane, Kidlington, Oxford OX5 1GB, United Kingdom

Library of Congress Cataloging-in-Publication Data
A catalog record for this book is available from the Library of Congress

British Library Cataloguing-in-Publication Data
A catalogue record for this book is available from the British Library

ISBN 978-0-12-813092-6

Publisher: Candice Janco
Acquisition Editor: J. Scott Bentley
Editorial Project Manager: Barbara Makinster
Production Project Manager: Maria Bernard
Designer: Christian J. Bilbow

Typeset by SPi Global, India

Biophysical Measurement in Experimental Social Science Research

Dedication

For my mother.

Contents

Contributors

Numbers in parentheses indicate the pages on which the authors' contributions begin.

Tom Beesley (1,279), Department of Psychology, Lancaster University, Lancaster, United Kingdom

David John Butler (167), Griffith Business School, Griffith University, Gold Coast, QLD, Australia

Stephen L. Cheung (167), School of Economics, The University of Sydney, Sydney, NSW, Australia

Weili Ding (225), Queen's University, Kingston, ON, Canada; NYU-Shanghai, Shanghai, China

Jonas Fooken (305), Centre for the Business and Economics of Health, The University of Queensland, Brisbane, QLD, Australia

Gigi Foster (267), School of Economics, University of New South Wales, Sydney, NSW, Australia

Ben Hardy (105), SOAS University of London, London, United Kingdom

Niree Kodaverdian (47), Pomona College, Claremont, CA, United States

Mike Le Pelley (1,279), School of Psychology, UNSW Sydney, Sydney, NSW, Australia

Steven F. Lehrer (225), Queen's University, Kingston, ON, Canada; NYU-Shanghai, Shanghai, China; National Bureau of Economic Research, Cambridge, MA, United States

Anthony Newell (149), Queensland University of Technology, Brisbane, QLD, Australia

Lionel Page (149), Queensland University of Technology, Brisbane, QLD, Australia

Stacey L. Parker (305), School of Psychology, The University of Queensland, Brisbane, QLD, Australia

Daniel Pearson (1,279), School of Psychology, UNSW Sydney, Sydney, NSW, Australia

Stuart N. Soroka (85), University of Michigan, Ann Arbor, MI, United States

Benno Torgler (197), Queensland University of Technology, Brisbane, QLD, Australia

Agnieszka Tymula (31), School of Economics, University of Sydney, Sydney, NSW, Australia

Foreword

In this timely book edited by Gigi Foster, nine teams of researchers bring us up to date with the frontiers in biophysical measurement. The gravity point is economics-oriented applications and experiments but the net is cast wide, covering neural processes, eyes, sweat, steroids, genes, and social communication. Each chapter hints at the larger field beyond economics in which biologists, psychologists, and marketers have been slaving away with these techniques for decades, if not centuries.

In this Foreword I review the nine chapters individually, focusing on the key question of whether the methods discussed in each chapter are truly useful for economics and the progress of our societies. I argue that many of the discussed techniques have promising futures, but that these futures will involve interests and designs that differ from how they are used and presented in much of the current literature. We researchers may think we own the future of our devices, but once created they become part of the larger, ancient dance of power.

Beesley, Pearson, and Le Pelley tackle eye trackers in Chapter 1. The field of eye-tracking is ancient, as one does not, in principle, need a machine to monitor eye movements. With the introduction of machines, eye tracking improved but limitations persisted due to needing to hold the head fixed and requiring a very controlled environment in order to know where individuals are looking. Automatic tracking on small devices has improved by leaps and bounds in the era of laptops and mobile phones, and this means that it has become very cheap to track where individuals look in very defined environments, such as when they are looking at screens that have an eye-tracking camera.

The authors express the hope that new techniques will soon allow us to use eye-tracking everywhere. There are limitations to how much data we can collect outside of laboratory settings because the problem remains that the researcher cannot track everything in the general environment outside of a lab, which means the researcher does not know what people are looking at. Yet, even "in the field" we can learn some things from just tracking the eye itself rather than the object of its focus. Gaze and blink intensity measure mental concentration, for example, which can be a useful means of tracking whether students or employees are paying attention.

The speed with which eyes are drawn to particular images on a screen apparently tells us how rewarding some signals seem, offering marketers a means of finding out how to maximally annoy us with advertisements. Most importantly, the eyes and the face betray our emotions, which means emotional tracking of whole populations without the need for surveys may eventually come into view (so to speak).

An interesting topic to come out of the eye-tracking literature is the general point that humans react more quickly than they can reflect, moved by value-measuring systems that make judgments we are not consciously aware of. Our eye is literally drawn to what we desire (or fear). We also seem to learn subconsciously, finding patterns in images that we cannot articulate but that nonetheless help us decipher subsequent images, a finding that provides some basic knowledge of learning processes. This evidence of humans' reliance on quick systems to make decisions should make us a bit humbler about claiming that individuals are conscious maximizers.

In Chapter 2, Tymula reminds us that both monkey brains and human brains think in terms of reward functions, not preference maps, showing the empirical failure of the choice axioms invented in the 1930s through to the 1950s that claimed the existence of such maps. Tymula also makes the case that perceptions and valuations change with context, essentially because our mental systems are set up to notice and exploit local differences in stimuli, rather than absolute levels. She thus courageously notes that the basis for microeconomics should shift towards context-dependent value functions rather than nonexistent fixed preference maps. As Clark, Frijters, and Shields (2008) note, the preference theories of the 1930s and 1940s have never been used because preferences maps cannot be measured. We now know this is because they do not exist, and by implication that the field of preference axioms should now be recognized as a failed theory, consigned to history.

In Chapter 3, Kodaverdian talks us through the use of fMRI, which essentially treats blood flows measured in brain regions as indicators of mental activity. Like Tymula, Kodaverdian notes how looking at brain activity makes it clear we think in terms of reward values, not preference maps. Moreover, the brain adapts its signal-response intensity to the circumstances, a reference-dependence that fits ancient theories of social status already noted in the writings of Adam Smith and Karl Marx, but is still avoided in most of mainstream economics because it reduces the importance of economic growth as a measure of human progress. If it is relative rather than absolute signals that drive reward, then as growth increases we will adapt to higher levels of input, rather than feeling better off in the long run as a result of those higher levels.

Kodaverdian is a bit less strident than Tymula in drawing implications for economists' fundamental approach to modeling decision-making, focusing more on specific theories like that of Kahneman and Tversky (1979) who point to the difference between subjective and objective probability, as well as the issue of regret. Kodaverdian claims that neuroscientific evidence supports these scholars' theories, which is debatable: the studies she quotes do not find an exact correspondence of any kind between subjective and objective probabilities. The core problem is that there is just too much noise in actual laboratory data to validate theories in any but the crudest sense. The key implication from examining the neuroscientific evidence through the lens of subjective-versus-objective probabilities is that choices depend upon how problems are presented, and that a lot goes on in the choosing brain that does not fit any existing published theory.

Kodaverdian is hesitant to drive home the theoretical implications of her claim that things such as discount rates and preference maps do not really exist in the brain. She focuses more on whether neuroscientific evidence supports making various distinctions, such as between risk and ambiguity, between regret and disappointment, and between risk aversion and betrayal aversion. This call for the recognition of many distinctions is reminiscent of the growing lists of behavioral anomalies claimed by researchers in behavioral economics more generally. This creates a very different problem for those wishing to understand aggregate behavior, which is that we do not have the analytical tools to deal with so much diversity. Simplifications have their uses, and from a scientific perspective it would be helpful to be advised about the degree to which certain simplifications are more or less reasonable than others.

In Chapter 4, Soroka talks us through the use of skin conductance as a measure of emotional arousal (good and bad), an approach underpinning the 160-year-old field that gave us the lie detector. The big selling point of using skin conductance is that it measures the arousal level of the subconscious and thus is somewhat independent of the face someone displays. The disadvantages are that there is a one-to-three second delay between stimulus and response, that there is huge natural variation between individuals and across individuals over time, and that it is not obvious which emotion is being measured (although additional analysis of just what is in the sweat helps to address that limitation). The measures one can derive from this technique are thus very noisy.

The main point Soroka makes is similar to that made in the preceding chapters: individuals often make quick emotional judgments outside of their more reflective deliberations, and then rationalize those judgments afterwards. Soroka illustrates a particular example of how skin conductance could be used to optimize the content of negative political advertising to have maximum impact, a use to which it might be put already by marketing companies.

Hardy tells us in Chapter 5 about the measurement of steroids such as cortisol and testosterone, which have very different effects at different parts of the life cycle—in utero, in adolescence, in adulthood, and in old age. He also points out just how variable steroid levels are across humans, over various cycles (day/night, menstrual), and in response to factors such as diet and quality of sleep. After convincing us that steroids are one of the most variable measures of almost anything, he details the role of steroids in preparing humans for immediate action.

Perhaps the most interesting story in this chapter is Wingfield's "challenge hypothesis", that holds that men (but not women) see testosterone levels rise when facing a challenge, increasing further for the winner and reducing for the loser. This matters because it shows how levels of motivation change over time and are socially mediated (in this case, winning is largely in the eyes of others). It, of course, also suggests a means for the powerful to suppress the rest: that is, by giving them testosterone-reducing chemicals. I seem to remember this was indeed suggested in the 1960s among radical American politicians as a means of pacifying particular groups.

In considering what we have learned about steroids that is of real value for future scientific discoveries, Hardy points to the literature suggesting that stock-market bubbles are caused by testosterone-charged male traders, a literature whose natural conclusion is that we should replace them with females or suppress their testosterone if we want to avoid bubbles and their subsequent crashes. It is disappointing commentary on this field if 80 years of studying steroids has led to the simple conclusion that the vagaries of financial markets are just a function of traders' testosterone, not the type of regulation applied to these markets or the role of these markets in the whole economic system.

In Chapter 6, Newell and Page walk us through the research on "interoceptiveness", which essentially means how good someone is at guessing their own heart rate, interpreted in this nascent field as a proxy for awareness of one's internal body processes. The authors document how more interoceptive people are better than others at many cognitive and social tasks, concluding based on the existing evidence that traders who are more interoceptive appear to get better financial results.

The literature review in this chapter highlights a problem with studying very small phenomena in isolation from the larger context in which they occur: the bigger phenomena that are also in play can become "black-boxed" and reset to very conservative representations. This reductionism of the larger picture in service to emphasizing the importance of the small phenomenon under study can in fact regress science, and as such, it is the most alarming aspect of present social scientific research using biophysical measurement. This is something Kahneman (2003) warned us of in his article on the contribution of psychology to economics. As an example, Newell and Page's chapter points to the Efficient Market Hypothesis as the "accepted theory" of economics about how financial markets work, and then reviews evidence suggesting that interoceptive people beat the market, running counter to the implications of the EMH's oversimplified view of how markets operate. By implication then, we could manipulate markets by selecting traders on the (supposedly fixed) trait of interoceptive ability, a potentially seductive suggestion that crowds out the attention that might otherwise be paid to adjusting other aspects of financial markets.

Butler and Cheung's presentation in Chapter 7 goes even further. The authors acknowledge the large degree of uncertainty and the conflicting findings of different studies, but they still review a series of authors who suggest that it would help significantly to adjust what are likely to be small aspects of the problem in the grand scheme of things, such as to have fewer male financial traders. Neither the authors nor the papers they review appear to seriously entertain the idea that financial booms and busts might have everything to do with the system and nothing to do with the particular traders, which is what the disciplines of finance and economics have argued for 300 years. The authors' presentation, reflective of the view taken in many papers in the literature in this field, is captured in their section on market design:

> *Human traders, in particular the young males who dominate the world's trading floors, face a maelstrom of emotions when facing risk and reward … cortisol and testosterone have an inverted U-shaped dose response curve for performance. Financial markets must thus navigate a tightrope of instability, seeking to avoid waves of optimism and pessimism that threaten to sweep away these young males with consequences for us all. To limit the damage caused by market instability, can we engineer the choice architecture of financial markets to be safer for human traders, as we design cars with myriad safety features to be robust to human drivers?*

Note the implicit view that financial phenomena are driven by traders, rather than by other, larger aspects of the system such as regulations or incentives.

In their narrow focus on hormones and gut feelings, the subliteratures reviewed by Hardy, Newell and Page, and Butler and Cheung accentuate each other in that all three omit mention of the intricate theories of financial markets in the theoretical and empirical literature that has burgeoned after the GFC (e.g., the works of Piketty, which essentially propose a rent-seeking theory of financial markets). The findings reviewed in these chapters should be seen not as pointing the way to a brave new world in which chemical or neurological differences explain whole-system movements, but rather as curiosities whose marginal impact on important phenomena is surely dwarfed by the impact of major institutional factors. Keynes' interest rate theory, 300 years of economic thinking about the structure of markets, Basel III, Glass-Steagall, the interplay of incentives for banks and investors, the concept of limited liability and the seniorage role of printing money all go far further, individually and together, in explaining our world. The omission of such ideas may leave the undiscerning reader of these literatures with the idea that financial markets are much simpler than they really are, and the overly simplistic notion that the booms and busts we have had for the last 200 years across the capitalist world are the mere by-product of employing the wrong traders. Hoping to avoid bad macro-level financial shocks by selecting individual market actors with particular levels of circulating chemicals and psychological traits is akin to hoping that wars might be avoided by replacing all the men staffing the military tanks, planes, and ships of the world with women.

When they ignore big institutional factors—a virtual necessity when operating in a controlled experimental laboratory—researchers who find that biophysical markers such as hormones and interoception relate to individual traders' actions can risk being dismissed in monetary and financial circles. To be of more use, researchers looking to explain whole-of-financial-market dynamics need to work on the boundary of our understanding of markets, for instance by focusing more on the psychology of the revolving door between financial markets and their regulators (i.e., interrogating the temptations of power).

In Chapter 8, Torgler helpfully discusses new portable devices that social scientists have been using to measure the heart rates, conversations, feelings, and choices of people in their daily lives. I am personally most excited by the "sociometer" developed and used by an MIT group led by Alex Pentland. The portable devices involved can be worn by a whole community and, inter alia, can be used to analyze the content and effects of conversations.

A particularly interesting aspect of this is the possibility of measuring bilateral power relations using the fact that, on average, the subservient partner in an interaction uses a higher pitch and speaks faster while the more dominant partner speaks more slowly and deeply. Coupled with measures of emotional arousal and content recognition, this insight offers the possibility of mapping power relations in defined communities like villages, and especially inside organizations. I can see a huge potential here for employers and social researchers to finally crack the perennial problem of just how to measure power relations in a complex environment. I can also see how this could be used for good (e.g., to measure who is being bullied) or bad (e.g., to more effectively bully).

In Chapter 9 Lehrer and Ding discuss the burgeoning world of genetics, including Genome Wide Association (GWA) studies. The authors provide a helpful summary of how researchers now measure the "genetic distance" between pairs of individuals, essentially by counting how many of the millions of known genetic mutations present in a population are shared between them. These genetic proximity scores can then be used to see how involved genes (G) are in educational attainment, IQ, crime, and other socially important outcomes and abilities.

While the authors are clearly optimistic about the eventual ability of this field to understand not merely social science's traditional preoccupation with the importance of "environment" (E), but also how that environment interacts with the unique DNA of every individual (G*E), I was particularly struck by the limitations of this field. After hugely expensive studies involving millions of respondents, the field at point of writing is reportedly only able to explain no more than 0.43% of educational outcomes with only 72 genetic mutations, and furthermore cannot yet explain how these 72 work. Given that discussions of heritability have been around since Francis Dalton over a century ago, this is a somewhat meager outcome. It is clear from reading the chapter that we have not yet come close to solving the G*E puzzle.

Lehrer and Ding usefully discuss many aspects of the brave new world of genetic predictions, including genetic price discrimination and mate selection. I want to add another one that requires no new techniques at all: to identify suboptimal nurturing of children. If all other inputs are optimized to suit the individual needs of every child, then the "genetic lottery" of Lehrer and Ding should explain all remaining variation in outcomes across those children once they become adults. This is indeed close to true for the middle classes, where the heritability of traits that have both genetic and environmental predictors, such as IQ and height, is around 80% (Turkheimer, Haley, Waldron, d'Onofrio, & Gottesman, 2003)—but it is apparently not true for the socioeconomically disadvantaged, for whom factors other than genes help to explain a very significant degree of the variation in outcomes.

This central finding can be flipped around and interpreted as saying not only that there is progress still to be made with disadvantaged children, but also that middle-class parents already know reasonably well how to nurture their (heterogeneous) children. Researchers might not know how to get the most out of a particular set of genes, but apparently many parents and communities do. Genetic measurement as a means of figuring out which people have more potential than their background has so far revealed seems to me the key application for the future, with wide implications for the state as well as for private organizations. Note that progress in this direction requires neither an understanding of which genes work, nor how they work, nor the specific details of G*E interactions.

A broader reflection on these nine chapters is that the subfields they review mainly look at the type of choices that economists have traditionally been uninterested in: what humans choose in a short space of time that is of limited value, such as the choice between a pear or an apple, or the choice between this stock or another. While such choices lend themselves to laboratory work, economists traditionally have been more interested in how to build systems, particularly systems in which people make drawn-out interactive choices such as organizing production, influencing politics, relocating, and bargaining over resources. Those choices crystallize over years, requiring extensive communication and coordination with others, and each individual act of communication, coordination, or choice is implicitly deemed to be too micro-level to be capable of explaining whole-of-system outcomes.

Marketers, not economists, are interested in questions such as which fizzy drink consumers prefer. Have the seductive limitations of the laboratory reduced "standard economics" to querying simple bilateral choices made in minutes, if not seconds? If this is true, it is of course partially the fault of economics, with its universalist pretentions embedded in the terminology of "preference axioms". Those pretentions were always waiting to be knocked down, and now they have been. Considering the main job of practicing economists, however, which is to design and think of whole systems, the main value to date of lab experiments has been to keep economists honest about the inadequacy of any behavioral assumption. Economics should go back to trying to discover what is likely to be "vaguely right" and steer clear of any pretense of discovering "precise" truth.

Stepping back even further, one might initially despair about the future of biophysical studies in the social sciences, which have attracted huge funding for decades with as yet no broad insights gained apart from keeping us honest about the fact that humans are far more complicated than any theory our discipline has so far put up. Following the policy prescriptions found in some of these literatures would promote a regression to very simplistic default theories of human behavior, such as that men make bad financial traders, big brains think more, and unknown genes matter for behavior.

From this perspective, the entrance of biophysical measurement techniques into social science has so far been mainly destructive, not constructive: researchers have been busy debunking the claims of others rather than building up new "vaguely right" claims that might be useful for understanding the system as a whole. The chapter on genes is the most optimistic about the eventual development of revised theories useful in understanding whole systems, but this subfield still has only little to show so far. Much of the literature seems caught in a classic focusing illusion: if all you study is a particular lump of cells or chemicals, you eventually find yourself arguing that the fate of the world hinges on the constituents of that lump. The whole middle bit of humanity that is too messy to study in the lab with these methods—unstructured interactions between millions of individuals influencing and manipulating each other—becomes lost from sight. Yet, just as the building of bridges is not applied quantum mechanics, so too is economics not applied physiology.

Can it be otherwise? We will never understand the economy by studying every single gene and neuron, but can we envisage a structural place for these techniques? I think the answer is "yes" and urge the researchers presently working in these fields to think much bigger. Consider some possibilities.

I imagine that 10 years from now it will be standard for cities and countries to measure the emotional state of school children and whole populations by means of computerized assessments of camera pictures, based on the link between facial/eye expressions and emotions. This is potentially a powerful tool, useful for grand social experiments and as a means of evaluating our leaders' policies. I also imagine that analyses of collected sweat, urine, and data on social interactions will become standard ways for companies and states to gauge things like aggregate drug use, stress levels, bullying, and political discontent. Genetic measurement will be useful in determining who has more potential than has been revealed so far, indicating suboptimal parenting or other suboptimal social investments in those people. Portable fMRI seems to carry good potential for use in schools and other learning environments to track developmental progress in emotion and cognitive abilities.

These uses will not be controlled by academic researchers and will also not necessarily be conducted for the common good, but they have one thing in common: they are on a massive scale and oriented towards big questions such as how well a population is doing, rather than towards explaining the choice between a pear and an apple. These applications are furthermore all in the realm of using measurement tools to aid the evaluation of long-term goals and feasible interventions to achieve them, not of whether a picture of a wombat leads to more neurons firing in the brain than a picture of a mouse.

In conclusion, I learned a lot from this book about the current state of play in biophysical measurement. The main function of work in these fields so far, it seems clear, has been to keep the rest of us honest by pointing out that pretty much any theory of human behavior is demonstrably wrong if you look closely enough. Yet, at present, the social scientific literature drawing on biophysical measurement risks regressing our understanding of higher-level phenomena because the effort involved in learning how the supermicro works seems to come at the expense of being able to simultaneously understand the macro and the meso. I predict that the economic and political system will nevertheless find quite prominent places outside the experimental laboratory for biophysical measurement techniques in the medium term, particularly automatic emotional recognition from visual and chemical cues. The literature reviewed in this book, and its two appendices that usefully walk us through the huge practical difficulties and interpretational uncertainties related to eye tracking (Pearson, Pelley, and Beesley) and heart rate variability (Fooken and Parker), will then be helpful background information regarding the limits and characteristics of the various measurement techniques that one might select from the toolbox.

Paul Frijters
London School of Economics

REFERENCES

Clark, A. E., Frijters, P., & Shields, M. A. (2008). Relative income, happiness, and utility: an explanation for the Easterlin paradox and other puzzles. *Journal of Economic Literature*, *46*(1), 95–144.

Kahneman, D. (2003). A psychological perspective on economics. *American Economic Review*, *93*(2), 162–168.

Kahneman, D., & Tversky, A. (1979). Prospect theory–analysis of decision under risk. *Econometrica*, *47*(2), 263–292.

Turkheimer, E., Haley, A., Waldron, M., d'Onofrio, B., & Gottesman, I. I. (2003). Socioeconomic status modifies heritability of IQ in young children. *Psychological Science*, *14*(6), 623–628.

Acknowledgments

Simon Graham and Brendan Wilson provided excellent editorial and research assistance in preparing this volume.

Chapter 1

Eye Tracking as a Tool for Examining Cognitive Processes

Tom Beesley*, Daniel Pearson† and Mike Le Pelley†
*Department of Psychology, Lancaster University, Lancaster, United Kingdom, †School of Psychology, UNSW Sydney, Sydney, NSW, Australia

INTRODUCTION

Our eyes are the window to the surrounding visual world and our sight is one of our most precious senses. Indeed, we experience a more intimate connection with vision than with our other senses—for example, our consciousness seems to reside behind our eyes (rather than in our ears, mouth, or fingertips). We carry out visual processing seemingly without significant effort, and typically feel as if we are in total control of how we choose to direct our vision from one moment to the next. Yet the complexities involved in our eye movements are largely opaque to introspection, and only truly reveal themselves through detailed measurement and analysis. Eye tracking tools are now commonplace in the laboratories of experimental psychologists. Recording the position of a person's gaze, often hundreds or thousands of times per second, can provide rich and precise data on the mechanisms and time course of cognitive processing. The analysis of eye movements in modern experimental research provides a surreptitious window into human sensitivities, desires, and biases. These tools have transformed cognitive psychology from the fields of visual perception, language processing and reading, to cognitive development, and many more. Here we describe the basic components of eye movements, the environmental factors, and internal cognitions that control these eye movements and why they occur. Through examples from empirical research, we demonstrate how the different components of eye movements can be used to make important inferences regarding cognitive function, exemplifying the benefit these methods can have for experimental psychology.

HISTORY AND MEASUREMENT

The ophthalmologist Louis Émile Javal (1839–1909) is widely credited with being the first to undertake a detailed, scientific analysis of eye movements.

Biophysical Measurement in Experimental Social Science Research. https://doi.org/10.1016/B978-0-12-813092-6.00002-2

By closely examining the eyes of people reading text, Javal noticed that their eye movements had a characteristic stop-start pattern of motion. The movement of the eyes would not sweep continually along the lines of text, but instead would flit seemingly from word to word as the text was read. This characteristic pattern of eye movements was later confirmed with the use of primitive "eye tracking' devices, first by Edmund Huey (1870–1913), and later in the pioneering work of the Russian psychologist Alfred Yarbus (1914–1986). Yarbus and colleagues developed some of the very first methods for precisely measuring eye movements. These extremely invasive systems involved anesthetizing the eye and placing a suction cup directly onto the surface. A mirror, attached to the suction cup, moved in concert with the eye, and by tracking a light reflected off the mirror, Yarbus could observe a rich display of the eye's movements across a scene. Examples of his famous demonstrations of the eye's "scan paths" across a visual scene are shown in Fig. 1, where the observer is given the same scene but with different instructions as to what information has to be gathered. Yarbus began to explore eye movements that were made when people viewed various visual stimuli (such as pictures of social scenes, or individual faces), examining the correspondence between movements elicited on repeated observations of the same image by a single observer, and the clear individual differences in eye movements between observers. Not only did Yarbus pioneer a successful technique for tracking the movement of the eyes, but he began to make the first notable connection between the patterns in these scan paths and the underlying psychological processes that gave rise to them.

Eye tracking techniques and equipment have continued to be developed and refined up to the present day. Modern systems provide rich and accurate data on eye movements with remarkable temporal resolution, and little or no discomfort to the participant (indeed, participants may not even be aware that their eyes are being tracked). These advances in technology, both in terms of the hardware used for recording gaze and the software for processing and analyzing the resulting data, have led to an explosion of interest in eye tracking for both research and commercial use. Even an experience as mundane as ordering a pizza in a restaurant can now be (supposedly) enhanced with the aid of eye tracking technology, with claims that gaze patterns can be used to deduce customers' topping-preferences before customers are even consciously aware of them (Henderson, 2014).

Modern eye trackers come in a variety of forms, but typically involve illuminating the eye using infrared light and recording it with an infrared camera. Computerized image analysis is then used to provide an accurate assessment of the changes in the orientation of the eye in space, and from this, the location of gaze on (for example) a computer monitor can be extrapolated. Eye tracking products differ in terms of how they are used in practice. Some trackers need to be mounted to the head (see Fig. 2 for an illustration of such a device), with cameras filming the eye from below the lower eyelid, while others have recording devices embedded into a computer monitor. The latest technology has now

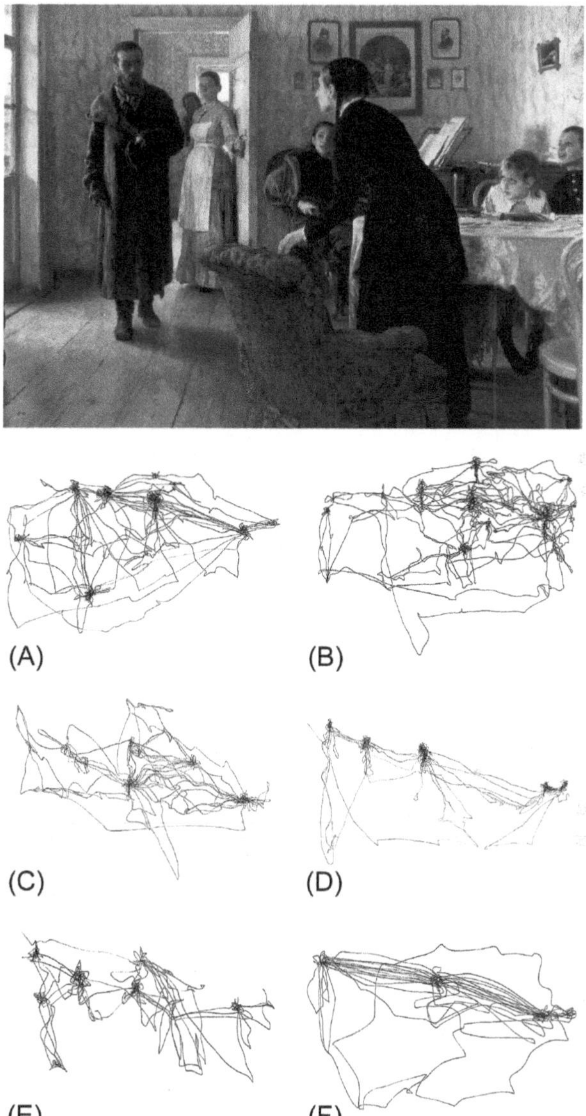

FIG. 1 The Unexpected Visitor, by Ilya Repin. Hand-drawn versions of scan-path data from Yarbus' study, courtesy of Julia Buntaine: www.juliabuntaine.com. Participants viewed the painting for three minutes under different instruction: (a) free examination; (b) estimate the material circumstances of the family; (c) surmise what the family had been doing before the arrival of the visitor; (d) give the ages of the people; (e) remember the clothes worn by the family; (f) estimate how long the unexpected visitor had been away.

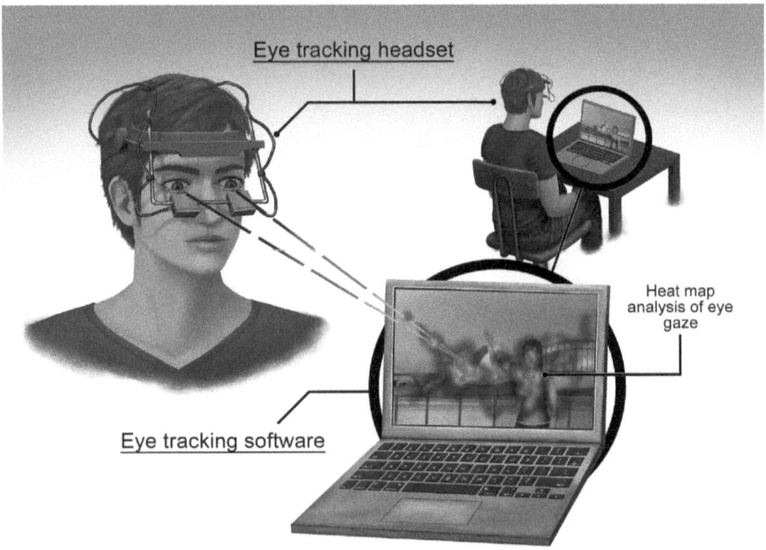

FIG. 2 An illustration of a head-mounted eye tracking and a heat-map analysis of eye fixations.

been miniaturized to the point that eye tracking systems can be embedded into laptop screens and even virtual reality headsets. As well as these practical differences, eye trackers vary in their technical abilities, such as how fast they sample the eye, the precision of recording measurements, and how quickly they send and receive data from a computer processing system. Appendix 1 contains a more detailed discussion of eye tracking hardware.

Before we review the benefits of eye trackers for social science research, we first discuss reasons why someone might *not* want to begin an eye tracking project. Eye trackers are still relatively expensive pieces of equipment for laboratories to purchase. The average computer workstation might set a researcher back $1000. With this workstation, a researcher can accurately measure manual responses made to visual stimuli. Combined with appropriate experimental procedures, this limited hardware allows the researcher to investigate all sorts of interesting questions about the processing of those stimuli to be investigated (e.g., by looking at the relative speed of one response compared to another). Eye trackers simply provide another way of studying visual processing by measuring the location of gaze, but they do so at a price; an eye tracking system suitable for research can cost anywhere from $15,000 to $100,000. In addition, using an eye tracker can require some expertise in computer programming. While many eye tracking systems will come with software that allows for the recording and analysis of eye movements "straight out of the box," most researchers will require a greater degree of flexibility, particularly in terms of the analysis of the resulting data (e.g., the data may require recalibration to stimulus positions, see Vadillo, Street, Beesley, & Shanks, 2015). Given that today's trackers can record eye movements at up to 2000 times per second, the resulting data files can be very large and often require custom analysis software to be written to parse the data. The financial cost of eye trackers may also lead to a cost in terms of time. For the price of a single eye tracker, a researcher may be able to instead buy 10 or more standard workstations. The resulting trade-off is between running 10 or more participants at a time on a study that does not require eye tracking (which may be finished in a week) or running one participant at a time on an eye tracking version of the same study (which may therefore take months to complete). These realities should be kept in mind when deciding if it will be useful to collect eye movement data in a particular study.

From Eye Tracking to Cognitive Science

What are the advantages of running an eye tracking study? Why is data on eye movements so important to experimental psychologists? Most psychology experiments measure behavior through recording overt intentional responses. Most commonly, these are keyboard responses made with the fingers, but could include written text or vocalizations by a participant. As an example, let us consider a *visual search task* in which participants have been given a target to search for (say, a letter "T") that is positioned within a scene that also contains several other objects that look similar to this target (say, a number of "L," "F," and "E" letters, known as distractors). In such a task, participants will be asked to press one response key if they detect the target in the search display, and another response key if the target is absent. The two critical components of the response are its *type* and its *timing*. We can use the response type to determine how accurately the participant was responding in the task, evaluating the proportion of times the "target present" key was pressed when the target was indeed present compared to when it was absent (i.e., hits versus false alarms). The timing of the response might also tell us something important about the underlying cognitive processes. For example, imagine that we increase the number of similar-looking distractor objects in the scene and we observe that the participant's response time increases. We might infer from this that perhaps more letters are being searched before the target is detected. This seems a natural conclusion, and is almost certainly right, but it cannot be inferred with certainty from the data collected. This is because response time, like response choice, represents a measurement at the terminal point of the psychological process. It comprises the accumulated time of all of the cognitive processing that precedes it, which may include (at least) the perception of the array of stimuli on the screen, the sequence of eye movements across the scene, the detection of the target, the decision about which response to make, and the execution of that response. An increase in response time might be attributed to a change in the time taken to complete any one of these steps in the chain of cognitive processes.

Due to these severe limitations in more traditional measurement of human behavior, eye movements can play a particularly important role in understanding cognitive processes. The recording of eye movements provides a continuous, real-time measure of stimulus processing throughout a series of cognitive processes. Eye tracking data provide moment-to-moment measurements of where the eyes are fixated throughout an experimental trial,[1] which may provide additional insight into the dynamic pattern of cognitive processes that were engaged during that trial. Gaze data also allow us to analyze, if we wish, particular sections of the visual search performance in our task. We may have a hypothesis that the L stimuli are viewed more than the E or F stimuli during the search process. Or we may be particularly interested in where the eyes move at the start of the trial when the stimuli are initially presented, or in evaluating how many distractors are fixated before a decision is made regarding whether the target is present (examining our initial intuition above). An analysis of eye movements will allow us to begin to answer these types of questions through isolating the processing that occurs in different periods of the trial.

Some of these questions about the contribution of certain psychological processes over a period of time might be answered by other means than an analysis of eye movements. Researchers could, for example, use clever experimental designs or sophisticated statistical modeling techniques to try to tease apart the contributions of each step in the chain. However, continuous eye movement data can provide a very compelling picture, not clouded by the complexities of these other techniques. At a basic level, a "heatmap" (see Fig. 3) of where the eyes were fixated most often during a trial procedure can provide an instant picture to aid the researcher in determining the cognitive processing that took place.

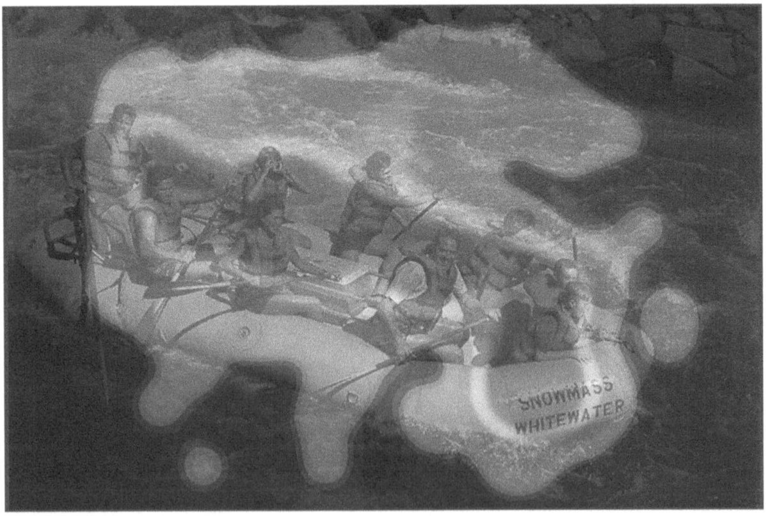

FIG. 3 A heatmap showing the density of eye fixations in space as observers view a photograph. *(Image courtesy of Olivier Le Meur (for details, see Le Meur, Le Callet, Barba & Thoreau, 2006).)*

1. The term "trial" here is intended to reflect the presentation of stimuli and the recording of a behavioral response. In typical experimental tasks, of the sort described here, many such trials will be used to minimize the effects of measurement error. Data from a set of trials are often grouped and analyzed in "blocks."

At a more granular level, what does eye tracking data enable us to deduce about cognitive processes? When we move our eyes across a scene, thus changing the sensory information falling on our retinas, our perception of that scene seems to change smoothly and continuously. Yet this experience is, to some degree, a trick of the brain's visual processing system. As Yarbus (1967) noted, eye movements are in fact a compilation of brief pauses known as fixations, and rapid eye movements, known as *saccades* (see Appendix 1 for a more complete discussion of the components of eye movements). Not only do these components of eye movements differ in their observable characteristics, but they fulfil different roles in information processing. Early work by vision scientists demonstrated that during a saccade from one stimulus to another, there is a general suppression of information in the visual system, such that the detection of objects that appear as we are making a saccade is impaired, or even abolished under certain conditions (e.g., Bridgeman, Hendry, & Stark, 1975; Volkmann, Schick, & Riggs, 1968). This "saccadic suppression" mechanism is important for maintaining a consistent visual percept. When the eyes are moved across a static scene, the location on the retina corresponding to every visual object will change. If visual input were active during this period, this would cause a flood of movement signals to inundate the visual processing system because all objects are moving from the perspective of the retina (see Fig. 4 for an illustration of the anatomy of the eye). The visual system would then need to devote significant processing resources in order to establish that it is the eyes that are moving, rather than (or in addition to) objects in the world. Suppressing visual input during a saccade effectively removes the need for this processing by censoring the period in which movement signaling occurs, and thus allows the visual system

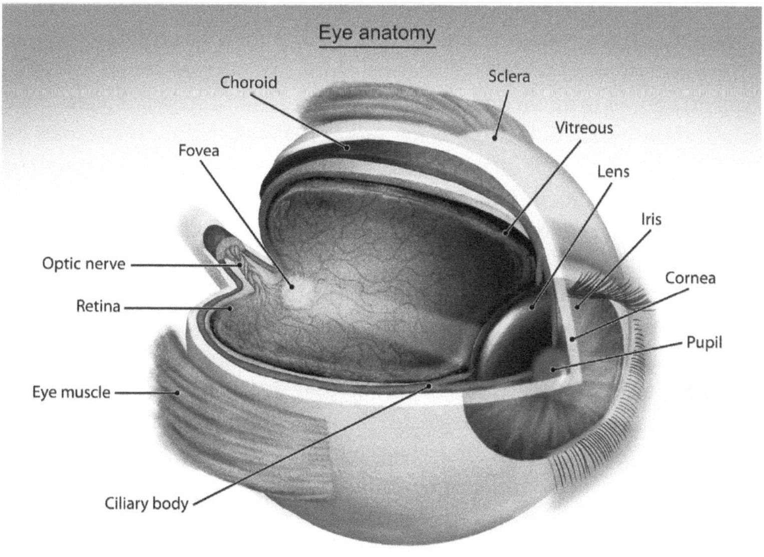

FIG. 4 The anatomy of the eye.

to more easily maintain a stable representation of the world. Many aspects of cognitive processing may be entirely restricted to periods of fixation. For example, it has been suggested that if a cognitive process such as object identification is interrupted by the initiation of a saccade, then object identification resumes only once that saccade is complete (Sanders & Houtmans, 1985).

It is perhaps unsurprising that saccadic eye movements and periods of fixation have different uses in the analysis of psychological processes. Due to the suppression of information processing during saccades, it is thought that fixations reflect the moments at which the observer is likely to be conducting meaningful information processing of a scene. Therefore, a great deal of experimental research has focused on the analysis of fixations, disregarding the moments where saccades occurred. Saccades on the other hand can provide an important measure of the selection of information and particularly the timing at which this information (i.e., a stimulus) comes to impinge on cognitive processing.

Before we discuss some typical uses of eye tracking in cognitive psychology, it is important to note one more limitation of studying eye movements. While fixations indicate those points in time and space at which observers are likely to be conducting meaningful information processing, this might not necessarily be the case in every instance of a fixation. It is quite possible to fixate your eyes while shifting your *attention* to another part of the environment. Try it for yourself; pick a word on this page to fixate and, without moving your eyes, shift the focus of your concentration to something far away from your chosen word, across the room in which you are sitting. This potential for decoupling of attention and eye movements has been studied extensively by cognitive psychologists. In what is now known as the classic "Posner cuing task," Posner and colleagues (e.g., Posner, 1980) asked participants to fixate on a central point, before an arrow appeared at that position, pointing either to the left or the right. After a short period, a target stimulus appeared on the screen, either in a position congruent with the direction of the arrow (e.g., to the left of a left-pointing arrow), or in an incongruent position (e.g., to the right of a left-pointing arrow). In these tasks, detection of the target is faster in congruent than incongruent positions, even though on each of these two trials, gaze was fixated on the central point of the screen. This demonstrates that we can maintain our gaze on a point of fixation, but nevertheless shift some of our processing resources towards another region of space.

Where does this leave us with respect to the measurement of eye movements? If the position of our eyes can be decoupled from the position of attentional processing, then what good is measuring eye movements? Thankfully, for the sake of research at least, the experience of decoupling one's eye position from attentional resources tends to be the exception, rather than the rule, of visual processing. As our demonstration will have illustrated, it takes effort to perform such a decoupling and, importantly, such a decoupling requires the eyes to be stationary; once the eyes are in motion, attentional processing and eye movements are tightly coupled (Deubel & Schneider, 1996). The upshot of this in practical terms is that for many types of experimental procedures, we can be confident that an analysis of eye position will provide a meaningful and accurate measurement of overt attentional processing. Nevertheless, the possibility of a decoupling of eye movements and attention, made possible by our ability to covertly attend to stimuli in the environment, is something that researchers should bear in mind when designing experimental procedures and when analyzing eye movement data.

EXAMPLES OF EYE TRACKING IN COGNITIVE SCIENCE

In this section we briefly describe some of the varied uses of eye tracking within experimental cognitive science and highlight the unique contributions that eye tracking technology has made to theoretical developments. This is then followed by a more detailed discussion of the use of eye tracking within the specific research area of attentional processing in human-associative learning.

Visual Search

First, we return to the simple example of understanding visual search behavior. This type of activity is fundamental to our daily lives: when we search for our keys in the morning, look for the TV remote at night, or scan for friends on a beach, we have to hold in mind a representation of a target object as we search and eliminate the distracting nontarget objects, often one-by-one until the target is located. Indeed, our health and safety can depend on the accuracy of visual search performance: think of radiologists searching X-rays for images of tumors, or airport security staff searching scans of suitcases for evidence of weapons or contraband. From a psychological perspective, the visual search task is certainly a nontrivial one, and there are a number of different perceptual and cognitive processes that are required for search to be efficient. For example, consider a difficult search task, such as finding one person on a beach full of hundreds of similar-looking people. In order to complete this task efficiently, we must avoid searching the same nontarget objects again and again in quick succession, because repetitive sampling of the same visual information does not provide a benefit and in many searches could lead to infinitely long search times. Instead it is better to move from one object to the next, searching for novel information that has not yet been processed. Our process of visual search does not appear to be random, but instead is controlled by mechanisms that constrain the possible objects that we might search next. "Inhibition of return" (Posner & Cohen, 1984) is one mechanism that has been proposed to operate, which simply stated is a mechanism that inhibits the further search of locations in visual space that have been recently searched, such that attention is prevented from returning to these locations in the future.

It is not straightforward to test whether inhibition of return occurs during visual search tasks (e.g., searching for a T among a group of L shapes) if we are restricted to using standard measurements of manual responses. One could have a second display of objects appear after the primary search has been completed and ask people to detect new stimuli (probes) that appear in positions that were previously occupied by the original search objects (e.g., Klein, 1988). However, the responses issued to these probes would come sometime after the original search has finished and so this test provides only an indirect test of inhibition of return. This test would therefore capture only the final or accumulated inhibition built up in the trial, but inhibition of return is likely to be a dynamic process that evolves over the course of search. This indirect method of testing the search process once it has terminated is therefore unlikely to give a complete picture of the underlying cognitive process.

Eye tracking provides a particularly useful measurement tool for examining this type of process, because, as we have noted, it provides a continuous real-time measurement of the search process that allows us to isolate the processing of each item in the display. As an example of this type of procedure and analysis, Gilchrist and Harvey (2000) tracked eye movements as observers searched for a target E shape within an array of 32 distractor letters. The researchers looked at the time between consecutive fixations on the same object, which allowed them to examine exactly when and how often objects were returned to during the search process. It was found that "refixations" of an object were very uncommon within the first 400 ms (approximately two fixations in this task) and which is comparable with a typical pattern of attentional processing in other tasks that have revealed inhibition of return (e.g., Posner & Cohen, 1984). Gilchrist and Harvey's data suggest that it was extremely rare for observers to fixate an object, saccade away from it, and then immediately re-fixate the object. Instead, several additional fixations are typically made prior to any return to the object. Thus, measures of eye movements provide compelling evidence of the operation of inhibition of return during visual search, where previous evidence, provided by more indirect means, had been less compelling. Furthermore, Gilchrist and Harvey's analysis provides a very rich data set; the inhibition of return process can be evaluated for each object that is fixated during search and not just at the terminal point of the entire search process.

Reading

The field in which eye tracking has arguably had the biggest impact in the cognitive sciences is the study of reading. By applying high resolution eye tracking techniques, researchers have been able to study the subtle eye movements that contribute to what becomes a very automatic behavior for the majority of people. A review of this literature is provided by Rayner (2009), but here we highlight just a few interesting findings which demonstrate the types of data and theoretical contributions that eye tracking has provided.

Expert readers—a group that includes most adults in developed countries—can rapidly process the visual patterns on a page and process them into meaningful linguistic information. The speed at which this happens gives the impression that we can take in many words at a time. Yet eye tracking reveals that reading is actually very effective even when we are restricted to a single word at a time. In fact, a number of "speed reading" programs claim to increase reading speeds by presenting individual words successively at a rapid rate (for an example, see http://www.readsy.co/). In the lab, eye tracking studies of reading can use real-time processing of eye movements to examine reading performance under conditions where word processing is restricted. For example, researchers can use data from the eye tracker to set a precise moving window around the point of fixation (this type of "gaze-contingent" task is discussed in more detail later). By doing so, it is possible to manipulate the size and position of this window, and therefore examine how these variables affect the accuracy and speed of reading. It has been observed, for example, that the reading of characters is biased to the right of fixation (at least for English readers) we take in just a few characters to the left of fixation, and four or five times that on the right of fixation (McConkie & Rayner, 1976).

Analysis of the pattern of eye movements under normal conditions also reveals interesting patterns in how words are processed. For example, as fixations run across the words of a sentence, the individual words on a line do not receive equivalent processing; eye tracking reveals that many words are in fact skipped as fixations jump between nonconsecutive words in a sentence. Analysis of the linguistic content of the words reveals that those words that are skipped tend to be function words, such as "is," "a," and "and," which suggests that these words that contain minimal semantic value are largely superfluous to the interpretation of text (e.g., "Larry fat cat sits mat" is largely interpretable without the addition of such function words).

Moreover, eye tracking has shown that semantic context influences the reading process. For example, Morris (1994) tracked participants' eye movements as they read sentences such as those below:

1. The friend talked as the person trimmed the moustache after lunch.
2. The friend talked as the barber trimmed the moustache after lunch.

Morris found that participants' gaze duration on the word "moustache" was significantly shorter when they read sentence 2 than when they read sentence 1. The critical difference is that, in sentence 2, "moustache" is semantically associated with a preceding word in the sentence ("barber"). The implication is that this preceding word automatically and rapidly activates its semantic associates, reducing the resources required for processing these associates if they are encountered subsequently (as occurs in sentence 2), hence speeding reading.

Similar findings of linguistic content (semantics) interacting with processing time are observed for reading garden path sentences, wherein a grammatically correct sentence presents a level of ambiguity resulting from different plausible local interpretations of word meaning. For example, in the sentence "The complex houses married and single soldiers and their families," the ambiguity that may initially arise is resolved by realizing that "houses," most commonly used as a noun, should here be interpreted as a verb. Analyzing eye movements allows researchers to investigate the time course of the linguistic processes implicated in parsing and disambiguating such sentences. Data suggest that readers fixate longer on critical disambiguating words and return to words that precede this ambiguous element (e.g., Frazier & Rayner, 1982). By analyzing the relationship between fixation durations and the syntactic structure of the material, it is possible to build more sophisticated process models of how eye movements are controlled during the process of reading (for a review, see Reichle, 2006).

One of the ultimate goals of reading and language processing research is to understand what happens when there are impairments in these skills, such as in the case of dyslexia. Eye movement data have also proved to be valuable here. It is now known that the sequenced pattern of eye movements is quite different in dyslexic and nondyslexic readers. Dyslexic readers exhibit longer fixations and shorter saccades, resulting in an overall pattern of eye movements that contains a greater number of fixations than observed in normal reading performance (e.g., Hutzler & Wimmer, 2004). This is coupled with slower reading times overall, but whether the unusual patterns of eye movements are a cause or result of dyslexia is unsettled.

In summary, the data provided by eye tracking have led to major advances in how psycholinguists understand the process of reading. The technological power of eye tracking systems has led to a major paradigm shift in the study of reading, shedding light on the mechanisms and processes of reading in ways that arguably would not have been possible with previous experimental techniques.

Infant Cognition

To see why eye tracking has also played such an important role in the study of infant cognition, consider first the difficult challenges a developmental psychologist faces when attempting to study how the mind of the infant functions and changes over time. Unlike for adult participants, it is often difficult or impossible for young children to verbalize their knowledge and beliefs about the world. It is also unreasonable to expect very young children to complete cognitive tasks suitable for adults. The sorts of tasks adults typically complete in psychology labs—whereby stimuli are presented repetitively for long periods, and manual responses are made—are clearly unsuitable for use with children; getting them to sit still for any test, let alone a boring one, is very difficult.

Eye tracking allows researchers to explore the preferences of very young children simply by assessing what they look at. It turns out quite usefully, that (other things being equal) infants show a preference for novel over familiar visual objects (Fantz, 1964). The more we present a single visual image to an infant, the less likely they are to look at that image compared to one that has not been previously seen. This simple "habituation" procedure demonstrates that some knowledge has been acquired by the infant; it demonstrates at least that the infant retains a memory of the familiar image, and this memory is sufficiently detailed to enable the familiar image to be discriminated from the novel image.

"Preferential looking" techniques have been widely applied as a research tool in developmental psychology. Here we will consider how it might be used to study the development of categorization; one of the basic components of mature cognitive processing in humans, and arguably in all animals. Categorization refers to the process by which ideas and objects are recognized, grouped, differentiated, and understood. It is an essential cognitive function because it stops us from treating each and every object we encounter as entirely unfamiliar. On a basic level, it allows us to transfer our knowledge appropriately; I do not treat each new banana I buy as different from the last, but rather I mentally group all bananas together as belonging to the same category. I can hence infer that they will share similar taste, smell, longevity, etc. This type of mental processing also allows for more flexible predictions about things that are unfamiliar. I have never eaten a jackfruit, but I have a fair idea of how it might taste from looking at its skin; I have never encountered a Bedlington Terrier, but I am confident as to what it might do if I throw it a stick. Learning how to partition the vast range of sensory information is not only required for efficiency, but is critical, even for newborns, so that they can execute appropriate behaviors at the right moments (e.g., crying, sucking, smiling).

How can these categorization processes be tested using procedures based on preferential looking? In adults, a standard way to test category knowledge is to present people with new test stimuli (probes) that contain properties that we want to examine and observe how they categorize these probe stimuli (e.g., are animals with spots more likely to be categorized as leopards or as tigers?). To the extent that there is overlap in the features of the probe stimulus and the participant's stored category knowledge, the participant will be inclined to classify that probe stimulus as a member of that category. We can conduct similar tests of category knowledge in infants if we assume that looking times correlate with the degree of overlap between features of the probe stimulus and the infant's knowledge of the category that has been built through previous experience. For example, Bomba and Siqueland (1983) conducted a study in which, during an initial "habituation phase," 3- and 4-month old infants were presented with a series of patterns of dots, in which the dots were formed into a simple geometric shape, such as a triangle. While the arrangement of dots presented in each pattern conformed to a triangular shape, each pattern varied slightly—e.g., the triangles varied in their internal angles and side lengths—such that several unique triangular stimuli were presented over the course of the habituation phase. The question then is to what extent the infants formed a mental representation of triangles over and above the instances of the individual triangles. One theory about the nature of category knowledge is that humans form mental "prototypes" of categories, represented by a single memory that reflects the most common or characteristic features of the category. To test this, Bomba and Siqueland examined preferential looking times for two shapes, one of which was a prototypical (equilateral) triangle, and the other a shape belonging to another category (e.g., a square). Both specific stimuli were novel—the prototypical triangle had never been shown during the habituation phase. Nevertheless, it was observed that infants were significantly less likely to look at the triangle than the other square; that is, they were less likely to look at the (novel) prototype of the familiar category. The implication is that exposure to specific examples of the category during the habituation phase led to infants abstracting general knowledge about the category of triangles, which in turn led to previously unseen examples of this category, and especially the "prototype" triangle, seeming somewhat familiar.

While such approaches based on eye tracking have proved very useful for examining cognitive processes in infants, they rely heavily on assumptions about what looking times mean in terms of the underlying hidden cognitive processing. Regarding Bomba and Siqueland's (1983) study of categorization, the interpretation offered above assumes that the looking preference for the novel prototype over the familiar prototype means that some category-level knowledge had previously been extracted. Alternative interpretations are possible. For example, perhaps the within-category differences between triangles are so slight as to render the prototype triangle indiscriminable, at least to an infant, from the instances encountered during the habituation phase. This account does not rely upon any learning of category-level knowledge, as differences in preferential looking times could result simply from the activation in memory of the individual training patterns that were seen earlier, rather than a unique prototype representation. Even if category-level knowledge was formed in the task, we are also far from knowing exactly what constitutes such knowledge, because all we know is that the familiar prototype is similar in some way to the other stimuli that have been experienced. While eye tracking provides a valuable source of measurement of infant preference, it does not provide a silver-bullet solution for unpicking the complexities of infant cognition (for further discussion of the pitfalls and restrictions of using preferential-looking data to make inferences about the operation of psychological processes, see Aslin, 2007).

Judgment and Decision Making

Eye tracking has been used widely to provide an "incidental" measure of how people form beliefs and execute decision responses. One of the most commonly observed findings from eye tracking research is that people tend to spend most of their time looking at information that has the highest utility. This is observed in the form of high-utility information receiving a greater number of fixations, as well as overall more looking time before other information is sought (e.g., Glaholt & Reingold, 2011). When deciding between different options, people's first fixation is more likely to be on the option that they will go on to choose.

Less surprisingly, they are also more likely to be looking at the to-be-chosen option at the time they make their choice (Krajbich & Rangel, 2011). Changes in the pattern of eye movements can hence be a consequence of decision making; we are more likely to look at options that we have decided are superior.

It has also been suggested that eye gaze may play a more active role in decision making, feeding into the decision making system and thereby influencing the choices that are made. That is, eye movements may also be a cause of changes in decision making. For example, Shimojo, Simion, Shimojo, and Scheier (2003) had participants perform a task in which they were shown a pair of faces on each trial and had to decide which face was more attractive. In a first experiment, participants viewed the two faces freely before making their decision. Consistent with Glaholt and Reingold's (2011) findings, during the viewing period participants showed a bias in eye gaze towards the face that they subsequently chose. This result is in line with the idea that choice influences gaze. Critically, in a subsequent experiment, Shimojo et al. manipulated the length of time that participants gazed at each of the faces in the pair by showing the faces one at a time, with one appearing for longer than the other. The researchers found that this manipulation of gaze influenced the decisions that participants made; they were more likely to choose the face that they had gazed at for longer. The implication is that biases in gaze can induce biases in preference (for more on this topic, see Newell & Le Pelley, 2018; Pärnamets et al., 2015). For anyone wanting to "nudge" our real-world preferences and decisions (politicians, advertising executives, etc.) an eye tracker may be a very useful tool.

How looking preferences relate to decision making is important not only for psychologists, but also for economists and marketeers, and eye tracking has had a long history in both commercial and academic spheres as a tool for measuring and understanding consumer decisions. As far back as the work of Nixon (1924), eye movements have been used to demonstrate that the size and layout of an advertisement affects the way in which viewers process it: what they pay attention to, and what they remember. Here we briefly describe two experimental tasks that have analyzed eye movement data in interesting ways in more applied settings.

Wedel, Pieters, and Liechty (2008) examined the effects of different processing goals on how people viewed advertisements taken from magazines. They hypothesized that the pattern of eye movements might be quite different if viewers were asked to memorize the content of the advertisement versus evaluate its content, or if they were asked to focus on a specific target detail versus focus on the global properties of the advertisement as a whole. Consistent with work-in-scene perception, Wedel et al. found that participants' initial viewing behavior tended to reflect a local processing state, with spatially dense groupings of fixations on specific details, before a transition was made to a global processing state, in which fixations were distributed more widely, thought to reflect processing of more holistic aspects of the advertisement. When asked to focus on memorizing or evaluating a specific target object, participants spent a greater proportion of time in the local processing state, compared to when asked to focus on memorizing or evaluating the advertisement as a whole. Interestingly, the instruction to memorize versus evaluate the advertisement or target feature also had a dramatic effect; memorizing the scene led to longer times in the local processing state, while the instruction to evaluate led viewers to spend longer in a global processing state. These eye movement data therefore reveal important details about the time course of different processing styles under intentional states of the viewer and could be used to redesign advertisements to maximize their effectiveness.

Up until this point, we have discussed how eye movement data can be useful in the examination of cognitive processes. Our next example uses pupillometry, which is the measurement of the size and reactivity of the pupil, provided by many modern eye trackers. Pupil size changes in response to the available light in the environment, but it is also known that cognitively challenging and stressful tasks lead to an unconscious dilation of the pupils. Pupil dilation therefore offers a surreptitious measure of cognitive effort or stress. Wang, Spezio, and Camerer (2010) used eye tracking to provide unique insights into how people make ethical decisions that affect the financial reward that others receive. In their task, participants were paired together playing a "sender–receiver" game. In this game, the sender transmits information about the current state of the game (states one through to five), that can either be truthful or misleading. The payoff for each player is determined by the action of the receiver, but the formulation of the payoff is different for each player. For the receiver, making an accurate prediction about the state provides the largest payoff, whereas the sender's payoff structure is such that, on some trials, the sender is inclined to mislead the receiver such that they overestimate the level of the state (i.e., guess three when the state is actually one)—this is beneficial for the sender but not for the receiver. Such tasks provide a nice experimental analog of real-world scenarios in which financial analysts seek to profit handsomely from exaggerating the value of financial products to clients. Wang et al. found that choice data unsurprisingly showed a high level of misleading advice provided by senders when it was beneficial for them to do so. Wang et al. also monitored senders' eyes to further examine the cognitive processes involved in their decision making. Most notable among their data were findings relating to the dilation of the pupil under different conditions. It is known that cognitively challenging and stressful tasks lead to a (unconscious) dilation of the pupils. Wang et al. also found this to be the case in their task; when senders were faced with a decision in which it was advantageous to lie (and in which they did in fact lie), pupils were more dilated compared to those trials in which lying was unnecessary. Moreover, the size of the lie—the difference between the communicated state and the true state—was positively correlated with pupil dilation.

IN-DEPTH EXAMPLE: ASSOCIATIVE LEARNING

Research in the field of associative learning has long considered the role that attention plays in shaping the learning process, and eye tracking has recently been used to great effect to answer specific questions on this theme.

Associative learning is the fundamental principle governing how mental representations become connected in memory and how they shape behavior. For example, in the famous case of Pavlov's (1927) studies of conditioning in dogs, a bell was rung each time food was about to be given to the dogs. Following repeat training of this kind, Pavlov noted that the ringing of the bell produced an anticipatory "conditioned response" in the dogs; salivation. In associative learning terms, the dogs had formed an association between the mental representation of the cue stimulus (the bell) and the outcome stimulus (the food). Once this association had formed, activating the representation of the cue (by ringing the bell) was sufficient to activate and retrieve the mental representation of the food even without food being presented, such that the cue elicited the appropriate response (in this case, salivating in anticipation of food).

Associative learning is thought to be the fundamental mechanism responsible for a vast array of behaviors in both human and nonhuman animals, underpinning much of our knowledge. For example, learning a language requires learning a set of associations between objects in the world (e.g., an apple), and the spoken and written forms of symbols (words) representing those objects. Associative learning also underpins many of our beliefs. For example, through experience we might form the belief that beer X is associated with a pleasant taste, whereas beer Y is not, that sunny weather is associated with crowds at the beach, or that politicians are associated with lying. Associative learning can also give rise to preferences. For example, expectant mothers commonly develop acute dislikes for certain foods that they have eaten at the same time as experiencing morning sickness. Similar effects are frequently reported by patients undergoing unpleasant medical treatments such as chemotherapy.

Learning, Blocking, and the Role of Attention

Researchers within the field of associative learning have questioned whether the learning process is shaped by the way in which we attend to events in the world, and this conjectured interaction between attention and learning has been investigated using eye tracking technology. For example, Beesley and Le Pelley (2011) trained participants with a task in which they learnt about the effects of drugs given to a fictitious patient. In Stage 1 of the task (see Table 1), participants learnt that treatment with chemical A led to nausea in the patient, and in Stage 2 that chemicals A and B also led to nausea. In a final test, participants are asked how likely they think it is that each of chemicals A and B—when used individually—will cause nausea. Unsurprisingly, participants report a strong belief that chemical A will cause nausea. However, participants typically do

TABLE 1 Design of the Study by Beesley and Le Pelley (2011)—Simplified

Stage 1	Stage 2	Stage 3
A—nausea X—headache	AB—nausea CD—headache	BD—dizziness

not tend to think that chemical B is likely to cause nausea, even though it has been paired with the occurrence of nausea many times (in Stage 2). This effect is known as "blocking"; the presence of chemical A blocks learning about chemical B during Stage 2. Blocking is one of the most widely studied phenomena in the field of associative learning and has been demonstrated in a wide range of animals including rats (Kamin, 1969), pigeons (Leyland & Mackintosh, 1978), honeybees (Blaser, Couvillon, & Bitterman, 2004), goldfish (Tennant & Bitterman, 1975) and snails (Prados et al., 2013). There are many theories that predict the blocking effect, and some of the more dominant theories suggest that the effect is a result of a change in the attention paid to the stimuli (e.g., Mackintosh, 1975; Pearce & Hall, 1980). These theories suggest that during Stage 1 of the task, participants learn that chemical A is a reliable predictor of the nausea, and then bias attention to that cue over chemical B during Stage 2 (as B is not a better predictor than A—it is redundant to the prediction). As a result of this attentional bias, chemical B is effectively ignored, and very little is therefore learnt about its relationship with nausea.

Using an eye tracker to record participants' gaze as they performed the blocking task, Beesley and Le Pelley (2011) were able to examine the role of attention in blocking, by measuring whether participants were more likely to direct their gaze (their "overt attention") towards chemical A rather than chemical B during Stage 2. This is exactly the pattern that was seen in the eye tracking data. As shown in panel A of Fig. 5, participants spent less time attending to the "blocked" cue B compared to both the "familiar" cue (A) and "control" cues that were novel during Stage 2 (C and D). This direct evidence from eye tracking provided a convincing demonstration that the blocking effect is, at least in part, attentional in nature (see also Kruschke & Blair, 2000; Wills, Lavric, Croft, & Hodgson, 2007).

Beesley and Le Pelley's study further examined the relationship between attention and learning in a third stage, in which cue B was paired with a control cue that had not received this "blocking" treatment in Stage 2 (cue D). These two cues were shown to predict a new reaction of dizziness in the patient. At the end of the task, participants were presented with each cue (B and D) individually and asked to rate how likely it would be for the outcome to occur given that cue alone. It was observed that people learned more about cue D than cue

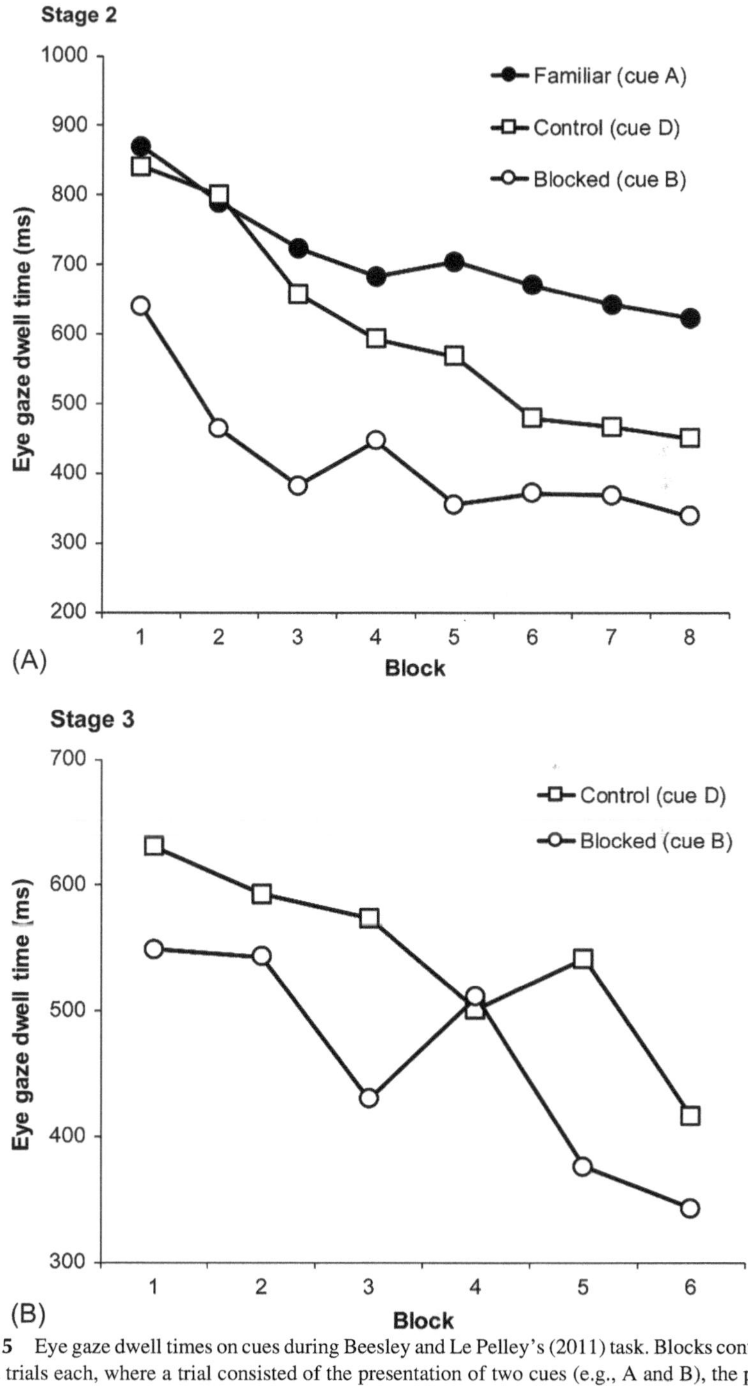

FIG. 5 Eye gaze dwell times on cues during Beesley and Le Pelley's (2011) task. Blocks contained eight trials each, where a trial consisted of the presentation of two cues (e.g., A and B), the participants issuing a response (e.g., "Nausea"), and the presentation of feedback (i.e., correct/incorrect).

B in this third stage (see also Griffiths & Le Pelley, 2009; Le Pelley, Beesley, & Griffiths, 2014; Le Pelley, Beesley, & Suret, 2007). Of critical interest here is the pattern of eye gaze to cues B and D during Stage 3, and how that related to how much was learnt about these cues. Fig. 5B shows that throughout Stage 3, participants also spent more time looking at cue D than cue B. The implication is that the bias in attention away from cue B, that was established in Stage 2, had a knock-on effect on the attention paid to this cue in Stage 3. Perhaps most importantly for attentional theories of learning (Mackintosh, 1975; Pearce & Hall, 1980), the extent of the bias away from cue B, and towards cue D, was positively correlated with the bias in learning during this stage; those participants showing the strongest attentional bias in their eye gaze data were the ones who learnt more about cue D over cue B. This result provides a nice demonstration of how eye tracking measures can consolidate our understanding of cognitive processing when used in tandem with traditional behavioral response measures.

Beesley and Le Pelley's (2011) study gives a clear demonstration of how eye tracking can provide a valuable complementary measure in behavioral tasks that would typically just measure response choice or response time. Eye tracking provided the ability to directly test the predictions of attentional accounts of blocking. It is also worth noting the value of the continuous nature of the eye tracking measure in this task. Fig. 5B shows how attention was distributed to cues B and D in Stage 3 of the task, plotted across the six training blocks of this stage. By measuring eye gaze throughout Stage 3, attentional processing can be monitored over the course of learning. One could alternatively collect response data to try to assess knowledge about cues B and D based on standard measurements. For example, we could ask participants what they believed B and D predicted (individually) after every training block, allowing us to draw a graph similar to Fig. 5B based on participants' reported knowledge. However, explicitly asking for this information may well have a considerable effect on behavior in the task. Prompting participants for their explicit judgments might alter the way in which they think about cues on the next trial (e.g., being asked what cue B predicts might prompt participants to focus more closely on learning about this cue in future, in a way that would not have happened naturally if they had not been asked). Eye tracking measures do not suffer from this type of problem, because once a calibration of the participant with the tracker is complete—typically at the very start of the task—the continuous recording and measurement of eye position can be completed in an unobtrusive manner.

The Automatic Capture of Attention by Reward

Beesley and Le Pelley's (2011) study demonstrates that an analysis of overall dwell time—a global measure of all fixations and saccades—provides a useful, broad measure of attentional processing that can yield insights into psychological processes. Finer-grained analyses of eye movements can provide a deeper understanding of the processes underlying our visual behavior. In an example of research using such an approach, Pearson et al. (2016) were interested in the effect of rewards on visual attention. If a mundane stimulus (say, a red circle) has been paired with rewards (e.g., money, food, or sex) in the past, does that stimulus become more likely to automatically grab our attention and dominate our behavior in the future? Understanding when people's attention will be captured, and what it will be captured by, is an important question. There are times when having our attention captured may be dangerous (e.g., while driving, we must try to prevent distraction by a roadside advertisement for a restaurant associated with tasty food), or harmful to health (e.g., an addict attempting to abstain from alcohol may try to ignore the bottles in the supermarket aisle—and a failure to do so may result in relapse: see Cox, Hogan, Kristian, & Race, 2002; Marissen et al., 2006; Wiers & Stacy, 2006). At other times, attentional capture is desirable; e.g., warning indicators in a plane's cockpit should be designed to attract attention as quickly as possible.

In their study, Pearson et al. (2016) used a visual search task in which, on each trial, participants were presented with an array of six objects on the screen and their task was to find the unique diamond among five circles (see Fig. 6). The task was controlled entirely with eye movements; participants simply looked at the diamond (known as the target) and once the eye tracker registered that their gaze had reached the target, the trial terminated. One additional layer of complexity was added to this otherwise simple task; on each trial, one of the circles was colored either red or green, with all other shapes (including the diamond) presented in gray. This brightly-colored circle was termed the distractor, and critically the color of this distractor signaled the size of the monetary reward that participants would receive for correctly making an eye movement to the target diamond. For half of the participants, if the distractor circle was red, then this signaled that a rapid eye movement to the diamond would receive a relative large reward (10 cents), whereas if the distractor was green, a rapid eye movement to the diamond would receive only a low reward (one cent). This relationship between colors and rewards was reversed for the other half of participants—i.e., for these participants, green was the high-reward color and red was the low-reward color. However, participants received their reward only for looking at the diamond target, not for looking at the colored distractor circle. In fact, the task was arranged such that if the eye tracker detected any gaze on or near the distractor circle before participants looked at the target, the reward that would otherwise have been delivered on that trial was canceled. Looking at the distractor was therefore counterproductive to participants' goal of maximizing their payoff. The worst thing a participant could do under these conditions is to look at a distractor in the high-reward color, because that resulted in loss of a larger reward. And yet that is exactly what people did. Over the course of the task, participants looked more at high-reward distractors than low-reward distractors. This difference cannot have been merely a consequence of participants' preference for one

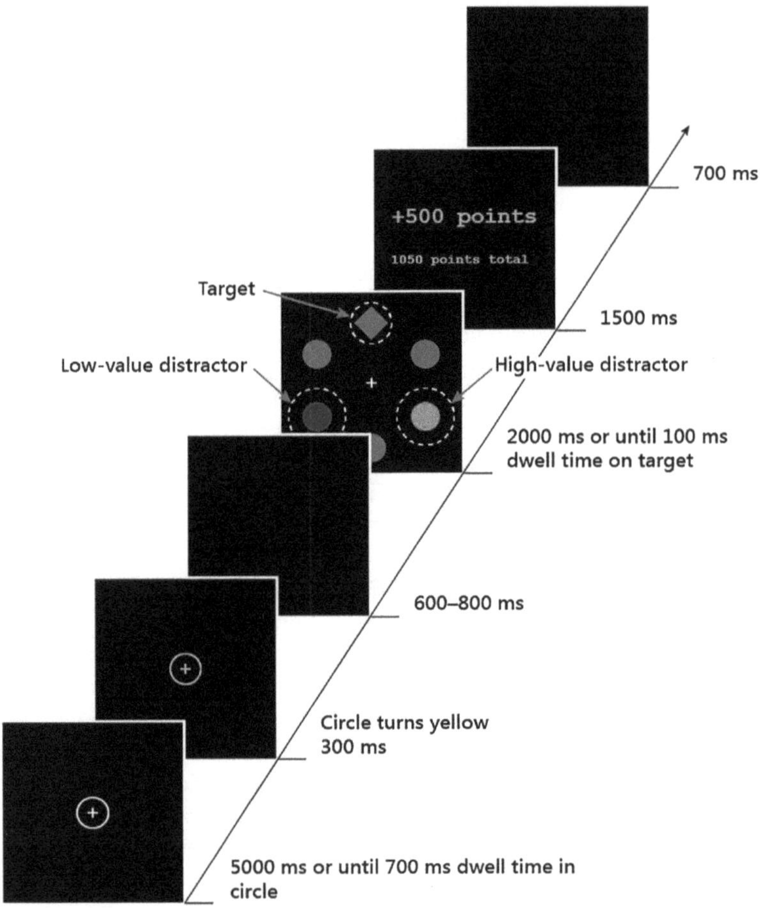

FIG. 6 The trial procedure of Pearson et al. (2016). Each square represents a part of the trial procedure. Participants were presented with a gaze-contingent fixation cross. Once gaze was registered in the center of the screen the fixation cross was removed and then followed by the search array. Participants moved their eyes to the diamond as quickly as possible. Reward was provided for accurate performance, the value of which was determined by the color of the distractor circle.

color over another, as the color of the high reward distractor was different for different participants (it was red for half of them, and green for the other half). Instead the findings must reflect the influence of people's experience of the rewards paired with each color. That is, it is more likely that gaze will be directed towards stimuli that have, in the past, signaled the availability of larger rewards—even if doing so results in a loss of reward! The broader implication is that we simply cannot help but look at things that tell us something nice might be about to happen. It is little wonder then that we struggle to avoid noticing those tempting treats in the supermarket queue.

Pearson et al.'s (2016) finding that high reward stimuli were more likely to capture eye movements (known as oculomotor capture) suggests that the extent to which we prioritize visual information is influenced by our previous experience with that information (in this case regarding rewards; supporting data using both reaction time and eye gaze measuresas provided by Le Pelley, Pearson, Griffiths, & Beesley, 2015). In subsequent analysis, Pearson et al. (2016) further explored the nature of this effect. In particular, they wanted to establish whether the effect of reward on attention reflected the operation of an automatic and involuntary process (in which the visual system prioritizes reward-related system in a "bottom-up" fashion), or a more controlled process wherein participants deliberately directed their attention towards reward-related stimuli in a "top-down" way. A hallmark of automatic influences on attention is that they are typically very rapid, whereas top-down influences are somewhat slower to take effect (Godijn & Theeuwes, 2002; Mulckhuyse, van Zoest, & Theeuwes, 2008). In an analysis of the time-course of the effect of reward on attention, Pearson et al. (2016) therefore focused on the very first saccade that participants made on each trial. In some trials, people would start moving their eyes very rapidly when the search array (the diamond and circles) appeared; that is, these trials had a short saccade latency. On other trials they would take longer to start moving their eyes, i.e., saccade latency was longer. Pearson et al. examined the direction of participants' first saccade as a function of its latency; the results of this analysis are shown in Fig. 7. This figure shows that, overall, participants' first saccade was more likely to go towards a high-reward distractor than a low-reward distractor—consistent with the findings described earlier. But notably, this influence of reward on oculomotor capture was most pronounced for the very fastest saccades that people made when the eyes started moving a mere 170 ms after the search array was presented. This shows that reward exerts an extremely rapid influence on behavior, suggesting that it reflects an automatic, bottom-up influence that operates at an early stage of the visual processing system. Fig. 7 also shows that the influence of reward on gaze was reduced at longer saccade latencies, suggesting that perhaps, given sufficient time, we might be able to prevent ourselves from having our behavior captured by reward-related stimuli—perhaps through the use of "cognitive control" processes (Kouneiher, Charron, & Koechlin, 2009; Miller, 2000; Posner & Snyder, 1975). Taken together, these results point to an interplay between rapid and automatic processes that promote capture by reward-related stimuli, and slower, more controlled processes that prevent it. These findings, and others like them (e.g., Luque, Vadillo, Le Pelley, & Beesley, 2017), shed valuable light on when we might expect stimuli to "take over" our behavior—which may have important implications for understanding and preventing maladaptive attentional biases, such as those associated with drug addiction (Field & Cox, 2008; Wiers & Stacy, 2006) and anxiety (Bar-Haim, Lamy, Pergamin, Bakermans-Kranenburg, & Van Ijzendoorn, 2007).

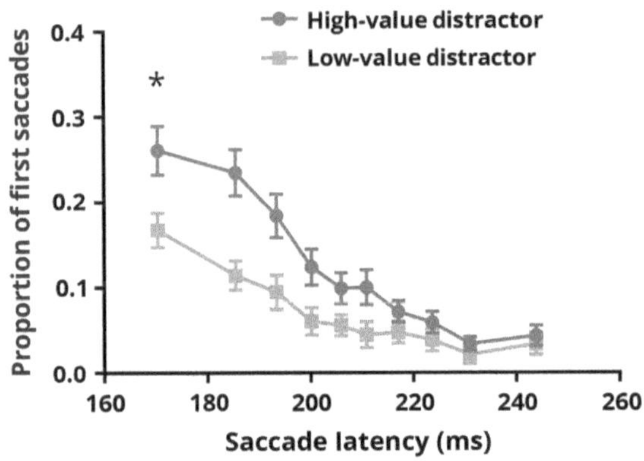

FIG. 7 Saccade data from Pearson et al. (2016), showing the proportion of first saccades towards the high value and low value distractors as a function of first saccade latency decile.

Gaze-Contingency

In this final section, we focus on the benefits of gaze-contingent eye tracking procedures for examining learning and attention. A gaze-contingent procedure is one in which eye tracking data are used to make changes to the task in real-time; events in the task procedure become contingent on the content of the gaze data. To achieve this, the gaze data are received by the computer system that is controlling stimulus presentation and then analyzed very rapidly (usually within a few milliseconds) to determine location, duration, and so on. The program then uses this information to make an adjustment to the procedure. It should be noted that gaze-contingent procedures will, somewhat inevitably, require a reasonable degree of technical expertise (see Appendix 1) to write custom routines that analyze data in real time to evaluate the characteristics of the eye data and determine the appropriate next step in the procedure.

We have already discussed in several places the benefits of gaze-contingent procedures: in studies of reading they have been used to control the number of words that are viewable at any one moment; in studies of infant development to control the presentation time of the stimuli; and in Pearson et al.'s oculomotor capture task, gaze-contingency was used primarily to determine the reward that was presented.

A gaze-contingent procedure can also be useful to help ensure that participants are performing a task in the way that we (as experimenters) want them to. For example, suppose we have a task in which, on each trial, we are going to present images scattered across the screen at various positions, and participants will be required to make a response (e.g., a button press, a spoken response, or an eye movement) to one of them—much as in Pearson et al.'s (2016) study described above. Under these circumstances, we would often want to be sure that participants begin the trial with their attention in the same place (typically the center of the screen), which makes it easier to compare performance between trials. For this reason, it is common to present a small image (often a cross) on the screen prior to the beginning of the trial, at the location where we want participants' attention to begin. Participants are asked to fix their gaze on this cross before the stimuli appear (hence this is known as the fixation period). Most participants will do this, most of the time. The question is what to do about occasions on which they do not—occasions on which their attention wanders prior to the trial, perhaps through boredom or because the participant is trying to second-guess where the stimuli will appear. Eye tracking can come to our aid here. One option is to take a passive approach. Here we record gaze during the fixation period and then, when the experiment is complete, we can analyze the gaze data offline to find those trials on which participants began the trial with their gaze on or near the fixation cross (we would include these trials in subsequent analyses), and those trials on which they did not (we would exclude these trials from subsequent analyses). This approach will work well, but the disadvantage is that if we have a particularly distractible or recalcitrant participant, we may end up discarding many trials on which the participant does not follow instructions and correctly fixate on the cross. An alternative is to use an active, gaze-contingent approach. Here we would record gaze during the fixation period and analyze the location of this gaze "online," perhaps once every few milliseconds. We can then keep the fixation cross on-screen (and delay the start of the trial) until we register that the participant is looking at or near this cross—the trial would then begin. The advantage of this approach is that we can be sure the participant begins every trial looking where we want them to be looking. The disadvantage is that it can be frustrating for participants if tracking is not accurate—a participant may in fact be looking at the fixation cross, but the tracker may sometimes fail to register this (e.g., because it has been poorly calibrated, or because it is unable to track the participants' eyes well—see Appendix 1) and the trial will therefore not begin. The study by Pearson et al. (2016) used a compromise approach; the trial began either after participants had accumulated 500 ms of gaze dwell time near the fixation cross, or after 5000 ms had elapsed, whichever came first.

Another good example of the value of gaze-contingent procedures is provided by Geringswald and Pollmann (2015). In this experiment, the authors examined a learning effect known as contextual cuing. In a typical contextual cuing experiment, participants are given a simple visual search task in which they are required to find a target "T" shape among an array of distractor "L" shapes, with some of the configurations of the search displays (the spatial arrangement of the Ls and the T) repeated across trials. Participants are not told that there is anything to learn about in the task, merely that they should locate and respond to the target. However, the term contextual cuing refers to the fact that the "context" of the environment (the arrangement of the Ls) cues the participant as to where the target (T) is positioned; participants are typically faster to find the target when it is presented in a repeated configuration (cued) as compared to a randomly arranged configuration (noncued). This effect demonstrates that even in a task that does not require an intentional strategy to learn (about the arrangement of distractors), we nevertheless do store these repeating patterns in memory such that they facilitate our behavior in the future (for a recent review of theories of contextual cuing, see Beesley, Vadillo, Pearson, & Shanks, 2016). Geringswald and Pollman were particularly interested in whether the contextual cuing effect was driven primarily by *foveal* or *extrafoveal* vision. The fovea is a small region of the retina on the back of the eye corresponding to the center of our field of vision. The fovea is densely packed with photoreceptor cells to provide for high visual acuity—when we change our point of fixation, we are shifting the visual information that is processed by the fovea. In contrast, the extrafoveal region corresponds to the periphery of our field of vision—there are fewer photoreceptors in this extrafoveal region such that items presented in the periphery are not perceived with such acuity. To examine the role of foveal and extrafoveal vision in contextual cuing, Geringswald and Pollman used a gaze-contingent procedure in which the visual display was altered at the point of fixation. For one group, the central visual region around the participant's fixation (~13 cm diameter) was masked, such that participants were unable to see objects falling in this central region. This provides an effective "scotoma" on the foveal region (a scotoma is an area of degraded visual acuity, such as that found in conditions such as macular degeneration). In another condition, participants experienced the opposite arrangement, where objects in peripheral vision were masked, while objects in the foveated region could be seen (creating a "tunnel vision" effect). Somewhat surprisingly, the researchers found that learning was significantly impaired in the case of the peripheral scotoma, in that not being able to see the peripheral objects of the scene was sufficient to abolish any learning of the scene's content (see also Zang, Jia, Müller, & Shi, 2015). In contrast, with a central scotoma (but intact peripheral vision), learning was largely unaffected. This suggests that contextual cuing is driven in large part by extrafoveal vision.

These results provide great insights into the way in which memory processes interact with, and rely upon, the information provided to the visual system. This is a clear example of where important theoretical questions in social science research—how impaired vision affects cognitive function—simply could not be answered without the technical advances brought about by eye tracking and gaze-contingent designs.

CONCLUSIONS AND FUTURE DIRECTIONS FOR EYE TRACKING

The eye tracker has been a useful tool in modern experimental psychology from its inception, and with the wide adoption of eye tracking in psychology labs across the world, there can be no doubt that it will continue to play a prominent role in the toolkit of experimental psychologists. Beyond simply providing a complementary measure, it offers insights into cognitive processes that cannot be attained from other behavioral measures. As we have demonstrated in many of the examples of research practices, this is primarily a result of the continuous measurement provided by the tracker, which allows researchers to conduct analyses over time as a chain of cognitive processes unfolds. This has provided major breakthroughs in a number of fields and advanced psychological theories. The ease of use of eye trackers means that they are starting to play a significant role in the work of many more researchers across a variety of fields. The costs of basic eye tracking devices are now a fraction of what they once were, and builtin software allows nonexpert researchers to collect gaze data and conduct basic data analyses.

What does the future hold for eye tracking research in the cognitive sciences? With eye trackers able to record at 2000 times per second and with a high degree of accuracy, it is unlikely that further improvements will have a considerable impact on the type of research that could be conducted. However, as with many computational advances, miniaturization of eye tracking technology will benefit users in a number of ways. Recent years have seen the emergence of small, portable eye trackers that can be attached to monitors on an ad-hoc basis, or even built into laptops, mobile phones, or specialized eyewear. These advances in technology may well change how we interact with personal computing devices. With the rise in popularity of virtual and augmented reality systems, it is also possible that eye tracking will find new applications to refine the experiences these devices provide.

For research purposes, today's miniature eye trackers are somewhat limited in terms of the temporal and spatial resolutions they provide (see Appendix 1 for a discussion), but that will almost certainly change in the near future. The advent of research-quality, highly portable eye trackers, as well as continuing reductions in cost, means eye trackers will become even more widespread and will offer exciting new possibilities for science. Rather than requiring participants to come to a lab where a bulky, fixed eye tracker is located, researchers will instead be able to take the portable eye tracker to the participants. This will be a boon for researchers studying populations in which people are not easily able to access a lab (e.g., remote communities, neurological patients, prisoners), or in which many participants are located at the same offsite location away from the lab (e.g., schools, companies).

REFERENCES

Aslin, R. N. (2007). What's in a look? *Developmental Science, 10*, 48–53.

Bar-Haim, Y., Lamy, D., Pergamin, L., Bakermans-Kranenburg, M. J., & Van Ijzendoorn, M. H. (2007). Threat-related attentional bias in anxious and nonanxious individuals: A meta-analytic study. *Psychological Bulletin, 133*, 1–24.

Beesley, T., & Le Pelley, M. E. (2011). The influence of blocking on overt attention and associability in human learning. *Journal of Experimental Psychology: Animal Behavior Processes, 37*, 114.

Beesley, T., Vadillo, M. A., Pearson, D., & Shanks, D. R. (2016). Configural learning in contextual cuing of visual search. *Journal of Experimental Psychology: Human Perception and Performance, 42*, 1173–1185.

Blaser, R. E., Couvillon, P. A., & Bitterman, M. E. (2004). Backward blocking in honeybees. *Quarterly Journal of Experimental Psychology Section B*, *57*, 349–360.

Bomba, P. C., & Siqueland, E. R. (1983). The nature and structure of infant form categories. *Journal of Experimental Child Psychology*, *35*, 294–328.

Bridgeman, B., Hendry, D., & Stark, L. (1975). Failure to detect displacement of the visual world during saccadic eye movements. *Vision Research*, *15*(6), 719–722.

Cox, W. M., Hogan, L. M., Kristian, M. R., & Race, J. H. (2002). Alcohol attentional bias as a predictor of alcohol abusers' treatment outcome. *Drug and Alcohol Dependence*, *68*, 237–243.

Deubel, H., & Schneider, W. X. (1996). Saccade target selection and object recognition: Evidence for a common attentional mechanism. *Vision Research*, *36*, 1827–1837.

Fantz, R. L. (1964). Visual experience in infants: Decreased attention to familiar patterns relative to novel ones. *Science*, *146*, 668–670.

Field, M., & Cox, W. M. (2008). Attentional bias in addictive behaviors: A review of its development, causes, and consequences. *Drug and Alcohol Dependence*, *97*, 1–20.

Frazier, L., & Rayner, K. (1982). Making and correcting errors during sentence comprehension: Eye movements in the analysis of structurally ambiguous sentences. *Cognitive Psychology*, *14*, 178–210.

Geringswald, F., & Pollmann, S. (2015). Central and peripheral vision loss differentially affects contextual cueing in visual search. *Journal of Experimental Psychology: Learning, Memory, and Cognition*, *41*, 1485.

Gilchrist, I. D., & Harvey, M. (2000). Refixation frequency and memory mechanisms in visual search. *Current Biology*, *10*, 1209–1212.

Glaholt, M. G., & Reingold, E. M. (2011). Eye movement monitoring as a process tracing methodology in decision making research. *Journal of Neuroscience, Psychology, and Economics*, *4*, 125.

Godijn, R., & Theeuwes, J. (2002). Programming of endogenous and exogenous saccades: Evidence for a competitive integration model. *Journal of Experimental Psychology: Human Perception and Performance*, *28*, 1039–1054.

Griffiths, O., & Le Pelley, M. E. (2009). Attentional changes in blocking are not a consequence of lateral inhibition. *Learning & Behavior*, *37*, 27–41.

Henderson, J. M. (2014). *Eyetracking technology knows your subconscious pizza desires … or not.* Available at: https://theconversation.com/eyetracking-technology-knows-your-subconscious-pizza-desires-or-not-35132.

Hutzler, F., & Wimmer, H. (2004). Eye movements of dyslexic children when reading in a regular orthography. *Brain and Language*, *89*, 235–242.

Kamin, L. J. (1969). Predictability, surprise, attention and conditioning. In B. A. Campbell & R. M. Church (Eds.), *Punishment and aversive behavior*. New York: Appleton-Century-Crofts.

Klein, R. (1988). Inhibitory tagging system facilitates visual search. *Nature*, *334*, 430–431.

Kouneiher, F., Charron, S., & Koechlin, E. (2009). Motivation and cognitive control in the human prefrontal cortex. *Nature Neuroscience*, *12*, 939–945.

Krajbich, I., & Rangel, A. (2011). Multialternative drift-diffusion model predicts the relationship between visual fixations and choice in value-based decisions. *Proceedings of the National Academy of Sciences*, *108*, 13852–13857.

Kruschke, J. K., & Blair, N. J. (2000). Blocking and backward blocking involve learned inattention. *Psychonomic Bulletin & Review*, *7*, 636–645.

Le Pelley, M. E., Beesley, T., & Suret, M. B. (2007). Blocking of human causal learning involves learned changes in stimulus processing. *Quarterly Journal of Experimental Psychology*, *60*, 1468–1476.

Le Pelley, M. E., Beesley, T., & Griffiths, O. (2014). Relative salience versus relative validity: Cue salience influences blocking in human associative learning. *Journal of Experimental Psychology: Animal Learning and Cognition*, *40*, 116.

Le Pelley, M. E., Pearson, D., Griffiths, O., & Beesley, T. (2015). When goals conflict with values: Counterproductive attentional and oculomotor capture by reward-related stimuli. *Journal of Experimental Psychology: General*, *144*, 158.

Leyland, C. M., & Mackintosh, N. J. (1978). Blocking of first- and second-order autoshaping in pigeons. *Animal Learning and Behavior*, *6*, 391–394.

Luque, D., Vadillo, M. A., Le Pelley, M. E., & Beesley, T. (2017). Prediction and uncertainty: Examining controlled and automatic components of learned attentional biases. *The Quarterly Journal of Experimental Psychology*, *70*, 1485–1503.

Mackintosh, N. J. (1975). A theory of attention: Variations in the associability of stimuli with reinforcement. *Psychological Review*, *82*, 276.

Marissen, M. A. E., Franken, I. H. A., Waters, A. J., Blanken, P., van den Brink, W., & Hendriks, V. M. (2006). Attentional bias predicts heroin relapse following treatment. *Addiction*, *101*, 1306–1312.

McConkie, G. W., & Rayner, K. (1976). Asymmetry of the perceptual span in reading. *Bulletin of the Psychonomic Society*, *8*(5), 365–368.

Miller, E. K. (2000). The prefontral cortex and cognitive control. *Nature Reviews Neuroscience*, *1*, 59–65.

Morris, R. K. (1994). Lexical and message-level sentence context effects on fixation times in reading. *Journal of Experimental Psychology: Learning, Memory, & Cognition*, *20*, 92–103.

Mulckhuyse, M., van Zoest, W., & Theeuwes, J. (2008). Capture of the eyes by relevant and irrelevant onsets. *Experimental Brain Research*, *186*, 225–235.

Newell, B. R., & Le Pelley, M. E. (2018). Perceptual but not complex moral judgments can be biased by exploiting the dynamics of eye-gaze. *Journal of Experimental Psychology: General*, *147*, 409–417.

Nixon, H. K. (1924). Attention and interest in advertising. *Archives of Psychology*, *72*, 5–67.

Pärnamets, P., Johansson, P., Hall, L., Balkenius, C., Spivey, M. J., & Richardson, D. C. (2015). Biasing moral decisions by exploiting the dynamics of eye gaze. *Proceedings of the National Academy of Sciences of the United States of America*, *112*, 4170–4175.

Pavlov, I. P. (1927). *Conditioned Reflexes (translated by G. V. Anrep)*. London: Oxford University Press.

Pearce, J. M., & Hall, G. (1980). A model for Pavlovian learning: Variations in the effectiveness of conditioned but not of unconditioned stimuli. *Psychological Review*, *87*(6), 532.

Pearson, D., Osborn, R., Whitford, T. J., Failing, M., Theeuwes, J., & Le Pelley, M. E. (2016). Value-modulated oculomotor capture by task-irrelevant stimuli is a consequence of early competition on the saccade map. *Attention, Perception, & Psychophysics*, *78*, 2226–2240.

Posner, M. I. (1980). Orienting of attention. *Quarterly Journal of Experimental Psychology*, *32*, 3–25.

Posner, M. I., & Cohen, Y. (1984). Components of visual orienting. *Attention and Performance X: Control of Language Processes*, *32*, 531–556.

Posner, M. I., & Snyder, C. R. R. (1975). Attention and cognitive control. In R. L. Solso (Ed.), *Information processing and cognition: The Loyola symposium*: Lawrence Erlbaum.

Prados, J., Alvarez, B., Acebes, F., Loy, I., Sansa, J., & Moreno-Fernández, M. M. (2013). Blocking in rats, humans and snails using a within-subjects design. *Behavioral Processes*, *100*, 23–31.

Rayner, K. (2009). Eye movements and attention in reading, scene perception, and visual search. *The Quarterly Journal of Experimental Psychology*, *62*, 1457–1506.

Reichle, E. D. (Ed.), (2006). Models of eye movement control in reading [special issue]. *Cognitive Systems Research*, *7*, 1–96.

Sanders, A. F., & Houtmans, M. J. M. (1985). There is no central stimulus encoding during saccadic eye shifts: A case against general parallel processing notions. *Acta Psychologica*, *60*, 323–338.

Shimojo, S., Simion, C., Shimojo, E., & Scheier, C. (2003). Gaze bias both reflects and influences preference. *Nature Neuroscience*, *6*(12), 1317–1322.

Tennant, W. A., & Bitterman, M. E. (1975). Blocking and overshadowing in two species of fish. *Journal of Experimental Psychology: Animal Behavior Processes*, *1*(1), 22.

Vadillo, M. A., Street, C. N. H., Beesley, T., & Shanks, D. R. (2015). A simple algorithm for the offline recalibration of eye tracking data through best-fitting linear transformation. *Behavior Research Methods*, *47*, 1365–1376.

Volkmann, F. C., Schick, A. M., & Riggs, L. A. (1968). Time course of visual inhibition during voluntary saccades. *Journal of the Optical Society of America*, *58*, 562–569.

Wang, J. T., Spezio, M., & Camerer, C. F. (2010). Pinocchio's pupil: Using eyetracking and pupil dilation to understand truth telling and deception in sender-receiver games. *American Economic Review*, *100*, 984–1007.

Wedel, M., Pieters, R., & Liechty, J. (2008). Temporal dynamics of scene perception: Goals influence switching between attention states. *Journal of Experimental Psychology: Applied*, *14*, 129–138.

Wiers, R. W., & Stacy, A. W. (2006). Implicit cognition and addiction. *Current Directions in Psychological Science*, *15*, 292–296.

Wills, A. J., Lavric, A., Croft, G. S., & Hodgson, T. L. (2007). Predictive learning, prediction errors, and attention: Evidence from event-related potentials and eye tracking. *Journal of Cognitive Neuroscience*, *19*, 843–854.

Yarbus, A. L. (1967). *Eye movements and vision*. New York: Plenum Press.

Zang, X., Jia, L., Müller, H. J., & Shi, Z. (2015). Invariant spatial context is learned but not retrieved in gaze-contingent tunnel-view search. *Journal of Experimental Psychology: Learning, Memory, and Cognition*, *41*, 807.

Chapter 2

Brain Morphometry for Economists: How do Brain Volume Constraints Affect Our Choices?

Agnieszka Tymula
School of Economics, University of Sydney, Sydney, NSW, Australia

---

> *"The task is to replace the global rationality of economic man with a kind of rational behavior that is compatible with the access to information and the computational capacities that are actually possessed by organisms."*
>
> (Herbert Simon, 1955, p. 241)

INTRODUCTION

While most economic models of choice assume that decision makers have unlimited computational ability to evaluate and choose from the available choice sets, in reality people's ability to process information is limited. Our brains consist of a limited number of cells that have a bounded capacity for conveying information. This implies that many seemingly irrational behaviors may be, in fact, due to the limitations of otherwise rationally acting human nervous systems. The idea that behavioral biases can be explained by the features of the nervous system dates back to Herbert Simon (1955), in writings that long preceded the development of tools to study the structural and functional properties of living brains. In this chapter, I first briefly review the theoretical literature from economics that derives optimal behavior given biological constraints. I point out that various modeling approaches arrive at the following similar insights: (1) capacity limitations on the nervous system should affect choice, and (2) widely observed behaviors, like those identified in the famous prospect theory of Kahneman and Tversky (1979), are the direct consequence of the limits of human cognition. Then I briefly describe the techniques and equipment used to estimate gray matter volume in the living brain and summarize the

Biophysical Measurement in Experimental Social Science Research. https://doi.org/10.1016/B978-0-12-813092-6.00001-0

empirical evidence that neuroeconomists have accumulated so far about the relationship between the limited neural capacities and economic decision making.

HOW IS INFORMATION ABOUT REWARD VALUE ENCODED IN THE BRAIN?

There are approximately 100 billion neurons in the human brain. These neurons transmit information by electrochemical impulses called action potentials. Fig. 1 illustrates the life course of a single action potential by plotting the voltage of a single neuron over time. This neuron reacts to some specific stimulus, such as brightness, contrast or, more relevant to economists, a prospective reward such as money or apple juice. In the figure, initially the neuron is shown to be at rest—its voltage is approximately −70 mV—meaning that there is no stimulus to convey information about. When the stimulus (for example, a glass of apple juice) appears, the voltage of the neuron starts moving towards zero. If the stimulus is strong enough that it passes the threshold of −55 mV, the neuron *fires* an action potential. All action potentials are of the same size. Either the stimulus is strong enough that the neuron fires, or it is not and the neuron remains at rest. This means that the size of the action potential cannot convey information about the intensity or the value of the stimulus. Such information is instead captured in the brain by the rate at which action potentials are created, the so-called *firing rate* of the neuron. For example, neurons in the visual cortex that are responsible for encoding brightness will fire at a faster rate if it gets brighter and at a slower rate when it gets darker. Value-encoding neurons, i.e., neurons in brain areas that change activity levels in response to rewards, will fire at a faster rate when faced by more valuable rewards. The rate at which

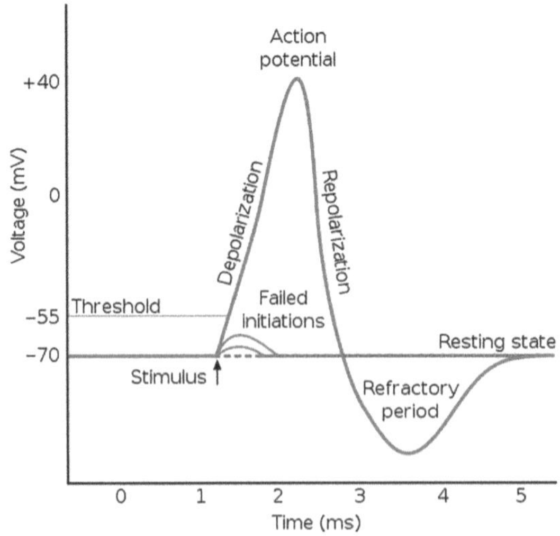

FIG. 1 Time course of an action potential.

a neuron can fire action potentials is biophysically limited to a maximum of 200 action potentials per second, a constraint that has serious consequences for how value is encoded in the brain.

Neuroeconomists have now accumulated vast evidence about the location of neurons whose firing rates correlate with the value that individuals attach to rewards. In their seminal research, Platt and Glimcher (1999) implanted electrodes in neurons in the lateral interparietal (LIP) area of monkeys' brains and recorded the activity of these neurons. They showed that neurons in the LIP are sensitive to both reward size and reward probability and fire at a faster rate as either the reward size and the probability of receiving it increases. These results have been replicated in numerous studies and are now treated as fact by neuroeconomists. These findings set the foundation for the new field of neuroeconomics by establishing that a utility-like object is represented by neuronal activity. Unlike utility in economics, which is usually thought of as an ordinal concept, the valuation of rewards in the brain is measured in units that have cardinal properties. Therefore, neuroeconomists refer to what economists call utility as *subjective value*, to differentiate it from the ordinal utility concept in economics.

In humans, the "neural signature" of value has been studied mainly using functional magnetic resonance imaging (fMRI), because implanting electrodes in the human brain is too invasive (although some data is available from studies conducted on patients who already have electrodes implanted in their brains for treatment purposes). fMRI relies on the fact that brain activity and cerebral blood flow are coupled. When neurons in a certain brain area become active, more blood flows to this area, a change that can be picked up by fMRI. Thousands of fMRI studies examining the neural signature of value in various contexts have been conducted, and they consistently identify the same value-encoding regions in the brain: the ventromedial prefrontal cortex (vmPFC), the striatum, and the posterior cingulate cortex (PCC) (for a review, see Bartra, McGuire, & Kable, 2013, for location of these brain regions see Fig. 2). Moreover, brain activity recorded in the fMRI scanner while people are passively observing rewards has successfully predicted what choices they will make later, outside the scanner (Levy, Lazzaro, Rutledge, & Glimcher, 2011; Smith, Bernheim, Camerer, & Rangel, 2014). This further confirms that in simple choice situations, our brains encode the subjective value of rewards, and that this subjective value causally leads to our choosing of rewards that trigger higher brain activity.

THEORETICAL FINDINGS ON THE IMPLICATIONS OF NERVOUS SYSTEM LIMITATIONS FOR VALUE ENCODING

The properties of the nervous system highlighted briefly above, specifically that (1) the firing rate of each neuron is restricted to a maximum of 200 action potentials per second and (2) the number of neurons in the value encoding areas (and more generally in the brain) is limited, have important implications for how the

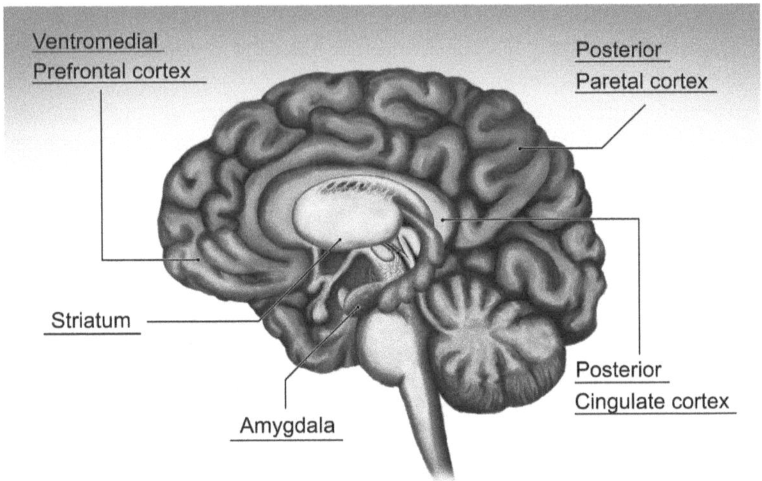

FIG. 2 Some relevant decision making areas of the brain.

encoding of value can be efficiently achieved in the brain. These two limiting properties taken together imply that a function mapping rewards to value has to be bounded—specifically, the values it maps to need to fall between some minimum and maximum that correspond to the brain's minimum and maximum level of response—because the total number of action potentials that can be created in response to a reward is constrained by both the number of neurons and their biophysical characteristics. These two properties alone would not be overly problematic from the perspective of modeling; one could just imagine a monotonic mapping from all possible rewards (x) to their subjective values ($V(x)$) with fixed upper and lower bounds, for example a linear function such as that depicted in Fig. 3A.

However, another feature of neurons is that their activity is, to a significant degree, stochastic. This means that if reward $\times 1$ is offered to a chooser at different times, the chooser's brain activity in response to this reward is likely to differ slightly each time. Instead of a thin line, as in Fig. 3A, a hypothetical linear mapping of rewards to value in the brain would be better represented by a much thicker line, as in Fig. 3B. When an individual is asked to choose between alternatives, the fact that neural activity is noisy may cause errors and intransitivity in decision making for certain choice sets, with the severity of these phenomena depending on the slope of the value function and the size of the error term. In Fig. 3B, the noise in the coding of subjective value is represented by the thickness of the subjective value function.

For example, imagine a chooser selecting between rewards $x1$ and $x2$, as illustrated in Fig. 3B. While $x2$ is of higher quality and would be selected in a noiseless world, when one accounts for neural noise, every now and then

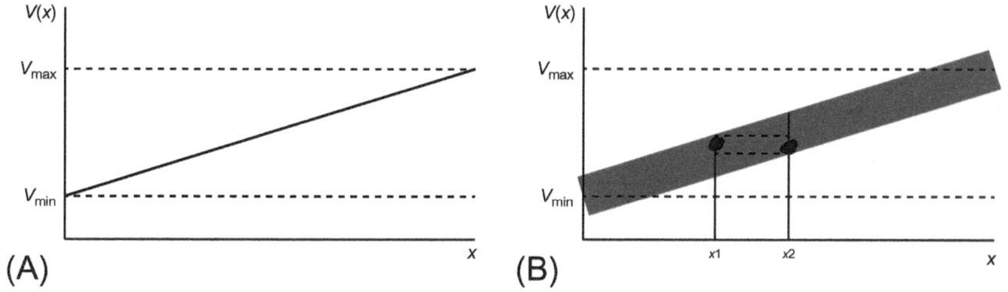

FIG. 3 Hypothetical ways to represent value in the brain (A) if there is no noise in the neural signal and (B) if there is noise in the neural signal.

the individual's brain would respond with higher brain activity to $x1$ than to $x2$, and therefore the individual would choose $x1$ over $x2$. One could propose that such disadvantageous decision making could be mitigated by increasing the upper bound on the value function, for example by adding more neurons which would increase the range of the possible number of action potentials produced and thus make the value function steeper, to increase discriminability. However, this is not feasible because neurons are extremely costly. The brain only accounts for approximately 3% of our body mass, but it uses about 20% of the total calories consumed by the body. It is essentially impossible to provide people with enough calories to increase the capacity of their brains sufficiently to make them noiseless choosers. Nevertheless, individuals differ in terms of the number of neurons they possess and the distribution of those neurons in the brain. This raises the possibility that individual differences in gray matter volume could help explain why different people make different decisions—for example, why some people are willing to tolerate more risks, or are more patient, or seem more 'irrational' than others.

Theoretical work in economics has investigated the features of efficient value coding in the face of the limited capacities of the value-encoding instrument, such as those depicted in Fig. 3b. Rayo and Becker (2007) referred to the output of this instrument as "bounded happiness." The common conclusion from the papers assuming a bounded happiness function of the type depicted in Fig. 3B is that the value function should dynamically adjust so that its slope is steepest around the values between which the individual is currently choosing (Netzer, 2009; Rayo & Becker, 2007; Robson & Whitehead, 2016; Woodford, 2012). In other words, the optimal value function is S-shaped with dynamically adjusting reference points, as shown in Fig. 4.

In neuroscience and neuroeconomics, the canonical neural computation that achieves such dynamic adjustment in the value function in response to the distribution and the history of experienced rewards is known as *divisive normalization* (Glimcher & Tymula, 2017; Khaw, Glimcher, & Louie, 2017; Louie & De Martino, 2013; Louie, Khaw, & Glimcher, 2013; Steverson, Brandenburger, & Glimcher, 2016). Divisive normalization has been shown to explain a wide range of behaviors, including prospect-theory-like behaviors

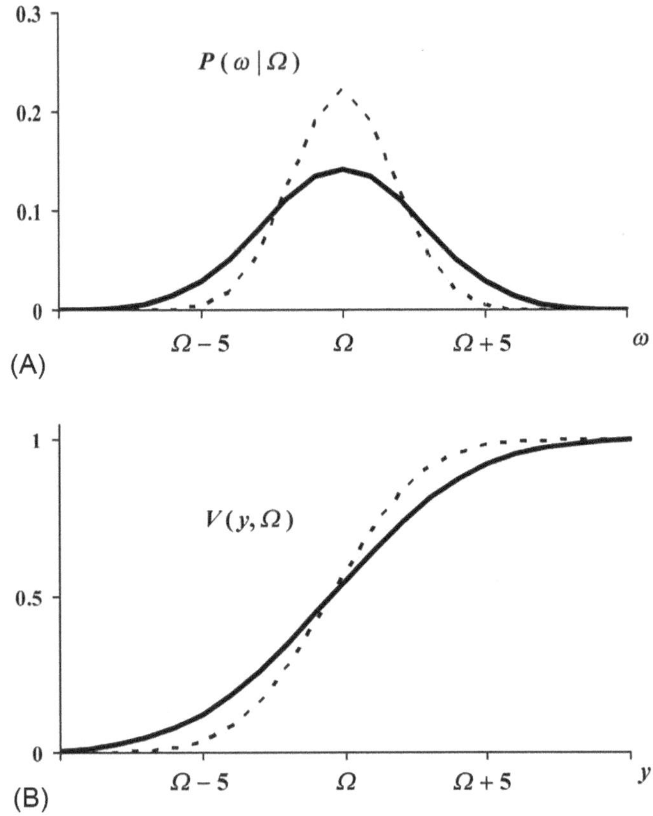

FIG. 4 Optimal value coding: (A) distribution of the rewards, and (B) corresponding optimal "happiness" function. *(From Rayo, L., & Becker, G. S. (2007). Evolutionary efficiency and happiness.* Journal of Political Economy, 115*(2), 302–337.)*

(Glimcher & Tymula, 2017) and choice-set effects, such as choice overload and asymmetric dominance (Louie & Glimcher, 2012; Louie, Glimcher, & Webb, 2015).

From a theoretical perspective, the limitations of neurons in encoding the value of rewards have significant predictive relevance. These limitations have been shown theoretically to be a potential source of decision making biases and "suboptimal" (i.e., not strictly expected-value-maximizing) behaviors. Recent methodological developments in neuroscience have allowed us to measure the density of neurons in the brains of living individuals, which in turn has led to the emerging literature on the associations between gray matter volume and economic behavior.

APPROACHES TO BRAIN ANATOMY

The history of studying morphological features of the brain dates from long before noninvasive techniques to look into the brains of living humans were developed. In the fourth century BC, Hippocrates first hypothesized that mental activity takes place in the brain rather than the heart. The first postmortem brain dissections date back to Herophilus (300 BCE to 250 BCE). There was a long break in the study of neuroanatomy from the third to the fifteenth century AD, due to the dominance of religious proscriptions that deemed the body unworthy of study, but at the end of the fifteenth century, interest in the brain returned and scientists begun again to dissect human brains post mortem. Many studies of neuroanatomy and the organizational structure of the brain have since been published.

Voxel-Based Morphometry

With the introduction of magnetic resonance imaging (MRI) technology, it is now possible to study associations between individual characteristics and behaviors, and the volumes of predefined regions (voxels) of the cortex in *living* humans. The central nervous system consists of two types of tissue: *gray matter*, that contains the neuronal cell bodies, and *white matter*, made of axons connecting different parts of gray matter to each other. It is possible to separate white matter from gray matter in the pictures obtained using MRI technology because they have different water content and thus different magnetic properties.

Specific locations in the brain are identified in MRI research using a three-dimensional coordinate space in which x corresponds to the sagittal, y to the horizontal (axial), and z to the coronal planes. Fig. 5 illustrates these different planes. This standardized mapping creates a common language for neuroscientists to describe and compare the brain areas between studies. The MRI scanner takes a sequence of pictures of the brain on these three planes. Special statistical techniques have been developed to allow scientists to estimate the surface area of the cortex, as well as its thickness, from these images. The structural MRI scan is a relatively quick measurement: it takes approximately 10 min to take all the measurements required to estimate the gray matter volume in every part

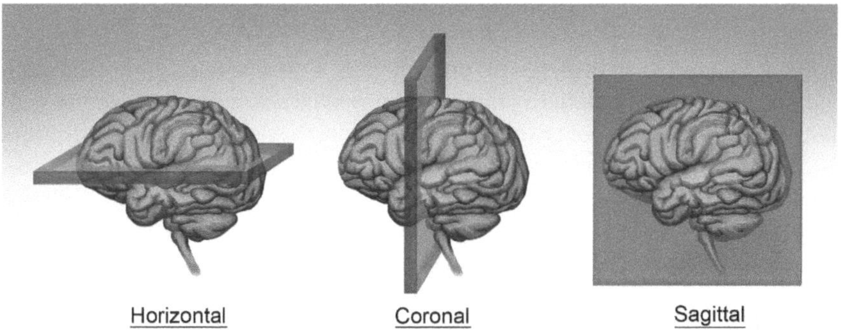

FIG. 5 The three planes of section in the brain.

of the brain. The technique is noninvasive and safe provided that no metal is brought into the vicinity of the scanning room.

In recent years, scientists have begun asking whether such neuroanatomical measurements are related, across participants, to their individual characteristics. The studies in this area can be classified into two types: exploratory studies and hypothesis-driven studies. Exploratory analysis involves searching the whole brain for regions in which gray matter volume correlates with the behavioral feature of interest, without any a priori hypothesis. This is also referred to as whole-brain analysis, and involves splitting the brain into many small regions (voxels) and regressing the gray matter volume in these voxels on the behavioral variable of interest, in search for the regions where such regressions reveal a significant correlation. Given the large number of regressions that are run in such an analysis, it is very important to use appropriate statistical correction procedures to avoid false-positive results. Such corrections are now a standard feature of the statistical software commonly used for such analysis (for example, Statistical Parametric Mapping: http://www.fil.ion.ucl.ac.uk/spm/).

In hypothesis-driven testing, on the other hand, prior knowledge about brain function and structure is used to focus the analysis on only selected, pre-defined brain areas. Such studies have revealed that the gray matter volume is an individual-specific feature that is stable in the short-to-medium term, but can be altered in the medium-to-long term through experience (Maguire, Woollett, & Spiers, 2006), ageing (Resnick, Pham, Kraut, Zonderman, & Davatzikos, 2003), or illness (Goodkind et al., 2015).

THE LINKS BETWEEN GRAY MATTER VOLUME AND BEHAVIOR

The empirical literature on the neuroanatomical basis of choice is still in its infancy, but a selection of studies in neuroeconomics has now established that, in principle, one can link fundamental preferences to gray matter volume. Here, we review several studies that focus on the correlations between gray matter volume and risk preferences, time preferences, and rationality in choice.

Risk Attitudes

In 2014, Gilaie-Dotan et al. (2014) published the first study describing the associations between gray matter volume and individual risk attitudes. Using a standard, incentive-compatible experimental method, they elicited the risk attitudes of 28 young adults (15 women and 13 men) of an average age of 25 (SD = 6). On all of these individuals, they also performed a structural MRI scan. With this information, they ran an exploratory whole-brain analysis, looking for regions of the brain where the gray matter volume correlated with individuals' tolerance of monetary risks. This analysis revealed that gray matter volume in the posterior parietal cortex (PPC) (see Fig. 2) correlated with risk attitudes: the more neurons people had in this region, the more risk-tolerant they were. In the same paper, Gilaie-Dotan et al. (2014) then replicated this finding in a different sample of 33 individuals (20 women and 13 men), of an average age of 21.34 (SD = 2.35), whose data was collected in a different laboratory and using a different MRI scanner.

This study builds on a now long-standing association between PPC function and decision making processes. In studies with monkeys that directly recorded brain activity using electrodes implanted in the brain, the activity of neurons in the PPC was shown to encode the subjective desirability of lotteries, delayed rewards, and social rewards (Dorris & Glimcher, 2004; Klein, Deaner, & Platt, 2008; Louie & Glimcher, 2010; Platt & Glimcher, 1999; Sugrue, Corrado, & Newsome, 2004). In humans, activity in the PPC has been shown to be correlated with levels of uncertainty about the reward (Huettel, 2005), and with individuals' risk tolerance (Huettel, Stowe, Gordon, Warner, & Platt, 2006).

Remarkably, it is also known that both gray matter volume and risk attitudes change as people age in ways that are consistent with these findings. As they age, adults become more risk averse (Tymula, Rosenberg Belmaker, Ruderman, Glimcher, & Levy, 2013; von Gaudecker, van Soest, & Wengström, 2011) and they also lose gray matter volume (Resnick et al., 2003). This raises the possibility that age-related changes in risk attitude could be attributed in part to changes in brain structure rather than only to chronological ageing per se. This is precisely the hypothesis that Grubb, Tymula, Gilaie-Dotan, Glimcher, and Levy (2016) tested in a sample of 52 adults (30 women and 22 men) whose ages spanned seven decades (18–88 years old). First, in line with previous findings, they confirmed that when studied separately, both higher chronological age and lower gray matter volume in the PPC were associated with less risk taking. More striking, they showed that once gray matter volume differences between the participants were accounted for, chronological age had no additional predictive power over risk attitudes—only gray matter volume was predictive of an individual's level of risk tolerance. These results suggest that, in the same way that the number of wrinkles or gray hairs we have is a more accurate predictor of how old we look than is our chronological age, the condition of our brain is a better predictor of our behavior than how old we are.

Another recent study (Hoon Jung, Lee, Lerman, & Kable, 2018) found that the gray matter volume of the amygdala, as well as the strength of structural and functional connections between the amygdala and the ventromedial prefrontal cortex (vmPFC) region of the brain, are predictive of risk attitudes. As the authors argue, these findings are consistent with an extensive literature that has shown that amygdala-vmPFC interactions play an important role in the evaluation of potential outcomes in decision making and learning.

Discounting

Several studies have investigated whether the rate at which people discount the future is related to gray matter volume. The tendency to make more impulsive decisions has been associated with less gray matter volume in the lateral prefrontal cortex (Bjork, Momenan, & Hommer, 2009), superior frontal gyrus (Schwartz et al., 2010), and putamen (Cho et al., 2013; Dombrovski et al., 2012). Yet this tendency has also been associated with *more* gray matter volume in the ventral striatum and posterior cingulate cortex (Schwartz et al., 2010), medial prefrontal regions and anterior cingulate cortex (Cho et al., 2013), and prefrontal cortex (Wang et al., 2016). The lack of consensus in these findings highlights the need for replication of the results and bigger sample sizes.

In what is perhaps the largest study of neuroanatomy and economic preferences (427 youths), Pehlivanova et al. (2017) found that impulsive choice in adolescence is associated with less gray matter volume in the following decision making areas of the brain: the ventromedial prefrontal cortex, the orbitofrontal cortex, the temporal pole, and the temporoparietal junction.

Rationality in Choice

One of the foundations of neoclassical economic theory is the assumption that people obey the generalized axiom of revealed preference (GARP). Obeying GARP is a necessary and sufficient condition for utility maximization (Samuelson, 1938). GARP assumes that if an apple is weakly revealed-preferred to a banana and a banana is weakly revealed-preferred to a cherry, then when asked to choose between an apple and a cherry, a cherry should not be strictly preferred to an apple. Behavioral studies show that individuals generally do very well in obeying GARP. Even children (Harbaugh, Krause, & Berry, 2001) and individuals under the influence of alcohol (Burghart, Glimcher, & Lazzaro, 2013) obey GARP. Naturally-occurring hormonal variations along the menstrual cycle also do not impact individuals' ability to obey GARP (Lazzaro, Rutledge, Burghart, & Glimcher, 2016). However, an impaired ability to obey GARP has been discovered in patients with lesions in the frontal lobe (Camille, Griffiths, Vo, Fellows, & Kable, 2011), highlighting the importance of this brain region for exhibiting what economists view as rational choice. Previous studies have found older adults to be less consistent and more likely to show impaired financial decision making than younger adults (for example, Agarwal, Driscoll, Gabaix, & Laibson, 2009; Tymula, Belmaker, Ruderman, Glimcher, & Levy, 2015), a result which could perhaps be driven by age-related decline in the volume of gray matter in a particular brain area.

To test directly whether rationality in choice is linked to gray matter volume, Chung, Tymula, and Glimcher (2017) recruited 39 healthy older adults (14 women and 15 men), aged 65 to 92 years old (average age 72.4). These participants performed a standard incentive-compatible task to test their rationality (Harbaugh et al., 2001) and were also scanned in the MRI scanner to obtain their gray matter volume. Chung et al. (2017) showed that lower gray matter volume in the ventrolateral prefrontal cortex correlates with less rationality as measured behaviorally by either the number or the severity of GARP violations.

THE RELEVANCE OF BRAIN STRUCTURE MEASUREMENTS TO ECONOMICS

The recently discovered associations between brain structure and economic decision making provide empirical support for the conjecture that neural measures could potentially serve as primitives in building economic theory, or at the very least for the argument that they should be incorporated somehow into economic modeling (as for example in Netzer, 2009; Rayo & Becker, 2007; Robson & Whitehead, 2016; Webb, Glimcher, & Louie, 2016; Woodford, 2012). Existing findings point to new constraints on the possible mechanisms that underlie observed risk attitudes, patience, and rationality in choice. One could even argue that although the research on the relationship between brain structure and decision making is still in its infancy, our current knowledge of the limitations of the nervous system is sufficient reason to call for a revolution in the economic modeling of choice. Some signs of such change in economic modeling—where the exogenously given preferences that are the foundation of mainstream economic models of choice are replaced with biological variables and concepts—are already present in the literature (Glimcher & Tymula, 2017; Netzer, 2009; Rayo & Becker, 2007; Robson & Whitehead, 2016; Webb et al., 2016; Woodford, 2012). The advantage of such a neuro-economic approach to modeling of decision making is that it maintains the biological realism of how choice actually proceeds. Replacing exogenously-given preferences with observable features of the nervous system should allow us, over time, to capture and predict more accurately the heterogeneity in behavior observed both between and within individuals.

Second, the short-term stability and medium-to-long-term malleability of gray matter volume make this particular measure an especially promising variable to act upon using behavior-altering policy interventions. Just as we can exercise to increase our muscle mass and become stronger, perhaps 1 day we will discover how to exercise our gray matter volume to, for example, maintain rationality in choice as we age, or overcome the self-control problems. As proof of concept, one study has shown that finger differentiation exercises, which might initially be thought of as unrelated to math skills, improved performance in mathematics in first-grade children (Gracia-Bafalluy & Noel, 2008). Many labs around the world are currently investigating whether cognitive training can improve our decision making, but we need to wait for the rigorous results of this research before being confident of policy recommendations in this area.

Third, these findings and future results in this area may help unite numerous previously documented associations between a host of brain-changing variables (age, illness, addiction, medication use) and economic behavior into one coherent theory. If there are several, even seemingly unrelated, factors that affect gray matter volume in a certain brain area that is known to determines behavior, it should not be surprising that all of these factors would change behavior in a similar way.

Finally, MRI technology opens up the opportunity for economists to draw inferences about behavior from completely new datasets. Billions of brains are captured on MRI scans every year for medical purposes. This data has so far been used only for diagnosis and treatment-prescription purposes. The early results relating gray matter volume to behavior suggest that this data could also be useful to economists wishing to characterize behavior in large samples and/or hard-to-access populations.

CAVEATS

Despite its promise for creating a new research agenda for social scientists, MRI technology has been used so far in only a few papers relating gray matter volume to behavior. Moreover, due to high labor and equipment usage costs, these papers have been based usually on very low samples. The standard sample size for papers using voxel-based morphometry (VBM) analysis is about 30–40 participants (with some exceptions, such as Pehlivanova et al. (2017) which used over 400 participants). With such low sample sizes, it has to be expected that some of the published results will not replicate and that some existing relationships will not be discovered. More studies, of broader populations, are needed to confirm and extend current findings.

Integrating existing datasets from various research sites could be a partial solution to the problem of small sample size. However, one can be concerned that structural brain measurements strongly depend on the properties of the scanner and procedures used and have urged caution in merging the data collected using different MRI scanners. This problem may be not as grave as once believed: recent research has shown high test-retest reliability among different scanners and scanning sites (Schnack et al., 2010).

When interpreting the results of VBM studies, it is important to keep in mind that the findings do not imply a fixed deterministic relation between genetics and preferences. Our environments and our own behaviors have been shown to affect brain structure. In fact, the malleability of the brain's structure may be the key property that makes VBM measurement interesting to economists as it implies the possibility of neurologically-informed treatment for behavioral problems.

Finally, existing studies do not allow us to infer causal relationships. For example, it may be that having more gray matter volume in the PPC region makes people more risk tolerant, but it is also possible that people who take more risks end up with a thicker cortex.

Despite these caveats, the study of how brain gray matter volume and more broadly brain structure, including connections between different brain regions, relates to economic behavior is promising and exciting. It has the potential to inform choice theorists about how to improve existing approaches to economic modeling of decision making by enriching these approaches with neural variables, as well as to inform policy makers about how to help people become better decision makers. Time will tell as to whether this potential gets fulfilled.

References

Agarwal, S., Driscoll, J. C., Gabaix, X., & Laibson, D. I. (2009). The age of reason: Financial decisions over the life-cycle with implications for regulation. *Brookings Papers on Economic Activity*, *2009*(2), 51–117. https://doi.org/10.2139/ssrn.973790.

Bartra, O., McGuire, J. T., & Kable, J. W. (2013). The valuation system: A coordinate-based meta-analysis of BOLD fMRI experiments examining neural correlates of subjective value. *NeuroImage*, *76*, 412–427.

Bjork, J. M., Momenan, R., & Hommer, D. W. (2009). Delay discounting correlates with proportional lateral frontal cortex volumes. *Biological Psychiatry*, *65*(8), 710–713. https://doi.org/10.1016/j.biopsych.2008.11.023.

Burghart, D. R., Glimcher, P. W., & Lazzaro, S. C. (2013). An expected utility maximizer walks into a bar. *Journal of Risk and Uncertainty*, *46*(3), 215–246.

Camille, N., Griffiths, C. A., Vo, K., Fellows, L. K., & Kable, J. W. (2011). Ventromedial frontal lobe damage disrupts value maximization in humans. *The Journal of Neuroscience*, *31*(20), 7527–7532. https://doi.org/10.1523/JNEUROSCI.6527-10.2011.

Cho, S. S., Pellecchia, G., Aminian, K., Ray, N., Segura, B., Obeso, I., et al. (2013). Morphometric correlation of impulsivity in medial prefrontal cortex. *Brain Topography*, *26*(3), 479–487. https://doi.org/10.1007/s10548-012-0270-x.

Chung, H. -K., Tymula, A., & Glimcher, P. (2017). The reduction of ventrolateral prefrontal cortex gray matter volume correlates with loss of economic rationality in aging. *The Journal of Neuroscience*, *37*(49), 12068–12077. https://doi.org/10.1523/JNEUROSCI.1171-17.2017.

Dombrovski, A. Y., Siegle, G. J., Szanto, K., Clark, L., Reynolds, C. F., & Aizenstein, H. (2012). The temptation of suicide: Striatal gray matter, discounting of delayed rewards, and suicide attempts in late-life depression. *Psychological Medicine*, *42*(6), 1203–1215. https://doi.org/10.1017/S0033291711002133.

Dorris, M. C., & Glimcher, P. W. (2004). Activity in posterior parietal cortex is correlated with the relative subjective desirability of action. *Neuron*, *44*(2), 365–378. https://doi.org/10.1016/j.neuron.2004.09.009.

Gilaie-Dotan, S., Tymula, A., Cooper, N., Kable, J., Glimcher, P., & Levy, I. (2014). Neuroanatomy predicts individual risk attitudes. *Journal of Neuroscience*, *34*(37).

Glimcher, P. W., & Tymula, A. A. (2017). *Expected subjective value theory (ESVT): A representation of decision under risk and certainty*. Working papers 2016-08 NSW, Australia: School of Economics, University of Sydney.

Goodkind, M., Eickhoff, S. B., Oathes, D. J., Jiang, Y., Chang, A., Jones-Hagata, L. B., et al. (2015). Identification of a common neurobiological substrate for mental illness. *JAMA Psychiatry*, *72*(4), 305. https://doi.org/10.1001/jamapsychiatry.2014.2206.

Gracia-Bafalluy, M., & Noel, M. (2008). Does finger training increase young children's numerical performance? *Cortex*, *44*(4), 368–375. https://doi.org/10.1016/j.cortex.2007.08.020.

Grubb, M. A., Tymula, A., Gilaie-Dotan, S., Glimcher, P. W., & Levy, I. (2016). Neuroanatomy accounts for age-related changes in risk preferences. *Nature Communications*. *7*, https://doi.org/10.1038/ncomms13822.

Harbaugh, W. T., Krause, K., & Berry, T. R. (2001). GARP for kids: On the development of rational choice behavior. *American Economic Review*, *91*(5), 1539–1545.

Hoon Jung, W., Lee, S., Lerman, C., & Kable, J. W. (2018). Amygdala functional and structural connectivity predicts individual risk tolerance. *Neuron*, *98*, 1–11.

Huettel, S. A. (2005). Decisions under uncertainty: Probabilistic context influences activation of prefrontal and parietal cortices. *Journal of Neuroscience*, *25*(13), 3304–3311.

Huettel, S. A., Stowe, C. J., Gordon, E. M., Warner, B. T., & Platt, M. L. (2006). Neural signatures of economic preferences for risk and ambiguity. *Neuron*, *49*(5), 765–775.

Kahneman, D., & Tversky, A. (1979). Prospect theory—analysis of decision under risk. *Econometrica*, *47*(2), 263–292.

Khaw, M. W., Glimcher, P. W., & Louie, K. (2017). Normalized value coding explains dynamic adaptation in the human valuation process. *Proceedings of the National Academy of Sciences*, *114*(48), 12696–12701. https://doi.org/10.1073/pnas.1715293114.

Klein, J. T., Deaner, R. O., & Platt, M. L. (2008). Neural correlates of social target value in macaque parietal cortex. *Current Biology: CB*, *18*(6), 419–424. https://doi.org/10.1016/j.cub.2008.02.047.

Lazzaro, S. C., Rutledge, R. B., Burghart, D. R., & Glimcher, P. W. (2016). The impact of menstrual cycle phase on economic choice and rationality. *PLoS One*, *11*(1).

Levy, I., Lazzaro, S. C., Rutledge, R. B., & Glimcher, P. W. (2011). Choice from non-choice: Predicting consumer preferences from blood oxygenation level-dependent signals obtained during passive viewing. *Journal of Neuroscience*, *31*(1), 118–125.

Louie, K., & De Martino, B. (2013). The neurobiology of context-dependent valuation and choice. In P. W. Glimcher & E. Fehr (Eds.), *Neuroeconomics: Decision making and the brain* (2nd ed., pp. 455–476). Academic Press.

Louie, K., & Glimcher, P. W. (2010). Separating value from choice: Delay discounting activity in the lateral intraparietal area. *The Journal of Neuroscience*, *30*(16), 5498–5507. https://doi.org/10.1523/JNEUROSCI.5742-09.2010.

Louie, K., & Glimcher, P. W. (2012). Set-size effects and the neural representation of value. In R. J. Dolan & T. Sharot (Eds.), *Neuroscience of preference and choice: Cognitive and neural mechanisms* (pp. 143–169). London: Academic Press.

Louie, K., Glimcher, P. W., & Webb, R. (2015). Adaptive neural coding: From biological to behavioral decision-making. *Current Opinion in Behavioral Sciences*, *5*, 91–99. https://doi.org/10.1016/j.cobeha.2015.08.008.

Louie, K., Khaw, M. W., & Glimcher, P. W. (2013). Normalization is a general neural mechanism for context-dependent decision making. *Proceedings of the National Academy of Sciences of the United States of America*, *110*(15), 6139–6144. https://doi.org/10.1073/pnas.1217854110.

Maguire, E. A., Woollett, K., & Spiers, H. J. (2006). London taxi drivers and bus drivers: A structural MRI and neuropsychological analysis. *Hippocampus*, *16*(12), 1091–1101.

Netzer, N. (2009). Evolution of time preferences and attitudes toward risk. *American Economic Review*, *99*(3), 937–955. https://doi.org/10.1257/aer.99.3.937.

Pehlivanova, M., Wolf, D. H., Sotiras, A., Kaczkurkin, A., Moore, T. M., Ciric, R., et al. (2017). Dimished cortical thickness is associated with impulsive choice in adolescence. *The Journal of Neuroscience*. pii 2200-17.

Platt, M. L., & Glimcher, P. W. (1999). Neural correlates of decision variables in parietal cortex. *Nature*, *400*(6741), 233–238. https://doi.org/10.1038/22268.

Rayo, L., & Becker, G. S. (2007). Evolutionary efficiency and happiness. *Journal of Political Economy*, *115*(2), 302–337.

Resnick, S. M., Pham, D. L., Kraut, M. A., Zonderman, A. B., & Davatzikos, C. (2003). Longitudinal magnetic resonance imaging studies of older adults: A shrinking brain. *The Journal of Neuroscience*, *23*(8), 3295–3301.

Robson, A., & Whitehead, L. A. (2016). *Rapidly adaptive hedonic utility*. Working paper Canada: Simon Fraser University.

Samuelson, P. A. (1938). A note on the pure theory of Consumer's behaviour. *Economica*, *5*(17), 61. https://doi.org/10.2307/2548836.

Schnack, H. G., van Haren, N. E. M., Brouwer, R. M., van Baal, G. C. M., Picchioni, M., Weisbrod, M., et al. (2010). Mapping reliability in multicenter MRI: Voxel-based morphometry and cortical thickness. *Human Brain Mapping*, *31*(12), 1967–1982. https://doi.org/10.1002/hbm.20991.

Schwartz, D. L., Mitchell, A. D., Lahna, D. L., Luber, H. S., Huckans, M. S., Mitchell, S. H., et al. (2010). Global and local morphometric differences in recently abstinent methamphetamine-dependent individuals. *NeuroImage*, *50*(4), 1392–1401. https://doi.org/10.1016/j.neuroimage.2010.01.056.

Simon, H. (1955). A behavioral model of rational choice. *The Quarterly Journal of Economics*, *69*(1), 99–118.

Smith, A., Bernheim, B. D., Camerer, C., & Rangel, A. (2014). Neural activity reveals preferences without choices. *American Economic Journal. Microeconomics*, *6*(2), 1–36. https://doi.org/10.1257/mic.6.2.1.

Steverson, K., Brandenburger, A., & Glimcher, P. (2016). *Rational imprecision: information processing, neural, and choice-rule perspectives*. Working paper New York: Institute for the Study of Decision Making, New York University.

Sugrue, L. P., Corrado, G. S., & Newsome, W. T. (2004). Matching behavior and the representation of value in the parietal cortex. *Science (New York, NY)*, *304*(5678), 1782–1787. https://doi.org/10.1126/science.1094765.

Tymula, A., Belmaker, L. A. R., Ruderman, L., Glimcher, P. W., & Levy, I. (2015). Erratum: Like cognitive function, decision making across the life span shows profound age-related changes (Proceedings of the National Academy of Sciences of the United States of America (2013) 110 (17143-17148) DOI: 10.1073/pnas.1309909110). *Proceedings of the National Academy of Sciences of the United States of America*. *112*(40). https://doi.org/10.1073/pnas.1517212112.

Tymula, A., Rosenberg Belmaker, L., Ruderman, L., Glimcher, P. W., & Levy, I. (2013). Like cognitive function, decision making across the life span shows profound age-related changes. *Proceedings of the National Academy of Sciences of the United States of America*, *110*(42), 17143–17148. https://doi.org/10.1073/pnas.1309909110.

von Gaudecker, H. -M., van Soest, A., & Wengström, E. (2011). Heterogeneity in risky choice behavior in a broad population. *American Economic Review*, *101*(2), 664–694.

Wang, Q., Chen, C., Cai, Y., Li, S., Zhao, X., Zheng, L., et al. (2016). Dissociated neural substrates underlying impulsive choice and impulsive action. *NeuroImage*, *134*, 540–549. https://doi.org/10.1016/j.neuroimage.2016.04.010.

Webb, R., Glimcher, P. W., & Louie, K. (2016). Rationalizing context-dependent preferences: Divisive normalization and neurobiological constraints on choice. *SSRN Electronic Journal*. https://doi.org/10.2139/ssrn.2462895.

Woodford, M. (2012). Prospect theory as efficient perceptual distortion. *American Economic Review*, *102*(3), 41–46. https://doi.org/10.1257/aer.102.3.41.

Chapter 3

fMRI in Economics: What Functional Imaging of the Brain Can Add to Behavioral Economics Experiments

Niree Kodaverdian
Pomona College, Claremont, CA, United States

INTRODUCTION

Among the best known biophysical measurement methods is functional magnetic resonance imaging (fMRI). Since the introduction of the magnetic resonance imaging (MRI) machine in health care in the 1980s, MRI has provided doctors with an unparalleled look into the body, beyond the possibilities available with other imaging techniques, such as X-ray radiography, ultrasonography, or computed tomography (CT). About a decade after its introduction to the clinic, seminal papers by researchers at Bell Laboratories and the Martinos Center introduced to the world a new use for the MRI machine: fMRI (Belliveau et al., 1991; Kwong et al., 1992; Ogawa, Lee, Nayak, & Glynn, 1990). This pioneering technique allowed for the measurement of neural activity. It did not take long for neuroeconomists, who until then had been measuring firing rates of individual neurons in monkeys, to see the value of fMRI in economic research. Equipped with a powerful new tool, the nascent field of neuroeconomics began directly testing economic theories with human subjects. This chapter will begin with a discussion of the economic theories relevant to fMRI technology, continue with some background on the brain and fMRI technology, and then examine the progress and current limitations of neuroeconomic research using fMRI.

ECONOMIC THEORIES RELEVANT TO FMRI TECHNOLOGY

Studying the choices of individuals and society in the face of scarcity, economics is invariably concerned with the human decision making process. As decision making can occur under different circumstances, such as under risk, across

Biophysical Measurement in Experimental Social Science Research. https://doi.org/10.1016/B978-0-12-813092-6.00005-8

time, or in social contexts, different theories exist to describe and to predict people's decisions. Additionally, alternate theories have been proposed within each context based on field and experimental observations of human behavior. fMRI technology has provided economists with an unmatched ability to test individual theories, and to resolve competing theories. Below (also in Tymula, 2018) is an overview of the different topics that neuroeconomists have delved into. These will be discussed in more detail later in the chapter.

Subjective value: Every decision has a benefit and a cost. The fundamental basis of economic decision making is individuals' desire to maximize benefits while minimizing costs. While people can agree on the relative values of different monetary benefits (for example, we can agree that $10 is better than $5), the same dollar amount may have a different subjective value for different people. Furthermore, benefits (and costs) do not always take the form of money. Sometimes, benefits come in the form of goods, other times in the form of services, or in the form of experiences. Economic theory builds on the understanding that people desire to maximize their subjective value, or utility. Using fMRI technology, economists can assess the neural basis of subjective value and understand the value computation and comparison processes more deeply.

Decision making under uncertainty: Most decisions are made under conditions of uncertainty. Whereas risk and ambiguity are both types of uncertainty, since Knight (1921) they have been considered distinct by decision scientists in psychology and economics. Risk is usually defined as uncertainty about which of several possible outcomes will eventuate when the probability of each is known, while ambiguity is defined as the uncertainty about which of several possible outcomes will eventuate when the probability of each is unknown. Daniel Ellsberg famously demonstrated the difference between risk and ambiguity in a 1961 paper, in what was later named the Ellsberg paradox (Ellsberg, 1961). This distinction is, unfortunately, overlooked sometimes and the terms are used interchangeably. For example, the Balloon analog risk task (BART) and the sequential investment task (SIT) used in psychology experiments do not present subjects with explicit probabilities, making the decisions ambiguous rather than risky. Using fMRI, economists have been able to provide neural evidence for the distinction between these two concepts of uncertainty.

Loss aversion: A widely-observed aspect of human decision making, absent from standard economic theory, is a strong aversion to potential loss. For example, experimental evidence shows that the cost of losing one dollar is greater than the value of gaining one dollar (Kahneman & Tversky, 1979). This aversion is formalized in prospect theory through an asymmetric value function, where the function is steeper for losses than for gains. One of the main controversies in understanding loss aversion regards whether the process is driven by one system, or by two systems: one responsible for reasoned comparisons, and another for emotional decision making. A second controversy concerns the source of loss aversion. Does loss aversion reflect a stable underlying preference function, or rather a fearful overreaction at the time of choice? Neuroeconomic research can help distinguish between these hypotheses.

Regret aversion: Experiments with fMRI can also help distinguish between expected utility theory and another set of alternative theories, namely, regret-based theories. As we know, expected utility theory assumes that the decision maker is fully rational. One implication of rationality is that a decision maker's choices reflect an underlying transitivity in preferences. However, when subjects expect to be provided with post-decision feedback in experiments, their decisions are significantly affected, and transitivity is violated (Bleichrodt & Wakker, 2015; Zeelenberg, 1999). This observation is consistent with taking anticipated regret into account when making an initial decision, an idea formalized in regret theory, which was simultaneously developed in 1982 by Graham Loomes and Robert Sugden, Robert E. Bell, and Peter C. Fishburn. Current forms of regret theory reconcile expected utility theory with these empirical observations by incorporating anticipated regret into the utility function. Using fMRI, economists can not only examine the neural substrates of regret and disappointment, but also determine the role of these emotions in decision making: i.e., how exactly does regret affect future choices?

Other reference dependence: According to standard economic theory, a rational person should not be swayed by any reference point, such as one that enables a distinction to be made between gains and losses. Another reference point is that of ownership: whether a person owns an item or not should be inconsequential to that person's valuation of the item. Behavioral experiments, however, have widely reported the presence of an endowment effect, which is the tendency to place greater value on items that one owns than on items that one does not own (Kahneman, Knetsch, & Thaler, 1991). This violates the reference-independence assumption commonly made in standard economic theories of choice. Another widely observed phenomenon is status quo bias, observed and coined as a term by Samuelson and Zeckhauser (1988), which refers to people's likelihood of accepting a default choice option regardless of its optimality. fMRI experiments can provide insight into the validity and source of these reference-dependent behaviors.

Intertemporal decision making: Economic theory has implications about decisions made for, or in, different points in time—what is referred to as intertemporal decision making. According to the standard model of economic decision making (Samuelson, 1937), people apply constant discounting rates which depend only on the length of the delay until a benefit or cost is realized, implying consistency in the choices made at all time periods. However, empirical evidence points to problems with this exponential time discounting function. For example, Thaler (1981) reported empirical evidence for dynamic inconsistency, finding that discount rates varied depending on the length of time between the immediate and delayed reward: a direct contradiction of the implications of the exponential time discounting function. The hyperbolic discount function accounts for dynamic inconsistency by including a discounting rate that decreases as the benefit or cost realization occurs further in the future, fitting experimental data better than the exponential functional form (as reviewed in Frederick, Loewenstein, & O'Donoghue, 2002). The quasi-hyperbolic discount function was later adopted by Laibson (1997) and O'Donoghue and Rabin (1999) to additionally account for present bias—people's tendency to place additional weight or value on an option with an immediate payoff. Economists can test the soundness of these different theories by having subjects make intertemporal choices in the fMRI scanner.

Social decision making: Traditionally, economic theory makes the assumption that people are self-regarding. In turn, most research on decision making tends to focus on individuals making choices outside of a social context. There is a large body of experimental evidence, however, suggesting a role for other-regarding preferences in economic decisions (Camerer, 2011; Fehr & Fischbacher, 2003): people's preferred choices are based on a positive or negative concern for the welfare of others, on what they believe about other players, and on what they believe other players believe about them (Fehr & Camerer, 2007). Where economic theory predicts defection, distrust, and betrayal, experimental evidence suggests the existence of cooperation and trust, at least some of the time. By studying social decision making in the scanner, neuroeconomists attempt to understand the brain processes that govern these regular deviations from purely self-interested behavior (Fehr & Camerer, 2007).

HOW THE BRAIN WORKS

The human brain contains billions of nerve cells called neurons. Neurons are arranged in patterns that coordinate thought, emotion, behavior, movement, and sensations. Although neurons vary in size and shape, each neuron has a cell body (called the soma) and various "processes" (appendages or protrusions) that extend from the cell body. A single, branched process (called an axon) extends from one side of the cell body and several branched processes (called dendrites) extend from around the cell body. Neurons also contain specialized structures for the purpose of communicating with other neurons: "signals" (called neurotransmitters) and signal releasing stations (called axon terminals). While all the parts of the brain work together through neuronal communication, each part is responsible for a specific function.

Although neurons are different from other cells in the body in structure and purpose, they are also similar in fundamental ways. Like any cell in the human body, neurons obtain virtually all of their energy via the aerobic metabolism of glucose. Because this requires a large amount of oxygen, the brain requires a high blood flow, as oxygen is carried in blood. Specifically, oxygen is transported with the assistance of red blood cells. Red blood cells contain a protein called hemoglobin, each molecule of which forms an unstable, reversible bond to oxygen. When oxygen is bound to hemoglobin, bright red oxyhemoglobin is formed and is carried in arterial blood to neurons, and cells generally. After the oxygen molecules are unloaded to cells, the deoxygenated hemoglobin molecule (which is called deoxyhemoglobin) is purple-blue in color.

The Hemodynamic Response

The concentration of deoxyhemoglobin changes in response to changes in neural activity. When neurons in the brain are activated, the immediate effect is an increase in metabolic activity. As metabolism occurs, the concentrations of oxyhemoglobin and deoxyhemoglobin change in the nearby vasculature—there is an increase in the concentration of deoxyhemoglobin and a decrease in the concentration of oxyhemoglobin, as oxygen is used in metabolism. Because the magnetic resonance (MR) signal depends on oxygen in the blood (called the blood oxygen-level dependent or BOLD signal), the relative decrease of oxyhemoglobin causes a dip in the signal.

As a secondary response, the neural activity also triggers an increase in blood flow to the area in order to provide neurons with additional oxyhemoglobin and for metabolism. As oxyhemoglobin pours in, the concentrations of oxy- and deoxyhemoglobin change again. As a result, the initial dip in the relative concentration of oxyhemoglobin and hence in the MR signal is followed a few seconds later by a significantly greater increase in this concentration, and the MR signal.

According to one widely-held belief, the inflow of blood "actually overcompensates for the amount of oxygen being extracted, so that an oversupply of oxygenated blood is delivered" (Heeger & Ress, 2002, p. 144). While there is an apparent mismatch between blood flow and oxygen consumption, blood flow is proportional to glucose consumption, as brain activity is supported by oxidative and nonoxidative glucose metabolism (glycolosis) alike (Heeger & Ress, 2002). A second view is that the blood flow provides sufficient and not excessive amounts of oxygen to cells, as extracting oxygen from the blood is less efficient when blood flows at a higher rate (Heeger & Ress, 2002).

As time passes and neurons carry out their metabolic activity, the once-oxygenated hemoglobin particles lose their oxygen molecule, becoming deoxyhemoglobin particles. This creates an "undershoot" following neural activity, where the MR signal falls below its equilibrium level. The cause of this post-stimulus undershoot is poorly understood, widely debated, and assumed to covary in amplitude with the primary response (Mullinger, Mayhew, Bagshaw, Bowtell, & Francis, 2013).

Excitatory Versus Inhibitory Activity

Neuronal activity can be excitatory or inhibitory. The brain is an interconnected place, with neurons often making numerous connections with each other. Neurons communicate with one another by passing electrical messages, or more commonly, by sending chemical messages to one another. Chemical messages are transmitted in the form of neurotransmitters, released from vesicles of one neuron, through the gap between the two neurons (the synaptic cleft), to ultimately bind to receptors on the second neuron. There are two categories of chemical gaps, or synapses, that can exist between neurons: excitatory synapses and inhibitory synapses. In excitatory synapses, a neurotransmitter binds to the receptor of the second neuron, increasing the likelihood that the neuron will "fire," or the probability that the neuron will generate an action potential. The neurotransmitter that generally binds to excitatory receptors is glutamate. In the case of inhibitory synapses, a neurotransmitter—typically gamma-aminobutyric acid (GABA)—binds to the receptor of the second neuron, decreasing the likelihood that the neuron will fire.

Excitatory activities and inhibitory activities both require energy. Excitatory activity requires energy directly and also leads to a greater demand in energy, as it increases the likelihood of many neurons firing in sequence. The eventual effect of synaptic inhibition is a decrease in neuronal activity. With inhibitory activity initially demanding metabolic activity, and then inhibiting the demand for further metabolic activity in the inhibited regions, the net effect of this category of activity is unclear. In a couple of studies discussed by Attwell and Iadecola (2002), it was found that inhibition of hippocampal pyramidal and auditory cells was associated with increased glucose usage. However, in a study by Waldvogel, Van Gelderen, Muellbacher, and Ziemann (2000), it was found that inhibition evoked no measurable change in the MR signal. Whether the net effect of inhibition on neuronal activity is null or positive, how do the energy requirements of inhibition compare with that of excitation?

Theoretically, one might predict that excitation demands more glucose metabolism than inhibition. At the individual neuron and aggregate brain level, more energy is required for excitation compared to inhibition (as discussed in Attwell & Iadecola, 2002). Waldvogel et al. (2000) conducted an fMRI study to test the relative metabolic demands of excitation and inhibition. As predicted, they found that in their task, unlike excitation, inhibition evoked no measurable change in the MR signal in the motor cortex, "indicating that inhibition is less metabolically demanding" and in turn suggesting that "the 'activation' seen in functional imaging studies probably results from excitation rather than inhibition" (Waldvogel et al., 2000, p. 995). Neural simulation results suggest a more complicated answer, with evidence that the effect of neuronal inhibition on brain imaging measures depends on several factors (Tagamets & Horwitz, 2001).

THE METHOD AND APPLICATION OF FMRI TECHNOLOGY

fMRI is based on the same technology as MRI: both types of imaging employ the same machine. Using a powerful magnet and radio waves, the machine takes advantage of the magnetic property of atomic nuclei to produce images. When not exposed to a strong magnetic field, as when outside the MRI machine, protons in the nuclei of atoms face in different directions. When exposed to a powerful magnet, as when inside the MRI machine, protons align themselves with the direction of the machine's magnetic field. As protons possess the quantum property of "spin" (they have "angular momentum"), being aligned in a way does not mean they face a certain direction in a fixed fashion, but rather that the axis along which they precess, or around which they orbit, is fixed. In the case of the MRI machine, exposed protons precess about the axis created by the machine's applied magnetic field (as shown in Fig. 1).

Radio frequency (RF) pulses emitted from the machine orthogonal to the direction of the static field then "hit" cells, causing protons to precess together in the new direction. As these protons release the energy absorbed from the RF pulses, returning, or relaxing, to their initial alignment with the static magnetic field, information is collected by the machine on the rate of their relaxation. There are two types of relaxation that occur: longitudinal, as the protons return to alignment with the direction of the static field, and transverse, as the protons return to spinning about the axis as before. Depending on the type of image desired (anatomical or functional), the sequence of RF pulses and sampling of relaxation rates emphasizes one of these two relaxations, and a Fourier transformation of these data produces the anatomical (MRI) or functional (fMRI) images on the linked computer screen.

The main difference between these two methods lies in what they enable us to view. MRI images the anatomical structure (of various body parts), while fMRI images the metabolic function (of the brain), a proxy for neural activity. How is the brain's metabolic function captured with this technology? Although we can have anaerobic metabolism in other parts of the body, neurons obtain virtually all of their nutrition via aerobic metabolism—which requires oxygen, by definition. As such, changing concentrations of oxygen can give us an idea about the changing levels of metabolic activity occurring in different regions of the brain.

However, fMRI cannot directly detect oxygen and instead, we look to hemoglobin, the protein located inside red blood cells that carries oxygen to cells in the brain and body (and carbon dioxide to the lungs). Oxyhemoglobin is slightly repelled by the fMRI machine's magnetic field (i.e., it is diamagnetic), similar to the rest of the brain, and thus will not produce contrasting magnetic susceptibilities. Deoxyhemoglobin, however, is attracted by the fMRI machine's magnetic field (i.e., it is paramagnetic). Paramagnetic materials, which stand in contrast to the diamagnetic tissues of the brain, allow us to capture images of brain activity. Changing proportions of deoxyhemoglobin affect the MR signal by affecting relaxation rates of protons—specifically, as the proportion of deoxyhemoglobin to oxyhemoglobin decreases, the MR signal increases.

WHAT HAVE WE LEARNED FROM FMRI EVIDENCE?

Below, I will discuss the findings from neuroeconomic experiments using fMRI. As many of the results I discuss involve regions of the brain, I have included two illustrations of the brain below (side view of the outside of the brain on the left, sagittal view of the inside of the brain on the right). If you encounter an unfamiliar brain term, please refer to Fig. 2 to aid in your comprehension.

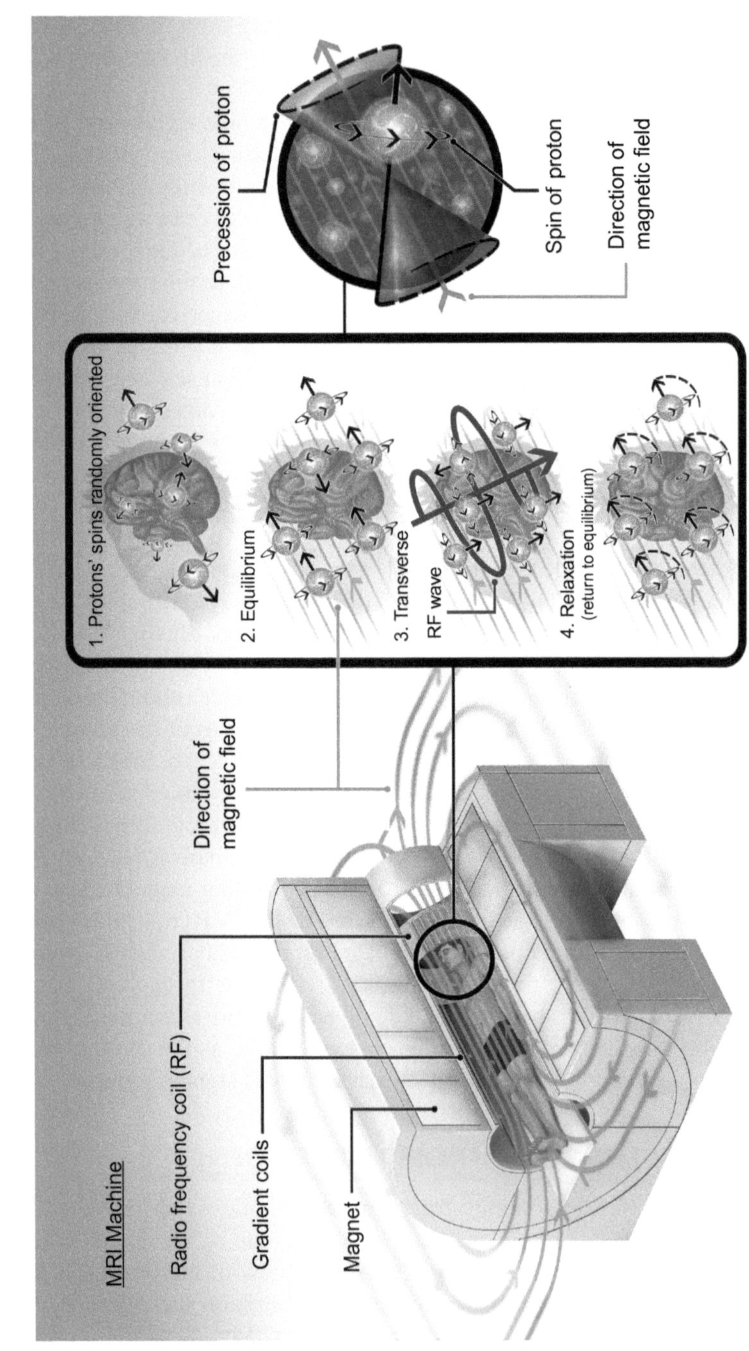

FIG. 1 Illustration of a subject in an MRI machine (left); Orientation of protons outside an MRI machine (top center) and during different phases of a scan (center); Precession of a proton around MRI machine's magnetic field (right).

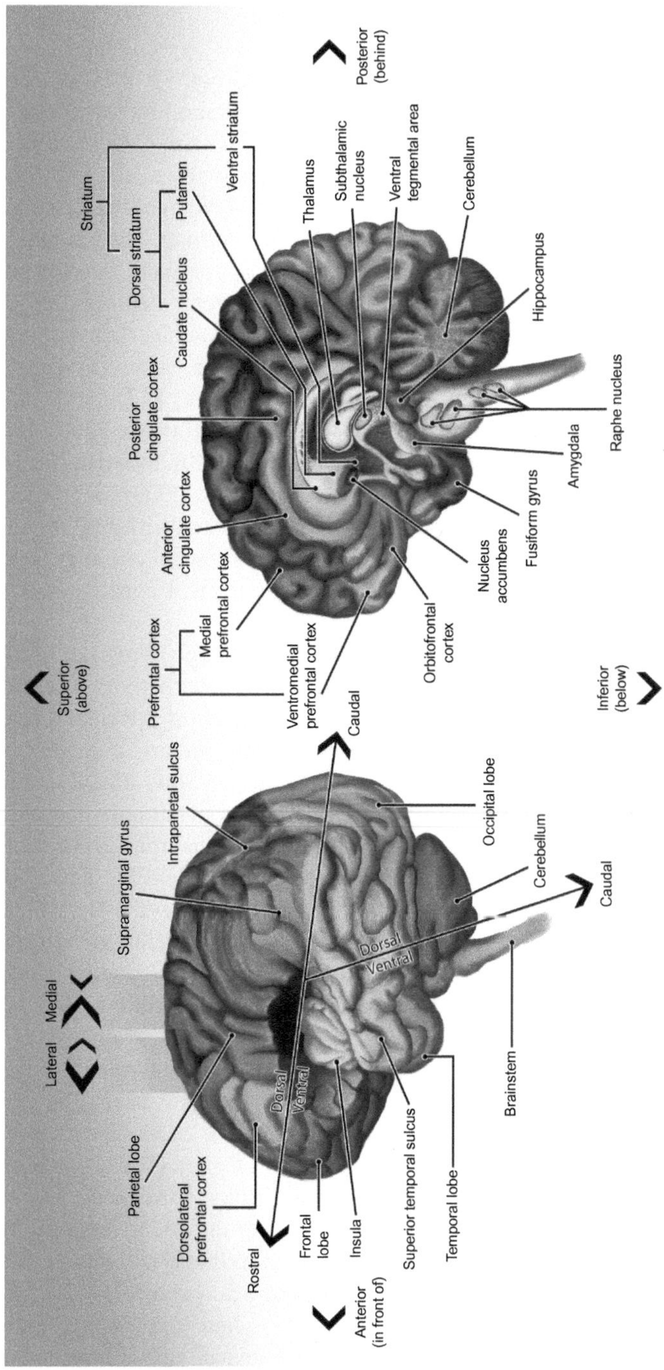

FIG. 2 Lateral (left) and sagital view (right) of the brain.

Subjective Value in the Brain

One way to experimentally elicit subjective values is by using the Becker-DeGroot-Marschack (BDM) method (Becker, DeGroot, & Marschak, 1964). Although there are several variations, the most common flavor of this method is as follows: (1) the subject formulates a bid for an item, (2) a random number generator determines a price to which the bid is compared, and (3) if the bid is higher than the price, the subject pays the price and receives the item, and if the bid is lower, the subject pays nothing and receives nothing. The optimal strategy is to bid exactly the amount one is willing to pay for each item (as shown in Chib, Rangel, Shimojo, & O'Doherty, 2009). Several neuroimaging studies have used the BDM method to elicit subjective values from subjects (as reviewed in Peters & Büchel, 2010). In these studies, subjects were asked to make bids for food snacks (Chib et al., 2009; Hare, O'Doherty, Camerer, Schultz, & Rangel, 2008; Plassmann, O'Doherty, & Rangel, 2007), donations (Hare, Camerer, Knoepfle, O'Doherty, & Rangel, 2010), lotteries (De Martino, Kumaran, Holt, & Dolan, 2009), monies (Chib et al., 2009), or trinkets (Chib et al., 2009). Subjective value was found to be correlated with activity in regions previously indicated as forming part of the brain's reward circuitry such as the orbitofrontal cortex (OFC) and ventromedial prefrontal cortex (vmPFC) (see Fig. 2), as reviewed in Peters and Büchel (2010).

A second way to measure subjective value is through liking ratings. By having subjects rate how much they like each of several alternatives on a scale, such as the Likert scale (named after its inventor, psychologist Rensis Likert), one can obtain a rough measure of subjects' subjective values. In a neuroimaging study with different wines, Plassmann, O'Doherty, Shiv, and Rangel (2008) find a positive correlation between liking ratings of stimuli and activity in the medial orbitofrontal cortex (mOFC). Many other neuroimaging studies find a positive correlation between activity in the mOFC/vmPFC and a subject's liking rating of a perceived stimulus (for a review, see Peters & Büchel, 2010). A subset of these studies also finds a positive correlation between liking ratings and activation in the lateral/central OFC, and a smaller subset still, between liking ratings and activation in the ventral striatum (see Peters & Büchel, 2010).

Yet another way to measure subjective value experimentally is through a subject's choices. Over the course of multiple identical trials, the frequency with which a subject chooses an option is revealing of his/her preference for the option. McClure, Laibson, Loewenstein, and Cohen (2004) study subjects' choices in the scanner for culturally familiar drinks (Coke and Pepsi, specifically). Similar to the findings from studies using the BDM method, McClure et al. (2004) find that activity in the OFC is correlated with subjective value, as measured by choice frequency: the more times a subject chose Coke, the more OFC activity was observed (relatively) when Coke was presented. In another study (Kable & Glimcher, 2007), subjects make repeated choices between immediate and delayed rewards in the scanner. Kable and Glimcher (2007) find a "clear match" between subjects' subjective preferences and their neural activity in the ventral striatum, mPFC, and posterior cingulate cortex (pCC), providing support for the role of preferences in making choices, as modeled in economics.

Regardless of the method used for value elicitation, there is strong evidence for the correlation of activation in the mOFC/vmPFC (as well as other more lateral parts of the OFC, the ventral striatum, and the pCC) and subjective values. An individual facing a choice must not only determine his subjective values for each alternative, according to the standard economic framework, but must also compare the different values to select the alternative with the highest one. fMRI experiments can shine a light here: does neural evidence support this two-part view of the decision making process?

Using repeated binary choices and a logit analysis, FitzGerald, Seymour, and Dolan (2009) extract subjective values for each of a pair of alternatives for each subject. They find that activation in the mOFC and perhaps in the pCC is correlated with the difference in subjective value between the presented options (FitzGerald et al., 2009). This finding suggests that beyond merely tracking the subjective value of a single option, the mOFC encodes value comparisons. Other studies support this finding, reporting that vmPFC, and sometimes intraparietal sulcus (IPS), signals reflect the difference in value between chosen and unchosen options during decision making (Boorman, Behrens, Woolrich, & Rushworth, 2009; De Martino, Fleming, Garrett, & Dolan, 2013; Hunt et al., 2012; Kolling, Behrens, Mars, & Rushworth, 2012; Philiastides, Biele, & Heekeren, 2010; Rushworth, Noonan, Boorman, Walton, & Behrens, 2011).

A related question is whether the brain computes choices by comparing the values of stimuli directly in "goods space" (e.g., comparing the values of items shown on either side of a participant's screen), or instead by first assigning values to the actions required to obtain those goods (e.g., comparing the values of the actions required to obtain the items shown on either side of the screen), and then making a choice over those actions (Wunderlich, Rangel, & O'Doherty, 2010). Wunderlich et al. (2010) found a correlation between the value of the chosen option and activity in the vmPFC prior to participants knowing what action would be required to obtain the option. Their findings provide support for the hypothesis that the brain can make choices in the space of goods without first transferring values into action space.

fMRI can take us one step further, by helping to expose the neural mechanism of this value comparison. While many studies have found activity in the vmPFC to be correlated with values and with value differences, implying that value comparison is taking place, the mechanism by which this comparison takes place has remained unknown. Economic theory does not model the mechanism underlying the comparison of values. Different classes of mechanisms have been suggested in the decision-neuroscience literature.

One popular proposed mechanism of value comparison involves competition by mutual inhibition, where neurons encoding the value of an alternative inhibit neurons of the competing alternative(s). Other classes of models involving inhibition include the feedforward inhibition model (Shadlen & Newsome, 2001) and the pooled inhibition model (simplified from Wang, 2002). In a study by Jocham, Hunt, Near, and Behrens (2012), the role of the vmPFC in value-based decision making is studied under the predictions of neural competition by mutual inhibition. They show that vmPFC levels of GABA (inhibitory neurotransmitters) and glutamate (excitatory neurotransmitters) in humans are predictive of both behavioral and neural data, as the predictions of this class of models would imply (Jocham et al., 2012). Chau, Kolling, Hunt, Walton, and Rushworth (2014) test a three-alternative version of a mutual inhibition model in the scanner. They find that in the presence of a third distractor alternative, there was greater difficulty choosing between the other two options. This difficulty was observed both behaviorally and neurally, with a decreased vmPFC signal in the presence of the distractor alternative, suggesting that people's choices are in fact affected by the presence of irrelevant alternatives (contra the conventional independence of irrelevant alternatives [IIA] assumption in economics [Ray, 1973; Arrow, 1963]).

Another popular mechanism for choice underpinned by value comparison involves accumulation (and not inhibition). This is embodied in stochastic models—such as the drift diffusion class of models (DDM; Ratcliff, 1978; Ratcliff & McKoon, 2008) and its variants, including the attentional drift diffusion model (aDDM; Krajbich & Rangel, 2011; Krajbich, Armel, & Rangel, 2010) which incorporates attention, as captured by eye-tracking devices (for more on using eye-tracking in economics experiments, see Beesley, Pearson, and Le Pelley (2018)) and the neural drift diffusion model (Turner, Van Maanen, & Forstmann, 2015)—as well as ballistic models, such as the linear ballistic accumulator (LBA) model (Brown & Heathcote, 2005, 2008), and single-trial linear ballistic accumulator (STLBA) model (Van Maanen et al., 2011). The basic DDM model assumes that decisions are made by a noisy process that accumulates information over time from a starting point, "drifting" toward one of two boundaries. For value-based decision making, the noisy evidence comes from the computation and comparison of the alternatives' values. The rate of accumulation of information is called the drift rate. When one of the boundaries is reached, a response is made. Using fMRI and electroencephalogram (EEG) recordings, Frank et al. (2015) show that decision making is well described by the DDM. However, their neural findings suggest an improvement to the model: namely, that the decision threshold is not fixed across trials, but varies as a function of activity in certain areas, representing decision conflict. Turner et al. (2015) propose another improvement to the DDM. They develop and test the neural DDM, which incorporates neural data into the model. They show that the neural DDM outperforms the traditional DDM, as it combines response time, choice accuracy, and the BOLD response (Turner et al., 2015).

With neural evidence in support of both classes of models (inhibition and accumulation), the question remains as to what mechanism underlies choice selection. In a review paper, Bogacz, Brown, Moehlis, Holmes, and Cohen (2006) compare six different classes of models, including the DDM and the inhibition models mentioned above, and in a subsequent study, Van Ravenzwaaij, Van der Maas, and Wagenmakers (2012), compare inhibition and DDM models. Both studies find that neural inhibition models can mimic the DDM and produce optimal decisions (Bogacz et al., 2006; Van Ravenzwaaij et al., 2012).

Decision Making Under Uncertainty

fMRI evidence suggests that the distinction between risk and ambiguity has neural bases. While there is neural evidence for a common system (involving the ventral striatum and mPFC) representing subjective values in both risky and ambiguous settings (Levy & Glimcher, 2012), there is also evidence for distinct systems being involved in the two concepts. For example, Huettel, Stowe, Gordon, Warner, and Platt (2006) find that individuals' preferences for risk and ambiguity predict different types of brain activation associated with decision making. Specifically, they find that activation within the lateral prefrontal cortex (lPFC) is predicted by ambiguity preference while activation of the posterior parietal cortex is predicted by risk preference. This difference "indicates that decision making under ambiguity does not represent a special, more complex case of risky decision making; instead, these two forms of uncertainty are supported by distinct mechanisms" (Huettel et al., 2006, p. 765). Similarly, Hsu, Bhatt, Adolphs, Tranel, and Camerer (2005) compared conditions of ambiguity to conditions of risk, and found that certain regions (the OFC, amygdala, and dorsomedial PFC) were relatively more sensitive to ambiguity, while another region (the striatum) was relatively more sensitive to risk. More recently, Congdon et al. (2013) compared activation patterns during decisions in BART and the angling risk task (ART), which measures risk preferences, in the scanner and also found a neural distinction, although their findings of increased fronto-cingulate activation during ambiguity (i.e., during BART) as compared to risk (i.e., during ART risky choice trials) do not map precisely onto those of Hsu et al. (2005).

In addition to providing evidence for distinct processes involved in risk and ambiguity, experiments with fMRI can help us understand the risky decision process. There are two general views of this decision process. The first is that when faced with a decision under risk, the brain computes a single-dimensional index for each option (as per expected utility theory or prospect theory), and the other is that the brain decomposes risk into its features of expected reward and variance (as per financial decision theory). In an fMRI study, Preuschoff, Bossaerts, and Quartz (2006) varied expected reward and risk (modeled as variance) orthogonally across trials, so as to identify subcortical (below the cortex) regions correlated with those two separate aspects of the decision problem. They found that activations in reward-related areas of the brain (specifically, areas such as the ventral striatum that receive dopamine, a neurotransmitter involved in reward-motivated behavior) were correlated with each mathematical parameter (expected reward and variance of expected reward) in a spatially and temporally differentiated way, providing support for the second view of the decision process. Other studies have found additional evidence for the distinct neural coding of value and risk (Knutson, Taylor, Kaufman, Peterson, & Glover, 2005; Tobler, O'Doherty, Dolan, & Schultz, 2007).

Furthermore, fMRI technology has allowed economists to horserace the bases of standard and alternative theories of risky decision making using neural evidence. Decision making under conditions of risk is typically explained as the result of utility maximization, first proposed by Daniel Bernoulli in 1738. The theory, later developed by Von Neumann and Morgenstern (1945), assumes that humans will assess options based on the utility they expect to gain from each. According to this theory, expected utility is linear in the objective probabilities of the possible options. However, observations of people's choices inside and outside the laboratory—as most famously demonstrated by the Allais Paradox—contradict this fact, at least at the tail ends of the probability distribution: people tend to overweight small probabilities and underweight large probabilities (as illustrated in studies including Gonzalez & Wu, 1999; Hershey & Schoemaker, 1980; Kahneman & Tversky, 1979). People's behavior in experiments has consistently revealed a four-fold pattern of risk preferences: risk-seeking for low-probability gains and high-probability losses, coupled with risk aversion for high-probability gains and low-probability losses. The Allais paradox and the four-fold pattern of risk preferences is neatly packaged in prospect theory (Kahneman & Tversky, 1979), which relaxes the linearity assumption by introducing the notion of a probability weighting function. fMRI-based experimental evidence can lend support to either expected utility theory or prospect theory.

Several neuroimaging studies have found evidence for the nonlinear weighting of probabilities predicted by prospect theory. In one study, subjects made binary choices between a gamble and a sure outcome on each trial (Paulus & Frank, 2006). The gamble was altered in successive trials to estimate each subject's certainty equivalent (i.e., the amount of money offered for certain that would make the subject indifferent between accepting that certain option and taking the proposed gamble). The certainty equivalent was then used to estimate the nonlinearity of each subject's probability weighting function. Across-subject analyses revealed that activity in the anterior cingulate cortex (aCC) was found to be correlated with the nonlinearity parameter, such that participants with more aCC activity for high compared to low prospects also showed more nonlinear weighting of probabilities. Nonlinearities in probability weighting were also examined by Hsu, Krajbich, Zhao, and Camerer (2009). In this experiment, subjects were scanned while they made binary choices between simple gambles, which varied in outcome magnitude and probability. As per the predictions of prospect theory, activity in the striatum during the valuation of monetary gambles was found to be nonlinear in probabilities. Moreover, analysis of individual differences revealed a significant correlation between behavioral nonlinearity and nonlinearity of striatal response across participants.

In a nonchoice neuroimaging study, subjects were scanned as they viewed visual stimuli which varied in shape and color, representing reward magnitude and probability, respectively (Tobler, Christopoulos, O'Doherty, Dolan, & Schultz, 2008). The activation patterns of dorsolateral frontal cortex regions were consistent with the overweighting of small probabilities and underweighting of large probabilities, whereas ventral frontal regions showed the opposite patterns. Probability weighting distortion for aversive outcomes was examined by Berns, Capra, Chappelow, Moore, and Noussair (2008). In a first phase, participants passively viewed prospects that specified the magnitude and probability of an electric shock. In a second phase, participants chose between pairs of lotteries. A quantity was estimated (the "neurological probability response ratio," NPRR) that indexed the response to a lottery with probability less than one using the response to a lottery with a probability of one as the numeraire. For the passive phase, NPRR was significantly nonlinear for most regions examined (including regions in the dorsal striatum, PFC, insula, and aCC). Recorded activity from the passive phase was then used to predict choices during the second phase. The fMRI signals from the passive phase provided significant predictive power, particularly for lotteries that were near a subject's indifference point. Thus, there appears to be fairly wide-scale overweighting of low-probability aversive events involving a number of brain regions.

Loss Aversion

Along with the above neural evidence for the phenomenon of subjective probability weighting, there is neural support for another conjecture of prospect theory. While standard economic theory suggests that people will accept a mixed gamble if the potential gain is equal to the potential loss, behavioral evidence suggests an asymmetric sensitivity to losses—specifically, by a factor of two, so that the potential gain must be at least twice as large as the potential loss for the gamble to be accepted (Tom, Fox, Trepel, & Poldrack, 2007). This phenomenon, called loss aversion, is captured in prospect theory by an asymmetric value function that is relatively steeper for losses than for gains.

One question is whether the same neural regions are involved in evaluating losses and gains. If common regions are found to be involved in the evaluation of each, then the question is whether there is evidence for a steeper loss function than gain function, or as Kahneman and Tversky (1979) originally put it, whether "losses loom larger than gains." If different regions are activated in the evaluation of losses and gains, a question we can address using neural evidence is whether the avoidance of potential losses reflects a fearful overreaction at the time of choice, or rather a stable component of preferences.

There is evidence for a common neural system underlying the evaluation of potential gains and potential losses. Several neuroimaging studies, where subjects make gambling choices in the scanner, find that activity in a broad set of areas displays joint sensitivity to prospective gains and losses (Canessa et al., 2013; Tom et al., 2007). While some of these areas (such as the ventral striatum, vmPFC, OFC, and aCC) displayed increased activation with potential gains and decreased activation with potential losses (Canessa et al., 2013; Tom et al., 2007), some other areas (posterior insula, parietal operculum) displayed decreased activation with potential gains and increased activation with potential losses (Canessa et al., 2013). In a neuroimaging study where subjects made intertemporal choices in the scanner (Xu, Liang, Wang, Li, & Jiang, 2009), it has again been found that common regions (lPFC, posterior parietal) are activated when evaluating potential gains and losses, with stronger activation when evaluating future losses as compared to when evaluating future gains.

With common regions of activation for losses and for gains, the shape of the value function can be interrogated: is prospect theory correct in proposing a steeper function for the loss domain as compared to the gain domain? Tom et al. (2007) find that a number of regions (including the ventral striatum) have a decrease in activity for losses that is steeper than their increase in activity for gains. Similarly, Canessa et al. (2013) find that the slope of the activation (in the right posterior insula and parietal operculum) for increasing losses is greater than the slope of the deactivation in these regions for increasing gains.

Conversely, there is evidence for the activation of distinct systems for the evaluation of losses. In line with a lesion study, where two patients with amygdala damage showed a dramatic reduction in loss aversion compared to normal controls (De Martino, Camerer, & Adolphs, 2010), Sokol-Hessner, Camerer, and Phelps (2012) find that amygdala activity is indicative of one's degree of loss aversion during a gambling task in the scanner: specifically, they find that amygdala activity in response to loss versus gain outcomes correlates with estimates of behavioral loss aversion, although due to their design it was not possible to independently analyze BOLD responses to potential losses versus potential gains at the point of a subject's decision.

Other studies also find support for dissociable systems for evaluating gain- and loss-related value. Employing a guessing task in the scanner, Yacubian et al. (2006) find that activation in the ventral striatum activation correlates with expected value (and prediction error) but only for the gain domain. In contrast, loss-related expected value and the associated prediction error are correlated with activity in the amygdala. Weber et al. (2007) use a design in which participants either buy or sell MP3 songs in a BDM auction. In their procedure, an individual bid his minimum buying or selling price in a second-price auction against a randomly drawn number. Comparing selling trials and buying trials revealed greater amygdala and dorsal striatal activity in the former, and greater activity in the parahippocampal gyrus (the region surrounding the hippocampus) in the latter. The researchers interpret the comparatively stronger activation of the amygdala during selling trials relative to buying trials as neural evidence for loss aversion. A lesion study by Weller, Levin, Shiv, and Bechara (2007) provides more evidence for dissociable systems, but the role of the amygdala appears to be the opposite of that found in the above studies. They find that patients with lesions to the amygdala display impaired decision making involving the consideration of potential gains but are unimpaired in making decisions involving the consideration of potential losses (Weber et al., 2007).

As the amygdala is instrumental in emotional processing and learning (as reviewed in Sergerie, Chochol, & Armony, 2008 and in Phelps & LeDoux, 2005), these findings suggest that loss anticipation may activate a Pavlovian response, inhibiting action to avoid the potentially aversive outcome (Phelps & LeDoux, 2005). Findings by Xu et al. (2009) support the conclusion that potential losses engage emotional systems. They find that regions previously found to be associated with emotion processing (e.g., the insula, thalamus, and dorsal striatum) were more activated during intertemporal choices involving losses as compared to those involving gains, leading to the inference that "enhanced sensitivity to losses may be driven by negative emotions" (Xu et al., 2009, p. 65).

The engagement of these structures in the processing of aversive stimuli and experiences raises the question of whether loss represents a transient fearful overreaction elicited by choice-related information, or rather a stable component of preferences. In a recent study, Canessa et al. (2017) scanned subjects' brains during a resting state: when they were not making decisions, but simply lying down in the scanner. They found that activity during this resting state in the same regions (ventral striatum, right posterior insula/supramarginal gyrus) that previously demonstrated patterns consistent with neural loss aversion was correlated with subjects' degree of behavioral loss aversion. This finding indicates that loss aversion may be a stable component of an individual's preferences.

Regret Aversion

Regret and disappointment are both negative emotions, experienced on the back of undesirable decision outcomes. The difference is that regret (or conversely, relief) is mediated by counterfactual thinking, a complex cognitive process that involves making comparisons between an actual outcome and an imagined better but unrealized outcome.

There is no room for feelings of regret in expected utility theory: when faced with a choice among alternatives, an expected utility maximizer will choose the one with the highest expected utility, regardless of the likelihood of future regret (Von Neumann & Morgenstern, 1945). However, from personal, anecdotal, and experimental evidence, we know that people behave differently. People appear to be inherently regret-averse, and in turn, may attempt to minimize future regret when making decisions.

Several models of regret have been proposed, beginning with those by Loomes and Sugden (1982), Bell (1982), and Fishburn (1982). Regret models resolve expected utility theory with observations of regret by incorporating anticipated regret in the utility function, as shown below. The question this poses to neuroeconomics researchers is whether this incorporation is physiologically valid, or whether it represents instead an as-if approximation to a different underlying mechanism.

$$\varphi[v(x) - v(y)] \tag{1}$$

Here, φ is the regret function representing the comparison between the value (v) of a choice (x) and the value of a rejected alternative (y). The function φ then purportedly appears in the utility function (U):

$$U(x, y) = v(x) + \varphi[v(x) - v(y)] \tag{2}$$

Besides looking for a neurological marker for anticipated regret, neuroimaging studies can answer important questions, beginning with whether regret and disappointment are neurally distinct from one another. Second, how exactly does regret affect future decisions? Does experienced regret affect subsequent decisions through anticipated regret, as modeled in regret theory? Is there a mechanism of cognitive control that jumps in to enforce an action, or is the anticipation of regret enough to steer future choices away from undesirable outcomes? Third, regret-related brain activity is dependent on free choice. Is this activity also a function of the degree of responsibility a decision maker has for his choice? What is the role of agency in the feeling of regret, and can experimental manipulations of agency pinpoint its role in the experience of regret? The evidence on each of these questions is reviewed below.

Regret is typically studied using a gambling task (called the "wheels of fortune" task), which is a binary choice gambling task with two feedback conditions: partial and complete. This feedback manipulation aims to disentangle feelings of disappointment from those of regret. In complete feedback trials, subjects are shown the outcome of their choice as well as that of the unchosen alternative, which is sometimes relatively worse (presumably triggering relief), or better (presumably triggering regret). In partial feedback trials, subjects are only shown the outcome of their choice, which may be bad (disappointment), or good (relief). Another task used for studying regret is a sequential decision making task where subjects are asked to open a series of boxes consecutively and decide when to stop. Opening a box can reveal a reward (gold) or an adverse stimulus (devil). All but one of the boxes contain gold, while the remaining box contains the devil. Opening a box to reveal gold adds it to the participant's accumulated gold. However, if a participant opens a box containing the devil, he loses all of his previously-accumulated gold. When participants decide to stop, the position of the devil is shown, revealing the number of collected gains and missed chances. Subjects are paid based on the amount of gold they collect.

To try to identify the neural basis of regret, researchers have administered the wheels of fortune task (Chua, Gonzalez, Taylor, Welsh, & Liberzon, 2009; Coricelli et al., 2005) and the sequential gold-devil task (Brassen, Gamer, Peters, Gluth, & Büchel, 2012; Liu et al., 2016) to subjects in the scanner. Corroborating past evidence from patients with brain lesions (Camille et al., 2004; Levens et al., 2014), where patients with lesions in the OFC brain region did not report feelings of regret, some of these neuroimaging studies report enhanced OFC (lateral OFC in Chua et al., 2009; mOFC in Coricelli et al., 2005) activity with experienced regret. Additionally, these studies report enhanced activation in the aCC (Brassen et al., 2012; Coricelli et al., 2005), anterior hippocampus (Coricelli et al., 2005), anterior insula (Chua et al., 2009), dmPFC (Chua et al., 2009; Liu et al., 2016), and left superior temporal gyrus (Liu et al., 2016) with experiences of regret. OFC activation is also observed in a nonmonetary setting with aversive stimuli, lending support to the notion that OFC is fundamental to regret in a general sense. In this study, subjects were shown three closed doors and an indicator of how many of the doors had shocks behind them (Chandrasekhar, Capra, Moore, Noussair, & Berns, 2008). After a delay, all of the doors would open, and the subject was either shocked or not shocked depending on their choice. In some of the trials, all doors had shocks, in other trials, none of the doors had shocks, and in other trials, one or two of the doors had shocks. Chandrasekhar et al. (2008) reported greater OFC activation with regret, namely, in those trials where subjects chose a door with a shock but not all doors had shocks.

Importantly, the neural basis of regret is found to be different than that of disappointment, and also different than that of reward processing. Coricelli et al. (2005) find that activity in response to experiencing regret (in the mOFC, aCC, and anterior hippocampus) is distinct from activity seen with disappointment (in the middle temporal gyrus and dorsal brainstem), and also distinct from activity seen with mere outcome evaluation (in the ventral striatum). While Chua et al. (2009) find that both regret and disappointment are associated with more activation in the anterior insula and dmPFC relative to fixation (i.e., times during which participants are staring at a point or cross, typically in the center of their screen, rather than viewing choices), they report that activation in these regions was greater in regret.

Neuroimaging studies have also deepened our understanding of the underlying mechanisms by which regret affects future decisions. One insight has come through the comparison of activation patterns during experienced and anticipated regret—which have proven to be similar. While an influential view (Bechara, Damasio, & Damasio, 2000; Bechara, Tranel, & Damasio, 2000) restricts the role of the OFC to the anticipatory phase of decision making, neuroimaging evidence points to a role for the OFC during the outcome phase as well (Coricelli et al., 2005). It has also been found that subjects not only experience regret but become increasingly regret-aversive as an experimental session goes on—"a cumulative effect reflected in enhanced activity within medial orbitofrontal cortex and amygdala" (Coricelli et al., 2005, p. 1255). Notably, this pattern of activity reoccurred before subjects made a choice, suggesting that the neural circuitry that mediates experienced regret also mediates its anticipation (Coricelli et al., 2005).

Another insight about the mechanism of regret's effect on future decisions is provided by a neuroimaging study where subjects played a regret gambling task and observed another's play of the same task (Canessa et al., 2009). In this way, subjects experienced regret first-hand and observed another's experience of regretful outcomes. Canessa et al. (2009) found that observing the regretful outcomes of someone else's choices activates the same regions that are activated during a first-person experience of regret—the vmPFC, aCC, and hippocampus—indicating a possible role of a mirror-like mechanism beyond basic self-referential emotions. Taken together, these findings suggest that subjects are affected by regretful decisions by summoning similar feelings of regret when anticipating new decisions.

Because the hippocampus is involved in memory formation and retrieval, the finding that the hippocampus is activated during regret (Canessa et al., 2009; Coricelli et al., 2005) supports the idea that regret requires memory. This is corroborated by evidence from a neuroimaging study specifically interested in brain activation differences between periods of episodic thinking and counterfactual thinking (Van Hoeck et al., 2012). As predicted, results confirmed that episodic and counterfactual thinking share a common brain network, involving a core memory network (comprised of the hippocampal area, temporal lobes, midline, and lateral parietal lobes) as well as prefrontal areas that might be related to mentalizing (mPFC) and performance monitoring (right PFC). In contrast to episodic thinking, however, counterfactual thinking is associated with stronger and more extensive activation in some of these areas, and also with activation of the bilateral inferior parietal lobe and posterior medial frontal cortex.

Yet another insight into how regret modulates future behavior comes from a neuroimaging study by Lohrenz, McCabe, Camerer, and Montague (2007). In this study, subjects play a sequential gambling task in the scanner. Lohrenz et al. (2007) find that fictive error signals, or counterfactual signals that involve rewards not received from actions not taken, are positively correlated with neural activity in the ventral caudate. These fictive error signals, which are theoretically and neurally distinct from experiential rewards mediated by the dopamine system, may be interpretable as a proxy for the regret represented in models of regret.

Moreover, neuroimaging studies have given insight into the enforcement of regret-induced learning in subsequent choices. Coricelli et al. (2005) observed enhanced responses in the right dorsolateral prefrontal cortex (dlPFC), right lateral OFC, and right inferior parietal lobe during a choice phase immediately following the experience of regret. This is indicative of a cognitive control, as negative emotions have been shown to recruit right-hemisphere responses (Simon-Thomas, Role, & Knight, 2005).

Finally, the role of personal responsibility in regret is studied in several neuroimaging studies. Intuitively, the experience of regret is greater when one feels more responsible for the choice that led to the regrettable outcome. Called the "actor effect," this idea was initially highlighted by Kahneman and Tversky (1982). In their paradigmatic example, subjects were presented with two scenarios involving a stockbroker sustaining a dramatic loss in his share portfolio. In the first scenario, the stockbroker had moved his stock from one company to another (after which he experienced the dramatic loss), whereas in the second scenario, the stockbroker had considered moving his stock but had ultimately decided against it. Subjects judge that the stockbroker in the first scenario will experience more regret. Personal agency and responsibility thus may play a fundamental role in feelings of regret.

Camille et al. (2010) scanned volunteers as they played a task involving choices between two wheel-of-fortune gambles. As a manipulation of personal responsibility, subjects were given the opportunity to change their minds before the gamble was resolved. Subjects' ratings of satisfaction with the outcome of their choice were correlated with the difference between actual and unobtained outcomes. More interestingly, ratings following losses were lower for those trials where subjects had been given the opportunity to change their minds—suggesting that subjects experienced greater regret when there was the sense of greater personal agency. The neural patterns showed that activity in the striatum and OFC was positively correlated with satisfaction ratings. The striatal response was modulated by the agency manipulation following losses, whereby the striatal signal was significantly lower when the subject had had the opportunity to change his mind. In another study (Nicolle, Bach, Driver, & Dolan, 2011) of a gambling task, researchers found a reduction in ventral striatal activity for regret-related relative to relief-related outcomes, but only when subjects were responsible for the bet (the alternative being forced-bet trials). These results support the involvement of frontostriatal regions in counterfactual thinking and highlight the sensitivity of the striatum to the perception of personal responsibility.

In another fMRI study, Liu et al. (2016) manipulate agency using a different design. Subjects play a sequential task, where at the start of each trial they receive advice about what to do next. Behaviorally, participants felt less regret when they chose not to follow the advice than when they did. At the neural level, striatal, vmPFC/mOFC, and ventral anterior cingulate cortex (vaCC) activations were associated with greater relief, while activity in the dmPFC and left superior temporal gyrus was associated with greater regret.

Regret might affect future decisions in an unexpected way. In two different neuroimaging studies (Giorgetta et al., 2013; Nicolle, Bach, Driver, et al., 2011), subjects exhibit counterintuitive behavior following regretful outcomes.

In the MEG study by Giorgetta et al. (2013), subjects made risker choices following regretful outcomes. In the fMRI study by Nicolle, Bach, Driver, et al. (2011), subjects exhibited "chasing" behavior (in line with the gambler's fallacy [Breen & Zuckerman, 1999]), sticking to the same choices even though they had previously led to regretful outcomes. Activity in the dorsal striatum was indicative of an influence of previous regret on participants' subsequent choices: increased activity was observed when regret-related choices were repeated, versus avoided, on the next trial. These findings indicate that regret can lead to repetition of choices, possibly in the hope of making up for our mistakes, and in so doing may lead to subsequent chasing behavior.

Reference Dependence

According to standard economic theory, a decision maker should not be swayed by a reference point, for example of ownership: whether a person owns an item or not should be inconsequential to the person's valuation of that item. Behavioral experiments, however, have widely reported the presence of an endowment effect, which refers to people's tendency to place greater value on items they own. This particular reference dependence can be attributed to loss aversion (see section on "Loss Aversion" above). In an fMRI study where participants' willingness to accept and willingness to pay were elicited for different items (some of which were given to them initially), Knutson et al. (2008) find an association between insula activation and a subject's susceptibility to the endowment effect.

Another widely-observed choice phenomenon is status quo bias, which refers to people's disproportionate likelihood of accepting a default choice option, regardless of its relative optimality. Although this bias is well-established behaviorally (Fernandez & Rodrik, 1991; Kahneman et al., 1991; Samuelson & Zeckhauser, 1988), the neural mechanisms underlying it are less clear. Behavioral evidence suggests the emotion of regret is higher when errors arise from rejection rather than acceptance of a status quo option. Such asymmetry in the genesis of regret might drive status quo bias in subsequent decisions, if indeed erroneous rejections of a status quo have a greater neuronal impact than erroneous acceptances of a status quo.

Status quo bias has been examined in the scanner using a "tennis line-judgement" task—a difficult perceptual decision task, where subjects have to determine whether a fast-disappearing ball appeared "in" or "on" one of two rectangles on their screen (Fleming, Thomas, & Dolan, 2010; Nicolle, Fleming, Bach, Driver, & Dolan, 2011). In the face of heightened decision difficulty, subjects are found to favor the default option (Fleming et al., 2010). Moreover, if subjects choose the nondefault judgement on these trials, they experience increased subthalamic nucleus (STN) activity, which is neurally similar to suppressing one's response, in turn suggesting that neural effort is involved in choosing to shift from the status quo. In a subsequent study

(Nicolle, Fleming, et al., 2011), researchers modify the task from Fleming et al. (2010) to incorporate feedback after each trial. They find that behaviorally, experienced regret (as measured through post-hoc subjective reports of regret based on a nine-point Likert scale) was higher after nondefault choices that were erroneous compared to after default choices that were erroneous, and at the same time, the anterior insula and mPFC showed disproportionally increased activity after nondefault choices that were erroneous.

Intertemporal Decision Making

Intertemporal decision making, or decision making involving outcomes to be experienced at different points in time, requires the evaluation of future rewards. As such, one fundamental question that fMRI can help answer is how the value of a delayed reward is computed. Using discounting tasks in the scanner, several studies (for example, Ballard & Knutson, 2009; Kable & Glimcher, 2007) have found that the same neural regions (the mesolimbic system, sometimes referred to as the reward system in the brain, and its closely-related regions: NAcc, mPFC, and pCC) that are generally more activated with immediate reward are also more activated with future reward.

Relatedly, there has been a consistent interest in the neural mechanisms underlying the construction of value in intertemporal choices as they relate to specific functional forms. Different models of intertemporal decision making have been proposed by choice theorists, including the exponential discounting model (3), the quasi-hyperbolic model (4), and the hyperbolic model (5), shown below. The fMRI method can help in discriminating among these competing models.

$$V = Ae^{-\rho D} \tag{3}$$

$$V = A\beta\delta^{D} \tag{4}$$

$$V = \frac{A}{1+kD} \tag{5}$$

Here, V is the subjective value of reward of amount (A) available after (D) time units. (ρ), (β), (δ), and (k) are discount parameters.

In one study (McClure et al., 2004), subjects made a series of intertemporal choices in the scanner between sooner and later monetary rewards, where the sooner option always had a lower undiscounted value than the later option. They found that two separate neural systems were involved in such decisions. One system, the mesolimbic system (including the ventral striatum, mPFC, and mOFC), was preferentially activated for choices in which the sooner option represented immediately available rewards. A second, fronto-parietal system (including the lPFC and parietal areas), was preferentially activated while making choices regardless of the immediacy of the sooner reward. Additionally, these researchers found that the relative engagement of the two systems depends on the subject's choice. Their basic results were replicated in a later study with liquid rewards (fruit juice or water) (McClure, Ericson, Laibson, Loewenstein, & Cohen, 2007). These findings provide support for the dual parameter model of quasi-hyperbolic discounting.

Other studies have also found support for a dual system, although not always with similar patterns of activation. In a study by Hariri et al. (2006), subjects made intertemporal choices outside of the scanner and performed a task in the scanner involving positive and negative feedback with monetary rewards. They found that increased preference for smaller immediate rewards over larger delayed rewards is predicted by a hyper-reactive ventral striatum, a part of the mesolimbic system. In a study by Xu et al. (2009), subjects made intertemporal choices inside the scanner that involved future gains as well as future losses. Similar to earlier findings (McClure et al., 2007, 2004), their study revealed that the fronto-parietal network was activated when discounting future prospects. Tanaka et al. (2004) employed a Markov decision task in the scanner to test whether the brain mechanisms for reward prediction at different time scales differed. When subjects learned actions on the basis of immediate rewards, significant activity was seen in the lateral OFC and the striatum. However, when subjects learned to act on the basis of large future rewards while incurring small immediate losses, the dlPFC, inferior parietal cortex, dorsal raphe nucleus, and cerebellum were also activated. Wittmann, Leland, and Paulus (2007) also found evidence for a dual system, reporting that some areas were more activated for shorter relative to longer delays (such as the head of the left caudate nucleus and putamen) while others were more activated when individuals selected the delayed relative to the immediate reward (such as the bilateral posterior insular cortex).

Challenging the dual system processing theory, several studies have found evidence for an integrative system representing both immediate reward values and delayed rewards (Ballard & Knutson, 2009; Pine et al., 2009). Kable and Glimcher (2007) find that neural activity in the ventral striatum, mPFC, and pCC is related to the revealed subjective value of both immediate and delayed monetary rewards. In a later study, Kable and Glimcher (2007) find that neural activity in the same group of regions (ventral striatum, mPFC, and pCC) tracks the subjective value of the reward for both immediate and delayed rewards. They also find that subjects do not necessarily behave as predicted by quasi-hyperbolic discounting; they were impatient, but there was no special effect of immediacy as is predicted by quasi-hyperbolic discounting. Taken together, their behavioral and neural results support an alternative discounting model which they call "ASAP" in which subjective value declines hyperbolically relative to the soonest available time (rather than relative to the present).

Social Decision Making

There are broadly two viewpoints in the economic and biological sciences about why prosocial behavior occurs. One view is that prosociality or cooperation is a reflex and a reflection of bounded rationality when observed in one-shot interactions, as humans have adapted to cooperate in the repeated interactions of real life. The other view is that prosocial behavior reflects robust social preferences for treating others generously or reciprocally, similar to preferences for other kinds of primary and secondary rewards (Fehr & Camerer, 2007). Neuroeconomic evidence can help evaluate the respective validity of these two broad viewpoints.

In support of the latter view, neuroimaging studies have found common patterns of neural activation for both cooperative outcomes and individual rewards. One of the most frequently utilized tasks in social decision making is the Prisoner's Dilemma (PD) game. Although it is well known that defection in every one-shot PD game is the unique dominant-strategy Nash equilibrium, cooperation is often observed in repeated PD games. The reward hypothesis would imply that the cooperative behavior in repeated games is a reflection of an additional reward brought about by cooperative play. One possible way of evaluating this conjecture would be to investigate whether mutual cooperation yields higher utility than unilateral defection, which could be done by comparing levels of activation in the brain's reward circuitry under either scenario. The problem with this approach, however, is that it would be difficult to disentangle differences that are due to the fact that the scanned player cooperates in one scenario and defects in another from those due to the fact that cooperation is more rewarding that defection. In one of the first neuroimaging studies, Rilling et al. (2002) use a design that circumvents this potential problem. Subjects played a repeated PD game with a human partner and then with a computer partner, while in the scanner. Higher levels of activation were reported in reward processing centers (anteroventral striatum and vmPFC) when subjects experienced mutual cooperation with a human partner compared to when they experienced mutual cooperation with a computer partner. In a subsequent study, Rilling, Sanfey, Aronson, Nystrom, & Cohen (2004) employed a one-shot PD game, played repeatedly with different partners (or at least from the viewpoint of the subject—in reality, subjects were always playing against the computer), as they scanned subjects. Again, they found that activation in the vmPFC and ventral striatum correlated more strongly with subjects' experience of mutual cooperation with a human partner than with cooperation experienced with a computer partner. In a specially designed computer game with cooperative and competitive conditions, Decety, Jackson, Sommerville, Chaminade, and Meltzoff (2004) also find evidence for the reward hypothesis, reporting increased activation in reward-related regions (specifically, left mOFC) during cooperation.

Neural evidence has suggested that the effect of cooperation on reward-related centers is strong enough to work indirectly. In a study by Singer, Kiebel, Winston, Dolan, and Frith (2004), subjects viewed faces of people who had been introduced as "fair" (cooperating) or "unfair" (defecting) players through repeated play of a sequential PD game. To manipulate moral responsibility, the fair and unfair players were introduced as either intentionally or unintentionally so. Relative to neutral faces, the faces of those presented as intentional cooperators resulted in increased activity in reward-related areas of subjects who viewed them (specifically, in the left amygdala, bilateral insula, fusiform gyrus, and STS).

Human prosociality is also reflected in donations. Charitable giving is observed in daily life as well as in behavioral experiments, where standard theory would predict no giving. Again, according to the reward hypothesis, giving could be explained by an additional reward that is experienced by the giver. Neuroimaging studies of donations report similar engagement of reward-related areas (VTA and striatal areas) when subjects donate to charities as when they receive the reward themselves (Harbaugh, Mayr, & Burghart, 2007; Moll et al., 2006), indicating that giving brings its own reward. Moll et al. (2006) also find that across subjects, those who make more costly donations also exhibit more activity in the striatum. Neural evidence can also help clarify the relative importance of "pure" altruism and "warm-glow" (termed by Andreoni, 1989, 1990) motives for charitable giving, where pure altruism is defined as giving for the sake of giving, while warm glow refers to the positive emotional feeling people get from helping others. To try to distinguish between these two, Harbaugh et al. (2007) included both forced-donation trials as well as voluntary-donation trials in their study. They report findings consistent with pure altruism as well as warm-glow. Consistent with the pure altruism motivation, they find that even mandatory, tax-like transfers to a charity elicit neural activity in reward-related areas. Consistent with the warm glow motivation, they find that neural activity further increases when people make voluntary transfers.

Neuroimaging studies also find evidence for the rewarding nature of equity. A preference for equity—or equivalently, an aversion to inequity—can be studied using the ultimatum game. In this game, there are two players, A and B. Player A gets a sum of money and decides how much of it he wants to offer Player B. Player B either accepts or rejects the offer; if he accepts, both players get the amounts proposed by Player A, but if he rejects, neither player receives anything. The rational strategy for Player B is to accept any offer, as something is better than nothing. However, it has been shown that people often reject offers, which has frequently been interpreted to indicate that people reject offers they consider unfair (Oosterbeek, Sloof, & Van De Kuilen, 2004). In a study by Tabibnia and Lieberman (2007) employing the ultimatum game, it is found that the fairness of a bargaining offer—controlling for the absolute size of the monetary gain—is associated with activations in reward regions (the ventral striatum, specifically) in subjects.

Social preference theories also predict that subjects prefer to punish an opponent's unfair behavior in public good games, PD games, and three-stage trust games (described below), as the disutility of leaving an unfair act unpunished is higher than that of punishing (Fehr & Camerer, 2007). As such, when subjects punish their opponent's defection, there should be greater activation in their reward circuitry. In a PET imaging study (De Quervain, Fischbacher, Treyer, & Schellhammer, 2004) subjects played a three-stage trust game. In the standard trust game, there are two players, A and B, each of whom has an initial endowment. First, player A decides whether to keep his endowment or to send it to player B. If player A decides to keep his endowment, the game ends and each player goes home with his or her initial endowment. If, however, player A decides to send his endowment to player B, the experimenter increases the transfer payment by a multiple (of three, typically). Player B observes player A's action and decides whether to keep her endowment or to send it to A. Again, if player B decides to send her endowment, the experimenter increases the transfer payment by a multiple. Both players would be better off if they each decide to send their endowment to the other. However, knowing the game ends after the second action, player B has a strong incentive to keep her endowment regardless of whether or not A transferred his; if A anticipates this behavior, however, he has a strong incentive to keep his endowment as well. Hence, a mutually beneficial exchange can only take place if A is trusting and B is trustworthy. In the three-stage trust game implemented in De Quervain et al. (2004), player A has the opportunity to punish player B after observing player B's behavior. There were three conditions in the study: in condition C it was costly for player A to punish B, in condition F it was free for player A to punish B, and in condition S the punishment was only symbolic, and not costly to either player. The dorsal striatum of player A—a region implicated in reward processing (O'Doherty, 2004)—was more strongly activated in both the C and F conditions as compared to the S condition, suggesting that effective punishment (but not symbolic punishment) was neurally rewarding for the punisher.

Besides providing evidence for the hypothesis that cooperation and the punishment of unfair behavior provide direct rewards, neuroeconomic studies can answer the question of whether social uncertainty is fundamentally different than nonsocial uncertainty. Economic theory does not differentiate between different types of uncertainty. However, behavioral evidence suggests that people view risky social situations (i.e., those involving "strategic" uncertainty) differently than risky nonsocial situations (i.e., those involving "state" uncertainty) (Aimone, Houser, & Weber, 2014). Using the fMRI tool, economists can identify the neural foundations of strategic uncertainty and understand trusting and distrusting behavior more deeply—is distrust a reflection of aversion to risk (i.e., uncertainty about states of the world), or aversion to betrayal (i.e., uncertainty about what another person is going to do)?

This question can be answered by employing the standard trust game to determine which neural regions are associated with trust, as well as which regions are associated with distrust, giving insight into the sources of these behaviors. In a neuroimaging study employing the trust game with both human and computer counterparts, McCabe, Houser, Ryan, Smith, and Trouard (2001) report that within a group of cooperating subjects, prefrontal regions are more active when subjects played with a human than when they played with a computer following a fixed (and known) probabilistic strategy. Comparing findings from studies with social risk and those with nonsocial risk, Aimone et al. (2014) conclude that decisions in the former seem to involve the lateral PFC, while decisions in the latter seem to recruit relatively greater posterior parietal cortex activation (Bach, Seymour, & Dolan, 2009; Hsu et al., 2005; Huettel et al., 2006). Moreover, a study by Lauharatanahirun, Christopoulos, and King-Casas (2012) focused on the amygdala in decisions involving different types of uncertainty (i.e., social versus nonsocial risk). They found that individuals' level of risk aversion in the social context was related to their amygdala activity in the nonsocial context; specifically, individuals who were more risk averse socially had less amygdala activity during the nonsocial risk task.

LIMITATIONS

In terms of spatial resolution, fMRI is relatively strong. Although its resolution is decidedly inferior to that of invasive procedures such as single-unit electrodes, MRI, in general, has better spatial resolution than other noninvasive techniques (such as EEG and magnetoencephalography, MEG). In terms of temporal resolution, however, fMRI is relatively weak. This weakness stems from the sluggish hemodynamic response to metabolic changes, although higher resolution can be achieved by designing studies with jittered event-related stimuli and using appropriate methods of analysis (Glover, 2011). Because of this, it is not straightforward to say whether the representations of value reported in the brain, for example, are due to the computational process of value comparison or other computational processes that covary closely with value computation (Hunt et al., 2012). In a study with humans, Hunt et al. (2012) use a technology with higher spatial resolution than fMRI to better understand the value-based decision process. Using MEG, the researchers interrogate the representation of value and value difference in the brain. They find that several areas exhibited value-dependent activity (as found in other studies), but that none of those regions matched well with predictions from the model they were considering (a specific inhibition-based decision process model called the biophysical cortical attractor network model, as in Wang, 2002), leading the researchers to hypothesize that the activation in those regions might be due to correlates of value computation, such as attention or response preparation, rather than to the value-computation process itself.

Aside from limits to the spatial and temporal resolution of measurement, there exists heterogeneity across individuals' brains, and variance in nomenclature across studies. While researchers often agree in their terminology at a broad level (for example, when referring to one of the four lobes of the brain), there is inconsistency when referring to regions that are not well-defined by their structure. The vmPFC is one example of such a region, which is by some researchers referred to as mOFC or ventromedial orbitofrontal cortex (vmOFC).

CONCLUSION

Despite its limitations, fMRI is a valuable tool for economic experiments, helping to elucidate the biological mechanisms of choice under uncertainty, across time, and in social contexts. With fMRI, we can help to establish the neural foundations of economic principles and theories, identify the most biologically-supported theory in the case of competing theories, and inform the development of new theories.

Neuroeconomists have consistently found activation in reward-related areas of the brain correlating with subjective value, regardless of how subjective value was defined. Different models of decision making have been tested with fMRI techniques and although there has been supportive evidence for many models, these studies have helped neuroeconomists improve the models. For example, neural data has pointed to a flexible rather than fixed decision threshold for the standard DDM. The neural DDM was developed in response to this finding, and upon testing, was found to outperform the standard DDM. In the context of decision making under uncertainty, neural data supports the theorized distinction between risk and ambiguity. Furthermore, fMRI has allowed neuroeconomists to study decision making under uncertainty, through which evidence has been found for the distinct coding of value and risk, instead of a single computation of expected utility that takes value and risk into account in combination. Neuroeconomists have also been able to test the assumptions of different theories of decision making under risk, such as prospect theory compared to expected utility theory, and here they have found evidence for the nonlinear weighting of outcome probabilities. Another aspect of prospect theory has been tested with fMRI studies: loss aversion. Some studies that have found common regions of activation for the evaluation of gains and losses have also found evidence for greater deactivation for losses than activation for gains. However, other studies have found evidence for dissociable systems responsible for the evaluation of gains and losses. In these studies, the amygdala was often preferentially activated during the evaluation of losses, suggesting an emotional aspect of decisions involving potential losses.

Neuroeconomists have also studied aversion to nonpreferred scenarios. Here, they have found that regret is neurally distinct from disappointment. By studying neural activations during the anticipation of regret and during the experience of regret, neuroeconomists have been better able to understand the mechanism through which regret affects future decisions. Specifically, they have found similar patterns of activation when people are anticipating regret as when they have experienced regret (or even when they have viewed someone else's experience of regret). Evidence of the activation of memory structures during decisions that might lead to future regret has suggested that regretful experiences are brought to mind when making future decisions. Neuroeconomists have also studied status quo bias in the scanner, finding that structures involved in emotional processing (such as the STN and amygdala) are activated during these decisions. In line with studies specifically studying loss aversion, these findings suggest that emotional considerations are involved in decisions that involve a change from the status quo.

In the context of intertemporal decision making, fMRI studies have found conflicting evidence. In support of a dual system of intertemporal processing (in line with the quasi-hyperbolic discounting model), some have found activation in distinct regions associated with sooner options versus later options. In support of an integrated system model, however, other studies have found activation in common regions regardless of reward delay. Based on neural and behavioral findings, an alternative discounting model, "ASAP," has been proposed which aims to reconcile these disparate findings.

Additionally, neuroeconomists have studied decision making in social contexts. Here, many studies have found that pro-sociality, cooperation, and equity activate similar regions as do rewards, as predicted by the reward hypothesis of pro-sociality, as mentioned above. Studies have also found that punishing unfair behavior activates these same regions. Neuroeconomists have also been able to ask whether distrust is a reflection of risk aversion or betrayal aversion. Findings from fMRI studies point to the latter, with socially-mediated risk and nonsocially-mediated risk found to be associated with different patterns of neural activation.

In conclusion, fMRI is a powerful tool that has been used in hundreds of neuroeconomic studies in the past several decades. Although neuroeconomists have been able to provide resounding support for certain aspects of decision making, the jury is still out on other aspects, as fMRI studies have provided conflicting evidence. However, sometimes what seems like conflicting evidence can make sense when looking at the whole picture. By combining fMRI with other biophysical tools in the lab, such as eye tracking and skin conductance, social scientists can get a better view of the bigger picture and continue to try to answer these fascinating questions about how people make decisions.

REFERENCES

Aimone, J. A., Houser, D., & Weber, B. (2014). Neural signatures of betrayal aversion: an fMRI study of trust. *Proceedings of the Royal Society B*, *281*(1782), 2013–2127.

Andreoni, J. (1989). Giving with impure altruism: applications to charity and Ricardian equivalence. *Journal of Political Economy*, *97*(6), 1447–1458.

Andreoni, J. (1990). Impure altruism and donations to public goods: a theory of warm-glow giving. *The Economic Journal*, *100*(401), 464–477.

Arrow, K. J. (1963). Social choice and individual values. In (2nd Ed.). New Haven: Yale University Press.

Attwell, D., & Iadecola, C. (2002). The neural basis of functional brain imaging signals. *Trends in Neurosciences*, *25*(12), 621–625.

Bach, D. R., Seymour, B., & Dolan, R. J. (2009). Neural activity associated with the passive prediction of ambiguity and risk for aversive events. *Journal of Neuroscience*, *29*(6), 1648–1656.

Ballard, K., & Knutson, B. (2009). Dissociable neural representations of future reward magnitude and delay during temporal discounting. *NeuroImage*, *45*(1), 143–150.

Bechara, A., Damasio, H., & Damasio, A. R. (2000). Emotion, decision making and the orbitofrontal cortex. *Cerebral Cortex*, *10*(3), 295–307.

Bechara, A., Tranel, D., & Damasio, H. (2000). Characterization of the decision making deficit of patients with ventromedial prefrontal cortex lesions. *Brain*, *123*(11), 2189–2202.

Becker, G. M., DeGroot, M. H., & Marschak, J. (1964). Measuring utility by a single-response sequential method. *Systems Research and Behavioral Science*, *9*(3), 226–232.

Beesley, T., Pearson, D., & Le Pelley, M. E. (2018). Eye-tracking as a tool for examining cognitive processes. In G. Foster (Ed.), *Biophysical measurement in experimental social science research*. Oxford, UK: Elsevier.

Bell, D. E. (1982). Regret in decision making under uncertainty. *Operations Research*, *30*(5), 961–981.

Belliveau, J. W., Kennedy, D. N., McKinstry, R. C., Buchbinder, B. R., Weisskoff, R., Cohen, M. S., et al. (1991). Functional mapping of the human visual cortex by magnetic resonance imaging. *Science*, *254*(5032), 716–719.

Berns, G. S., Capra, C. M., Chappelow, J., Moore, S., & Noussair, C. (2008). Nonlinear neurobiological probability weighting functions for aversive outcomes. *NeuroImage*, *39*(4), 2047–2057.

Bleichrodt, H., & Wakker, P. P. (2015). Regret theory: a bold alternative to the alternatives. *The Economic Journal*, *125*(583), 493–532.

Bogacz, R., Brown, E., Moehlis, J., Holmes, P., & Cohen, J. D. (2006). The physics of optimal decision making: a formal analysis of models of performance in two-alternative forced-choice tasks. *Psychological Review*, *113*(4), 700.

Boorman, E. D., Behrens, T. E., Woolrich, M. W., & Rushworth, M. F. (2009). How green is the grass on the other side? Frontopolar cortex and the evidence in favor of alternative courses of action. *Neuron*, *62*(5), 733–743.

Brassen, S., Gamer, M., Peters, J., Gluth, S., & Büchel, C. (2012). Don't look back in anger! Responsiveness to missed chances in successful and nonsuccessful aging. *Science*, 1217516.

Breen, R. B., & Zuckerman, M. (1999). Chasing'in gambling behavior: personality and cognitive determinants. *Personality and Individual Differences*, *27*(6), 1097–1111.

Brown, S., & Heathcote, A. (2005). A ballistic model of choice response time. *Psychological Review*, *112*(1), 117.

Brown, S. D., & Heathcote, A. (2008). The simplest complete model of choice response time: linear ballistic accumulation. *Cognitive Psychology*, *57*(3), 153–178.

Camerer, C. F. (2011). *Behavioral game theory: Experiments in strategic interaction*. Princeton: Princeton University Press.

Camille, N., Coricelli, G., Sallet, J., Pradat-Diehl, P., Duhamel, J. R., & Sirigu, A. (2004). The involvement of the orbitofrontal cortex in the experience of regret. *Science*, *304*(5674), 1167–1170.

Camille, N., Pironti, V. A., Dodds, C. M., Aitken, M. R. F., Robbins, T. W., & Clark, L. (2010). Striatal sensitivity to personal responsibility in a regret-based decision making task. *Cognitive, Affective, & Behavioral Neuroscience*, *10*(4), 460–469.

Canessa, N., Crespi, C., Baud-Bovy, G., Dodich, A., Falini, A., Antonellis, G., et al. (2017). Neural markers of loss aversion in resting-state brain activity. *NeuroImage*, *146*, 257–265.

Canessa, N., Crespi, C., Motterlini, M., Baud-Bovy, G., Chierchia, G., Pantaleo, G., et al. (2013). The functional and structural neural basis of individual differences in loss aversion. *Journal of Neuroscience*, *33*(36), 14307–14317.

Canessa, N., Motterlini, M., Di Dio, C., Perani, D., Scifo, P., Cappa, S. F., et al. (2009). Understanding others' regret: a FMRI study. *PLoS One*, *4*(10).

Chandrasekhar, P. V., Capra, C. M., Moore, S., Noussair, C., & Berns, G. S. (2008). Neurobiological regret and rejoice functions for aversive outcomes. *NeuroImage*, *39*(3), 1472–1484.

Chau, B. K., Kolling, N., Hunt, L. T., Walton, M. E., & Rushworth, M. F. (2014). A neural mechanism underlying failure of optimal choice with multiple alternatives. *Nature Neuroscience*, *17*(3), 463–470.

Chib, V. S., Rangel, A., Shimojo, S., & O'Doherty, J. P. (2009). Evidence for a common representation of decision values for dissimilar goods in human ventromedial prefrontal cortex. *Journal of Neuroscience*, *29*(39), 12315–12320.

Chua, H. F., Gonzalez, R., Taylor, S. F., Welsh, R. C., & Liberzon, I. (2009). Decision related loss: regret and disappointment. *NeuroImage*, *47*(4), 2031–2040.

Congdon, E., Bato, A. A., Schonberg, T., Mumford, J. A., Karlsgodt, K. H., Sabb, F. W., et al. (2013). Differences in neural activation as a function of risk-taking task parameters. *Frontiers in Neuroscience*, *7*, 173.

Coricelli, G., Critchley, H. D., Joffily, M., O'Doherty, J. P., Sirigu, A., & Dolan, R. J. (2005). Regret and its avoidance: a neuroimaging study of choice behavior. *Nature Neuroscience*, *8*(9), 1255.

De Martino, B., Camerer, C. F., & Adolphs, R. (2010). Amygdala damage eliminates monetary loss aversion. *Proceedings of the National Academy of Sciences*, *107*(8), 3788–3792.

De Martino, B., Fleming, S. M., Garrett, N., & Dolan, R. J. (2013). Confidence in value-based choice. *Nature Neuroscience*, *16*(1), 105–110.

De Martino, B., Kumaran, D., Holt, B., & Dolan, R. J. (2009). The neurobiology of reference-dependent value computation. *Journal of Neuroscience*, *29*(12), 3833–3842.

De Quervain, D. J., Fischbacher, U., Treyer, V., & Schellhammer, M. (2004). The neural basis of altruistic punishment. *Science*, *305*(5688), 1254.

Decety, J., Jackson, P. L., Sommerville, J. A., Chaminade, T., & Meltzoff, A. N. (2004). The neural bases of co-operation and competition: an fMRI investigation. *NeuroImage*, *23*(2), 744–751.

Ellsberg, D. (1961). Risk, ambiguity, and the savage axioms. *The Quarterly Journal of Economics*, 643–669.

Fehr, E., & Camerer, C. F. (2007). Social neuroeconomics: the neural circuitry of social preferences. *Trends in Cognitive Sciences*, *11*(10), 419–427.

Fehr, E., & Fischbacher, U. (2003). The nature of human altruism. *Nature*, *425*(6960), 785–791.

Fernandez, R., & Rodrik, D. (1991). Resistance to reform: status quo bias in the presence of individual-specific uncertainty. *The American Economic Review*, 1146–1155.

Fishburn, P. C. (1982). Nontransitive measurable utility. *Journal of Mathematical Psychology*, *26*(1), 31–67.

FitzGerald, T. H., Seymour, B., & Dolan, R. J. (2009). The role of human orbitofrontal cortex in value comparison for incommensurable objects. *Journal of Neuroscience*, *29*(26), 8388–8395.

Fleming, S. M., Thomas, C. L., & Dolan, R. J. (2010). Overcoming status quo bias in the human brain. *Proceedings of the National Academy of Sciences*, *107*(13), 6005–6009.

Frank, M. J., Gagne, C., Nyhus, E., Masters, S., Wiecki, T. V., Cavanagh, J. F., et al. (2015). fMRI and EEG predictors of dynamic decision parameters during human reinforcement learning. *Journal of Neuroscience*, *35*(2), 485–494.

Frederick, S., Loewenstein, G., & O'Donoghue, T. (2002). Time discounting and time preference: a critical review. *Journal of Economic Literature*, *40*(2), 351–401.

Giorgetta, C., Grecucci, A., Bonini, N., Coricelli, G., Demarchi, G., Braun, C., et al. (2013). Waves of regret: a MEG study of emotion and decision making. *Neuropsychologia*, *51*(1), 38–51.

Glover, G. H. (2011). Overview of functional magnetic resonance imaging. *Neurosurgery Clinics of North America*, *22*(2), 133–139.

Gonzalez, R., & Wu, G. (1999). On the shape of the probability weighting function. *Cognitive Psychology*, *38*(1), 129–166.

Harbaugh, W. T., Mayr, U., & Burghart, D. R. (2007). Neural responses to taxation and voluntary giving reveal motives for charitable donations. *Science*, *316*(5831), 1622–1625.

Hare, T. A., Camerer, C. F., Knoepfle, D. T., O'Doherty, J. P., & Rangel, A. (2010). Value computations in ventral medial prefrontal cortex during charitable decision making incorporate input from regions involved in social cognition. *Journal of Neuroscience*, *30*(2), 583–590.

Hare, T. A., O'Doherty, J., Camerer, C. F., Schultz, W., & Rangel, A. (2008). Dissociating the role of the orbitofrontal cortex and the striatum in the computation of goal values and prediction errors. *Journal of Neuroscience*, *28*(22), 5623–5630.

Hariri, A. R., Brown, S. M., Williamson, D. E., Flory, J. D., de Wit, H., & Manuck, S. B. (2006). Preference for immediate over delayed rewards is associated with magnitude of ventral striatal activity. *Journal of Neuroscience*, *26*(51), 13213–13217.

Heeger, D. J., & Ress, D. (2002). What does fMRI tell us about neuronal activity? *Nature Reviews. Neuroscience*, *3*(2), 142.

Hershey, J. C., & Schoemaker, P. J. (1980). Risk taking and problem context in the domain of losses: An expected utility analysis. *Journal of Risk and Insurance*, 111–132.

Hsu, M., Bhatt, M., Adolphs, R., Tranel, D., & Camerer, C. F. (2005). Neural systems responding to degrees of uncertainty in human decision making. *Science*, *310*(5754), 1680–1683.

Hsu, M., Krajbich, I., Zhao, C., & Camerer, C. F. (2009). Neural response to reward anticipation under risk is nonlinear in probabilities. *Journal of Neuroscience*, *29*(7), 2231–2237.

Huettel, S. A., Stowe, C. J., Gordon, E. M., Warner, B. T., & Platt, M. L. (2006). Neural signatures of economic preferences for risk and ambiguity. *Neuron*, *49*(5), 765–775.

Hunt, L. T., Kolling, N., Soltani, A., Woolrich, M. W., Rushworth, M. F., & Behrens, T. E. (2012). Mechanisms underlying cortical activity during value-guided choice. *Nature Neuroscience*, *15*(3), 470–476.

Jocham, G., Hunt, L. T., Near, J., & Behrens, T. E. (2012). A mechanism for value-guided choice based on the excitation-inhibition balance in prefrontal cortex. *Nature Neuroscience*, *15*(7), 960–961.

Kable, J. W., & Glimcher, P. W. (2007). The neural correlates of subjective value during intertemporal choice. *Nature Neuroscience*, *10*(12), 1625.

Kahneman, D., Knetsch, J. L., & Thaler, R. H. (1991). Anomalies: the endowment effect, loss aversion, and status quo bias. *The Journal of Economic Perspectives*, *5*(1), 193–206.

Kahneman, D., & Tversky, A. (1979). Prospect theory: an analysis of decision under risk. *Econometrica*, *47*, 263–291.

Kahneman, D., & Tversky, A. (1982). The psychology of preferences. *Scientific American*, *246*(1), 160–173.

Knight, F. (1921). *Risk, uncertainty, and profit. Hart Schaffner and Marx Prize Essays no 31*. Boston and New York: Houghton Mifflin.

Knutson, B., Taylor, J., Kaufman, M., Peterson, R., & Glover, G. (2005). Distributed neural representation of expected value. *Journal of Neuroscience*, *25*(19), 4806–4812.

Knutson, B., Wimmer, G. E., Rick, S., Hollon, N. G., Prelec, D., & Loewenstein, G. (2008). Neural antecedents of the endowment effect. *Neuron*, *58*(5), 814–822.

Kolling, N., Behrens, T. E., Mars, R. B., & Rushworth, M. F. (2012). Neural mechanisms of foraging. *Science*, *336*(6077), 95–98.

Krajbich, I., Armel, C., & Rangel, A. (2010). Visual fixations and the computation and comparison of value in simple choice. *Nature Neuroscience, 13*(10), 1292.

Krajbich, I., & Rangel, A. (2011). Multialternative drift-diffusion model predicts the relationship between visual fixations and choice in value-based decisions. *Proceedings of the National Academy of Sciences, 108*(33), 13852–13857.

Kwong, K. K., Belliveau, J. W., Chesler, D. A., Goldberg, I. E., Weisskoff, R. M., Poncelet, B. P., et al. (1992). Dynamic magnetic resonance imaging of human brain activity during primary sensory stimulation. *Proceedings of the National Academy of Sciences, 89*(12), 5675–5679.

Laibson, D. (1997). Golden eggs and hyperbolic discounting. *The Quarterly Journal of Economics, 112*(2), 443–478.

Lauharatanahirun, N., Christopoulos, G. I., & King-Casas, B. (2012). Neural computations underlying social risk sensitivity. *Frontiers in Human Neuroscience, 6*, 213.

Levens, S. M., Larsen, J. T., Bruss, J., Tranel, D., Bechara, A., & Mellers, B. A. (2014). What might have been? The role of the ventromedial prefrontal cortex and lateral orbitofrontal cortex in counterfactual emotions and choice. *Neuropsychologia, 54*, 77–86.

Levy, D. J., & Glimcher, P. W. (2012). The root of all value: a neural common currency for choice. *Current Opinion in Neurobiology, 22*(6), 1027–1038.

Liu, Z., Li, L., Zheng, L., Hu, Z., Roberts, I. D., Guo, X., et al. (2016). The neural basis of regret and relief during a sequential risk-taking task. *Neuroscience, 327*, 136–145.

Lohrenz, T., McCabe, K., Camerer, C. F., & Montague, P. R. (2007). Neural signature of fictive learning signals in a sequential investment task. *Proceedings of the National Academy of Sciences, 104*(22), 9493–9498.

Loomes, G., & Sugden, R. (1982). Regret theory: an alternative theory of rational choice under uncertainty. *The Economic Journal, 92*(368), 805–824.

McCabe, K., Houser, D., Ryan, L., Smith, V., & Trouard, T. (2001). A functional imaging study of co-operation in two-person reciprocal exchange. *Proceedings of the National Academy of Sciences, 98*(20), 11832–11835.

McClure, S. M., Ericson, K. M., Laibson, D. I., Loewenstein, G., & Cohen, J. D. (2007). Time discounting for primary rewards. *Journal of Neuroscience, 27*(21), 5796–5804.

McClure, S. M., Laibson, D. I., Loewenstein, G., & Cohen, J. D. (2004). Separate neural systems value immediate and delayed monetary rewards. *Science, 306*(5695), 503–507.

Moll, J., Krueger, F., Zahn, R., Pardini, M., de Oliveira-Souza, R., & Grafman, J. (2006). Human fronto-mesolimbic networks guide decisions about charitable donation. *Proceedings of the National Academy of Sciences, 103*(42), 15623–15628.

Mullinger, K. J., Mayhew, S. D., Bagshaw, A. P., Bowtell, R., & Francis, S. T. (2013). Poststimulus undershoots in cerebral blood flow and BOLD fMRI responses are modulated by poststimulus neuronal activity. *Proceedings of the National Academy of Sciences, 110*(33), 13636–13641.

Nicolle, A., Bach, D. R., Driver, J., & Dolan, R. J. (2011). A role for the striatum in regret-related choice repetition. *Journal of Cognitive Neuroscience, 23*(4), 845–856.

Nicolle, A., Fleming, S. M., Bach, D. R., Driver, J., & Dolan, R. J. (2011). A regret-induced status quo bias. *Journal of Neuroscience, 31*(9), 3320–3327.

O'Doherty, J. P. (2004). Reward representations and reward-related learning in the human brain: Insights from neuroimaging. *Current Opinion in Neurobiology, 14*(6), 769–776.

O'Donoghue, T., & Rabin, M. (1999). Doing it now or later. *American Economic Review, 89*(1), 103–124.

Ogawa, S., Lee, T. M., Nayak, A. S., & Glynn, P. (1990). Oxygenation-sensitive contrast in magnetic resonance image of rodent brain at high magnetic fields. *Magnetic Resonance in Medicine, 14*(1), 68–78.

Oosterbeek, H., Sloof, R., & Van De Kuilen, G. (2004). Cultural differences in ultimatum game experiments: evidence from a meta-analysis. *Experimental Economics*, *7*(2), 171–188.

Paulus, M. P., & Frank, L. R. (2006). Anterior cingulate activity modulates nonlinear decision weight function of uncertain prospects. *NeuroImage*, *30*(2), 668–677.

Peters, J., & Büchel, C. (2010). Neural representations of subjective reward value. *Behavioral Brain Research*, *213*(2), 135–141.

Phelps, E. A., & LeDoux, J. E. (2005). Contributions of the amygdala to emotion processing: from animal models to human behavior. *Neuron*, *48*(2), 175–187.

Philiastides, M. G., Biele, G., & Heekeren, H. R. (2010). A mechanistic account of value computation in the human brain. *Proceedings of the National Academy of Sciences*, *107*(20), 9430–9435.

Pine, A., Seymour, B., Roiser, J. P., Bossaerts, P., Friston, K. J., Curran, H. V., et al. (2009). Encoding of marginal utility across time in the human brain. *Journal of Neuroscience*, *29*(30), 9575–9581.

Plassmann, H., O'Doherty, J., & Rangel, A. (2007). Orbitofrontal cortex encodes willingness to pay in everyday economic transactions. *Journal of Neuroscience*, *27*(37), 9984–9988.

Plassmann, H., O'Doherty, J., Shiv, B., & Rangel, A. (2008). Marketing actions can modulate neural representations of experienced pleasantness. *Proceedings of the National Academy of Sciences*, *105*(3), 1050–1054.

Preuschoff, K., Bossaerts, P., & Quartz, S. R. (2006). Neural differentiation of expected reward and risk in human subcortical structures. *Neuron*, *51*(3), 381–390.

Ratcliff, R. (1978). A theory of memory retrieval. *Psychological Review*, *85*(2), 59.

Ratcliff, R., & McKoon, G. (2008). The diffusion decision model: theory and data for two-choice decision tasks. *Neural Computation*, *20*(4), 873–922.

Ray, P. (1973). Independence of irrelevant alternatives. *Econometrica: Journal of the Econometric Society*, 987–991.

Rilling, J. K., Gutman, D. A., Zeh, T. R., Pagnoni, G., Berns, G. S., & Kilts, C. D. (2002). A neural basis for social co-operation. *Neuron*, *35*(2), 395–405.

Rilling, J. K., Sanfey, A. G., Aronson, J. A., Nystrom, L. E., & Cohen, J. D. (2004). Opposing BOLD responses to reciprocated and unreciprocated altruism in putative reward pathways. *Neuroreport*, *15*(16), 2539–2543.

Rushworth, M. F., Noonan, M. P., Boorman, E. D., Walton, M. E., & Behrens, T. E. (2011). Frontal cortex and reward-guided learning and decision making. *Neuron*, *70*(6), 1054–1069.

Samuelson, P. A. (1937). A note on measurement of utility. *The Review of Economic Studies*, *4*(2), 155–161.

Samuelson, W., & Zeckhauser, R. (1988). Status quo bias in decision making. *Journal of Risk and Uncertainty*, *1*(1), 7–59.

Sergerie, K., Chochol, C., & Armony, J. L. (2008). The role of the amygdala in emotional processing: a quantitative meta-analysis of functional neuroimaging studies. *Neuroscience & Biobehavioral Reviews*, *32*(4), 811–830.

Shadlen, M. N., & Newsome, W. T. (2001). Neural basis of a perceptual decision in the parietal cortex (area LIP) of the rhesus monkey. *Journal of Neurophysiology*, *86*(4), 1916–1936.

Simon-Thomas, E. R., Role, K. O., & Knight, R. T. (2005). Behavioral and electrophysiological evidence of a right hemisphere bias for the influence of negative emotion on higher cognition. *Journal of Cognitive Neuroscience*, *17*(3), 518–529.

Singer, T., Kiebel, S. J., Winston, J. S., Dolan, R. J., & Frith, C. D. (2004). Brain responses to the acquired moral status of faces. *Neuron*, *41*(4), 653–662.

Sokol-Hessner, P., Camerer, C. F., & Phelps, E. A. (2012). Emotion regulation reduces loss aversion and decreases amygdala responses to losses. *Social Cognitive and Affective Neuroscience*, *8*(3), 341–350.

Tabibnia, G., & Lieberman, M. D. (2007). Fairness and co-operation are rewarding. *Annals of the New York Academy of Sciences*, *1118*(1), 90–101.

Tagamets, M. A., & Horwitz, B. (2001). Interpreting PET and fMRI measures of functional neural activity: the effects of synaptic inhibition on cortical activation in human imaging studies. *Brain Research Bulletin*, *54*(3), 267–273.

Tanaka, S. C., Doya, K., Okada, G., Ueda, K., Okamoto, Y., & Yamawaki, S. (2004). Prediction of immediate and future rewards differentially recruits cortico-basal ganglia loops. *Nature Neuroscience*, *7*(8), 887.

Thaler, R. (1981). Some empirical evidence on dynamic inconsistency. *Economics Letters*, *8*(3), 201–207.

Tobler, P. N., Christopoulos, G. I., O'Doherty, J. P., Dolan, R. J., & Schultz, W. (2008). Neuronal distortions of reward probability without choice. *Journal of Neuroscience*, *28*(45), 11703–11711.

Tobler, P. N., O'Doherty, J. P., Dolan, R. J., & Schultz, W. (2007). Reward value coding distinct from risk attitude-related uncertainty coding in human reward systems. *Journal of Neurophysiology*, *97*(2), 1621–1632.

Tom, S. M., Fox, C. R., Trepel, C., & Poldrack, R. A. (2007). The neural basis of loss aversion in decision making under risk. *Science*, *315*(5811), 515–518.

Turner, B. M., Van Maanen, L., & Forstmann, B. U. (2015). Informing cognitive abstractions through neuroimaging: the neural drift diffusion model. *Psychological Review*, *122*(2), 312.

Tymula, A. (2018). Brain morphometry for economists: how do brain volume constraints affect our choices? In G. Foster (Ed.), *Biophysical measurement in experimental social science research*. Oxford, UK: Elsevier.

Van Hoeck, N., Ma, N., Ampe, L., Baetens, K., Vandekerckhove, M., & Van Overwalle, F. (2012). Counterfactual thinking: an fMRI study on changing the past for a better future. *Social Cognitive and Affective Neuroscience*, *8*(5), 556–564.

Van Maanen, L., Brown, S. D., Eichele, T., Wagenmakers, E. J., Ho, T., Serences, J., et al. (2011). Neural correlates of trial-to-trial fluctuations in response caution. *Journal of Neuroscience*, *31*(48), 17488–17495.

Van Ravenzwaaij, D., Van der Maas, H. L., & Wagenmakers, E. J. (2012). Optimal decision making in neural inhibition models. *Psychological Review*, *119*(1), 201.

Von Neumann, J., & Morgenstern, O. (1945). *Theory of games and economic behavior*. Princeton, NJ: Princeton University Press.

Waldvogel, D., Van Gelderen, P., Muellbacher, W., & Ziemann, U. (2000). The relative metabolic demand of inhibition and excitation. *Nature*, *406*(6799), 995.

Wang, X. J. (2002). Probabilistic decision making by slow reverberation in cortical circuits. *Neuron*, *36*(5), 955–968.

Weber, B., Aholt, A., Neuhaus, C., Trautner, P., Elger, C. E., & Teichert, T. (2007). Neural evidence for reference-dependence in real-market-transactions. *NeuroImage*, *35*(1), 441–447.

Weller, J. A., Levin, I. P., Shiv, B., & Bechara, A. (2007). Neural correlates of adaptive decision making for risky gains and losses. *Psychological Science*, *18*(11), 958–964.

Wittmann, M., Leland, D. S., & Paulus, M. P. (2007). Time and decision making: differential contribution of the posterior insular cortex and the striatum during a delay discounting task. *Experimental Brain Research*, *179*(4), 643–653.

Wunderlich, K., Rangel, A., & O'Doherty, J. P. (2010). Economic choices can be made using only stimulus values. *Proceedings of the National Academy of Sciences, 107*(34), 15005–15010.

Xu, L., Liang, Z. Y., Wang, K., Li, S., & Jiang, T. (2009). Neural mechanism of intertemporal choice: from discounting future gains to future losses. *Brain Research, 1261*, 65–74.

Yacubian, J., Gläscher, J., Schroeder, K., Sommer, T., Braus, D. F., & Büchel, C. (2006). Dissociable systems for gain-and loss-related value predictions and errors of prediction in the human brain. *Journal of Neuroscience, 26*(37), 9530–9537.

Zeelenberg, M. (1999). Anticipated regret, expected feedback and behavioral decision making. *Journal of Behavioral Decision Making, 12*(2), 93.

Chapter 4

Skin Conductance in the Study of Politics and Communication☆

Stuart N. Soroka
University of Michigan, Ann Arbor, MI, United States

INTRODUCTION

The last decade has seen a marked increase in the use of skin conductance in social scientific research, both as a real time measure of reactions to stimuli, and as an indicator of underlying predispositions connected to a range of political, economic and social behaviors. Recent work explores, for instance, psychological responses to "liking" and sharing on social media (Alhabash, Almutairi, Lou, & Kim, 2018); asymmetries in the impact of losses versus gains in economic experiments focusing on the "Monty Hall Problem" (Massad, dos Santos, da Rocha, & Stupple, 2018); and the relationship between threat sensitivity and politicians' preferences for government spending (Arceneaux, Dunaway, & Soroka, 2018). There is increasing interest in the use of skin conductance as a measure of unconscious, real-time psychophysiological activation, across the social sciences.

This chapter provides an introduction to the use of skin conductance in social scientific work, with a particular emphasis on political science and communication studies. It begins by describing what we mean by the term "skin conductance." The chapter then considers some of the most common interpretations of skin conductance in the social sciences, and outlines some of the advantages—both methodological and substantive—of skin conductance over some more typical measures in the study of political science and communication. We then turn to an expository example of the use of skin conductance in

☆ This work draws on ongoing collaborative projects with Patrick Fournier, Lilach Nir, and Johanna Dunaway. Data gathering was supported by the Social Sciences and Humanities Council of Canada and the LSA at the University of Michigan. Research assistants for this project were Amanda Hampton, Sydney Foy, Heidi Payter, and Autumn Szczepanski.

Biophysical Measurement in Experimental Social Science Research. https://doi.org/10.1016/B978-0-12-813092-6.00007-1

work on political communication, using data from recent psychophysiological experiments on reactions to negative versus positive network news in the United States.

WHAT EXACTLY IS SKIN CONDUCTANCE?

Skin conductance is one element of a broader psychophysiological quantity, electrodermal activity (EDA), which refers to changes in electrical activity at the skin surface. The study of EDA has a long legacy, including Carl Jung's (1969[1906]) word-association experiments, but the recent period of research using EDA, following somewhat more systematic methods of recoding and measurement, started in the early 1970s (see, for example, Lykken & Venables, 1971; Prokasy & Raskin, 1973). Most recent work focuses on skin conductance (SC), one measure of electrodermal activity focused on the ease with which an electrical current passes through the skin.[1] Because water is a good conductor, changes in the moisture produced by eccrine sweat glands, typically on a participant's fingers or hand, produce differences in conductance (see Fig. 1). Increases (or decreases) in sweat gland activity are interpreted

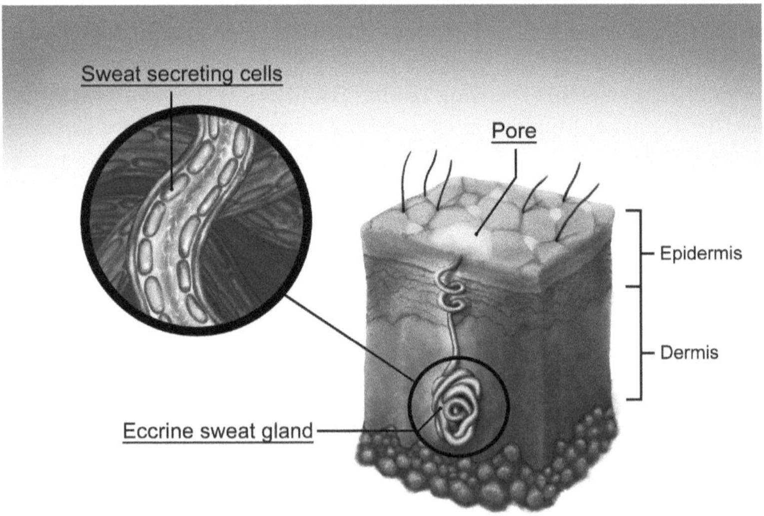

FIG. 1 Cross-section of skin.

1. An alternative measure of a similar quality can be captured through the analysis of skin potential (SP) rather than skin conductance (SC), although the former is less frequent in the social sciences.

in psychophysiological work as increases (or decreases) in "activation" or "arousal," broadly defined.

What exactly does "activation," as captured by skin conductance, reflect? Why consider a measure of skin conductance in social scientific research? In short, skin conductance reflects changes in both information processing and/or emotional arousal; and as an implicit (i.e., not requiring active consideration by participants), automatic (i.e., not easily open to manipulation or reporting bias), and low-cost measure of real-time reactions to stimuli, skin conductance is able to capture these quantities in real time and without the need for conscious feedback from participants. SC thus has both methodological and substantive appeal for researchers interested in, for instance, attentiveness, information processing, and the effects of exposure to media messages. Substantive contributions offered by work on SC are the focus of the section that follows. This section focuses first on the methodological strengths and weaknesses of using SC as an indicator of psychophysiological activation.

Where measurement is concerned, the advantages of SC are straightforward. First, in comparison with some other physiological measures such as heart rate and facial myography, there is a relatively clear connection between SC and the sympathetic nervous system (SNS). The SNS, along with the parasympathetic nervous system (PNS), is a component of the autonomic nervous system (ANS), which regulates unconscious actions. The primary function of the SNS is mobilization, or "fight-or-flight." This is in contrast with the PNS, the primary function of which is "rest-and-digest." (For a particularly clear description of the physical mechanics of skin conductance, including its connection with the SNS, and the particular importance of eccrine sweat glands on the hand, see Dawson, Schell, & Filion, 2007.) Some psychophysiological measures, including heart rate, are governed jointly by the SNS and PNS. This can make the interpretation of these measures complicated as the SNS and PNS can pull in opposite directions, often in complex, interactive ways (see for example, work on autonomic space, e.g., Berntson, Cacioppo, Quigley, & Fabro, 1994). This is not a problem where SC is concerned—SC is governed predominantly by the SNS, and changes in SC are thus a clear signal of activation within the SNS. (And, as the next section describes, there are good reasons for social scientists to be interested in sympathetic activation.)

The second advantage is that measurement of SC is both inexpensive and straightforward. Most physiological encoders—i.e., the machines used to capture physiological measures such as SC—monitor a very small electrical current passed between two electrodes placed on the ends of two fingers (more specifically, the distal phalanx, typically on a respondent's nondominant hand). If the voltage is held constant, changes in the current flow capture conductance, which fluctuates with sweat. The placement of electrodes will vary based on the technology being used; so too will the need for electrode paste (or not), and the complexity of the computer system required to both capture the physiological measure and present the stimuli. This chapter does not go into the details of data

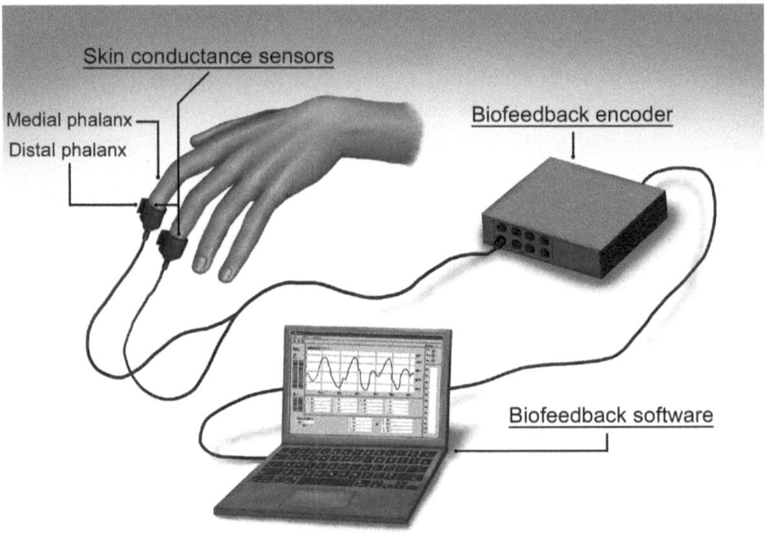

FIG. 2 Measuring skin conductance.

gathering methods given the extensive variation in available systems. Suffice to say that SC data can be captured at a very high frequency using a relatively simple encoder attached to no more than a standard laptop computer. Fig. 2 offers an illustration of the measurement of SC with the kind of simple sensors and physiological encoder used for the experiments described below. For a more detailed discussion of the biological and physiological sources of SC, and further mechanics of measuring it see, for example, Andreassi (2007) and Dawson et al. (2007).

Most importantly, as with other psychophysiological measures, SC allows social scientists the opportunity to capture attitudes both implicitly and in real time. Survey responses and self-reports are limited in their ability to capture nonconscious predispositions. They also face constraints when the focus is on attitudes that participants may be uncomfortable revealing. (For a useful discussion, see Wagner et al., 2014.) SC is not limited in these ways. In addition, SC allows researchers to capture reactions in real time, without the need for any pausing or conscious effort on the part of participants. This facilitates, for instance, the study of activation in the context of decision making games, or second-by-second as a person views a news video.

There are some measurement-related weaknesses to the use of SC as well, of course. It is of some significance that SC activity is often but need not necessarily be related to emotion or affect. As we shall see below, there is a good deal of work that interprets heightened SC as an indication of affective or emotional arousal, but there also is work suggesting that heightened SC can reflect interest, attention, or cognitive effort (e.g., Lang, Greenwald, Bradley, & Hamm, 1993).

Relatedly, it also matters that when SC captures emotion, it captures the intensity but not what is termed the valence of affect. In more common language, SC captures the magnitude of a reaction, but not whether that reaction is positive (e.g., happiness) or negative (e.g., fear). Heightened SC may thus reflect both interest and affect, and *if* it reflects affect, that affect may be either positive or negative. Any interpretation of SC must consequently recognize this potential blending of attention and affect. In particular, when valence matters for research hypotheses, the identification of valence in SC measures must rely either on (1) additional psychophysiological measures such as EMG (electromyography) data, which by capturing a smile or a furrowed brow can point towards positive or negative affect, or (2) stimuli that are very clearly valenced, such a photos that pretests suggest consistently evoke disgust (vomit), fear (an attacking snake), or happiness (a puppy), as is the objective of work relying on the International Affective Picture System (IAPS; see, for example, Bradley & Lang, 2007). The selection of stimuli that are clearly valenced can in many instances be straightforward, and assumptions about the valence of SC reactions can be similarly straightforward. Furthermore, a good number of research questions exist for which simple physiological activation—i.e., evidence of a reaction (or not) from the SNS—is all that is required.

WHAT CAN WE LEARN FROM SKIN CONDUCTANCE?

What have existing literatures learned from measures of skin conductance? SC has been an especially relevant quantity for researchers interested in affective activation, and particularly *negative* affective activation. Work in psychophysiology typically considers SC as a measure of responsivity to what Schell, Dawson, and Marinkovic (1991) refer to as "potentially phobic" or "fear relevant" stimuli. The tendency for fear-inducing stimuli to produce a reaction in SC has been well established, in large part by early work by Ohman and colleagues (e.g., Öhman, Fredrikson, & Hugdahl, 1978). This link to negativity fits well with the fact that the SNS is concerned with fight-or-flight reactions. Heightened SC in response to negative rather than positive stimuli fits with recent work linking SC to activity in the amygdala, a section of the brain linked to emotional reactions, particularly those related to fear and anxiety (e.g., Cheng, Knight, Smith, & Helmstetter, 2006; Phelps et al., 2001).[2]

SC has thus featured prominently in psychological work focused on negative reactions to stimuli. For instance, Dotsch and Wigboldus (2008) explore "impulsive prejudiced behavior," based on measures of SC recorded while participants interacted with White versus Moroccan avatars in a virtual environment, where heightened SC is interpreted as indicating higher levels of prejudice. (Note this is a particularly valuable example of the advantages of

2. Note also that SC has played a central role in the argument for an evolutionary basis of emotional response to information (Öhman, 1986).

using SC to capture attitudes that participants may not reveal through standard questionnaires. For a review of earlier work in this area, see Guglielmi, 1999.) Romero-Martínez, Lila, Williams, González-Bono, and Moya-Albiol (2013) find that participants with a history of violence towards intimate partners show higher SC levels during periods surrounding a stress test (in this case, involving a verbal presentation and a mental math problem), and suggest that there may be biological correlates of abusive behavior. Hein, Lamm, Brodbeck, and Singer (2011) find that participants who exhibit higher levels of SC activation while observing another person's pain are more likely to choose to help in subsequent rounds, even when that help is costly (see also Krebs, 1975).

Work spanning the fields of psychology and economics has used SC as a means of exploring the role of affect in decision making.[3] There is a considerable body of work linking SC to various aspects of decision making under risk (e.g., Bechara, Damasio, Tranel, & Damasio, 1997; Tchanturia et al., 2007; Tomb, Hauser, Deldin, & Caramazza, 2002). Studer and Clark (2011) offer a recent example, in which they explore SC during a gambling task, and find links between SC and the need to make an active choice, the magnitude of wins or losses, and the chances of winning. Here, and in related work (e.g., Dawson, Schell, & Courtney, 2011; Palomäki, Kosunen, Kuikkaniemi, Yamabe, & Ravaja, 2013), high-risk and/or negative outcomes are associated with higher activation. The same is true for work exploring skin conductance during the ultimatum games commonly played in economic experiments (e.g., Hewig et al., 2011; Wu, Luo, Broster, Gu, & Luo, 2013).

The emphasis on SC as an indication of information processing or cognitive effort is especially evident in work in communication studies. Work by Lang and colleagues has been particularly influential in this area. They find, for instance, that participants exhibit higher levels of activation when confronted with risky rather than nonrisky products, and that this heightened activation is correlated with increased recall of those products. The link between physiological activation and information processing is especially clear in these authors' interpretation of their results: "risky products are capable of eliciting arousal in viewers that, in turn, results in the automatic allocation of mental resources to processing the messages" (Lang, Chung, Lee, & Zhao, 2005, p. 297). Earlier work using video stimuli similarly finds that arousal is positively related to recall (Lang, Dhillon, & Dong, 1995, p. 1999).

Where politically-focused work is concerned, Wang, Morey, and Srivastava (2014) use skin conductance as an indication of attentiveness to political ads from those who both support or do not support the advertised party; while Daignault, Soroka, and Giasson (2013) use skin conductance to explain what appears to be the heightened impact of negative advertising. For news content, Soroka (2014) and Soroka and McAdams (2015) use skin conductance to

3. For an introduction to the use of SC in this area, see Dawson et al. (2011).

explore heightened attentiveness to negative news content as one account for the prevalence of negative news. Other work explores gender differences in reactivity to news content as a means of explaining the gender gap in political interest and knowledge (Grabe & Kamhawi, 2006; Soroka Gidengil, Fournier, & Nir, 2016).

A recent body of work in political science focuses on skin conductance not just as a measure of real time reactivity to information, or as an indication of either affective or cognitive processes, but rather as a measure with which to explore underlying predispositions in reactivity to information. Most prominent is recent work by Hibbing and colleagues, which uses skin conductance responses to images to capture either threat sensitivity or disgust sensitivity, and then explores the political correlates of each. There is a small but growing body of work that connects threat and/or disgust sensitivity to conservative political attitudes in the United States (e.g., Dodd et al., 2012; Hibbing Smith, & Alford, 2014; Oxley et al., 2008; Smith, Oxley, Hibbing, Alford, & Hibbing, 2011; see also Arceneaux et al., 2018). (This is line with early work in the field focusing on skin conductance as measure of reactivity to *racial* threat, although results in that case led researchers to be somewhat skeptical of psychophysiological measures; see Wahlke & Lodge, 1972.) Other recent work highlights a connection between heightened reactivity to images and increased political participation (Gruszczynski, Balzer, Jacobs, Smith, & Hibbing, 2012), as well as a correlation between heightened skin conductance levels in response to images of Barack Obama and the expressed intensity of attitudes towards both the candidate and his health care policy: "...our findings," Wagner et al. (2014, p. 313) note, "suggest that people's opinions of the job being done by President Obama or of health-care reform are shaped not just by conscious feelings but by nonconscious subprocesses."

The existing literature thus highlights many different interpretations of SC. One might distinguish views of SC as being on the one hand about measuring affective reactions or cognitive activation, and on the other hand about measuring real time information processing or "nonconscious subprocesses." These approaches are not contradictory. Given the importance of emotion to "rational" thinking (see in particular Damasio, 2005),[4] there is no reason to expect psychophysiological activation to capture just one or the other. Additionally, the fact that SC captures automated physiological reactions is what facilitates both the real-time information-processing perspective *and* the notion that SC indicates something subconscious that regular survey questioning (and answering) cannot reveal.

The value of SC as a measure in communication and political science hinges then on whether psychophysiological activation, representing some combination of affective and/or cognitive reactivity, is of importance in the study of

4. Note the parallels between Damasio's seminal work and Potter and Bolls (2011, p. 31) argument that SC research hinges on a belief that "cognitive processes can be inferred from bodily reactions."

information processing, media effects, and/or political preferences. It clearly is. There are large groups of literature focused on attentiveness to political news content, the impact of political advertising, and the ways in which people remember (or do not remember) political information. There is a growing body of work on the importance of emotion in news choice, in political decision making, and on subsequent behavior. SC measures offer an opportunity to further explore how affect is important in decision making, or the situations for which, or individuals for whom, affect is likely to play a greater or lesser role. It may also capture deep-seated, otherwise unmeasurable reactions that structure how we react to our (political) world. SC also offers an unobtrusive way to capture reactivity to information over time. It is for these reasons that SC has been of increasing interest in research on communications and political behavior.

NEGATIVITY BIASES IN REACTIONS TO NETWORK NEWS

The sections that follow offer an expository analysis of SC, focused on reactions to television news programming. There is a good deal of work in political communication documenting high and/or increasing levels of negativity in news content (e.g., Cappella & Jamieson, 1997; Farnsworth & Lichter, 2007; Patterson, 1994; Sabato, 1991). There is also research suggesting that people are more activated by, and pay more attention to, negative news (e.g., Soroka, 2014; Trussler & Soroka, 2014). Whether this prevalence of, and attraction to, negative news is problematic is unclear. On the one hand, negativity may encourage attentiveness to political issues, particularly problematic issues that require attention. There is evidence that cynicism may be positively rather than negatively related to mobilization (de Vreese, 2005), and that conflict may increase participation (Martin, 2008; Schuck, Vliegenthart, & de Vreese, 2014). On the other hand, it may be that biases in human information processing are enhanced by media organizations, whose primary purpose is after all to produce news that will attract an audience. The end result may be the provision of disproportionately negative information, and as a result, decreasing political interest and engagement. (The debate about the direction of the relationship between negative versus positive information and turnout has been particularly rich in work on political advertising. See, for example, Ansolabehere, Iyengar, Simon, & Valentino, 1994; Brooks, 2006; Finkel & Geer, 1998; Lau, Sigelman, Heldman, & Babbitt, 1999.)

There is accordingly a need for work that seeks to better understand (1) the widespread tendency for news consumers to be more attentive to negative information, and (2) what this tendency means for the encoding and recall of political information, and for political behavior more broadly. The sections that follow focus on (1), exploring the possibility that American television news viewers will be more psychophysiologically activated by negative than by positive news content. Stronger psychophysiological activation in response to negative news content may help account for the decidedly negative nature of news content and political campaigns. If the aim of news programs is to find an activated and attentive audience, and if negativity tends to increase psychophysiological activation, then it makes sense that news programs would come to focus more on negative information. Considering this possibility and understanding how these findings matter for political psychology and behavior more broadly, is a critical area for future work. In a concluding section, results are discussed with these issues in mind.

METHODS

This study replicates and extends recent work exploring skin conductance in response to television news content (Soroka & McAdams, 2015). While this past work focuses on a relatively small student sample in Canada, the analyses that follow rely on a larger, more representative sample in the United States. Analyses are based on 116 female and 69 male respondents, where 110 were recruited from an undergraduate student participant pool, and 75 were recruited from a more representative pool managed primarily for medical research.

The experimental protocol combines a physiological study and a computer-based survey. We focus here on variations in skin conductance during the physiological study, a video experiment involving seven randomly-ordered BBC television news stories. A list of all stories used in the experiment is shown in Table 1. All respondents are shown the two domestic stories, one of which is positive and one negative. They also see a random draw of five of the international stories. As there are a total of eight possible international stories, four positive and four negative, respondents can end up with a broadcast that is predominantly positive or negative; but each will see at least two positive and two negative stories. Most see three of one valence and four of the other. The order of stories is entirely randomized, so that effects of one story are not influenced by any single preceding story. Stories range from roughly two and a half to under four minutes long. Depending on the randomization, the entire study takes between 20 and 30 minutes.

Stories are coded for valence in several ways. They are first categorized by research assistants as either predominantly negative or positive; this is done as part of the story selection stage. After stories are selected, they are coded second-by-second on a five-point scale of valence by three expert coders. (Details on coding are available in Soroka & McAdams, 2015.) The average tone is then the averaged either across the entire story, or five second interval, depending on the level of analysis. This coding of stories is further confirmed by postexperimental questions asking respondents to rate each story on several dimensions, including negativity. Subjects' mean ratings, on a scale of one to seven, are in the last column of Table 1. The correlation between the two sets of ratings is 0.95.

Coder-rated valence is thus the principal independent variable in our analysis. The dependent variable is skin conductance level (SCL). An illustrative

TABLE 1 Video Stimuli

Title	Description	Valence	Coder Rating (−2 to 2)	Participant Rating (1 to 7)
International				
Peru	Small town of Chimbote burns down	Negative	0.859	4.783
May Day	May Day protests following economic downturn	Negative	0.688	3.161
Niger	Food Shortages in Niger	Negative	1.071	5.082
UN Sri Lanka	UN investigations in war crimes in Sri Lanka	Negative	1.253	5.157
Gorillas	Gorillas are released into wild	Positive	−1.053	1.541
Folding car	New electric, folding car intended to reduce congestion	Positive	−0.356	1.456
Young director	11-year old makes stop-motion films	Positive	−1.053	1.073
Cured liver disease	Young child recovers from liver disease	Positive	−0.540	1.625
Domestic				
Homeless	A homeless man is battered and shot by police	Negative	1.059	5.739
Bagpipes	A US man learns how to make bagpipes	Positive	−0.693	1.184

SCL time series is shown in Fig. 3, from one participant, over the first 150 five-second intervals of the experiment. (Note that SCL values typically lie somewhere between 2 and 20 microseimens.) The task of the current project is to explore to what degree the increases and decreases evident in Fig. 3 are related to the experimental stimuli—in this case, news content.

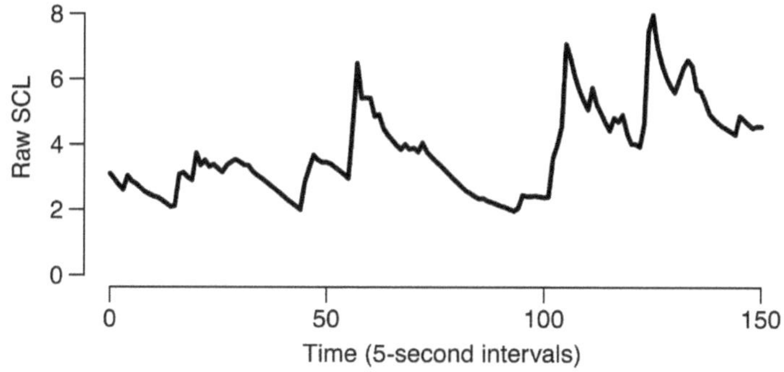

FIG. 3 One respondent's SCL, at five-second intervals.

Skin conductance is captured using a ProComp encoder from Thought Technology and is originally sampled 256 times per second. The data is first downsampled by taking averages over 125-ms intervals, and then smoothed slightly, using Lowess smoothing. The smoothing matters relatively little in this case given that the analysis focuses on five-second and full story intervals. For work that explores skin conductance responses at much smaller time intervals, however, appropriate smoothing and the removal of outliers can be critical. Indeed, the construction of SC measures will in some instances be much more complex than what is presented here.

Where more complex analyses are concerned, it is worth distinguishing between work on skin conductance levels (SCL) and skin conductance responses (SCR), where the latter involves a counting of spikes in the SC signal, and/or a detailed analysis of the shape of individual SCR. Indeed, Dawson et al. (2007) review a range of different possibilities where the analysis of SC is concerned, including levels, changes, frequency of SCR, SCR amplitude, habituation, and so on. Some work also uses a combination of SCL and SCR as means of distinguishing different cognitive processes (e.g., Cacioppo & Sandman, 1978). (The spikes in Fig. 3 reflect SCRs, although we do not see the full shape of individual SCRs when data are averaged over five-second intervals.) It is also generally true that SCL and SCR are associated with the tonic (long-term) and phasic (short-term) components of SC respectively; and for those using SC as a millisecond-to-millisecond signal of cognitive processing, separating SC levels from responses, and responses from each other, can be a complex statistical problem (e.g., Bach, Flandin, Friston, & Dolan, 2009; Benedek & Kaernbach, 2010; Lim et al., 1997). Much like the study that follows, however, a good deal of work in political science, communications, and economics has focused on mean levels of SC over longer time periods (from five-second periods upwards), lumping together a combination of tonic and phasic components.

"Normalizing" the skin conductance signal is crucial regardless of time interval. The objective of this procedure is to take into account the fact that different individuals will exhibit rather different mean levels of skin conductance, due not just to demographic differences but also time of day and room temperature (e.g., Venables & Mitchell, 1996). Not taking these inter-individual differences into account can make identifying stimulus effects rather difficult. The bare minimum standard approach to normalizing SC data—and the one used here—is to use measures of a participant's skin conductance during the stimulus relative to skin conductance levels recorded during a prestimulus period.

In the current experiment, the first news story is preceded by two-minutes of gray screen, and then for 40 seconds a gray screen appears between each succeeding pair of stories. The options given this setup are to express skin conductance levels relative to either (1) the first two-minute baseline period, or (2) the baseline period that precedes each story. The advantages of the latter are twofold: not only does it remove individual-level differences in skin conductance levels, by allowing the baseline level to change between stories, but it also partly accounts for the tendency of SCL to decrease over the course of longer experiments. This may be a consequence of measurement issues with the electrode, and/or it may be related to participants' habituation to the experimental environment or the decreasing impact of stimuli. Regardless, one simple correction is to detrend the SCL measure (e.g., Soroka & McAdams, 2015). Another is to include the impact of time in regression models. Another still is to allow the baseline to shift from one story to the next, which will, at least in part, remove trends in SCL over the course of an experiment. This is one major advantage to normalizing stimulus period SC using the baseline period that precedes each story. (There is a long-standing and valuable literature on different approaches to normalizing SC measures, in terms of both baselines and variances. For early work, see, for example, Ben-Shakhar, 1985; Lykken, 1972; Stemmler, 1987.)

The estimation used here is relatively simple, in part because a good deal of work in the social sciences takes a similarly simple approach. We explore the effects of story valence on SCL by estimating a panel model in which each respondent-video combination is a case. There are seven stories for each respondent, and each of those stories is associated with both a mean valence, and mean SCL. The analyses that follow explore the within-subject relationship between these two mean values. This approach prevents us from looking in detail at what exactly in a video provokes a skin conductance response; it only explores the possibility that, overall, a negative story will provoke higher levels of activation than a positive story. More detailed analyses are certainly possible, connecting SCL to specific moments in videos, and/or modeling individuals' reactions using more complex time-series methods. There also may be interesting differences in either levels or reactivity of SCL across gender, age, political interest and so on, but those are not the focus of the analysis that follows.

The simple model used here is as follows:

$$SCL_{i,s} = \alpha + \beta_1 valence_{i,s} + \beta_2 order_{i,s} + \beta_3 length_{i,s} + \varepsilon_{i,s}, \qquad (1)$$

where *SCL* and *valence* for individual *i* and story *s* are as they are described above; *order* is an ordinal variable representing the place of story *i* in the series of stories viewed by the participant, to capture the possibility that respondents' reactions change based on the number of stories they have seen thus far; and *length* is an interval-level variable counting the number of five-second intervals in each story, in case the length of a story leads to lower or higher average SCL. (We might, for instance, imagine that longer stories eventually become less engaging, and lead to lower average SCL.) We do not add demographic variables to the model, partly because they are not the focus of our analysis, but also because they should not be critical to revealing the impact of valence: level differences that are a consequence of demographics will be accounted for by normalizing the SC signal within subject.[5]

RESULTS

A simple *t*-test comparing SCL during positive versus negative stories finds that the mean of the former is −0.69 while the latter is −0.001. Note that both values are negative, reflecting the tendency for SCL, following activation at the start of a news story, to decrease over the course of the story. However, the decrease in SCL during negative stories is marginal, in comparison with the notable decrease during positive stories. (The t-statistic for a difference in means test is −2.94, which is statistically significant at $P < .01$.) Already, this is evidence that SCL is higher for negative than for positive news stories.

The impact of valence is further explored in Table 2, which shows results from the panel model described above. The model was estimated with both fixed and random effects, but only the latter are included here, because a Hausman test suggests no significant difference with the addition of the fixed effects. (This is as we should expect given that the data is normalized, of course.) Estimates suggest no impact of story length on mean SCL. The order of videos does matter however: each additional story in the newscast is associated with a decrease in SCL of −0.051. Valence also matters. Valence is measured on a five-point scale, from −2 to +2, but these estimates are based on averages across whole stories, so the observed range of tone is closer to −1.5 to +1.5. Based on the estimates in Table 1, moving from one extreme of this range to the other is associated with a roughly −0.15 change in SCL. This is illustrated in Fig. 4, where the black line shows the estimated SCL

5. The same is not true for differences in variance across subjects, of course. Some work "normalizes" to account for different variances as well, expressed all SC in standard deviations (for each individual), above or below the baseline period. The difficulty with this approach is that it assumes that all respondents exhibit equal levels of activation, i.e. the highest (lowest) level they reach during the experiment is the height of their activation. This is a rather strong assumption, so this work avoids normalizing variances across individuals.

TABLE 2 The Impact of Story Valence on SCL

	DV: SCL
Valence	−0.050* (0.025)
Order	−0.051*** (0.011)
Length	−0.001 (0.003)
Constant	0.161** (0.061)
N	1183
Rsq	0.026

Cells contain OLS regression coefficients with standard errors in parentheses.
** P < .05; ** P < .01; *** P < .001.*

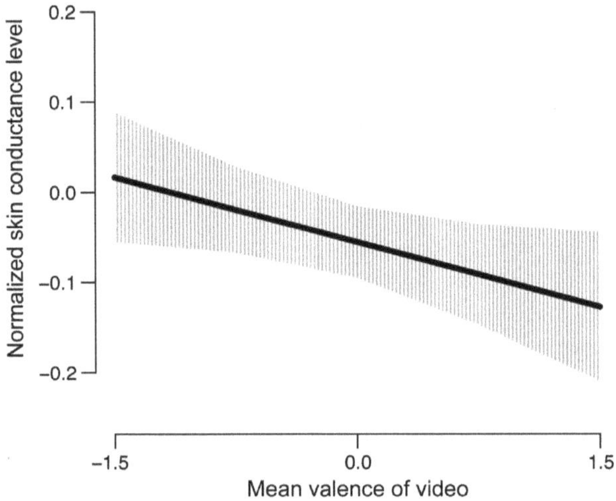

FIG. 4 The impact of story tone on SCL.

and the shaded area shows 95% confidence intervals, and where negative values for valence indicate negative valence.

Fig. 4 offers a simple illustration of the tendency for Americans to be more activated by negative than by positive news content. Note that the regression line captures the average effect over the entire story, so a predicted value of just over zero when valence is −1.5 combines (1) typically very high activation at the beginning, and then intermittently over the course of the story, and (2) other periods during which SCL is declining. The figure thus gives a highly averaged and highly stylized view of the communication process. As noted above there are ways to look in more detail at the impact of news coverage on psychophysiological activation. One approach is to move to a repeated-measures structure in which each respondent is his or her own panel, and every five-second interval is an observation. Given the number of participants and the length of the news stories, this leads to a rather large dataset (~50,000 five-second intervals for each of 175 respondents). The estimated impact of valence in a time-series panel estimation relying on these data is not statistically different from what we have seen above—activation increases with negative content and decreases with positive content—although the estimation must be more complex to deal with the existence of multiple observations per subject; see Soroka and McAdams (2015) for an example using similar data.

Rather than estimate the impact of valence, however, we can also explore models in which SCL, across all respondents, is estimated as a function of within-story time, included as a categorical variable. The advantage of this approach is that it makes no assumptions about what affects activation—it offers simple descriptive information on the impact of news content on SCL, averaged across all respondents. Each story is modeled separately, as follows,

$$SCL_{i,t} = \alpha + \beta_1 \, time_t + \varepsilon_{i,t}, \tag{2}$$

where time simple counts through the five-second intervals t. To be clear, the model estimates average SCL and margin of error across all participants for every five-second interval in each story. Fig. 5 shows the estimated trends for one negative (Sri Lanka) and one positive (Young Director) story.

The difference between the negative and positive story in Fig. 5 is very clear. These are among the clearest examples. Stories that are not as consistently negative or positive will produce trends that are not quite as clear as what we see here. These two stories are included because they are paradigmatic examples of SC during a negative and positive story: the negative story about Sri Lanka leads to levels of SC that are marginally higher than the baseline value; while the positive story about the young director leads to a steadily declining activation. Results here thus confirm the tendency for negative news to be more activating than positive news.

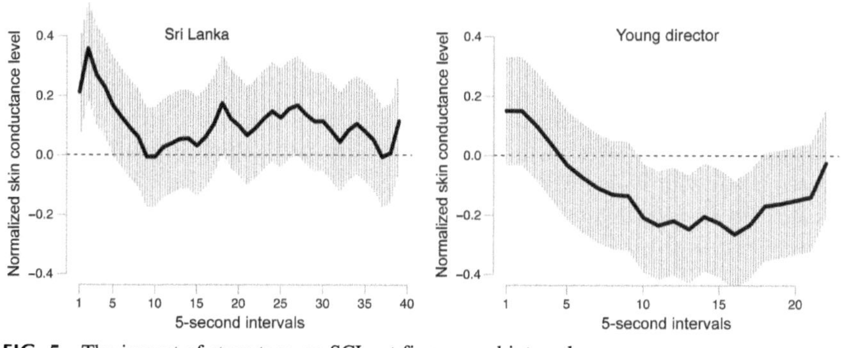

FIG. 5 The impact of story tone on SCL, at five-second intervals.

DISCUSSION

Results as shown in Fig. 5 are exactly as we should expect given what we know about the impact of negativity on skin conductance in other fields, but Fig. 5 offers an especially clear illustration of why we might expect news content, and perhaps political campaigns as well, to focus more on negative than on positive information. Insofar as skin conductance reflects not just physiological activation, but an affective reaction, or a change in the way in which we process information, or both, there may be good reason for news producers to focus primarily on negative news—i.e., it generates larger audiences, and/or holds people's attention longer, and/or has a more lasting impact.

This conclusion depends on the belief that physiological activation will be positively correlated with news selection, or consumption, or recall. Whether this is actually the case is unclear, however. Past work in psychophysiology and neurology gives us good reason to connect heightened skin conductance with affect. As discussed above, there is a considerable body of work that finds a connection between skin conductance and other measures of heightened (primarily negative) affect. There is also good evidence that heightened skin conductance reflects a change in information processing. As we have seen, work in economics and psychology has shown how decisions change when information is interpreted during heightened activation, and there is a good amount of evidence suggesting that recall is better when activation is higher. Nevertheless, we do not yet fully understand the degree to which actual news consumption and political behavior are affected by whether or not news content is physiologically activating.

One might imagine several possibilities. Negative content might prove more interesting and be better remembered, and provoke an active consideration of political attitudes, or even participation. Alternatively, negative content might be activating, but in a way that encourages avoidance and disengagement, so that citizens withdraw not just from news content but from politics more broadly. Existing work focused on information processing would seem to suggest the former, insofar as negative information seems be more activating, and more easily recalled. However, none of the existing literature has focused explicitly on political stimuli.

We thus cannot be sure whether increased activation as a consequence of negative news content will produce more or less political engagement and participation. This is of some significance, as one predominant modern concern in politics and political communication is that negative content is leading to disaffection and withdrawal from politics. Work using SC is not yet well-equipped to offer answers on this critical issue, because our ability to link skin conductance to behavior outside the lab has been limited.[6]

6. Note that asking people about their intentions where political behavior is concerned is straightforward, but the link between intended and actual subsequent behavior is rather weak.

SC-focused work can nevertheless offer valuable information on the aspects of media content that provoke activation, affect, information processing, and/or cognitive effort. The fact that SC captures reactions in real time is of special importance for those interested in work on media effects, or in information processing during games (i.e., during economics experiments). The additional fact that SC captures reactions implicitly means that researchers avoid the problems of self-assessments, at least for quantities that are indicated through nonconscious psychophysiological reactions. For these reasons, the analysis of SC provides a uniquely simple means by which to explore the ways in which affect and information processing matter for learning and decision making, not just in political science and communication but across the social sciences.

REFERENCES

Alhabash, S., Almutairi, N., Lou, C., & Kim, W. (2018). Pathways to virality: psychophysiological responses preceding likes, shares, comments, and status updates on Facebook. *Media Psychology*, 1–21. First View.

Andreassi, J. L. (2007). *Psychophysiology: Human behavior and physiological response*. Lawrence Erlbaum.

Ansolabehere, S., Iyengar, S., Simon, A., & Valentino, N. (1994). Does attack advertising demobilize the electorate? *American Political Science Review*, *88*, 829–838.

Arceneaux, K., Dunaway, J., & Soroka, S. (2018). Elites are people, too: the effects of threat sensitivity on policymakers' spending priorities. *PLoS One*, *13*(4).

Bach, D. R., Flandin, G., Friston, K. J., & Dolan, R. J. (2009). Time-series analysis for rapid event-related skin conductance responses. *Journal of Neuroscience Methods*, *184*(2), 224–234.

Bechara, A., Damasio, H., Tranel, D., & Damasio, A. R. (1997). Deciding advantageously before knowing the advantageous strategy. *Science*, *275*(5304), 1293–1295.

Benedek, M., & Kaernbach, C. (2010). A continuous measure of phasic electrodermal activity. *Journal of Neuroscience Methods*, *190*(1), 80–91.

Ben-Shakhar, G. (1985). Standardization within individuals: a simple method to neutralize individual differences in skin conductance. *Psychophysiology*, *22*(3), 292–299. https://doi.org/10.1111/j.1469-8986.1985.tb01603.x.

Berntson, G. G., Cacioppo, J. T., Quigley, K. S., & Fabro, V. T. (1994). Autonomic space and psychophysiological response. *Psychophysiology*, *31*(1), 44–61.

Bradley, M. M., & Lang, P. J. (2007). The international affective picture system (IAPS) in the study of emotion and attention. In *Handbook of emotion elicitation and assessment* (pp. 29–46). New York, NY: Oxford University Press.

Brooks, D. J. (2006). The resilient voter: moving toward closure in the debate over negative campaigning and turnout. *Journal of Politics*, *68*(3), 684–696.

Cacioppo, J. T., & Sandman, C. A. (1978). Physiological differentiation of sensory and cognitive tasks as a function of warning, processing demands, and reported unpleasantness. *Biological Psychology*, *6*(3), 181–192.

Cappella, J. N., & Jamieson, K. H. (1997). *Spiral of cynicism: The press and the public good*. New York: Oxford University Press.

Cheng, D. T., Knight, D. C., Smith, C. N., & Helmstetter, F. J. (2006). Human amygdala activity during the expression of fear responses. *Behavioral Neuroscience*, *120*(6), 1187–1195.

Daignault, P., Soroka, S., & Giasson, T. (2013). The perception of political advertising during an election campaign: a preliminary study of cognitive and emotional effects. *Canadian Journal of Communication*, *38*(2), 167–186.

Damasio, A. (2005). *Descartes' error: Emotion, reason, and the human brain*. New York, NY: Penguin.

Dawson, M. E., Schell, A. M., & Courtney, C. G. (2011). The skin conductance response, anticipation, and decision-making. *Journal of Neuroscience, Psychology, and Economics*, *4*(2), 111–116.

Dawson, M. E., Schell, A. M., & Filion, D. M. (2007). The electrodermal system. In J. T. Cacioppo, L. G. Tassinary, & G. Berntson (Eds.), *Handbook of psychphysiology* (pp. 159–181). New York: Cambridge University Press.

de Vreese, C. H. (2005). The spiral of cynicism reconsidered. *European Journal of Communication*, *20*(3), 283–301.

Dodd, M. D., Balzer, A., Jacobs, C. M., Gruszczynski, M. W., Smith, K. B., & Hibbing, J. R. (2012). The political left rolls with the good and the political right confronts the bad: connecting physiology and cognition to preferences. *Philosophical Transactions of the Royal Society of London B: Biological Sciences*, *367*(1589), 640–649.

Dotsch, R., & Wigboldus, D. H. J. (2008). Virtual prejudice. *Journal of Experimental Social Psychology*, *44*(4), 1194–1198.

Farnsworth, S. J., & Lichter, S. R. (2007). *The nightly news nightmare: Television's coverage of U.S. Presidential Elections, 1988–2004*. Lanham, MD: Rowman & Littlefield Publishers.

Finkel, S. E., & Geer, J. G. (1998). A spot check: casting doubt on the demobilizing effect of attack advertising. *American Journal of Political Science*, *42*(2), 573–595.

Grabe, M. E., & Kamhawi, R. (2006). Hard wired for negative news? Gender differences in processing broadcast news. *Communication Research*, *33*(5), 346–369.

Gruszczynski, M. W., Balzer, A., Jacobs, C. M., Smith, K. B., & Hibbing, J. R. (2012). The physiology of political participation. *Political Behavior*, *35*(1), 135–152.

Guglielmi, R. S. (1999). Psychophysiological assessment of prejudice: past research, current status, and future directions. *Personality and Social Psychology Review*, *3*(2), 123–157.

Hein, G., Lamm, C., Brodbeck, C., & Singer, T. (2011). Skin conductance response to the pain of others predicts later costly helping. *PLoS One*, *6*(8).

Hewig, J., Kretschmer, N., Trippe, R. H., Hecht, H., Coles, M. G. H., Holroyd, C. B., et al. (2011). Why humans deviate from rational choice. *Psychophysiology*, *48*(4), 507–514.

Hibbing, J. R., Smith, K. B., & Alford, J. R. (2014). Differences in negativity bias underlie variations in political ideology. *Behavioral and Brain Sciences*, *37*(3), 297–307. https://doi.org/10.1017/S0140525X13001192.

Jung, C. G. (1969). *Studies in word association* (1st ed.). London: Routledge & Kegan Paul PLC.

Krebs, D. (1975). Empathy and altruism. *Journal of Personality and Social Psychology*, *32*(6), 1134–1146.

Lang, A., Chung, Y., Lee, S., & Zhao, X. (2005). It's the product: do risky products compel attention and elicit arousal in media users? *Health Communication*, *17*(3), 283–300.

Lang, A., Dhillon, K., & Dong, Q. (1995). The effects of emotional arousal and valence on television viewers' cognitive capacity and memory. *Journal of Broadcasting & Electronic Media*, *39*(3), 313–327.

Lang, P. J., Greenwald, M. K., Bradley, M. M., & Hamm, A. O. (1993). Looking at pictures: affective, facial, visceral, and behavioral reactions. *Psychophysiology*, *30*(3), 261–273.

Lau, R. R., Sigelman, L., Heldman, C., & Babbitt, P. (1999). The effects of negative political advertisements: a meta-analytic assessment. *The American Political Science Review*, *93*(4), 851–875.

Lim, C. L., Rennie, C., Barry, R. J., Bahramali, H., Lazzaro, I., Manor, B., et al. (1997). Decomposing skin conductance into tonic and phasic components. *International Journal of Psychophysiology*, *25*(2), 97–109.

Lykken, D. T. (1972). Range correction applied to heart rate and to GSR data. *Psychophysiology*, *9* (3), 373–379.

Lykken, D. T., & Venables, P. H. (1971). Direct measurement of skin conductance: a proposal for standardization. *Psychophysiology*, *8*(5), 656–672.

Martin, P. S. (2008). The mass media as sentinel: why bad news about issues is good news for participation. *Political Communication*, *25*(2), 180–193.

Massad, E., dos Santos, P. C. C., da Rocha, A. F., & Stupple, E. J. N. (2018). The Monty Hall problem revisited: autonomic arousal in an inverted version of the game. *PLoS One*, *13*(3).

Öhman, A. (1986). Face the beast and fear the face: animal and social fears as prototypes for evolutionary analyses of emotion. *Psychophysiology*, *23*(2), 123–145.

Öhman, A., Fredrikson, M., & Hugdahl, K. (1978). Orienting and defensive responding in the electrodermal system: palmar-dorsal differences and recovery rate during conditioning to potentially phobic stimuli. *Psychophysiology*, *15*(2), 93–101.

Oxley, D. R., Smith, K. B., Alford, J. R., Hibbing, M. V., Miller, J. L., Scalora, M., et al. (2008). Political attitudes vary with physiological traits. *Science*, *321*(5896), 1667–1670.

Palomäki, J., Kosunen, I., Kuikkaniemi, K., Yamabe, T., & Ravaja, N. (2013). Anticipatory electrodermal activity and decision making in a computer poker-game. *Journal of Neuroscience, Psychology, and Economics*, *6*(1), 55–70.

Patterson, T. E. (1994). *Out of order*. New York: Vintage Books.

Phelps, E. A., O'Connor, K. J., Gatenby, J. C., Gore, J. C., Grillon, C., & Davis, M. (2001). Activation of the left amygdala to a cognitive representation of fear. *Nature Neuroscience*, *4*(4) nn0401_437.

Potter, R. F., & Bolls, P. (2011). *Psychophysiological measurement and meaning: Cognitive and emotional processing of media* (1st ed.). New York: Routledge.

Prokasy, W. F., & Raskin, D. C. (1973). *Electrodermal activity in psychological research*. Oxford, England: Academic Press.

Romero-Martínez, A., Lila, M., Williams, R. K., González-Bono, E., & Moya-Albiol, L. (2013). Skin conductance rises in preparation and recovery to psychosocial stress and its relationship with impulsivity and testosterone in intimate partner violence perpetrators. *International Journal of Psychophysiology*, *90*(3), 329–333.

Sabato, L. (1991). *Feeding frenzy: How attack journalism has transformed American politics*. New York: The Free Press.

Schell, A. M., Dawson, M. E., & Marinkovic, K. (1991). Effects of potentially phobic conditioned stimuli on retention, reconditioning, and extinction of the conditioned skin conductance response. *Psychophysiology*, *28*(2), 140–153.

Schuck, A. R. T., Vliegenthart, R., & de Vreese, C. H. (2014). Who's afraid of conflict? The mobilizing effect of conflict framing in campaign news. *British Journal of Political Science*, 1–18. First View.

Smith, K. B., Oxley, D., Hibbing, M. V., Alford, J. R., & Hibbing, J. R. (2011). Disgust sensitivity and the neurophysiology of left-right political orientations. *PLoS One*, *6*(10).

Soroka, S., & McAdams, S. (2015). News, politics, and negativity. *Political Communication*, *32*(1), 1–22.

Soroka, S. N. (2014). *Negativity in democratic politics: Causes and consequences*. New York, NY: Cambridge University Press.

Soroka, S., Gidengil, E., Fournier, P., & Nir, L. (2016). Do women and men respond differently to negative news? *Politics & Gender*, *12*(2), 344–368. https://doi.org/10.1017/S1743923X16000131.

Stemmler, G. (1987). Standardization within subjects: a critique of Ben-Shakhar's conclusions. *Psychophysiology*, *24*(2), 243–246.

Studer, B., & Clark, L. (2011). Place your bets: psychophysiological correlates of decision-making under risk. *Cognitive, Affective, & Behavioral Neuroscience*, *11*(2), 144–158.

Tchanturia, K., Liao, P. -C., Uher, R., Lawrence, N., Treasure, J., & Campbell, I. C. (2007). An investigation of decision making in anorexia nervosa using the Iowa Gambling Task and skin conductance measurements. *Journal of the International Neuropsychological Society*, *13*(4), 635–641.

Tomb, I., Hauser, M., Deldin, P., & Caramazza, A. (2002). Do somatic markers mediate decisions on the gambling task? *Nature Neuroscience*, *5*(11), 1103–1104.

Trussler, M., & Soroka, S. (2014). Consumer demand for cynical and negative news frames. *The International Journal of Press/Politics*, *19*(3), 360–379. https://doi.org/10.1177/1940161214524832.

Venables, P. H., & Mitchell, D. A. (1996). The effects of age, sex and time of testing on skin conductance activity. *Biological Psychology*, *43*(2), 87–101.

Wagner, M. W., Deppe, K. D., Jacobs, C. M., Friesen, A., Smith, K. B., & Hibbing, J. R. (2014). Beyond survey self-reports: using physiology to tap political orientations. *International Journal of Public Opinion Research*, *27*(3), 303–317.

Wahlke, J. C., & Lodge, M. G. (1972). Psychophysiological measures of political attitudes and behavior. *Midwest Journal of Political Science*, *16*(4), 505–537.

Wang, Z., Morey, A. C., & Srivastava, J. (2014). Motivated selective attention during political ad processing the dynamic interplay between emotional ad content and candidate evaluation. *Communication Research*, *41*(1), 119–156.

Wu, T., Luo, Y., Broster, L. S., Gu, R., & Luo, Y. (2013). The impact of anxiety on social decision-making: behavioral and electrodermal findings. *Social Neuroscience*, *8*(1), 11–21.

Chapter 5

Steroid Hormones in Social Science Research

Ben Hardy
SOAS University of London, London, United Kingdom

INTRODUCTION

The sociologist Emil Durkheim knew, reasonably accurately, how many people would commit suicide each year. His problem was that he did not know who these people were. So, it is with much social science: we know what people will do on average but struggle to predict what a given individual will do. The gap between aggregate prediction and individual behavior has proved both vexatious and fruitful for social scientists. Whilst it has frustrated attempts to predict individuals' actions, it has also given birth to new fields. In economics, for example, this disparity between aggregate and individual behaviors helped give birth to the field of behavioral economics.

Behavioral economics, like much of social science, stops at the skin. The mechanisms of how and why people act the way they do is inferred from behavior and dissected through cunningly-wrought experiments. What is often missing is an understanding of what actually happens inside a person's body when they do the things that the social scientist is interested in. More recently this has begun to change. Disciplines such as neuroeconomics have attempted to tease apart the processes by which preferences are formed and maintained (see, for example, Chapters 2 and 3 of this volume). Psychologists have used functional magnetic resonance imaging (fMRI) and electroencephalograms (EEG) to evaluate the brain processes underpinning behavior. Despite this, many social scientists still adhere to the precept that what really matters are the inputs into the body and the subsequent behavioral outputs.

Like much of this book, this chapter aims to get under the skin of human behavior by looking at some of the physiological processes underpinning it. This chapter specifically examines the role of steroid hormones. Hormones are chemical messengers that travel around the body, changing the way cells behave. Steroid hormones are a subset of this group that affect every nucleated cell in the body—including those in the central and peripheral nervous systems.

Biophysical Measurement in Experimental Social Science Research. https://doi.org/10.1016/B978-0-12-813092-6.00008-3

Consequently, steroid hormones have profound effects on many of the processes that social scientists are interested in. By studying them we can peek inside the black box of human behavior and understand more fully the mechanisms that underpin it.

Human physiological mechanisms are similar across individuals. Evolution has produced systems that enable the organism to regulate and maintain its internal milieu, and these systems are highly conserved. This has two important implications for social scientists. First, factors such as culture or race are largely irrelevant physiologically—so physiological principles are applicable across groups. Second, it means that the consequences of physiological processes may be felt not only at an individual level but at a societal one too (see Coates, Gurnell, & Sarnyai, 2010; Coates, 2012). If, for example, an entire society becomes stressed, for example by a financial crisis or war, then this may alter hormone levels which, in turn, alter behavior, potentially meaning that hormonal responses have profound implications for the economy.

This chapter aims to do three things: provide a basic overview of steroid hormones, explain how they might be useful in social science research, and outline how researchers might go about integrating steroid hormone measures into their research programs. This chapter begins with an explanation of what hormones are and how they work, and then reviews the measurement of steroid hormones. Once we have established the what and the how of steroid hormone research, we then turn to the why. This section looks at the different ways in which steroid hormones are used in social science research, and the reasons for their use. Following this, we turn to the practicalities of conducting hormone research and examine some common pitfalls. This then leads into an assessment of the limitations of hormonal research, as well as an appreciation of how it can complement other forms of research. Finally, we will discuss some future directions for steroid hormone research.

The central proposition of this chapter is that measuring and manipulating steroid hormones can offer insights into the bodily processes that underpin a number of phenomena observed in social science. Moreover, because of the ubiquity of steroid hormones, many of these insights are applicable universally across the species.

UNDERSTANDING STEROID HORMONES

What Are Steroid Hormones?

Hormones are chemical messengers that move between cells, coordinating activity across cells. There are three broad classes of hormones, but we are going to focus on one of them—steroid hormones—because of their pervasive effects. Steroid hormones are derived from cholesterol and this makes them soluble in lipids (fats), which means that they can easily pass through the fatty membrane that surrounds animal cells.

The ubiquity of steroid hormones means that they are readily measured, not just in blood but also in other bodily fluids, such as saliva or urine. This means that they can be measured without poking holes in peoples' bodies—a considerable benefit to the social science researcher.

We are going to focus on two major classes of steroid hormones: stress hormones and sex hormones. Stress hormones, with cortisol as the archetype, are produced in response to a wide variety of physical and environmental threats (Selye, 1936). Sex hormones differ between men and women. In men, the predominant sex hormone is the androgen (from the Greek, *andros*—man and *gennein*—to produce) testosterone. In women, the picture is more complex. Hormones such as the estrogens[1] (e.g., estradiol) and progesterone are classic female sex hormones, but women also produce testosterone and other androgens such as dehydroepiandrosterone (DEHA) and its sulfated derivative (DHEAs). Both stress and sex hormones have profound effects on bodily and mental function. These effects will be outlined later in this chapter.

Hormones do not simply affect the individual in the here-and-now; they also leave lasting imprints on the body, particularly during development (Phoenix, Goy, Gerall, & Young, 1959). For the purposes of research, it is helpful to think about these two classes of effects separately. The developmental effects, which leave lasting physical changes, affect the way the body is organized and so are known as "organizational effects." The more transient effects of fluctuations in hormone levels affect behavior in real time, and so are known as "activational effects."

Understanding the production and effects of steroid hormones is crucial to effective research. Failure to take account of basic biological processes such as the organizational effects of steroid hormones, fluctuating hormone levels, or factors affecting measurement, may produce research results that are statistically valid but scientifically—and practically—worthless. With this as motivation, we will now examine some of the biological processes underpinning steroid hormones' impacts on human physiology and behavior.

Organizational Effects of Steroid Hormones

Steroid hormones begin their influence in utero. They switch on and switch off various cellular processes, fundamentally changing fetal development. Most research on the organizational effects of steroid hormones has concentrated on the sex hormones, specifically the androgen testosterone. Relatively little work has been done on the in utero effects of female hormones (Bakker & Baum, 2008), but estrogens are thought to have little effect, probably because both sexes are exposed to them from the mother (Berenbaum & Beltz, 2011).

1. Estrogens are a group of hormones, of which estradiol is probably the best known, but there are other members, such as estrone and estriol. Often these are referred to colloquially as estrogen.

To describe the organizational effects of testosterone as profound is to rather understate the case. The SRY gene, a gene located on the Y chromosome (which only males have), turns the indifferent gonad into a testis at around 6 weeks of gestation. This, in turn, produces male androgens, principally testosterone, which produce the male primary and secondary sexual characteristics. The SRY gene is the initiator, but testosterone and other androgens organize the cellular and consequent tissue changes needed to produce a male. In short, testosterone is what makes males males.

The patterning effect of testosterone occurs between 12 and 18 weeks of gestation, when testosterone levels in the male fetus' bloodstream reach nine times those of females, causing morphological alterations in the brain and spinal cord and the formation of male external genitalia (Cohen-Bendahan, van de Beek, & Berenbaum, 2005). As well as these substantial effects, androgen exposure in utero influences the ratio of lengths of the second (index) and fourth (ring) fingers (Lutchmaya, Baron-Cohen, Raggatt, Knickmeyer, & Manning, 2004; Manning, Scutt, Wilson, & Lewis-Jones, 1998) in both males and females. This marker of androgenic patterning is readily measured in adults and can, as we shall see, serve as an independent and mediating/moderating variable in social science studies.

Another organizational effect of testosterone can be seen in the relationship between facial width (measured between the left and right zygion, i.e., the most lateral point of the left and right cheekbone) and height (measured by the distance between the brow and upper lip). This facial width-to-height ratio (fWHR) appears to reflect a combination of pre-natal (Whitehouse et al., 2015) and pubertal (Welker, Bird, & Arnocky, 2016) testosterone exposure. Again, this marker is easy to measure and, although it is not without controversy (see Hodges-Simeon, Hanson Sobraske, Samore, Gurven, & Gaulin, 2016), it can serve as a useful metric in analyses.

The organizational effects of the stress hormone cortisol have also been investigated. The developing fetus is to some extent protected from maternal cortisol levels, but this protection is not absolute, particularly when maternal levels are greatly elevated (Cao-Lei et al., in press). This means that fetuses are susceptible to the influence of maternal cortisol and these maternal levels may, in turn, impact fetal development. In contrast to testosterone and other androgens, there are no readily observable markers of prenatal cortisol exposure. The only evidence of its effect comes from inferential studies that correlate perceived population-level stressors on pregnant women with pathologies observed subsequently in their offspring. For example, the 5-day invasion of the Netherlands in 1940 is thought to have resulted in elevated levels of schizophrenia amongst those Dutch people in utero at the time (van Os & Selten, 1998). There is some circumstantial evidence of the organizing effects of cortisol but, in the absence of an observable marker of prenatal exposure, it is rather speculative.

An intriguing possibility is that stress and cortisol exposure leave chemical marks on the genome. The genome is the complete set of genes encoded by DNA. The emerging field of epigenetics offers an interesting halfway house between the baked-in nature of genetics and the malleability of dynamic responses to the environment. Epigenetics is a somewhat disputed term (Greally, 2018), but in this case we are using it to define modifications "on or around the gene" (i.e., epi+genetics in Greally's terminology) to describe alterations to the totality of the genome (genome = the complete set of genes)—which may have consequences for the expression of genes (i.e., the way they are turned into proteins), but does not alter the underlying DNA sequence. There is evidence that environmental factors can alter part of the structure of the genome—for example by adding a methyl group (methylation) to certain genes—and that this, in turn, affects gene expression. For example, partner violence in pregnancy has been linked to epigenetic changes to the glucocorticoid (cortisol is a glucocorticoid) receptor gene (Radtke et al., 2011). Although this field is in its infancy, it may be that exploring methylation patterns in an individual's DNA may help us better understand the organizing effects of steroid hormones.

One way to think of the organizing effects of steroid hormones is to think of them as affecting the wiring of the individual. Steroid hormones affect how various biological systems are configured. Exposure to maternal hormones affects the way we develop, which has consequences for later life. This is true for both the stress hormones (Bale & Epperson, 2015) and the sex hormones (Berenbaum & Beltz, 2011, 2016). We may never know the full scale and scope of this configuring process but there are proxies available that allow us to speculate—profitably—on the role of early hormone exposure in driving behavior. If the organizing effects are the wiring, then we also need to investigate what is flowing through the wires. This, then, brings us to the activational effects of steroid hormones—the effects that transient fluctuations in hormone levels have on behavior.

Activational Effects of Steroid Hormones

To understand the activational effects of steroid hormones it is important to understand how they are produced, as this explains how information from the external environment comes to be reflected in levels of circulating hormones. The brain is of fundamental importance in determining hormone levels. As the neuroscientist Bruce McEwen puts it, "The brain is the central organ of stress and adaptation to stress because it perceives and determines what is threatening, as well as the behavioral and physiological responses to the stressor" (McEwen, Eiland, Hunter, & Miller, 2012, p. 3). The same is true for the sex steroids, where perception of the external environment, both conscious and unconscious, can drive hormone levels (e.g., Booth, Shelley, Mazur, Tharp, & Kittok, 1989; Mazur, Booth, & Dabbs Jr, 1992).

The production of both sex and stress steroid hormones is initiated in the hypothalamus, a pea-sized structure at the base of the brain (see Fig. 1). This brain region integrates inputs from the autonomic nervous system, which we are not consciously aware of, and from conscious thought. The hypothalamus produces releasing hormones—gonadotrophin releasing hormone (GnRH) in the case of the gonadal sex steroids, and corticotropin releasing hormone (CRH) in the case of adrenal glucocorticoids (stress steroids). GnRH then promotes the synthesis and secretion of luteinizing hormone (LH) and follicle-stimulating hormone (FSH), which act on the ovaries in females to coordinate estrogen and progesterone synthesis/release during the estrous cycle (LH and FSH working in concert), and on the testes in males to regulate testosterone production (LH on its own). CRH promotes the synthesis and secretion of adreno-corticotropic hormone (ACTH), which stimulates the synthesis and release of adrenal glucocorticoids (e.g., cortisol in humans) (Melmed, Polonsky, Larsen, & Kronenberg, 2011).

Critically, this system is controlled through negative feedback loops. Elevated levels of cortisol will suppress CRH production, dampening down cortisol levels. Hormone levels will increase in response to perceived necessity. Effectively, this acts like a thermostat, with the hypothalamus acting as the householder regulating the temperature to suit environmental conditions and room usage. The aim of this process, as with the thrifty householder, is to ensure that steroid production is closely matched to bodily need. It is this matching process which makes the activational effects of steroid hormones so interesting to social scientists, as hormone levels reflect the impact of incoming environmental information.

Once produced, steroids act on the body through three different routes. The first, the "classical" pathway, is where the hormone interacts with the cell's genome to change the rate of protein synthesis, and so alters the structure and/or function of the cell and the tissue/organ that it makes up. This process, however, is relatively slow, and usually takes several hours, or even days (Gurnell, Burrin, & Chatterjee, 2010). The second route does not involve the genome, but instead targets proteins involved in cell-to-cell signaling. Altering signaling alters neuronal activity, both in the central (brain) and peripheral nervous systems. The timescale here is much shorter, falling in the range of minutes to hours, rather than hours to days. Steroid receptors using this route have been found on the outer membranes of cells in the hippocampus and many other brain areas (McEwen & Milner, 2007). The third route is less well understood. Neuroactive steroids are either produced endogenously within neurons themselves or arrive exogenously from endocrine glands and stimulate the central nervous system (CNS), swiftly altering brain function, emotions, and mood (Baulieu, 1997). Different individuals will exhibit different sensitivity to hormone levels as a result, for example, of differing levels of receptor expression or affinity for hormone binding (Melmed et al., 2011). This means that the same dose of hormone may produce somewhat different effects between individuals.

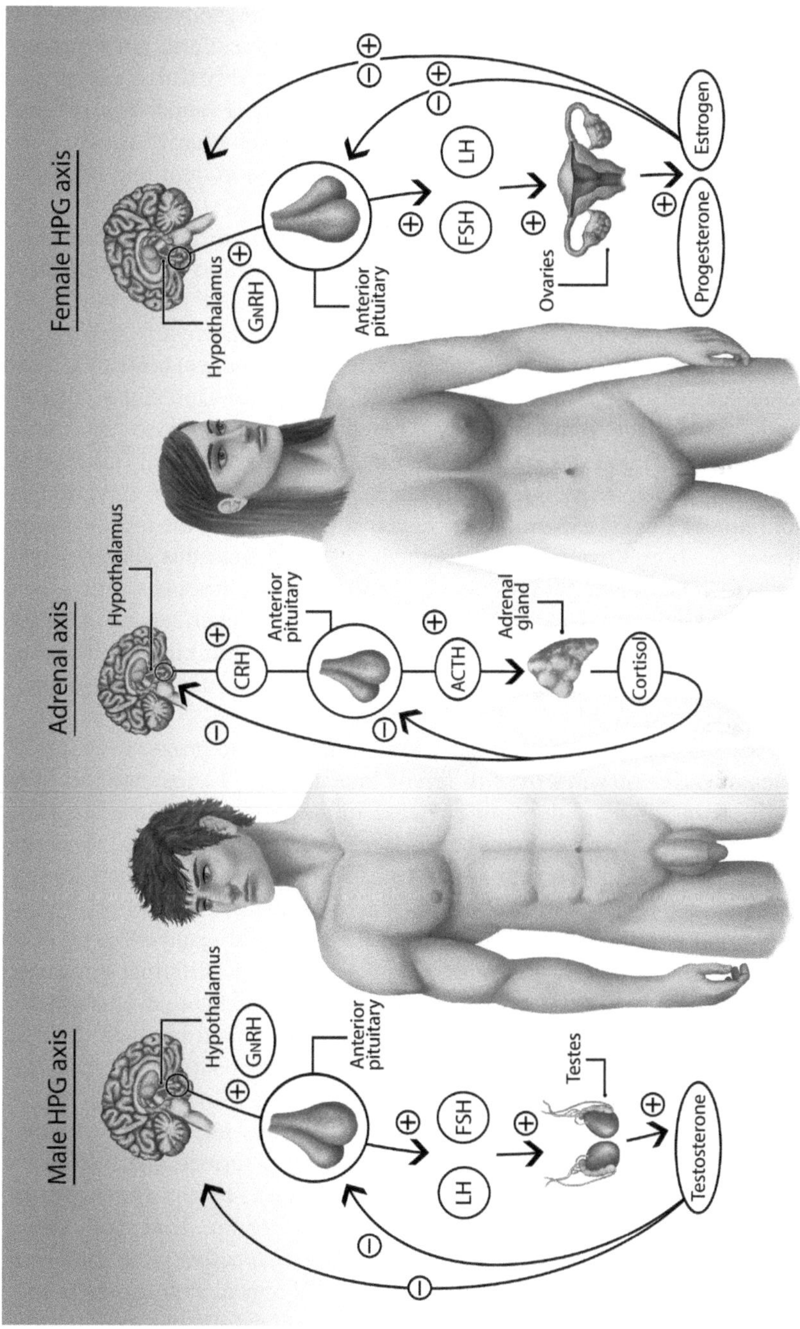

FIG. 1 Hormone production.

These different modes of action mean that steroids can have different effects. For example, transiently stressful situations might produce a quick "hit" of cortisol, which would operate through the second and third mechanisms, i.e., by altering neuronal activity. A chronically stressful situation can affect protein transcription, changing the nature of the cells themselves, not just the way they behave. The timescale over which the alteration in steroid hormone levels occurs affects the outcome of that alteration, and this needs to be borne in mind when evaluating hormone research.

Cortisol affects the body in different ways over these different timescales. The acute phase of corticosteroid elevation (i.e., minutes to hours) produces enhanced vigilance, alertness, arousal, and attention (de Kloet, Joels, & Holsboer, 2005) and may have rewarding properties (Sarnyai, McKittrick, McEwen, & Kreek, 1998). In the medium term (hours to days) cortisol affects the metabolism of glucose and proteins, breaking down stored precursors of glucose and muscle tissue so that the body is prepared for action and to repair possible damage. It also affects the immune system, damping down the inflammatory response (Rang & Dale, 2007). Chronic high-level elevation of cortisol (days to weeks) can produce a variety of effects, with the most extreme form being Cushing's syndrome. Individuals suffering from this display physical signs such as weight gain (especially abdominal fat), muscle wasting, and elevated blood pressure (Coates et al., 2010). There are also effects on the brain such as depression, psychosis (in extreme cases), and shrinking of the brain areas involved in learning and memory (such as the hippocampus) (Sapolsky, Romero, & Munck, 2000).

The sex steroids, principally testosterone, estrogen, and progesterone, similarly act in different ways over different time frames. Testosterone and its metabolites can stimulate dopamine release in the short term (Frye, Rhodes, Rosellini, & Svare, 2002; Sarnyai et al., 1998), which is rewarding. Over the medium to longer term testosterone increases lean muscle mass, bone density (Isidori et al., 2005), and levels of red blood cells (Matsumoto, 1990). Estradiol also has mood effects, but these have been predominantly studied in peri- or post-menopausal women, who are undergoing a once-in-a-lifetime hormonal pattern change and may not be representative of the population as a whole. Estrogens are thought to improve mood and cognitive performance (Miller, Conney, Rasgon, Fairbanks, & Small, 2002) as well as being a key factor in coordinating the estrous cycle with progesterones.

Steroid hormones' activational effects are affected by interactions with one another and with the organizational effects previously described. Excessive cortisol levels inhibit testosterone synthesis (Doerr & Pirke, 1976), whilst cortisol levels fluctuate across the menstrual cycle (Kirschbaum, Kudielka, Gaab, Schommer, & Hellhammer, 1999). The organizational/activational model of hormone action (Phoenix et al., 1959) suggests that prenatal exposure to testosterone affects sensitivity in adults to changes in circulating testosterone (Breedlove & Hampson, 2002).

Failing to account for these factors (short-term versus long-term effects, the interactions between hormones, the effects of previous exposure, etc.) can lead social scientists to incorporate steroid hormones into research in a way that produces a result—but a result that might be meaningless.

HOW CAN STEROID HORMONES BE MEASURED?

Steroid hormones are relatively easy to measure, when compared to peptide hormones, such as oxytocin, or amines, such as epinephrine (adrenaline). Indeed, this is one of the features that makes them so suitable for use in social scientific research. The organizational effects of steroid hormones can be evaluated by looking at the bodily markers they leave behind. We will begin by briefly looking at how organizational effects might be measured and then examine how activational effects might be explored.

Measuring the Organizational Effects of Steroid Hormones

Most of the research looking at the organizational effects of steroid hormones has focused on testosterone. There are two principal proxies that are used: the ratio of the lengths of the second and fourth fingers (2D:4D ratio), and facial width to height ratio (fWHR). Both are readily appraised, but both are also relatively crude measures.

2D:4D ratio is calculated simply by measuring the length of the second (index) finger and the fourth (ring) finger. This ratio can then be used as an independent variable, or a moderating variable in analyses. For typical outcomes such as risk taking (e.g., Garbarino, Slonim, & Sydnor, 2011) or violent behavior (e.g., Turanovic, Pratt, & Piquero, 2017) the effect sizes are small to moderate (Kemper & Schwerdtfeger, 2009) and so great care is needed to ensure accurate measurement. There has been a significant amount of research on how to obtain the most accurate measurement. Using photocopiers or flatbed scanners is quicker, reduces movement artifacts seen with direct measurement (Caswell & Manning, 2009), improves consensus between raters (Allaway, Bloski, Pierson, & Lujan, 2009), and allows a permanent record to be kept (Caswell & Manning, 2009; Manning, Fink, Neave, & Caswell, 2005). The 2D:4D ratios of the left and right hands are frequently not identical, with the right hand's ratio being thought to better reflect prenatal androgen exposure. Accordingly, the academic literature suggests that the right hand should be used (Hönekopp & Watson, 2010). Participants should remove finger jewelry and place the palmar surface of their relaxed hand lightly on the surface of the scanner without exerting pressure (Voracek, Manning, & Dressler, 2007). The second to fifth fingers should be held parallel and the tip of the middle finger aligned with the wrist and elbow (Allaway et al., 2009). The landmarks of interest are the midpoint of the crease nearest the palm at the base of the second and fourth digits (this may be enhanced with a fine black marker pen

(Voracek et al., 2007) and the tip of the relevant digit (contrast here may be enhanced when the back of the hand is covered with crumpled aluminum foil before photocopies or digital scans of the palm are made (Voracek et al., 2007). Researchers are advised to take measures using computer-assisted image analysis, such as the GNU Image Manipulation Program (2017), as this appears to produce more accurate results (Allaway et al., 2009). Taking multiple images is advised, as this enables the calculation of absolute-agreement intraclass correlation coefficients (ICCs) for assessing measurement repeatability (Voracek et al., 2007).

2D:4D ratios are thought to indicate the degree of exposure to testosterone in utero (Lutchmaya et al., 2004; Manning et al., 1998). Higher concentrations of testosterone produce lower 2D:4D ratios, with men typically having lower 2D:4D ratios than women (Manning et al., 1998; McIntyre, 2006). This measure is not without controversy, however, as factors such as ethnicity may also have considerable influence on the 2D:4D ratio (Manning, Stewart, Bundred, & Trivers, 2004). Brañas-Garza, Galizzi, and Nieboer (2018) provide an excellent review of the field.

More recently, other digit ratio measures have been explored, such as the relative length of the second digit to the sum of the lengths of all four fingers (known as "rel 2"), with some authors using it in preference to 2D:4D ratio (e.g., Nepomuceno, Saad, Stenstrom, Mendenhall, & Iglesias, 2016a, 2016b; Stenstrom, Saad, Nepomuceno, & Mendenhall, 2011). Other authors (e.g., Voracek, 2009) suggest that there is little difference between existing digit ratio measures.

Facial width-to-height ratio (fWHR) is used as a marker for aggression and dominance (Haselhuhn, Ormiston, & Wong, 2015; Wong, Ormiston, & Haselhuhn, 2011). In a number of studies there is a tacit implication that fWHR may relate, in some way, to testosterone. fWHR has been linked to 2D:4D ratio (Fink et al., 2005), and also to circulating levels of testosterone (Lefevre, Lewis, Perrett, & Penke, 2013). It may be that some of the organizational effects of testosterone only manifest in adolescence (Welker et al., 2016), although this is not clear cut (Hodges-Simeon et al., 2016).

fWHR is commonly assessed from photos. The individual needs to be facing directly square to the camera with a neutral expression. Bizygomatic width (BZW) is measured by the distance between the left and right zygion (Carré & McCormick, 2008b). The zygion is the most lateral point of the zygomatic bone (the cheekbone in common parlance). In practical terms, as the measurements are not being conducted on skulls, this often means the maximum distance between the left and right facial boundary (Lefevre et al., 2013). Upper facial height is measured differently in different papers. Many papers use "the distance between the upper lip and brow" (Carré & McCormick, 2008b, p. 2652). Determining the edge of the upper lip is relatively straightforward, but exactly what the "brow" means is often unclear. A number of authors do not define it but rather show a diagram (e.g., Carré, Putnam, & McCormick, 2009), while others use the highest point of the eyelids (e.g., Lefevre et al., 2013). In practical terms, it probably does not matter (Haselhuhn et al., 2015), at least within a given sample or study, as long as the same landmarks are used for all participants. After measurement is made, the ratio between width and height is calculated. Rotated shots or facial expressions may produce inaccurate measurement. For example, rotation may mean that the BZW is underestimated, while facial expression may distort the upper facial height (and potentially BZW as well).

The physical markers left behind by previous testosterone exposure relate to something that happened in the past but may also have important implications for the present, as testosterone's organizational effects may affect sensitivity to the activational effects of androgens (de Vries & Södersten, 2009). This type of interaction between organizational and activational effects may also hold for stress hormones and sex steroids other than androgens. The nascent field of epigenetics, for example, hints that historical cortisol exposure may affect subsequent development. The mechanisms for measuring this exposure are still expensive and experimental, but it may be that in years to come epigenetic markers of cortisol exposure will allow us to examine the lasting implications of stressful events.

Measuring the Activational Effects of Steroid Hormones

There are two broad parts to measuring the activational effects of steroid hormones. One is the actual process of measurement itself, and the other is the context in which the measurement occurs. Both parts require attention to enable hormone levels to be accurately interpreted. We will begin with the easier part: the measurement of steroid hormones.

Measuring Circulating Steroid Hormone Levels

Steroid hormones are relatively easy to collect and measure. This is because steroid hormones are relatively stable and their levels in an individual's saliva (which is readily accessible) reflect blood levels. Saliva is best obtained via the passive drool technique—which is exactly as it sounds. Participants passively drool into an appropriate container, such as a Salivette® (Sarstedt). This has been demonstrated to most accurately reflect circulating hormone levels for testosterone measurement (Fiers et al., 2014) and is likely to be best for other steroid hormones, as they share a similar chemical structure—which is what makes them steroid hormones. Before providing the sample, participants should rinse their mouths with water to remove food particles that could contaminate the sample. They should then wait about 10 minutes, so the water does not dilute salivary hormone levels. Participants cannot have any mouth or gum lesions, such as ulcers or gingivitis, as any blood or serum in the saliva sample can interfere with the measurement assay, giving a false reading. Some authors advocate chewing sugar-free gum or polyester wadding (e.g., Schultheiss, Wirth, & Stanton, 2004), but this introduces the risk of contamination with foreign material. Samples should be frozen as soon as possible. Some steroid hormones, such as cortisol, are quite robust but others, e.g., estradiol and progesterone, degrade at room temperature (Salimetrics, 2018). A conventional freezer should be sufficient for storage before shipping to a testing laboratory (Salimetrics, 2017). This also has the advantage of slowing bacterial growth, which makes the samples less foul smelling when they come to be processed.

There are a number of technical procedures using which salivary hormones can be measured. These include radioimmunoassay, enzyme-linked immunosorbent assay (ELISA), and mass spectrometry. A discussion of the relative merits of these different methods is beyond the scope of this chapter. Suffice to say that there are many reputable laboratories offering these services that also provide advice on collection and dispatch. Social scientists are best advised to use these services. Selecting an accredited laboratory that conforms to accepted international standards, such as Good Laboratory Practice (a set of rules governing the conduct of nonclinical safety studies to ensure the quality, integrity and reliability of study data [World Health Organization, 2009]) is recommended. British readers may also need to pay attention to the Human Tissue Act (2004), which defines saliva as a human tissue and imposes restrictions on handling and storage. Other countries may have analogous legislation.

Steroid hormones can alternatively be measured in the serum component of blood and also in hair (Staufenbiel, Penninx, Spijker, Elzinga, & van Rossum, 2013). Hair provides longer term information (Stalder et al., 2012) on cortisol levels (rather like an ice core can for historic CO_2 levels, see Barnola, Raynaud, Korotkevich, & Lorius, 1987), but is used relatively little compared to salivary and serum measures. Serum measures are used in clinical healthcare but involve venipuncture to withdraw several milliliters of blood, which may not be a skill many social scientists possess.

Accurate measurement of steroid hormones is critical but, as it lies outside most researchers' expertise, it is typically outsourced to those with greater clinical laboratory experience. Where researchers can profitably spend their time and effort is in ensuring that the context in which the hormones are measured is appropriate to the research question being asked.

Contextual Factors Affecting Steroid Hormone Measurement

Many contextual factors affect steroid hormone levels. The purpose of steroid hormones is to match the internal milieu of the body to the demands of the environment, and the environment produces many signals apart from the ones of interest in a particular research project. Separating the signal that we are interested in, from the noise produced as hormones play their principal role of keeping the body functioning, requires a detailed evaluation of the environment.

Some of this noise comes from "trait" factors, which are innate to the individual, and some from "state" factors, which are affected by the environment.

All too often, researchers take data that purports to measure hormone levels at face value, without digging into the circumstances surrounding the measurement. As the economist John Kay points out, one should always ask, "What is the question to which this number is the answer?" (Kay, 2011). Later in the same article, Kay wisely advises: "When the data seem to point to an unexpected finding, always consider the possibility that the problem is a feature of the data, rather than a feature of the world" (Kay, 2011).

Considering trait factors first, steroid hormone levels are affected by demographic variables such as age and gender. Levels of cortisol tend to increase over the lifespan (Feldman et al., 2002), whereas sex hormone levels tend to decline (Coates et al., 2010). Female hormones decline precipitously after menopause, a fact that some researchers have tried to exploit in order to remove the "noise" of sex hormones in hormone administration research (see, for example, Zethraeus et al., 2009). Gender also clearly affects sex hormone levels. Men typically have testosterone levels which are about ten times higher than those of premenopausal women (Wolf & Kirschbaum, 2002). Similarly, premenopausal women have higher and fluctuating levels of female sex hormones, such as estradiol and progesterone, than men.

Personality factors also appears to affect hormone levels. Daitzman and Zuckerman (1980) and Daitzman, Zuckerman, Sammelwitz, and Ganjam (1978) found that sensation seeking and impulsivity correlate positively with testosterone and estradiol levels. Cortisol levels have also been found to link to psychological dimensions such as locus of control (Pruessner et al., 1997).

Genetics and health status also affect hormone levels. Genes may affect both hormone levels and sensitivity to a given level of hormone. Cortisol (Wüst, Federenko, Hellhammer, & Kirschbaum, 2000) and testosterone (Meikle, Bishop, Stringham, & West, 1986) levels have a heritable component (although Bartels, Van den Berg, Sluyter, Boomsma, & de Geus, 2003, have some doubts about the power of the test in the Wüst paper). Sensitivity to androgens may also have a genetic component (Amrhein, Meyer, Jones, & Migeon, 1976), so genetics may impact the effect of any circulating hormone. Health may also affect hormone levels. Cortisol responses are altered in both acute and chronic disease states (Kudielka & Kirschbaum, 2003), and testosterone levels are affected by disease states such as strokes (Svartberg, Midtby, et al., 2003).

These "trait" factors need to be borne in mind when planning or reviewing steroid hormone research. Mismatching groups on the basis of age or gender may affect results, as may failing to control for health status. Care should also be taken when extrapolating results from women to men, or vice versa. Regrettably, there are numerous studies where testosterone has been administered to women in dosages that do not appear to mimic any natural physiological process. Researchers have simply given women some testosterone, observed how they behaved, and then published the results. The fact that women have not experienced the organizational effects of testosterone on the brain, and the fact that the dose rate is not related to any natural physiological parameter, mean that although the results might be statistically significant, they are practically meaningless as they do not mimic a state of affairs that occurs in the real world.

Turning now to "state" factors associated with short-term fluctuations in hormones levels, there are two broad groups of these: those related to natural dynamic variation, and exogenous influences.

There is a great deal of natural dynamic variation in steroid hormone levels. Perhaps the most relevant to social scientists is diurnal variation, whereby hormone levels fluctuate over the course of the day. The best-known example of this is the diurnal variation of cortisol (Whitehead & Miell, 2012). Levels of cortisol rise sharply (50%–160%) on waking and then fall back over the course of the day. A number of researchers assume that late afternoon is the optimal time to conduct research in which the hypothalamic–pituitary axis (HPA) is stimulated (for example using the Trier Social Stress Test, outlined later in this chapter), because ambient cortisol levels have dropped from their morning peak and are reasonably flat (Hermans, Putman, & van Honk, 2006). Testosterone (Brambilla, Matsumoto, Araujo, & McKinlay, 2009; Brambilla, O'Donnell, Matsumoto, & McKinlay, 2007) and estradiol (Bao et al., 2003) also exhibit diurnal variation.

Not only do steroid hormones vary across the course of the day but testosterone and cortisol exhibit inter-day variation (Brambilla et al., 2007; Rose, Kreuz, Holaday, Sulak, & Johnson, 1972; Rowe et al., 1974) which may introduce error into measurement. Female sex hormones also clearly fluctuate day-to-day due to the menstrual cycle, which is discussed in more detail below. Hormone levels, particularly those of the sex steroids, also show seasonal variation. Studies in Norway have shown that testosterone levels are lowest when temperatures are highest and daylight hours are longest (Svartberg, Jorde, Sundsfjord, Bønaa, & Barrett-Connor, 2003), which would be logical from an evolutionary perspective, as it makes sense to reduce the likelihood of offspring born when food supplies are scarce. Levels of cortisol have been shown to be highest in Scandinavia in February, March, and April, and lowest in July and August (Persson et al., 2008).

The most well-known fluctuation in steroid hormones is due to the female menstrual cycle, where a carefully orchestrated suite of hormones prepares the woman and her body for reproduction. There are five phases to the menstrual cycle, which is measured from the onset of menstruation (see Richardson, 1992)—the menstrual phase, the follicular phase, the ovulatory phase, the luteal phase, and the premenstrual phase. The menstrual phase is the start point for the cycle as the uterine lining sloughs and is excreted. This is followed by the follicular phase, when ovarian follicles develop, and the uterine lining is readied for the potential implantation of a fertilized egg. This is followed by the ovulatory phase, where the egg is released from the ovary into the fallopian tube and uterine body and can, potentially, be fertilized. The ovulatory phase is followed

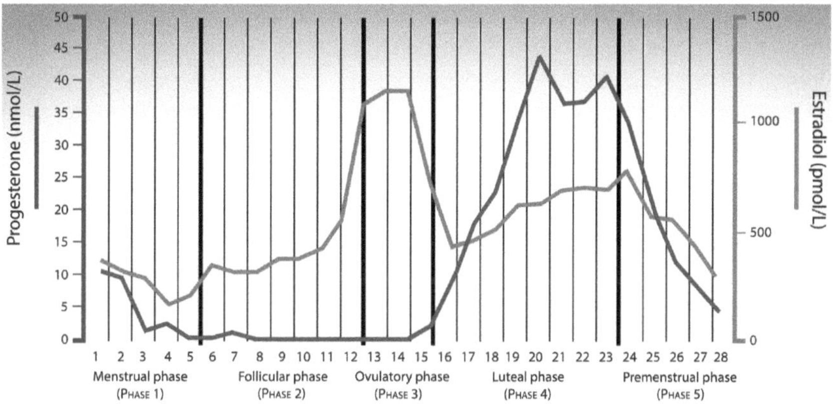

FIG. 2 Estradiol and progesterone levels over the menstrual cycle. Hormone levels are obtained from Buffet, Djakoure, Maitre, and Bouchard (1998).

by the luteal phase where the corpus luteum (literally, the "yellow body" developed from ovarian follicle) forms to maintain the pregnancy in the case of a fertilized egg implanting. In nonpregnant females, this then leads to the premenstrual phase where levels of estrogen and progesterone drop, in preparation for the menstrual phase.

Two ovarian sex steroids, estrogen and progesterone, are of particular interest in this cycle. Fig. 2 shows how they vary across the cycle. Researchers can exploit this natural variation as an independent variable in order to examine the effects of these hormones on behavior.

Levels of estrogens and progesterone may interfere with cortisol measurement, particularly in times of stress (Kirschbaum et al., 1999). As hormone levels fluctuate over the cycle it may be necessary to control for phase of the menstrual cycle either experimentally or statistically. This has implications for sample size, which may in turn explain the paucity of hormone research in females. McCarthy, Arnold, Ball, Blaustein, and De Vries (2012) offer some helpful advice to encourage researchers in this fruitful yet underexplored area.

Finally, a variety of exogenous factors also affect steroid hormone levels. The first of these is contraception. Chemical contraception in women involves manipulating hormone levels to either block conception or prevent implantation, and this manipulation interferes with hormone measurement (see Bröder & Hohmann, 2003; Buser, 2012).

Some substances stimulate the production of steroid hormones. Caffeine may stimulate the production of cortisol (Charney, Heninger, & Jatlow, 1985; Lovallo et al., 2005) and also, potentially, testosterone (Beaven et al., 2008). Nicotine consumption by mothers correlates with lower 2D:4D ratio in their offspring, reflecting an impact on fetal testosterone levels (Rizwan, Manning, & Brabin, 2007; Smith, Cloak, Poland, Torday, & Ross, 2003). Nicotine consumption may also affect HPA), which controls cortisol levels

(Kirschbaum, Strasburger, & Langkrär, 1993). Alcohol also affects testosterone production and metabolism (Gordon, Altman, Southren, Rubin, & Lieber, 1976).

Exercise also affects steroid hormone levels. Cortisol levels rise in the short term (Kuoppasalmi, Näveri, Härkönen, & Adlercreutz, 1980), but there is little effect on estradiol levels (Kuoppasalmi, Näveri, Rehunen, Härkönen, & Adlercreutz, 1976). The picture for testosterone is less clear, with some sources suggesting exercise raises testosterone levels (Cumming, Wall, Galbraith, & Belcastro, 1987) and others suggesting it lowers them (Kuoppasalmi et al., 1980). Given the potential effects of exogenous chemicals and exercise on hormone levels, Salimetrics, one of the commercial providers of salivary hormone testing, advocates that researchers record participants' consumption of alcohol, caffeine, nicotine, prescription/over-the-counter medications, and exercise for the 12 hours prior to testing (Salimetrics, 2017).

HOW CAN WE USE STEROID HORMONES IN SOCIAL SCIENCE RESEARCH?

Social science typically treats the body as something of a black box, inferring what the body is doing by looking at inputs into the body and behavioral outputs. Studying steroid hormones allows us to explore some of the biological processes that link inputs to outputs. Much attention has been focused on the neural components of decision making with techniques such fMRI and EEG looking at brain activity—see Chapter 3. What can be overlooked is that the brain sits in a bath of chemicals, such as steroid hormones, that can have profound effects on the way the brain functions and, in turn, on the physical and behavioral responses of the body.

The role of steroid hormones is to enable bodily systems to respond to the environment. The environment determines and constrains an organism's response, and the organism reciprocally shapes and alters its environment through these responses. Sociologists will recognize the parallels between this structure of constraint and influence, and Giddens' structuration theory (Giddens, 1984). Appreciating the role played by current, or past, levels of steroid hormones helps us better understand both the effect of external events on the body, and the consequences of internal events on the environment.

A useful way of classifying research is to think about the different ways in which social scientists arrange the variables in their studies. When examining the environment's impact on the individual's bodily processes (environment → hormone levels), the environment serves as the predictor and either historical or current hormone levels serve as the outcome of interest. When exploring the impact of hormone levels on the environment (hormone levels → environment), behavioral measures (such as the proclivity to take risks or make accurate predictions) serve as the focal outcomes, and historical or current hormone levels serve as the predictors. Hormone levels (either historical or current) may also influence the relationship between other variables of interest.

The following section considers each of these arrangements separately, maintaining the organizational/activational distinction whilst doing so.

Steroid Hormones as a Reflector of Environmental Inputs

Steroid hormone levels are affected by certain types of environmental factors and can leave lasting imprints on the body, as reviewed briefly above. The body, effectively, acts as a sensor for detecting the environmental factors that can affect steroid hormone levels in both the short (activational) and long (organizational) term.

Most research on the organizational effects of steroid hormones in early life has focused on cortisol. Despite 2D:4D ratio being an accepted marker of prenatal testosterone exposure, there is little work exploring what affects these levels. Therefore, we know the organizational effect, but we do not know the cause (i.e., what it is that explains different in-utero testosterone exposure across people). With cortisol, we know the cause—personal or maternal stress—but we are not as sure about the consequences or the mechanisms. The 5-day invasion of the Netherlands in 1940, for example, is thought to have resulted in elevated levels of schizophrenia amongst those Dutch people in utero at the time (van Os & Selten, 1998). Similarly, CEOs' early-life exposure to natural disasters, for example, seems to affect risk taking in their firms (Bernile, Bhagwat, & Rau, 2017). Work in rats and nonhuman primates suggests that mental health problems, such as schizophrenia, are associated with prenatal elevations in cortisol (Koenig et al., 2005; Kofman, 2002), and as reviewed above, similar results have been suggested in humans (van Os & Selten, 1998). What is lacking is a clear understanding of the processes by which prior stressful experiences trigger cortisol fluctuations and how these, in turn, affect current outcomes.

Epigenetics offers a possible mechanism through which stressful events exert long-term effects. The nascent field of epigenetics sits between and interleaves traditional ideas of nature and nurture, offering a mechanism by which nurture may affect nature. The exact mechanisms are still unclear (Maccari, Krugers, Morley-Fletcher, Szyf, & Brunton, 2014), but it is possible that early-life maternal stress results in alterations to the fetal genome, for example through DNA methylation (Maccari et al., 2014), and that this may account for behaviors observed in the offspring. In a recent meta-analysis, Palma-Gudiel, Córdova-Palomera, Eixarch, Deuschle, and Fañanás (2015) concluded that early-life stress correlated with methylation of a receptor gene for cortisol. It is important to emphasize that this whole area of research is in the early stages of development, so solid grounding points for theory or prediction are often not available. Nonetheless, epigenetics offers a mechanism to link environmental events such as wars, natural disasters, and recessions to the subsequent behaviors of those affected by them, and their children, through a pathway involving steroid hormones. The prediction of future behavior is the stock in trade of the economist and so epigenetics holds out the appealing prospect of uncovering more accurate mechanisms that can inform better predictions.

The effect of the environment on circulating levels of steroid hormones is much clearer. These activational effects are well documented, giving us confidence in using steroid hormone measures as a sensor for the environmental changes that trigger those hormones.

Testosterone is critical to male reproductive behavior. Males need to prepare their bodies for reproduction, attract a mate and, potentially, eliminate rivals (Archer, 2006). To do these things males need to signal to potential mates that reproducing with them will mean that the offspring will be successful and so, in turn, will get the chance to propagate their parents' genes further.

The manifestations of these reproductive fitness signals are of interest to social scientists for several reasons. As we shall see when we turn to the effect of hormone levels on behavior, testosterone levels affect the way males behave. However, the reverse is also true. Information about an individual's reproductive fitness gleaned from the external environment, whether consciously or not, has an effect on that individual. This means that circulating testosterone levels may be a useful sensor for detecting how male bodies interpret the external environment. The intensity of competition between males and socially mediated perceptions of status and power differences are therefore reflected in testosterone levels. Moreover, unlike self-report-based methods, testosterone levels are not subject to social desirability bias.

The role of testosterone in social competition has been elegantly synthesized by John Wingfield in his "Challenge Hypothesis." Drawing on animal models, he suggests that male testosterone rises to the minimum level required for reproduction but continues to rise beyond this when confronted by social challenge (Wingfield, Hegner, Dufty Jr., & Ball, 1990). Research in humans confirms that testosterone rises in response to challenge. Tennis players and wrestlers show rising testosterone levels before competition (Archer, 2006). Moreover, as in animal models, victory elevates testosterone levels still further. These results rely on physical competition, but similar results are found in settings featuring nonphysical competition, such as chess games (Mazur et al., 1992). This effect may also be mirrored in spectators: Bernhardt, Dabbs Jr, Fielden, and Lutter (1998) took testosterone samples from fans during a World Cup soccer match in which Brazil defeated Italy. Both sets of fans went into the game with elevated testosterone, but afterwards the Brazilian fans' testosterone rose while the Italians' fell. Geniole, Bird, Ruddick, and Carré (2017) confirmed the broad direction of Wingfield's hypothesis in a recent meta-analysis, with testosterone increasing before competition and then, after competition, rising for the winner but falling for the loser. These effects were noted only in men, and not in women.

Unsurprisingly, given testosterone's role in nonphysical competition, it is also involved in social status signaling. Saad and Vongas (2009) examined the effects on testosterone levels of driving either a Porsche 911 or alternatively a dilapidated Toyota Camry. Driving the Porsche elevated testosterone levels, whereas driving the Toyota either had no effect or lowered testosterone levels.

In sum, circulating testosterone levels are affected by the external environment. Physical and status competitions seem to be particularly effective in driving testosterone levels, which, in evolutionary terms, is unsurprising.

Cortisol is similarly affected by external events. Coates and Herbert (2008) evaluated hormone levels in traders, expecting to find that losses raised cortisol levels. Somewhat to their surprise, they found that traders' cortisol levels recovered quickly from losses. Rather than losses, the key determinant of cortisol levels was uncertainty. They evaluated the relationship between volatility in the German bond market and cortisol levels, finding a strong relationship ($r^2 = 0.86$, $P < .01$). Laboratory studies mirror this result, with uncertainty, manifest as uncontrollability or social threat, raising cortisol levels (Dickerson & Kemeny, 2004). Given hormones' homeostatic role of preparing the body to match the challenges of the external environment, described above, this finding is not surprising.

There is relatively little research on the effects of the external environment on female hormone levels (Geniole et al., 2017). Casto and Prasad (2017) suggest a number of reasons for this, including lower effect sizes in some studies, the menstrual cycle complicating analysis and requiring more participants, and the validity of immunoassays (particularly for testosterone). They cite McCarthy et al. (2012) who suggest that what most deters social scientists from including females in their studies are misconceptions about the difficulty of performing good studies, difficulties in comparing males and females, and the concern that they will not learn anything new.

Using steroid hormones as environmental sensors helps us understand the connection between incoming information and hormone levels. This link forms part of a feedback loop between the organism and its environment. The other part is the effect of hormones on behavior.

Steroid Hormones' Effect on Behavior

Studies of the organizational effects of steroid hormones involve identifying a marker of the organizational effects of the hormone (such as 2D:4D ratio and fWHR in the case of testosterone) and evaluating its impact on behavior. Studies of the activational effects of steroid hormones rely on manipulating hormone levels. There are two categories of manipulation. Levels of endogenous (i.e., naturally produced) hormone may be altered by changing the environment. This affects hormone levels which, in turn, affect behavioral outcomes. Exogenous hormone from outside the body may also be administered, for example by injection, to alter hormone levels so that the impact of these levels on behavioral outcomes can be examined.

We begin by evaluating the impact of organizational effects of steroid hormones on behavior. Most studies in this area tend to focus on testosterone as there are few organizational markers of exposure to other steroid hormones such as cortisol or estrogen. The most readily used marker of the organizational effects of testosterone is 2D:4D ratio.

2D:4D ratio has been used as an independent variable in a number of social science studies. These studies tend to focus on behavioral characteristics thought to be influenced by testosterone's presence, such as aggression, assertiveness, competitiveness, and risk taking, or its absence, such as verbal fluency or empathy.

Aggression is more likely to be displayed by men than women, possibly as a strategy to compete for access to mates (Hönekopp & Watson, 2011). Testosterone has been proposed as a candidate to account for this difference. There are a great number of studies examining the relationship between 2D:4D ratio and aggression, of which two meta-analyses have been performed. Both find a significant relationship albeit with a small effect size (Hönekopp & Watson, 2011). The relationship between 2D:4D ratio and other factors that may be linked to competing for mates, such as risk taking, sporting performance, and status, have also been explored.

Risk taking is an area of interest for a variety of social scientists, such as economists, criminologists and psychologists. The results linking 2D:4D ratios to risk taking are mixed, with Brañas-Garza et al. (2018) reporting that, in a series of ten studies, five pointed to a significant relationship between 2D:4D ratio and risk taking and five did not. Brañas-Garza et al. (2018) then report on their own large-scale study, which suggested that there is indeed a significant relationship. Recent research by Xie, Page, and Hardy (2017) suggests that 2D:4D ratio correlates with risk aversion in women, but that the relationship in men varies according to the measure of risk used.

Looking at real-world outcomes, Coates, Gurnell, and Rustichini (2009) found that traders with low 2D:4D ratios were likely to make greater profits and survive longer in the market. Sapienza, Zingales, and Maestripieri (2009) found that a lower 2D:4D ratio correlated with an increased likelihood of starting a career in finance. Bönte, Procher, and Urbig (2016) found a similar result for entrepreneurial intent, a finding replicated by Unger, Rauch, Weis, and Frese (2015) in actual entrepreneurs—but only when present together with a high need for achievement. 2D:4D ratio inversely correlates with dominance (Manning & Fink, 2008; Neave, Laing, Fink, & Manning, 2003) and number of sexual partners (Hönekopp & Schuster, 2010).

2D:4D ratio has been linked to athletic performance. A meta-analysis by Hönekopp and Schuster (2010) suggests that a lower 2D:4D ratio relates to improved athletic performance, with an inconsistent, low-to-moderate effect. Digit ratio also relates to a predilection for watching competitive sport

(Huh, 2011) and other forms of aggressive and sexual content in entertainment products. Nepomuceno and colleagues found that men with a lower 2D:4D ratio were more likely to give lingerie or "erotic gifts"[2] (Nepomuceno et al., 2016a) and participate in courtship-related consumption to acquire mates (Nepomuceno et al., 2016b). Conversely, women with high 2D:4D ratios indulged in greater courtship-related consumption to acquire mates and greater romantic gift giving (Nepomuceno et al., 2016b).

Prenatal testosterone exposure, reflected in 2D:4D ratios, has been linked to a number of behaviors and personality traits. The amount given in the standard version of the Dictator Game correlates with 2D:4D ratio (Brañas-Garza, Kovářík, & Neyse, 2013; Galizzi & Nieboer, 2015), suggesting that prenatal testosterone exposure may affect altruism. 2D:4D ratio has also been related to overconfidence (Dalton & Ghosal, 2014; Neyse, Bosworth, Ring, & Schmidt, 2016) and optimism (Xie et al., 2017). Lower 2D:4D ratios have been linked to lower agreeableness in men and women (Luxen & Buunk, 2005) and lower neuroticism in men (Manning & Fink, 2011). 2D:4D ratio has also been linked with intelligence, with those exposed prenatally to higher levels of testosterone scoring higher on numerical intelligence but lower on verbal intelligence (Luxen & Buunk, 2005).

The ease of measuring the 2D:4D ratio has led to a profusion of studies in all sorts of areas of social scientific research. Stanton (2017), however, urges caution in reviewing the literature, as the absence of published studies reporting null results leads him to suspect a "file drawer" problem (see Rosenthal, 1979)—i.e., researchers only publishing the research that yields positive results. Despite this concern, 2D:4D ratios remain an easy, albeit imperfect, method for exploring how the organizational effects of testosterone are associated with a variety of behaviors.

Facial width-to-height ratio (fWHR) has also been found to be related to variables of interest to social scientists. As with 2D:4D ratio, meta-analysis of a number of studies reveals a small, but significant and positive relationship between fWHR and aggression in men (Haselhuhn et al., 2015). A larger fWHR serves as a cue for selfish, pejorative, and aggressive behavior (Geniole, Denson, Dixson, Carré, & McCormick, 2015). Zilioli et al. (2015) evaluated how formidable Ultimate Fighting Championship (UFC) fighters appeared and found a positive correlation between perceived formidability and fWHR. This impression of formidability was borne out both in the ring and when composite faces were used to remove cues other than fWHR.

Other sorts of behavior that might signal sexual competitiveness or mating fitness have also been linked to fWHR. Arnocky et al. (2018) found that higher fWHR was related to higher sex drive in men and women, as well as male

2. The authors are disappointingly unforthcoming about the nature of these "erotic gifts."

sociosexual orientation (i.e., how comfortable men were in engaging in sex without love, commitment or emotional closeness) and intended infidelity.

Haselhuhn, Wong, Ormiston, Inesi, and Galinsky (2014) found that men with higher fWHR are less cooperative negotiators compared to men with smaller fWHR. This allows them to claim more value in negotiations, but makes them less likely to undertake creative and integrative bargaining. Wong et al. (2011) found that CEOs' fWHR predicted their companies' financial performance. Xie et al. (2017) found that women with higher fWHR were less risk averse. fWHR has also been found to predict trustworthiness (Kleisner, Priplatova, Frost, & Flegr, 2013; Stirrat & Perrett, 2010), although this effect is not consistent (Efferson & Vogt, 2013; Linke, Saribay, & Kleisner, 2016).

Both 2D:4D ratio and fWHR are relatively easy to appraise and so can be quickly and easily added to existing social science research projects. Because the measurements can be taken from scans or photographs, they can be added to studies where the participants are remote to the experimenter, such as internet-based studies (e.g., Manning, Trivers, & Fink, 2017).

The activational effects of steroid hormones on behavior can be studied in two ways. One is to exploit natural fluctuations in steroid hormone level due to environmental or individual variation. The other is to intentionally alter the environment to manipulate levels of circulating hormone. We begin by examining the literature on natural fluctuations in the sex steroids—testosterone, estrogens, and progesterone—and then turn to the stress steroid, cortisol.

Testosterone levels vary between—and possibly within—individuals, providing variance that can be used to assess the effect of testosterone on behavior. Although there is little relationship between prenatal testosterone exposure, as manifest in the 2D:4D ratio, and circulating hormone levels (Hönekopp, Bartholdt, Beier, & Liebert, 2007), testosterone's organizational and activational effects do interact (Arnold, 2009; Arnold & Breedlove, 1985). This interaction is typically not attended to in studies of circulating testosterone levels, but it probably should be, as it may allow for a more accurate depiction of the role of testosterone in behavior.

As with the organizational effects of testosterone, levels of circulating hormone have been linked to aggression. Two meta-analyses and one review article have demonstrated a small, but significant, relationship between testosterone levels and aggression (Book, Starzyk, & Quinsey, 2001).

Testosterone also affects decision making. High testosterone men (as determined by measurement of salivary or serum testosterone) are more likely to reject offers in the Ultimatum Game than low testosterone men (Burnham, 2007). Apicella et al. (2008) found a positive correlation between salivary testosterone levels and the decision to take economic risk. Stanton, Liening, and Schultheiss (2011) find a linear relationship between testosterone levels and risk taking in the Iowa Gambling Task, as do Evans and Hampson (2014). A number of authors have suggested that higher circulating testosterone is associated with more optimal economic choices (Apicella et al., 2008).

Derntl, Pintzinger, Kryspin-Exner, and Schöpf (2014) used a variety of risk assessment tasks and found no relationship between risk taking and testosterone levels. This may be due a nonlinear relationship between risk taking and testosterone. Stanton, Mullette-Gillman, et al. (2011) found that individuals with extreme levels of testosterone (more than 1.5 standard deviations from their gender mean) were risk and ambiguity neutral, and those with intermediate levels were risk and ambiguity averse.

Coates and Herbert (2008) found that amongst financial traders, 11 am testosterone level predicted the overall profitability of that day's trading. Putting this together with the observation of Apicella, Dreber, and Mollerstrom (2014) that testosterone changes following wins and losses affect future risk taking, a possible positive feedback loop emerges wherein success in the financial markets boosts testosterone levels, which elevate risk taking which, in turn, promotes success. This mechanism has been suggested as a possible hormonal driver of asset bubbles (Coates et al., 2010), an idea discussed more fully in Chapter 7.

As well as economic risk taking and other decision making, Carney and Mason (2010) found that those with higher testosterone levels were more likely, within the trolley problem paradigm[3], to kill one person to save five rather than the opposite, thereby making a utilitarian decision. Arnocky, Taylor, Olmstead, and Carré (2017) used a different task and did not find an association between circulating testosterone levels and utilitarian decision making.

Circulating testosterone levels also affect altruistic behavior, specifically parochial altruism—the tendency to be altruistic towards the in-group. Diekhof, Wittmer, and Reimers (2014) found that unfair offers in the Ultimatum Game were rejected more frequently by high testosterone men than fair proposals, and that altruistic punishment of out-groups increased. Increased in-group favoritism and out-group hostility were also observed. This testosterone-mediated behavior favoring in-groups over out-groups was also seen in a Prisoners' Dilemma task (Reimers & Diekhof, 2015).

When investigating the effect of naturally occurring hormonal fluctuations on behavior, there is one set of natural fluctuations that particularly stands out: that associated with the female menstrual cycle. The menstrual cycle's role in reproduction means that its effect on mate choice has been extensively investigated.

---

3. Trolley problems typically have a trolley careering along a railway track towards five people who are tied to the track. The decision maker is faced with a choice. In one scenario they are stood by a switch where they can divert the trolley to a branch line where there is one person tied to the track. By flipping the switch only one person will be killed, rather than five. Researchers style this as an *incidental* decision. A second version is more extreme in that the decision maker is stood on the bridge next to another person who, if they push them off the bridge, will jam the wheels of the runaway trolley, dying in the process but saving the lives of the five people tied to the track. This is classed as an *instrumental* decision. Both are utilitarian choices as they maximize the number of lives saved.

Gangestad and Thornhill (2008) concluded that women's mate choice shifts mid-cycle (i.e., around the time of ovulation, and hence peak fertility) to prefer a number of masculinized male traits, a finding similar to that of Jones et al. (2008). Alvergne and Lummaa (2010) also suggest that there is a shift in preference towards more masculine and symmetrical male features mid-cycle, but that this shift—the so called "ovulatory shift"—is obliterated by oral contraceptives. A meta-analysis by Wood, Kressel, Joshi, and Louie (2014) investigating the ovulatory shift finds that women prefer masculinized men at all stages of the menstrual cycle and that there is no evidence for a shift in preferences.

Moving from overt mating behavior to more covert behaviors, there is evidence that the menstrual cycle affects preferences for consumer goods. Durante, Griskevicius, Hill, Perilloux, and Li (2011) and Durante, Li, and Haselton (2008) find that women dress differently and prefer different products at different phases of their menstrual cycle, particularly after viewing pictures of attractive women. Peri-ovulatory women spend more on beauty related items and less on food than at other phases of the menstrual cycle (Saad & Stenstrom, 2012). Women in the peri-ovulatory phase also have a greater preference for goods that confer status, such as diamond rings and cars, than they do at other phases of their cycle (Durante, Griskevicius, Cantú, & Simpson, 2014). Durante and Arsena (2015) found that women in relationships preferred greater product variety in consumer goods (such as nail polish and high heels), particularly when primed to think about attracting other mates, which the authors related to a desire to seek mates outside the primary relationship in the pursuit of genetic diversity.

Some mating-focused research suggests that economic risk taking varies across the menstrual cycle. Chavanne and Gallup Jr (1998) find that women take less risk during the ovulatory phase but those on hormonal contraceptives do not, a finding that is replicated by Bröder and Hohmann (2003). Lazzaro, Rutledge, Burghart, and Glimcher (2016) find the opposite effect, with women taking more risk at times of peak fertility (i.e., around ovulation) and showing decreased loss aversion. Lazzaro et al. (2016) offer a more granular interpretation of cycle phases, rather than making two categories of "ovulation" and "non-ovulation," as Chavanne and Gallup Jr (1998) and Bröder and Hohmann (2003) do.

With auction bidding, Chen, Katuščák, and Ozdenoren (2013) find that women's bidding patterns are relatively stable across the cycle for naturally cycling women, with women bidding more than men. For those on hormonal contraception, bidding appears as a sine-like function across the menstrual cycle, peaking in the pre-ovulatory phase. Pearson and Schipper (2013) find that naturally cycling women bid more than men across the cycle, with the exception of the ovulatory phase, in which their bidding is similar to that of men. Women on hormonal contraception bid higher in all circumstances.

One intriguing study has looked at the effect of the menstrual cycle on men's behavior. Miller, Tybur, and Jordan (2007) recorded the estrous cycle of female lap dancers and related this to their earnings, which are comprised mostly of tips. Normally cycling dancers (i.e., those not using contraceptive pills) earned approximately US$335 for a 4-hour shift around ovulation, US$260 per shift during the luteal phase, and US$185 per shift during menstruation. Dancers using oral contraceptives did not demonstrate this pattern.

Given the ease with which natural fluctuations can be assessed, and the fact that women are roughly half the human population, research on the behavioral effects of the menstrual cycle seems an area ripe for exploration. Casto and Prasad (2017) make a number of suggestions as to how social scientists could effectively conduct research on women related to hormones and competition.

Cortisol exhibits natural diurnal variation. The influence of cortisol on risk taking and decision making has been less explored than that of testosterone. van Honk, Schutter, Hermans, and Putman (2003) found that low salivary cortisol levels predicted disadvantageous performance in the Iowa Gambling Task. Chumbley et al. (2014) found that cortisol levels in hair predicted reduced loss aversion in young men.

Alterations in diurnal variation can also have behavioral effects. Weller et al. (2014) showed that older adults with reduced diurnal variation (i.e., a less steep fall in cortisol levels from the morning peak) were more likely to make risky decisions. Kumari, Shipley, Stafford, and Kivimaki (2011) found that a flatter slope of cortisol decline was related to an increase in mortality.

Some researchers suggest that considering a single hormone is unwarrantedly simplistic and that hormones should be considered together. Mehta and Prasad (2015) propose a Dual Hormone Hypothesis, suggesting that testosterone promotes risk taking and status-seeking behavior when cortisol levels are low, but that this effect is blocked when they are high (Mehta, Welker, Zilioli, & Carré, 2015). Mehta, Mor, Yap, and Prasad (2015) found that rising levels of testosterone during negotiations were associated with success only when cortisol was simultaneously decreasing; when both hormone levels rose together, negotiations had poorer outcomes for the individual whose hormone levels were being measured. Van Den Bos, Golka, Effelsberg, and McClure (2013) found that high testosterone was associated with competitive bidding, but only when cortisol levels were low. Akinola, Page-Gould, Mehta, and Lu (2016) examined the hormonal profiles of whole groups, finding that groups with high testosterone and low cortisol outperformed other groups.

As well as exploiting natural hormone fluctuations, levels of circulating steroid hormones can be manipulated using the principles outlined in the section on the environment's impact on hormone levels. Testosterone levels can be manipulated by social challenge or the presence of potential mates, although they are not that commonly manipulated in this way because social challenge or the presence of potential mates is not a "clean" signal, for example, levels of epinephrine (adrenaline) and other hormones may also be raised in such settings. As a consequence, it is hard to tell whether solely testosterone levels are responsible for any effects observed, or whether instead other factors are causal.

There have nonetheless been some attempts to manipulate testosterone levels by manipulating the environment. In a field experiment, Ronay and Hippel (2010) asked young men to perform skateboarding tricks in front of either a male or attractive female experimenter. Subjects observed by the female experimenter produced elevated testosterone levels, and also increased risk taking.

The behavioral effects of changes in testosterone levels following competition (as discussed in the Challenge hypothesis, Wingfield, 2017), have been studied by Mehta and Josephs (2006) and Carré and McCormick (2008a), who find that changes in testosterone after competition predict subsequent competitive motivation. Carré, Baird-Rowe, and Hariri (2014) find that testosterone levels after competition predict how much participants trust neutral emotional faces, with higher testosterone leading to lower trust. Wu, Eisenegger, Sivanathan, Crockett, and Clark (2017) found that winning in competition increased preferences for high-status products and increased rejection of unfair Ultimatum Game offers.

Researchers often induce variation in cortisol levels through environmental manipulation. The Trier Social Stress Test (TSST) asks participants to perform the role of a job applicant in front of a committee of three people. The setup is designed to promote anxiety and uncertainty, and reliably raises cortisol levels (Kirschbaum, Pirke, & Hellhammer, 1993).

Another method of raising cortisol draws on Selye's observation that cortisol is produced in response to a diverse set of noxious agents (Selye, 1936). The cold pressor test (CPT) requires participants to place one hand up to the wrist in a bath of ice water for as long as they can, or up to a maximum of 1 minute. This is painful and elevates cortisol levels, although not as effectively as the TSST.

The TSST has been used to raise cortisol in a number of studies. Buckert, Schwieren, Kudielka, and Fiebach (2014) found that stress from the TSST increased risk taking but not ambiguity aversion. Cahlíková and Cingl (2017) found the opposite result—stress increased loss aversion and reduced risk taking. When the TSST is used in conjunction with the Iowa Gambling Task, those with elevated cortisol show increased risk taking and poorer performance (van den Bos, Harteveld, & Stoop, 2009). The TSST has also been used with the Game of Dice Task, a computerized game of chance simulating decision making under risk. Stressed individuals make less advantageous decisions than others (Pabst, Brand, & Wolf, 2013a; Pabst, Schoofs, Pawlikowski, Brand, & Wolf, 2013), although one study suggested a time-mediated effect, whereby the stressed group outperformed the control 5 and 18 minutes post-stressor, but the control subsequently outperformed 28 minutes after the stressor was administered (Pabst, Brand, & Wolf, 2013b). The TSST has also been used in a beauty contest task, with stressed individuals found to make more numerous and quicker decisions, suggesting a lack of strategy (Leder, Häusser, & Mojzisch, 2013).

Akinola and Mendes (2012) used a variant of the TSST whereby police officers were instructed that they would engage in a mock job interview, during which they would role play the part of a supervisor dealing with a disgruntled black citizen who was complaining about another officer. This effectively raised cortisol levels, but also raised testosterone levels. They then had to complete a shoot/don't shoot task requiring them to decide accurately whether to shoot or not shoot armed and unarmed black and white human targets. The larger the cortisol increase produced, the fewer errors the officers made when deciding to shoot armed black targets vs. armed white targets, suggesting that cortisol may elevate the attention paid to threat cues.

The CPT relies on the body producing cortisol in response to a diverse range of threats. Participants immerse their hand in iced water and this results in elevation of cortisol levels. The CPT has been examined in conjunction with the Balloon Analog Risk Task (BART)[4]. One study suggested that stressed individuals made fewer unsafe decisions than the control group (Lighthall, Mather, & Gorlick, 2009). Lighthall et al. (2012) found that CPT-induced stress led to greater reward collection and faster decision speed on the BART in males, but less reward collection and slower decision speed in females. The CPT also interferes with performance on working memory tasks requiring executive functions (Schoofs, Wolf, & Smeets, 2009).

CPT, TSST, and Akinola's modification of the TSST are "dirty" ways of raising cortisol levels because they may stimulate epinephrine (adrenaline) production and other factors that may be responsible for any effects observed. Moreover, it is obvious what the researcher is doing, so double-blind studies are difficult to engineer. Some of these problems can be overcome by administering steroid hormones directly.

As synthetic steroid hormones are readily available, they can be administered to alter circulating levels of steroid hormones. When designing hormone administration studies, great care needs to be taken to ensure that the conditions produced mimic those that actually occur in physiological systems. Regrettably, a number of studies using testosterone and cortisol are meaningless as they create levels of circulating hormones that do not mirror any situation that occurs in nature (Stanton, 2017).

Testosterone has frequently been used as an independent variable as it can be readily administered orally or transdermally (i.e., through the skin). However, much of the research using exogenous testosterone has been conducted in women. This is problematic for two reasons. First, women have not had the same androgenic exposure as men during their development (as discussed in

4. The BART is a computerized task which simulates blowing up a balloon. Each click of a button causes the balloon to inflate and also earns the participant a monetary reward. At some point, however, the balloon becomes over-inflated and bursts. When this happens, the participant loses any monetary reward accrued. So participants have to balance the size of reward with the risk of losing it.

the section on the organizational effects of steroid hormones) and so will not have undergone the neural architectural changes believed to accompany this exposure (see Breedlove, 1994; Breedlove & Hampson, 2002) which may in part determine how circulating testosterone affects behavior. Secondly, even if this evidence is ignored, administering 0.5 mg of testosterone, as per a commonly used protocol (Tuiten et al., 2000, is frequently cited as an authority) has not been shown to produce a state of affairs akin to anything occurring in nature. A dose of 0.5 mg testosterone has been shown to raise blood testosterone levels tenfold (van Honk, Peper, & Schutter, 2005), but there is no evidence that women's testosterone levels ever increase this much in nature. Even if they did, no conclusion could be drawn about the effects of administering a similar dose to men on the basis of these results. On top of this, giving the same dose to all women, irrespective of body size, means that their testosterone levels are not raised equally in these studies due to dilution effects.

The issue is further complicated as hormones tend not to have a simple monotonic relationship with behavior. Steroid hormones tend to have dose-response effects, such that a small elevation in a hormone may produce one effect, but a larger dose may produce a very different effect. In some cases, a supra-physiological dose (i.e., a dose that exceeds physiologically normal levels) may produce an effect that does not occur naturally.

What features would a good study need to have in order to convincingly address these issues? The key principle to uphold is ecological validity: is the hormone being administered in a manner which replicates a natural situation? To ensure ecological validity, researchers need to know the normal levels and patterns of hormonal secretion. They also need to know the environmental factors that affect levels of the hormone of interest. Researchers also need a clear idea about the appropriate dosage of directly-administered hormone, so that the biological effect created by administering it mimics the circumstances of interest. The appropriate dosage is likely to vary according to the subject's body weight and/or surface area.

For a number of years, testosterone researchers followed the protocol developed by Tuiten et al. (2000) for women, discussed above. More recently, Eisenegger, von Eckardstein, Fehr, and von Eckardstein (2013) administered 150 mg of testosterone gel topically to a number of men and observed its effects on testosterone levels. This gives some useful information about exogenous testosterone administration in men, but dose-response effects were not reported (dose-response effects can be seen through variation in body mass across participants while dosage is held constant). What is needed to put this field on a sound scientific footing is a well conducted dose-response study so that real-world settings can be better approximated in the laboratory.

The lack of verisimilitude of many administration studies means that the existing literature needs to be treated with a certain amount of caution. Studies administering testosterone to women may tell us something about what happens when you administer testosterone to women, but they tell us little about the effects of testosterone in men. Studies administering testosterone to men are, by definition, flawed, as we do not have the pharmacokinetic data to accurately mimic real-world conditions. However, that does not mean that they do not offer a glimpse of interesting insights for economists.

Zak et al. (2009) administered testosterone or a placebo to male participants in a within-subject design. They measured the participants' performance in the Ultimatum Game 16 hours later and found that testosterone administration caused them to make less generous offers and be more likely to punish those making stingy offers. This finding is echoed in work by Dreher et al. (2016) who found that men who had received exogenous testosterone were more likely to punish proposers in the Ultimatum Game, particularly those who made unfair offers. When testosterone-treated men received large offers, they were more likely to reward the proposer, which Dreher et al. (2016) regarded as evidence of prosocial behavior.

Cueva et al. (2015) administered testosterone and cortisol to groups of men and then had them play an asset trading game. They found that testosterone increased investment in riskier assets by making individuals more optimistic about future price changes. Nadler, Jiao, Johnson, Alexander, and Zak (2017) took this further, using a more developed trading simulation, finding that exogenous testosterone caused men to make higher bids and take longer to grasp an asset's fundamental value. This meant that testosterone administration generated larger and longer-lasting bubbles.

The administration of testosterone also appears to affect individuals' thought processes. Nave, Nadler, Zava, and Camerer (2017) examined the balance between system 1 and system 2 thinking (system 1 is the brain's fast, automatic, intuitive decision making system whereas system 2 is the slower, analytical mode, where reason dominates) using the Cognitive Reflection Test (CRT). The CRT estimates the capacity to override incorrect intuitive (system 1) judgments with more deliberated, correct (system 2) responses. They found testosterone tipped the balance towards the fast, instinctive processes of system 1, overriding the slower and more deliberative mechanisms of system 2.

Testosterone may also affect ethical aspects of behavior. Arnocky et al. (2017) administered 150 mg testosterone to 30 male participants and found that this increased utilitarian decision making overall. However, it increased utilitarian decision making for incidental moral dilemmas (i.e., dilemmas affecting others but not the individual himself), but decreased utilitarian decision making for instrumental moral dilemmas (i.e., those in which the individual himself was involved). Neither of these findings, however, reached statistical significance. Wibral, Dohmen, Klingmüller, Weber, and Falk (2012) found that administering 50 mg testosterone reduced lying.

There are fewer studies looking at the behavioral effects of administering cortisol. Like testosterone administration studies, many cortisol-administration studies do not take proper account of physiological processes. A number of studies have administered a fixed quantity of hydrocortisone (synthetic cortisol) and assessed the behavioral results. There is frequently no allowance for different body masses, so that a 50 kg woman and a 90 kg man would receive the same dose, producing very different effective dose rates. As with studies of the behavioral effects of testosterone administration, these studies are not perfect, but they offer glimpses of the ways in which hormone administration could help better understand individual behavior.

Putman, Antypa, Crysovergi, and Van Der Does (2010) found that administering 40 mg of hydrocortisone increased risky decision making when potentially big rewards were involved. This result was replicated by Kluen, Agorastos, Wiedemann, and Schwabe (2017), who found that 20 mg of hydrocortisone produced a "striking" increase in risk taking in men but not, interestingly, in women. Robertson, Immink, and Marino (2016) found similar results when 50 mg of hydrocortisone was administered to each of nine men.

When cortisol is administered in a market-type task, such as that used by Cueva et al. (2015), it appears to shift investment towards riskier assets. In contrast to testosterone, which had a significant effect on price expectations, cortisol did not have this effect and seemed instead to impact risk preferences directly.

Kandasamy et al. (2014) strove for ecological validity, aiming to replicate the 68% rise in cortisol levels observed in Coates and Herbert's (2008) trading floor study. Using a body-weight-derived dosing protocol from Mah et al. (2004), they were able to elevate participants' cortisol levels by 69% over an 8 day period. This study is notable for its verisimilitude and the fact that it examined both acute cortisol elevation and chronic (i.e., 8-day) administration. Acute cortisol elevation had little effect on risk taking, but chronic elevation (hypercortisolemia) profoundly reduced risk taking. Moreover, chronically elevated cortisol levels affected men differently to women, with men, but not women, overweighting small changes in probability.

LIMITATIONS OF STEROID HORMONE RESEARCH

One of the key limitations of using steroid hormones in social scientific research is, ironically, the very reason researchers are interested in them: namely, that these hormones are so pervasive. Cortisol, for example, affects every nucleated cell in the body and so can have profound effects on any number of behavioral parameters. Decision making and risk taking are obvious behaviors that may be affected by cortisol, but other variables, such as usage of healthcare or mortality rates, may also be affected by alterations in cortisol levels (Kumari et al., 2011). The diversity of effects of steroid hormones may mean that they are too entangled in physiological responses and human behaviors to use as a way of isolating specific mechanisms.

At present we still have an incomplete picture of the role of steroid hormones in social science. There are a number of reasons for this. The first is that we have an imperfect state of knowledge about some steroid hormones. Dehydroepiandrosterone (DHEA) and its sulfated form, DHEAS are some of the most abundant steroid hormones in the body (Barrett, Barman, Boitano, & Brooks, 2009), yet their role in normal physiological processes, let alone those relevant to social scientists, is unclear. The second is that the interactions between organizing and activation effects are difficult to tease out. At what point do alterations in protein transcription wrought by steroid hormones turn into organizational effects? In chronic cortisol elevation, for example, the classical pathway alters protein transcription but, at some point, this has a morphological effect as structure follows function (see, for example McEwen et al., 2012). It is also unclear how reversible these changes are. The third problem is that research using hormones can be startlingly expensive. At ten dollars per saliva sample, it is easy to see how sampling for multiple participants at multiple time points over multiple days can quickly add up, quite apart from the costs of overheads, personnel, standard participant payments, and so forth. Fourth, the difficulty of conducting studies, for example those needing synchronization of start times across multiple participants to avoid diurnal effects, may put researchers off. The fifth problem is that one cannot treat all participants equally. Men are not women, post-menopausal women are not the same as women who have menstrual cycles, and old men differ from young men. Sickness, exercise, and caffeine may also affect hormonal parameters in unpredictable ways. The sixth problem is a more general one; social scientists are not usually very well versed in physiology. When social scientists engage with the discipline of physiology, they can get it badly wrong (see Hardy, 2008). As with all interdisciplinary research, there is a danger of being enfiladed by reviewers from each discipline who either fail to understand other disciplines or deplore a perceived lack of disciplinary purity.

These caveats lead to the two big questions haunting steroid hormone research: how generalizable is it, and why should anyone care? The good news about generalizability is that hormones are ubiquitous; humans who do not have them die quickly. This means that aggregate findings are relatively generalizable across the species. The bad news is that they are not necessarily generalizable across groups, e.g., males/females, young/old. Moreover, because many basic elements of human behavior are refracted through conscious processes—that are themselves affected by cultural, institutional and other factors—these processes (often unmeasured in social science experiments) may alter the outputs of the basic physiological processes that hormones drive.

The "so what?" question asks whether hormone studies are just an academic frolic with no practical import. Leaving aside the standard argument about the value of the pursuit of knowledge per se, there is something useful to be gained from examining these processes. New theories or insights into individual and aggregate behavior can be suggested by dissecting hormonal events. For example, Coates et al. (2010) suggest that the winner effect might account for stock-market bubbles, and Coates and Gurnell (2017) extend this, suggesting a hormonal role in crashes. Such insights would not be possible without knowledge of steroid hormones.

COMPLEMENTARITY WITH OTHER RESEARCH AND DIRECTIONS FOR FUTURE RESEARCH

So where does all this leave steroid hormones in the pantheon of social scientific research? And what would a social science research program profitably incorporating steroid hormone measures look like? Because steroid hormones reach into every aspect of our lives—outwards to our behavior, and inwards into our bodies and even, through epigenetics, to our DNA—a successful research program could reach in a wide variety of directions. As an example, researchers trying to understand drug addiction may look at the social and environmental causes and consequences of drug use. However, they may also look at the behavioral patterns which drug use alters. They may examine the chemical and electrical changes that accompany addiction. At their most basic level, genetic differences may predispose individuals to misuse drugs. A research program that draws on and adds to converging lines of evidence leading to a theoretical paradigm has the potential to offer robust multi-level explanations for complex social problems.

A similar research project in economics might look at the social consequences of asset bubbles and crashes. If testosterone is associated with asset bubbles, as some authors have suggested (Coates, 2012), then we may see the consequences of excess testosterone in wider society. When population-level testosterone levels rise, is there an increase in risk taking, such as speeding, or in the incidence of sexually transmitted diseases? Are people more likely to divorce? There is the potential for sophisticated research programs that combine social data, to establish the phenomenon, with laboratory study, to isolate the mechanism, and field experiments, to explore possible remedies. Coates and Gurnell (2017) examine what a program of this sort would look like.

Steroid hormones can help social scientists understand complex problems in the world and propose novel solutions. For example, traders with a successful recent track record may be seen as being on a winning streak. A steroid hormone approach, however, would suggest that they may be caught up in a dangerous positive feedback loop, posing a danger. If seen as being on a winning streak, the trader may be given more money. If seen as a hormonal risk, they may be sent on holiday.

Research incorporating steroid hormones is not the answer to everything, but it does enable some of the processes going on within individuals to be more effectively explored. In doing so we gain a more nuanced understanding of social science problems, allowing us to pose better questions and improve our understanding of social scientific phenomena.

REFERENCES

Akinola, M., & Mendes, W. B. (2012). Stress-induced cortisol facilitates threat-related decision making among police officers. *Behavioral Neuroscience*, *126*(1), 167–174.

Akinola, M., Page-Gould, E., Mehta, P. H., & Lu, J. G. (2016). Collective hormonal profiles predict group performance. *Proceedings of the National Academy of Sciences of the United States of America, 113*(35), 9774–9779.

Allaway, H. C., Bloski, T. G., Pierson, R. A., & Lujan, M. E. (2009). Digit ratios (2D:4D) determined by computer-assisted analysis are more reliable than those using physical measurements, photocopies, and printed scans. *American Journal of Human Biology, 21*(3), 365–370.

Alvergne, A., & Lummaa, V. (2010). Does the contraceptive pill alter mate choice in humans? *Trends in Ecology & Evolution, 25*(3), 171–179.

Amrhein, J. A., Meyer, W. J., Jones, H. W., & Migeon, C. J. (1976). Androgen insensitivity in man: evidence for genetic heterogeneity. *Proceedings of the National Academy of Sciences, 73*(3), 891–894.

Apicella, C. L., Dreber, A., Campbell, B., Gray, P. B., Hoffman, M., & Little, A. C. (2008). Testosterone and financial risk preferences. *Evolution and Human Behavior, 29*(6), 384–390.

Apicella, C. L., Dreber, A., & Mollerstrom, J. (2014). Salivary testosterone change following monetary wins and losses predicts future financial risk-taking. *Psychoneuroendocrinology, 39*, 58–64. Suppl. C.

Archer, J. (2006). Testosterone and human aggression: an evaluation of the challenge hypothesis. *Neuroscience & Biobehavioral Reviews, 30*(3), 319–345.

Arnocky, S., Carré, J. M., Bird, B. M., Moreau, B. J. P., Vaillancourt, T., Ortiz, T., & Marley, N. (2018). The facial width-to-height ratio predicts sex drive, sociosexuality, and intended infidelity. *Archives of Sexual Behavior, 47*(5), 1375–1385. https://doi.org/10.1007/s10508-017-1070-x.

Arnocky, S., Taylor, S. M., Olmstead, A., & Carré, J. M. (2017). The effects of exogenous testosterone on men's moral decision-making. *Adaptive Human Behavior and Physiology, 3*(1), 1–13.

Arnold, A. P. (2009). The organizational-activational hypothesis as the foundation for a unified theory of sexual differentiation of all mammalian tissues. *Hormones and Behavior, 55*(5), 570–578.

Arnold, A. P., & Breedlove, S. M. (1985). Organizational and activational effects of sex steroids on brain and behavior: a reanalysis. *Hormones and Behavior, 19*(4), 469–498.

Bakker, J., & Baum, M. J. (2008). Role for estradiol in female-typical brain and behavioral sexual differentiation. *Frontiers in Neuroendocrinology, 29*(1), 1–16.

Bale, T. L., & Epperson, C. N. (2015). Sex differences and stress across the lifespan. *Nature Neuroscience, 18*, 1413.

Bao, A., Liu, R., van Someren, E., Hofman, M., Cao, Y., & Zhou, J. (2003). Diurnal rhythm of free estradiol during the menstrual cycle. *European Journal of Endocrinology, 148*(2), 227–232.

Barnola, J. M., Raynaud, D., Korotkevich, Y. S., & Lorius, C. (1987). Vostok ice core provides 160,000-year record of atmospheric CO_2. *Nature, 329*, 408.

Barrett, K. E., Barman, S. M., Boitano, S., & Brooks, H. L. (2009). *Ganong's review of medical physiology*. McGraw-Hill Medical. 23rd ed.

Bartels, M., Van den Berg, M., Sluyter, F., Boomsma, D. I., & de Geus, E. J. C. (2003). Heritability of cortisol levels: review and simultaneous analysis of twin studies. *Psychoneuroendocrinology, 28*(2), 121–137.

Baulieu, E. (1997). Neurosteroids: of the nervous system, by the nervous system, for the nervous system. *Recent Progress in Hormone Research, 52*, 1.

Beaven, C. M., Hopkins, W. G., Hansen, K. T., Wood, M. R., Cronin, J. B., & Lowe, T. E. (2008). Dose effect of caffeine on testosterone and cortisol responses to resistance exercise. *International Journal of Sport Nutrition and Exercise Metabolism, 18*(2), 131–141.

Berenbaum, S. A., & Beltz, A. M. (2011). Sexual differentiation of human behavior: effects of prenatal and pubertal organizational hormones. *Frontiers in Neuroendocrinology*, *32*(2), 183–200.

Berenbaum, S. A., & Beltz, A. M. (2016). How early hormones shape gender development. *Current Opinion in Behavioral Sciences*, *7*, 53–60.

Bernhardt, P. C., Dabbs, J. M., Jr., Fielden, J. A., & Lutter, C. D. (1998). Testosterone changes during vicarious experiences of winning and losing among fans at sporting events. *Physiology & Behavior*, *65*(1), 59–62.

Bernile, G., Bhagwat, V., & Rau, P. R. (2017). What doesn't kill you will only make you more risk-loving: early-life disasters and CEO behavior. *The Journal of Finance*, *72*(1), 167–206.

Bönte, W., Procher, V. D., & Urbig, D. (2016). Biology and selection into entrepreneurship—the relevance of prenatal testosterone exposure. *Entrepreneurship Theory and Practice*, *40*(5), 1121–1148.

Book, A. S., Starzyk, K. B., & Quinsey, V. L. (2001). The relationship between testosterone and aggression: a meta-analysis. *Aggression and Violent Behavior*, *6*(6), 579–599.

Booth, A., Shelley, G., Mazur, A., Tharp, G., & Kittok, R. (1989). Testosterone, and winning and losing in human competition. *Hormones and Behavior*, *23*(4), 556–571.

Brambilla, D. J., Matsumoto, A. M., Araujo, A. B., & McKinlay, J. B. (2009). The effect of diurnal variation on clinical measurement of serum testosterone and other sex hormone levels in men. *The Journal of Clinical Endocrinology & Metabolism*, *94*(3), 907–913.

Brambilla, D. J., O'Donnell, A. B., Matsumoto, A. M., & McKinlay, J. B. (2007). Intraindividual variation in levels of serum testosterone and other reproductive and adrenal hormones in men. *Clinical Endocrinology*, *67*(6), 853–862.

Brañas-Garza, P., Galizzi, M. M., & Nieboer, J. (2018). Experimental and self-reported measures of risk taking and digit ratio (2d:4d): evidence from a large, systematic study. *International Economic Review*, *59*(3), 1131–1157. https://doi.org/10.1111/iere.12299.

Brañas-Garza, P., Kovářík, J., & Neyse, L. (2013). Second-to-fourth digit ratio has a non-monotonic impact on altruism. *PLoS ONE*, *8*(4).

Breedlove, S. M. (1994). Sexual differentiation of the human nervous system. *Annual Review of Psychology*, *45*(1), 389–418.

Breedlove, S. M., & Hampson, E. (2002). Sexual differentiation of the brain and behavior. In J. B. Becker, S. M. Breedlove, D. Crews, & M. M. McCarthy (Eds.), *Behavioral endocrinology* (2nd ed., p. 776). Cambridge, MA; London: MIT Press.

Bröder, A., & Hohmann, N. (2003). Variations in risk taking behavior over the menstrual cycle: an improved replication. *Evolution and Human Behavior*, *24*(6), 391–398.

Buckert, M., Schwieren, C., Kudielka, B. M., & Fiebach, C. J. (2014). Acute stress affects risk taking but not ambiguity aversion. *Frontiers in Neuroscience*, *8*(82), 1–11.

Buffet, N. C., Djakoure, C., Maitre, S. C., & Bouchard, P. (1998). Regulation of the human menstrual cycle. *Frontiers in Neuroendocrinology*, *19*(3), 151–186. https://doi.org/10.1006/frne.1998.0167.

Burnham, T. C. (2007). High-testosterone men reject low ultimatum game offers. *Proceedings of the Royal Society B: Biological Sciences*, *274*(1623), 2327–2330.

Buser, T. (2012). The impact of the menstrual cycle and hormonal contraceptives on competitiveness. *Journal of Economic Behavior & Organization*, *83*(1), 1–10.

Cahlíková, J., & Cingl, L. (2017). Risk preferences under acute stress. *Experimental Economics*, *20*(1), 209–236.

Cao-Lei, L., de Rooij, S. R., King, S., Matthews, S. G., Metz, G. A. S., Roseboom, T. J., & Szyf, M. (in press) Neuroscience and biobehavioral reviews prenatal stress and epigenetics. Neuroscience and Biobehavioral Reviews. https://doi.org/10.1016/j.neubiorev.2017.05.016.

Carney, D. R., & Mason, M. F. (2010). Decision making and testosterone: when the ends justify the means. *Journal of Experimental Social Psychology*, *46*(4), 668–671.

Carré, J. M., Baird-Rowe, C. D., & Hariri, A. R. (2014). Testosterone responses to competition predict decreased trust ratings of emotionally neutral faces. *Psychoneuroendocrinology*, *49*, 79–83. Suppl. C.

Carré, J. M., & McCormick, C. M. (2008a). Aggressive behavior and change in salivary testosterone concentrations predict willingness to engage in a competitive task. *Hormones and Behavior*, *54*(3), 403–409.

Carré, J. M., & McCormick, C. M. (2008b). In your face: facial metrics predict aggressive behaviour in the laboratory and in varsity and professional hockey players. *Proceedings of the Royal Society B: Biological Sciences*, *275*(1651), 2651–2656.

Carré, J. M., Putnam, S. K., & McCormick, C. M. (2009). Testosterone responses to competition predict future aggressive behaviour at a cost to reward in men. *Psychoneuroendocrinology*, *34*(4), 561–570.

Casto, K. V., & Prasad, S. (2017). Recommendations for the study of women in hormones and competition research. *Hormones and Behavior*, *92*, 190–194.

Caswell, N., & Manning, J. T. (2009). A comparison of finger 2D:4D by self-report direct measurement and experimenter measurement from photocopy: methodological issues. *Archives of Sexual Behavior*, *38*(1), 143–148.

Charney, D. S., Heninger, G. R., & Jatlow, P. I. (1985). Increased anxiogenic effects of caffeine in panic disorders. *Archives of General Psychiatry*, *42*(3), 233–243.

Chavanne, T. J., & Gallup, G. G., Jr. (1998). Variation in risk taking behavior among female college students as a function of the menstrual cycle. *Evolution and Human Behavior*, *19*(1), 27–32.

Chen, Y., Katuščák, P., & Ozdenoren, E. (2013). Why can't a woman bid more like a man? *Games and Economic Behavior*, *77*(1), 181–213.

Chumbley, J. R., Krajbich, I., Engelmann, J. B., Russell, E., Van Uum, S., Koren, G., et al. (2014). Endogenous cortisol predicts decreased loss aversion in young men. *Psychological Science*, *25*(11), 2102–2105.

Coates, J. M. (2012). *The hour between dog and wolf: Risk-taking, gut feelings and the biology of boom and bust.* London: Fourth Estate.

Coates, J. M., & Gurnell, M. (2017). Combining field work and laboratory work in the study of financial risk-taking. *Hormones and Behavior*, *92*, 13–19. Suppl. C.

Coates, J. M., Gurnell, M., & Rustichini, A. (2009). Second-to-fourth digit ratio predicts success among high-frequency financial traders. *Proceedings of the National Academy of Sciences of the United States of America*, *106*(2), 623–628.

Coates, J. M., Gurnell, M., & Sarnyai, Z. (2010). From molecule to market: steroid hormones and financial risk-taking. *Philosophical Transactions of the Royal Society, B: Biological Sciences*, *365*(1538), 331–343.

Coates, J. M., & Herbert, J. (2008). Endogenous steroids and financial risk taking on a London trading floor. *Proceedings of the National Academy of Sciences of the United States of America*, *105* (16), 6167–6172.

Cohen-Bendahan, C. C. C., van de Beek, C., & Berenbaum, S. A. (2005). Prenatal sex hormone effects on child and adult sex-typed behavior: methods and findings. *Neuroscience & Biobehavioral Reviews*, *29*(2), 353–384.

Cueva, C., Roberts, R. E., Spencer, T., Rani, N., Tempest, M., Tobler, P. N., et al. (2015). Cortisol and testosterone increase financial risk taking and may destabilize markets. *Scientific Reports*, *5*, 1–16.

Cumming, D. C., Wall, S. R., Galbraith, M. A., & Belcastro, A. N. (1987). Reproductive hormone responses to resistance exercise. *Medicine and Science in Sports and Exercise, 19*(3).

Daitzman, R., & Zuckerman, M. (1980). Disinhibitory sensation seeking, personality and gonadal hormones. *Personality and Individual Differences, 1*(2), 103–110.

Daitzman, R. J., Zuckerman, M., Sammelwitz, P., & Ganjam, V. (1978). Sensation seeking and gonadal hormones. *Journal of Biosocial Science, 10*(04), 401–408.

Dalton, P. S., & Ghosal, S. (2014). *Self-confidence, overconfidence and prenatal testosterone exposure: Evidence from the lab.* CentER Discussion Paper, 2014-014.

de Kloet, E. R., Joels, M., & Holsboer, F. (2005). Stress and the brain: from adaptation to disease. *Nature Reviews Neuroscience, 6*(6), 463–475.

de Vries, G. J., & Södersten, P. (2009). Sex differences in the brain: the relation between structure and function. *Hormones and Behavior, 55*(5), 589–596.

Derntl, B., Pintzinger, N., Kryspin-Exner, I., & Schöpf, V. (2014). The impact of sex hormone concentrations on decision-making in females and males. *Frontiers in Neuroscience, 8*, 1–11.

Dickerson, S. S., & Kemeny, M. E. (2004). Acute stressors and cortisol responses: a theoretical integration and synthesis of laboratory research. *Psychological Bulletin, 130*(3), 355–391.

Diekhof, E. K., Wittmer, S., & Reimers, L. (2014). Does competition really bring out the worst? Testosterone, social distance and inter-male competition shape parochial altruism in human males. *PLoS ONE, 9*(7).

Doerr, P., & Pirke, K. M. (1976). Cortisol-induced suppression of plasma testosterone in normal adult males. *The Journal of Clinical Endocrinology & Metabolism, 43*(3), 622–629.

Dreher, J. C., Dunne, S., Pazderska, A., Frodl, T., Nolan, J. J., & O'Doherty, J. P. (2016). Testosterone causes both prosocial and antisocial status-enhancing behaviors in human males. *Proceedings of the National Academy of Sciences of the United States of America, 113*(41), 11633–11638.

Durante, K. M., & Arsena, A. R. (2015). Playing the field: the effect of fertility on women's desire for variety. *Journal of Consumer Research, 41*(6), 1372–1391.

Durante, K. M., Griskevicius, V., Cantú, S. M., & Simpson, J. A. (2014). Money, status, and the ovulatory cycle. *Journal of Marketing Research, 51*(1), 27–39.

Durante, K. M., Griskevicius, V., Hill, S. E., Perilloux, C., & Li, N. P. (2011). Ovulation, female competition, and product choice: hormonal influences on consumer behavior. *Journal of Consumer Research, 37*(6), 921–934.

Durante, K. M., Li, N. P., & Haselton, M. G. (2008). Changes in women's choice of dress across the ovulatory cycle: naturalistic and laboratory task-based evidence. *Personality and Social Psychology Bulletin, 34*(11), 1451–1460.

Efferson, C., & Vogt, S. (2013). Viewing mens' faces does not lead to accurate predictions of trustworthiness. *Scientific Reports, 3*, 1047.

Eisenegger, C., von Eckardstein, A., Fehr, E., & von Eckardstein, S. (2013). Pharmacokinetics of testosterone and estradiol gel preparations in healthy young men. *Psychoneuroendocrinology, 38*(2), 171–178.

Evans, K. L., & Hampson, E. (2014). Does risk-taking mediate the relationship between testosterone and decision-making on the Iowa Gambling Task? *Personality and Individual Differences, 61–62*, 57–62.

Feldman, H. A., Longcope, C., Derby, C. A., Johannes, C. B., Araujo, A. B., Coviello, A. D., et al. (2002). Age trends in the level of serum testosterone and other hormones in middle-aged men: longitudinal results from the Massachusetts male aging study. *The Journal of Clinical Endocrinology and Metabolism, 87*(2), 589–598.

Fiers, T., Delanghe, J., T'Sjoen, G., Van Caenegem, E., Wierckx, K., & Kaufman, J. -M. (2014). A critical evaluation of salivary testosterone as a method for the assessment of serum testosterone. *Steroids*, *86*, 5–9. Suppl. C.

Fink, B., Grammer, K., Mitteroecker, P., Gunz, P., Schaefer, K., Bookstein, F. L., et al. (2005). Second to fourth digit ratio and face shape. *Proceedings of the Royal Society B: Biological Sciences*, *272*(1576), 1995–2001.

Frye, C. A., Rhodes, M. E., Rosellini, R., & Svare, B. (2002). The nucleus accumbens as a site of action for rewarding properties of testosterone and its 5[alpha]-reduced metabolites. *Pharmacology Biochemistry and Behavior*, *74*(1), 119–127.

Galizzi, M. M., & Nieboer, J. (2015). Digit ratio (2D:4D) and altruism: evidence from a large, multi-ethnic sample. *Frontiers in Behavioral Neuroscience*, *9*(41), 1–8.

Gangestad, S. W., & Thornhill, R. (2008). Human oestrus. *Proceedings of the Royal Society B: Biological Sciences*, *275*(1638), 991–1000.

Garbarino, E., Slonim, R., & Sydnor, J. (2011). Digit ratios (2D,4D) as predictors of risky decision making for both sexes. *Journal of Risk and Uncertainty*, *42*(1), 1–26.

Geniole, S. N., Bird, B. M., Ruddick, E. L., & Carré, J. M. (2017). Effects of competition outcome on testosterone concentrations in humans: an updated meta-analysis. *Hormones and Behavior*, *92*, 37–50. Suppl. C.

Geniole, S. N., Denson, T. F., Dixson, B. J., Carré, J. M., & McCormick, C. M. (2015). Evidence from meta-analyses of the facial width-to-height ratio as an evolved cue of threat. *PLoS ONE*, *10*(7).

Giddens, A. (1984). *The constitution of society: Outline of the theory of structuration*. Cambridge: Polity Press.

GIMP (2017). *GNU Image Manipulation Program (GIMP)* (2.8.22 ed.). .

Gordon, G. G., Altman, K., Southren, A. L., Rubin, E., & Lieber, C. S. (1976). Effect of alcohol (ethanol) administration on sex-hormone metabolism in normal men. *New England Journal of Medicine*, *295*(15), 793–797.

Greally, J. M. (2018). A user's guide to the ambiguous word 'epigenetics'. *Nature Reviews Molecular Cell Biology*, *19*, 207.

Gurnell, M., Burrin, J., & Chatterjee, K. (2010). Principles of hormone action. In D. A. Warrell, T. M. Cox, & J. D. Firth (Eds.), *Oxford textbook of medicine*. (5th ed.). Oxford: Oxford University Press.

Hardy, B. (2008). Things should be made as simple as possible, but no simpler: integrating management and physiology. *Academy of Management Review*, *33*(4), 1007–1009.

Haselhuhn, M. P., Ormiston, M. E., & Wong, E. M. (2015). Men's facial width-to-height ratio predicts aggression: a meta-analysis. *PLoS ONE*, *10*(4).

Haselhuhn, M. P., Wong, E. M., Ormiston, M. E., Inesi, M. E., & Galinsky, A. D. (2014). Negotiating face-to-face: men's facial structure predicts negotiation performance. *The Leadership Quarterly*, *25*(5), 835–845.

Hermans, E. J., Putman, P., & van Honk, J. (2006). Testosterone administration reduces empathetic behavior: a facial mimicry study. *Psychoneuroendocrinology*, *31*(7), 859–866.

Hodges-Simeon, C. R., Hanson Sobraske, K. N., Samore, T., Gurven, M., & Gaulin, S. J. C. (2016). Facial width-to-height ratio (fWHR) is not associated with adolescent testosterone levels. *PLoS ONE*, *11*(4).

Hönekopp, J., Bartholdt, L., Beier, L., & Liebert, A. (2007). Second to fourth digit length ratio (2D:4D) and adult sex hormone levels: new data and a meta-analytic review. *Psychoneuroendocrinology*, *32*(4), 313–321.

Hönekopp, J., & Schuster, M. (2010). A meta-analysis on 2D:4D and athletic prowess: substantial relationships but neither hand out-predicts the other. *Personality and Individual Differences*, *48*(1), 4–10.

Hönekopp, J., & Watson, S. (2010). Meta-analysis of digit ratio 2D:4D shows greater sex difference in the right hand. *American Journal of Human Biology*, *22*(5), 619–630.

Hönekopp, J., & Watson, S. (2011). Meta-analysis of the relationship between digit-ratio 2D:4D and aggression. *Personality and Individual Differences*, *51*(4), 381–386.

Huh, H. (2011). Digit ratios and preferences for aggressive content in entertainment. *Personality and Individual Differences*, *51*(4), 451–453.

Human Tissue Act. (2004). (c. 30). United Kingdom.

Isidori, A. M., Giannetta, E., Greco, E. A., Gianfrilli, D., Bonifacio, V., Isidori, A., et al. (2005). Effects of testosterone on body composition, bone metabolism and serum lipid profile in middle-aged men: a meta-analysis. *Clinical Endocrinology*, *63*(3), 280–293.

Jones, B. C., DeBruine, L. M., Perrett, D. I., Little, A. C., Feinberg, D. R., & Law Smith, M. J. (2008). Effects of menstrual cycle phase on face preferences. *Archives of Sexual Behavior*, *37*(1), 78–84.

Kandasamy, N., Hardy, B., Page, L., Schaffner, M., Graggaber, J., Powlson, A. S., et al. (2014). Cortisol shifts financial risk preferences. *Proceedings of the National Academy of Sciences*, *111*(9), 3608–3613.

Kay, J. (2011). Sex, lies and pitfalls of overblown statistics. In *Financial times*. London: Financial Times Ltd.

Kemper, C. J., & Schwerdtfeger, A. (2009). Comparing indirect methods of digit ratio (2D:4D) measurement. *American Journal of Human Biology*, *21*(2), 188–191.

Kirschbaum, C., Kudielka, B. M., Gaab, J., Schommer, N. C., & Hellhammer, D. H. (1999). Impact of gender, menstrual cycle phase, and oral contraceptives on the activity of the hypothalamus-pituitary-adrenal axis. *Psychosomatic Medicine*, *61*(2), 154–162.

Kirschbaum, C., Pirke, K. M., & Hellhammer, D. H. (1993). The 'trier social stress test'—a tool for investigating psychobiological stress responses in a laboratory setting. *Neuropsychobiology*, *28*(1-2), 76–81.

Kirschbaum, C., Strasburger, C. J., & Langkrär, J. (1993). Attenuated cortisol response to psychological stress but not to CRH or ergometry in young habitual smokers. *Pharmacology Biochemistry and Behavior*, *44*(3), 527–531.

Kleisner, K., Priplatova, L., Frost, P., & Flegr, J. (2013). Trustworthy-looking face meets brown eyes. *PLoS ONE*, *8*(1).

Kluen, L. M., Agorastos, A., Wiedemann, K., & Schwabe, L. (2017). Cortisol boosts risky decision-making behavior in men but not in women. *Psychoneuroendocrinology*, *84*, 181–189.

Koenig, J. I., Elmer, G. I., Shepard, P. D., Lee, P. R., Mayo, C., Joy, B., et al. (2005). Prenatal exposure to a repeated variable stress paradigm elicits behavioral and neuroendocrinological changes in the adult offspring: potential relevance to schizophrenia. *Behavioural Brain Research*, *156*(2), 251–261.

Kofman, O. (2002). The role of prenatal stress in the etiology of developmental behavioural disorders. *Neuroscience & Biobehavioral Reviews*, *26*(4), 457–470.

Kudielka, B. M., & Kirschbaum, C. (2003). Awakening cortisol responses are influenced by health status and awakening time but not by menstrual cycle phase. *Psychoneuroendocrinology*, *28*(1), 35–47.

Kumari, M., Shipley, M., Stafford, M., & Kivimaki, M. (2011). Association of diurnal patterns in salivary cortisol with all-cause and cardiovascular mortality: findings from the Whitehall II study. *The Journal of Clinical Endocrinology & Metabolism*, *96*(5), 1478–1485.

Kuoppasalmi, K., Näveri, H., Härkönen, M., & Adlercreutz, H. (1980). Plasma cortisol, androstenedione, testosterone and luteinizing hormone in running exercise of different intensities. *Scandinavian Journal of Clinical & Laboratory Investigation*, *40*(5), 403–409.

Kuoppasalmi, K., Näveri, H., Rehunen, S., Härkönen, M., & Adlercreutz, H. (1976). Effect of strenuous anaerobic running exercise on plasma growth hormone, cortisol, luteinizing hormone, testosterone, androstenedione, estrone and estradiol. *Journal of Steroid Biochemistry*, *7*(10), 823–829.

Lazzaro, S. C., Rutledge, R. B., Burghart, D. R., & Glimcher, P. W. (2016). The impact of menstrual cycle phase on economic choice and rationality. *PLoS ONE*, *11*(1), 1–15.

Leder, J., Häusser, J. A., & Mojzisch, A. (2013). Stress and strategic decision-making in the beauty contest game. *Psychoneuroendocrinology*, *38*(9), 1503–1511.

Lefevre, C. E., Lewis, G. J., Perrett, D. I., & Penke, L. (2013). Telling facial metrics: facial width is associated with testosterone levels in men. *Evolution and Human Behavior*, *34*(4), 273–279.

Lighthall, N. R., Mather, M., & Gorlick, M. A. (2009). Acute stress increases sex differences in risk seeking in the balloon analogue risk task. *PLoS ONE*, *4*(7).

Lighthall, N. R., Sakaki, M., Vasunilashorn, S., Nga, L., Somayajula, S., Chen, E. Y., et al. (2012). Gender differences in reward-related decision processing under stress. *Social Cognitive and Affective Neuroscience*, *7*(4), 476–484.

Linke, L., Saribay, S. A., & Kleisner, K. (2016). Perceived trustworthiness is associated with position in a corporate hierarchy. *Personality and Individual Differences*, *99*(Suppl. C), 22–27.

Lovallo, W. R., Whitsett, T. L., al'Absi, M., Sung, B. H., Vincent, A. S., & Wilson, M. F. (2005). Caffeine stimulation of cortisol secretion across the waking hours in relation to caffeine intake levels. *Psychosomatic Medicine*, *67*(5), 734–739.

Lutchmaya, S., Baron-Cohen, S., Raggatt, P., Knickmeyer, R., & Manning, J. T. (2004). 2nd to 4th digit ratios, fetal testosterone and estradiol. *Early Human Development*, *77*(1-2), 23–28.

Luxen, M. F., & Buunk, B. P. (2005). Second-to-fourth digit ratio related to Verbal and Numerical Intelligence and the Big Five. *Personality and Individual Differences*, *39*(5), 959–966.

Maccari, S., Krugers, H. J., Morley-Fletcher, S., Szyf, M., & Brunton, P. J. (2014). The consequences of early-life adversity: neurobiological, behavioural and epigenetic adaptations. *Journal of Neuroendocrinology*, *26*(10), 707–723.

Mah, P. M., Jenkins, R. C., Rostami-Hodjegan, A., Newell-Price, J., Doane, A., Ibbotson, V., et al. (2004). Weight-related dosing, timing and monitoring hydrocortisone replacement therapy in patients with adrenal insufficiency. *Clinical Endocrinology*, *61*(3), 367–375.

Manning, J., Scutt, D., Wilson, J., & Lewis-Jones, D. (1998). The ratio of 2nd to 4th digit length: a predictor of sperm numbers and concentrations of testosterone, luteinizing hormone and oestrogen. *Human Reproduction*, *13*(11), 3000–3004.

Manning, J. T., & Fink, B. (2008). Digit ratio (2D,4D), dominance, reproductive success, asymmetry, and sociosexuality in the BBC Internet Study. *American Journal of Human Biology*, *20*(4), 451–461.

Manning, J. T., & Fink, B. (2011). Digit ratio (2D:4D) and aggregate personality scores across nations: data from the BBC internet study. *Personality and Individual Differences*, *51*(4), 387–391.

Manning, J. T., Fink, B., Neave, N., & Caswell, N. (2005). Photocopies yield lower digit ratios (2D:4D) than direct finger measurements. *Archives of Sexual Behavior*, *34*(3), 329–333.

Manning, J. T., Stewart, A., Bundred, P. E., & Trivers, R. L. (2004). Sex and ethnic differences in 2nd to 4th digit ratio of children. *Early Human Development*, *80*(2), 161–168.

Manning, J. T., Trivers, R., & Fink, B. (2017). Is digit ratio (2D:4D) related to masculinity and femininity? Evidence from the BBC internet study. *Evolutionary Psychological Science*, *3*(4), 316–324.

Matsumoto, A. (1990). Effects of chronic testosterone administration in normal men: safety and efficacy of high dosage testosterone and parallel dose-dependent suppression of luteinizing hormone, follicle-stimulating hormone, and sperm production. *The Journal of Clinical Endocrinology & Metabolism*, *70*(1), 282–287.

Mazur, A., Booth, A., & Dabbs, J. M., Jr. (1992). Testosterone and chess competition. *Social Psychology Quarterly*, *55*(1), 70–77.

McCarthy, M. M., Arnold, A. P., Ball, G. F., Blaustein, J. D., & De Vries, G. J. (2012). Sex differences in the brain: the not so inconvenient truth. *The Journal of Neuroscience*, *32*(7), 2241–2247.

McEwen, B. S., Eiland, L., Hunter, R. G., & Miller, M. M. (2012). Stress and anxiety: structural plasticity and epigenetic regulation as a consequence of stress. *Neuropharmacology*, *62*(1), 3–12.

McEwen, B. S., & Milner, T. A. (2007). Hippocampal formation: shedding light on the influence of sex and stress on the brain. *Brain Research Reviews*, *55*(2), 343–355.

McIntyre, M. (2006). The use of digit ratios as markers for perinatal androgen action. *Reproductive Biology and Endocrinology*, *4*(1), 10.

Mehta, P. H., & Josephs, R. A. (2006). Testosterone change after losing predicts the decision to compete again. *Hormones and Behavior*, *50*(5), 684–692.

Mehta, P. H., Mor, S., Yap, A. J., & Prasad, S. (2015). Dual-hormone changes are related to bargaining performance. *Psychological Science*, *26*(6), 866–876.

Mehta, P. H., & Prasad, S. (2015). The dual-hormone hypothesis: a brief review and future research agenda. *Current Opinion in Behavioral Sciences*, *3*, 163–168.

Mehta, P. H., Welker, K. M., Zilioli, S., & Carré, J. M. (2015). Testosterone and cortisol jointly modulate risk-taking. *Psychoneuroendocrinology*, *56*, 88–99.

Meikle, A. W., Bishop, D. T., Stringham, J. D., & West, D. W. (1986). Quantitating genetic and nongenetic factors that determine plasma sex steroid variation in normal male twins. *Metabolism*, *35*(12), 1090–1095.

Melmed, S., Polonsky, K. S., Larsen, P. R., & Kronenberg, H. M. (2011). *Williams textbook of endocrinology*. Elsevier Health Sciences 12th ed.

Miller, G., Tybur, J. M., & Jordan, B. D. (2007). Ovulatory cycle effects on tip earnings by lap dancers: economic evidence for human estrus? *Evolution and Human Behavior*, *28*(6), 375–381.

Miller, K. J., Conney, J. C., Rasgon, N. L., Fairbanks, L. A., & Small, G. W. (2002). Mood symptoms and cognitive performance in women estrogen users and nonusers and men. *Journal of the American Geriatrics Society*, *50*(11), 1826–1830.

Nadler, A., Jiao, P., Johnson, C. J., Alexander, V., & Zak, P. J. (2017). The bull of wall street: experimental analysis of testosterone and asset trading. *Management Science*, *64*(9), 4032–4051. https://doi.org/10.1287/mnsc.2017.2836.

Nave, G., Nadler, A., Zava, D., & Camerer, C. (2017). Single-dose testosterone administration impairs cognitive reflection in men. *Psychological Science*, *28*(10), 1398–1407.

Neave, N., Laing, S., Fink, B., & Manning, J. T. (2003). Second to fourth digit ratio, testosterone and perceived male dominance. *Proceedings of the Royal Society of London. Series B: Biological Sciences*, *270*(1529), 2167–2172.

Nepomuceno, M. V., Saad, G., Stenstrom, E., Mendenhall, Z., & Iglesias, F. (2016a). Testosterone & gift-giving: mating confidence moderates the association between digit ratios (2D:4D and rel2) and erotic gift-giving. *Personality and Individual Differences*, *91*, 27–30.

Nepomuceno, M. V., Saad, G., Stenstrom, E., Mendenhall, Z., & Iglesias, F. (2016b). Testosterone at your fingertips: digit ratios (2D:4D and rel2) as predictors of courtship-related consumption intended to acquire and retain mates. *Journal of Consumer Psychology*, *26*(2), 231–244.

Neyse, L., Bosworth, S., Ring, P., & Schmidt, U. (2016). Overconfidence, incentives and digit ratio. *Scientific Reports*, *6*, .

Pabst, S., Brand, M., & Wolf, O. (2013a). Stress effects on framed decisions: there are differences for gains and losses. *Frontiers in Behavioral Neuroscience*, *7*(142), 1–11.

Pabst, S., Brand, M., & Wolf, O. T. (2013b). Stress and decision making: a few minutes make all the difference. *Behavioural Brain Research*, *250*, 39–45. Suppl. C.

Pabst, S., Schoofs, D., Pawlikowski, M., Brand, M., & Wolf, O. T. (2013). Paradoxical effects of stress and an executive task on decisions under risk. *Behavioral Neuroscience*, *127*(3), 369–379.

Palma-Gudiel, H., Córdova-Palomera, A., Eixarch, E., Deuschle, M., & Fañanás, L. (2015). Maternal psychosocial stress during pregnancy alters the epigenetic signature of the glucocorticoid receptor gene promoter in their offspring: a meta-analysis. *Epigenetics*, *10*(10), 893–902.

Pearson, M., & Schipper, B. C. (2013). Menstrual cycle and competitive bidding. *Games and Economic Behavior*, *78*(0), 1–20.

Persson, R., Garde, A. H., Hansen, Å. M., Österberg, K., Larsson, B., Ørbæk, P., et al. (2008). Seasonal variation in human salivary cortisol concentration. *Chronobiology International*, *25*(6), 923–937.

Phoenix, C. H., Goy, R. W., Gerall, A. A., & Young, W. C. (1959). Organizing action of prenatally administered testosterone propionate on the tissues mediating mating behavior in the female guinea pig. *Endocrinology*, *65*(3), 369–382.

Pruessner, J. C., Gaab, J., Hellhammer, D. H., Lintz, D., Schommer, N., & Kirschbaum, C. (1997). Increasing correlations between personality traits and cortisol stress responses obtained by data aggregation. *Psychoneuroendocrinology*, *22*(8), 615–625.

Putman, P., Antypa, N., Crysovergi, P., & Van Der Does, W. A. J. (2010). Exogenous cortisol acutely influences motivated decision making in healthy young men. *Psychopharmacology*, *208*(2), 257–263.

Radtke, K. M., Ruf, M., Gunter, H. M., Dohrmann, K., Schauer, M., Meyer, A., et al. (2011). Transgenerational impact of intimate partner violence on methylation in the promoter of the glucocorticoid receptor. *Translational Psychiatry*, *1*, e21.

Rang, H. P., & Dale, M. M. (2007). *Rang & Dale's pharmacology* (6th ed.). Edinburgh: Churchill Livingstone.

Reimers, L., & Diekhof, E. K. (2015). Testosterone is associated with cooperation during intergroup competition by enhancing parochial altruism. *Frontiers in Neuroscience*, *9*(183), 1–9.

Richardson, J. T. E. (1992). The menstrual cycle, cognition, and paramenstrual symptomatology. In J. T. E. Richardson (Ed.), *Cognition and the menstrual cycle* (pp. 1–38). New York, NY: Springer New York.

Rizwan, S., Manning, J. T., & Brabin, B. J. (2007). Maternal smoking during pregnancy and possible effects of in utero testosterone: evidence from the 2D:4D finger length ratio. *Early Human Development*, *83*(2), 87–90.

Robertson, C. V., Immink, M. A., & Marino, F. E. (2016). Exogenous cortisol administration; effects on risk taking behavior, exercise performance, and physiological and neurophysiological responses. *Frontiers in Physiology*, *7*(640), 1–14.

Ronay, R., & Hippel, W. v. (2010). The presence of an attractive woman elevates testosterone and physical risk taking in young men. *Social Psychological and Personality Science*, *1*(1), 57–64.

Rose, R. M., Kreuz, L. E., Holaday, J. W., Sulak, K. J., & Johnson, C. E. (1972). Diurnal variation of plasma testosterone and cortisol. *Journal of Endocrinology*, *54*(1), 177–178.

Rosenthal, R. (1979). The file drawer problem and tolerance for null results. *Psychological Bulletin, 86*(3), 638–641.

Rowe, P. H., Lincoln, G. A., Racey, P. A., Lehane, J., Stephenson, M. J., Shenton, J. C., et al. (1974). Temporal variations of testosterone levels in the peripheral blood plasma of men. *Journal of Endocrinology, 61*(1), 63–73.

Saad, G., & Stenstrom, E. (2012). Calories, beauty, and ovulation: the effects of the menstrual cycle on food and appearance-related consumption. *Journal of Consumer Psychology, 22*(1), 102–113.

Saad, G., & Vongas, J. G. (2009). The effect of conspicuous consumption on men's testosterone levels. *Organizational Behavior and Human Decision Processes, 110*(2), 80–92.

Salimetrics (2017). Saliva collection and handling advice. Retrieved from:http://www.salimetrics.com/documents/Saliva_Collection_Handbook.pdf.

Salimetrics (2018). Maintaining analyte Integrity. Retrieved from:https://salimetrics.com/saliva-collection-handbook/#saliva-sample-integrity (Accessed 26 September 2018).

Sapienza, P., Zingales, L., & Maestripieri, D. (2009). Gender differences in financial risk aversion and career choices are affected by testosterone. *Proceedings of the National Academy of Sciences, 106*(36), 15268–15273.

Sapolsky, R. M., Romero, L. M., & Munck, A. U. (2000). How do glucocorticoids influence stress responses? Integrating permissive, suppressive, stimulatory, and preparative actions. *Endocrine Reviews, 21*(1), 55–89.

Sarnyai, Z., McKittrick, C. R., McEwen, B. S., & Kreek, M. J. (1998). Selective regulation of dopamine transporter binding in the shell of the nucleus accumbens by adrenalectomy and corticosterone-replacement. *Synapse, 30*(3), 334–337.

Schoofs, D., Wolf, O. T., & Smeets, T. (2009). Cold pressor stress impairs performance on working memory tasks requiring executive functions in healthy young men. *Behavioral Neuroscience, 123*(5), 1066–1075.

Schultheiss, O. C., Wirth, M. M., & Stanton, S. J. (2004). Effects of affiliation and power motivation arousal on salivary progesterone and testosterone. *Hormones and Behavior, 46*(5), 592–599.

Selye, H. (1936). A syndrome produced by diverse nocuous agents. *Nature, 138*(3479), 32.

Smith, L. M., Cloak, C. C., Poland, R. E., Torday, J., & Ross, M. G. (2003). Prenatal nicotine increases testosterone levels in the fetus and female offspring. *Nicotine & Tobacco Research, 5*(3), 369–374.

Stalder, T., Steudte, S., Miller, R., Skoluda, N., Dettenborn, L., & Kirschbaum, C. (2012). Intraindividual stability of hair cortisol concentrations. *Psychoneuroendocrinology, 37*(5), 602–610.

Stanton, S. J. (2017). The role of testosterone and estrogen in consumer behavior and social & economic decision making: a review. *Hormones and Behavior, 92*, 155–163. Suppl. C.

Stanton, S. J., Liening, S. H., & Schultheiss, O. C. (2011). Testosterone is positively associated with risk taking in the Iowa Gambling Task. *Hormones and Behavior, 59*(2), 252–256.

Stanton, S. J., Mullette-Gillman, O. D. A., McLaurin, R. E., Kuhn, C. M., LaBar, K. S., Platt, M. L., et al. (2011). Low- and high-testosterone individuals exhibit decreased aversion to economic risk. *Psychological Science, 22*(4), 447–453.

Staufenbiel, S. M., Penninx, B. W. J. H., Spijker, A. T., Elzinga, B. M., & van Rossum, E. F. C. (2013). Hair cortisol, stress exposure, and mental health in humans: a systematic review. *Psychoneuroendocrinology, 38*(8), 1220–1235.

Stenstrom, E., Saad, G., Nepomuceno, M. V., & Mendenhall, Z. (2011). Testosterone and domain-specific risk: digit ratios (2D:4D and rel2) as predictors of recreational, financial, and social risk-taking behaviors. *Personality and Individual Differences, 51*(4), 412–416.

Stirrat, M., & Perrett, D. I. (2010). Valid facial cues to cooperation and trust: male facial width and trustworthiness. *Psychological Science, 21*(3), 349–354.

Svartberg, J., Jorde, R., Sundsfjord, J., Bønaa, K. H., & Barrett-Connor, E. (2003). Seasonal variation of testosterone and waist to hip ratio in men: the Tromsø study. *The Journal of Clinical Endocrinology & Metabolism, 88*(7), 3099–3104.

Svartberg, J., Midtby, M., Bonaa, K., Sundsfjord, J., Joakimsen, R., & Jorde, R. (2003). The associations of age, lifestyle factors and chronic disease with testosterone in men: the Tromso Study. *European Journal of Endocrinology, 149*(2), 145–152.

Tuiten, A., Van Honk, J., Koppeschaar, H., Bernaards, C., Thijssen, J., & Verbaten, R. (2000). Time course of effects of testosterone administration on sexual arousal in women. *Archives of General Psychiatry, 57*(2), 149–153.

Turanovic, J. J., Pratt, T. C., & Piquero, A. R. (2017). Exposure to fetal testosterone, aggression, and violent behavior: a meta-analysis of the 2D:4D digit ratio. *Aggression and Violent Behavior, 33*, 51–61.

Unger, J. M., Rauch, A., Weis, S. E., & Frese, M. (2015). Biology (prenatal testosterone), psychology (achievement need) and entrepreneurial impact. *Journal of Business Venturing Insights, 4*, 1–5.

van den Bos, R., Harteveld, M., & Stoop, H. (2009). Stress and decision-making in humans: performance is related to cortisol reactivity, albeit differently in men and women. *Psychoneuroendocrinology, 34*(10), 1449–1458.

Van Den Bos, W., Golka, P., Effelsberg, D., & McClure, S. (2013). Pyrrhic victories: the need for social status drives costly competitive behavior. *Frontiers in Neuroscience, 7*(189), 1–11.

van Honk, J., Peper, J. S., & Schutter, D. J. L. G. (2005). Testosterone reduces unconscious fear but not consciously experienced anxiety: implications for the disorders of fear and anxiety. *Biological Psychiatry, 58*(3), 218–225.

van Honk, J., Schutter, D. J. L. G., Hermans, E. J., & Putman, P. (2003). Low cortisol levels and the balance between punishment sensitivity and reward dependency. *Neuroreport, 14*(15), 1993–1996.

van Os, J., & Selten, J. P. (1998). Prenatal exposure to maternal stress and subsequent schizophrenia. The May 1940 invasion of The Netherlands. *The British Journal of Psychiatry, 172*(4), 324–326.

Voracek, M. (2009). Comparative study of digit ratios (2D:4D and other) and novel measures of relative finger length: testing magnitude and consistency of sex differences across samples. *Perceptual and Motor Skills, 108*(1), 83–93.

Voracek, M., Manning, J. T., & Dressler, S. G. (2007). Repeatability and interobserver error of digit ratio (2D:4D) measurements made by experts. *American Journal of Human Biology, 19*(1), 142–146.

Welker, K. M., Bird, B. M., & Arnocky, S. (2016). Commentary: facial width-to-height ratio (fWHR) is not associated with adolescent testosterone levels. *Frontiers in Psychology, 7*(1745), 1–3.

Weller, J. A., Buchanan, T. W., Shackleford, C., Morganstern, A., Hartman, J. J., Yuska, J., et al. (2014). Diurnal cortisol rhythm is associated with increased risky decision making in older adults. *Psychology and Aging, 29*(2), 271–283.

Whitehead, S. A., & Miell, J. (2012). *Clinical endocrinology*. Banbury: Scion.

Whitehouse, A. J. O., Gilani, S. Z., Shafait, F., Mian, A., Tan, D. W., Maybery, M. T., et al. (2015). Prenatal testosterone exposure is related to sexually dimorphic facial morphology in adulthood. *Proceedings of the Royal Society B: Biological Sciences, 282*(1816), 1–9.

Wibral, M., Dohmen, T., Klingmüller, D., Weber, B., & Falk, A. (2012). Testosterone administration reduces lying in men. *PLoS ONE*, *7*(10).

Wingfield, J. C. (2017). The challenge hypothesis: where it began and relevance to humans. *Hormones and Behavior*, *92*, 9–12. Suppl. C.

Wingfield, J. C., Hegner, R. E., Dufty, A. M., Jr., & Ball, G. F. (1990). The "challenge hypothesis": theoretical implications for patterns of testosterone secretion, mating systems, and breeding strategies. *The American Naturalist*, *136*(6), 829–846.

Wolf, O. T., & Kirschbaum, C. (2002). Endogenous estradiol and testosterone levels are associated with cognitive performance in older women and men. *Hormones and Behavior*, *41*(3), 259–266.

Wong, E. M., Ormiston, M. E., & Haselhuhn, M. P. (2011). A face only an investor could love: CEOs' facial structure predicts their firms' financial performance. *Psychological Science*, *22*(12), 1478–1483.

Wood, W., Kressel, L., Joshi, P. D., & Louie, B. (2014). Meta-analysis of menstrual cycle effects on women's mate preferences. *Emotion Review*, *6*(3), 229–249.

World Health Organization (2009). *Handbook of good laboratory practice (GLP)* (2nd ed.). Geneva, Switzerland: World Health Organization.

Wu, Y., Eisenegger, C., Sivanathan, N., Crockett, M. J., & Clark, L. (2017). The role of social status and testosterone in human conspicuous consumption. *Scientific Reports*, *7*(1), 11803.

Wüst, S., Federenko, I., Hellhammer, D. H., & Kirschbaum, C. (2000). Genetic factors, perceived chronic stress, and the free cortisol response to awakening. *Psychoneuroendocrinology*, *25*(7), 707–720.

Xie, Z., Page, L., & Hardy, B. (2017). Investigating gender differences under time pressure in financial risk taking. *Frontiers in Behavioral Neuroscience*, *11*, 246.

Zak, P. J., Kurzban, R., Ahmadi, S., Swerdloff, R. S., Park, J., Efremidze, L., et al. (2009). Testosterone administration decreases generosity in the ultimatum game. *PLoS ONE*, *4*(12).

Zethraeus, N., Kocoska-Maras, L., Ellingsen, T., von Schoultz, B., Hirschberg, A. L., & Johannesson, M. (2009). A randomized trial of the effect of estrogen and testosterone on economic behavior. *Proceedings of the National Academy of Sciences*, *106*(16), 6535–6538.

Zilioli, S., Sell, A. N., Stirrat, M., Jagore, J., Vickerman, W., & Watson, N. V. (2015). Face of a fighter: bizygomatic width as a cue of formidability. *Aggressive Behavior*, *41*(4), 322–330.

Chapter 6

An Interoceptive Walk Down Wall Street

Anthony Newell and Lionel Page
Queensland University of Technology, Brisbane, QLD, Australia

INTRODUCTION

> *Two-thirds of professionally managed funds are regularly outperformed by a broad capitalization-weighted index fund with equivalent risk, and those that do appear to produce excess returns in one period are not likely to do so in the next. The record of professionals does not suggest that sufficient predictability exists in the stock market to produce exploitable arbitrage opportunities.*
>
> (Malkiel, 2007, 19)

Burton Malkiel's quote is in line with much of the historical and contemporary academic thinking on the subject of stockmarket returns. Unsurprisingly, many financial professionals do not hold this view. They, sometimes literally, bet the house on their belief that they can beat the market, and beat it resoundingly. It is clear, however, that some traders do better and stay in their jobs longer than others. The lore of the financial industry often puts this success down to "gut feelings". But how does one identify or even measure these instincts? One candidate is interoceptive ability, which is the conscious or unconscious awareness of internal bodily states. In the field of neurophysiology, interoceptive ability is often proxied by the tested ability to count one's heartbeats without finding a pulse with a finger, and is positively correlated with memory, intensity of emotion, empathy, and decision making (Critchley & Harrison, 2013). It is the decision making aspect of interoception that has piqued the interest of behavioral economists and their findings suggest that individuals with increased interoceptive sensitivity make better financial decisions under risk.

Whether investing in the stockmarket, asking for another card in blackjack, or placing $20 each way on Ocean Magic in race number nine at Flemington, we are making risky decisions. In pure economic terms, we risk an amount of money on a prospect with the hope that we will receive a larger amount of money in return. Whether we take the available bet or not will depend on our current wealth, the possible return, our tolerance for risk, and our

Biophysical Measurement in Experimental Social Science Research. https://doi.org/10.1016/B978-0-12-813092-6.00006-X

assessment of our chances of success. To assess the situation and find the best option, we may thoroughly investigate the company we are going to invest in, try to count the cards on the blackjack table, or bury ourselves in the racing form guide to guide our decision making. We may also use our instincts or gut feelings—at least in part—to choose the most appropriate course of action. Chapter 5 of this book (Butler & Cheung, 2018) provides a general overview of the study of the psychological and biophysical dimensions of behavior in the case of experimental asset markets.

Although gut feelings are typically thought of as a myth or flight of fancy, like a fabled "sixth sense", there is strong evidence from the fields of psychology and neurophysiology supporting their role in the decision making process. Gut feelings are closely associated with the concept of interoception. Interoception was proposed separately in theories of emotions by William James (1894) and Carl Lang (1885), who both contended that emotions are triggered by a physical reaction in the autonomic nervous system as a result of an external stimulus. For example, if someone says something unpleasant, this may increase our breathing rate, leading to an increase in heart rate and blood pressure. These changes in our physiological state in turn cause an emotion, such as anger. It is not the emotion that causes the changes in physiological state, which is the more conventional view of emotion as originally proposed by Cannon (1927). Schachter and Singer (1962) have found empirically that if physiological change by itself is not enough to trigger an emotion, it does significantly increase the strength of the emotion already being felt. While the James-Lang theory stipulates that these changes in bodily state should be perceived consciously in order to generate emotion, later work by Schachter and Singer (1962) and Damasio, Everitt, and Bishop (1996) suggest that they may also be perceived unconsciously.

Interoception has been formally defined in the literature as the mental ability to detect changes in the body's supportive, exchange and regulatory systems, either consciously or unconsciously (Dunn et al., 2010). It is based on the premise that our mental and psychological functions are inextricably linked to physiological factors, in such a way that the brain and the body interact, effect, and affect in a reciprocal fashion (Cameron, 2001). When we see a threatening object, such as a wild dog, our cognitive processes are bypassed and a fight/flight response is triggered. Our autonomic nervous system immediately kicks into action, increasing heart rate, blood pressure, and breathing, and releasing stress hormones. Fear is an extreme example, but this type of autonomic activity is continuously happening in our bodies. Physiological responses appropriate to encountered external stimuli can be learned unconsciously, in the classical conditioning sense, in a wide range of situations that we encounter in our day-to-day lives (Cameron, 2001).

In the sections below we first discuss how the role of interoception in decision making fits within the theories of behavior from economics and psychology, prefacing this discussion with a broad sketch of how behavioral theories in these disciplines have evolved over the course of the past century. We then explore in more detail the notion of interoception and describe how it is typically measured experimentally. Finally, we walk through an example of a study using interoception to investigate financial traders' ability to make good decisions.

FROM COLD TO WARM RATIONALITY

A Brief History of the Economic Study of Behavior

Economics is arguably one of the most formal and unified disciplines of the behavioral sciences (Gintis, 2007). When compared to psychology or sociology, economics is characterized by a relatively unified conceptual framework based on shared assumptions upon which formal models are built. The comparative formalism of the economic approach to understanding human behavior sets it apart from other behavioral disciplines. From the beginning of the 20th century, economics expelled most of psychology from its core theories to develop a study of economic choice based instead on the concept of "rational" decision makers (Bruni & Sugden, 2007).

This idea to abstract from all but the cold, calculating part of our brains was very much in tune with the positivist argument that science should only focus on what is observable (Hahn, Neurath, & Carnap, 1929). The human psyche was not observable, arguably, and should therefore be left outside of the realm of economics. Economists would just look at people's choices. The empirical study of what drives people's preferences was left to other disciplines, such as psychology. Economists instead opted to make minimal behavioral assumptions considered so reasonable that they could be called axioms (i.e., evidently true). Specifically, economists "only" assumed that people have preferences over goods (i.e., they know what they want) and that these preferences are consistent in some mathematically logical ways (i.e., not mutually contradictory).

From such a seemingly defensible starting point, formal mathematical methods could be used to determine what would be the best decisions for an agent given his preferences. Whether this approach was normative (describing what agents should do) or positive (describing what agents actually do) was not always clear. The models pointed to the best possible decisions that could be made by their modeled agents, so surely they were normative in the sense that deviating from these models' predictions would be worse in the sense implied by the models themselves. But models also became seen by some as ways of describing actual behavior. One practical reason for this shift is that modeling behavior in such a way was the only way economists knew of to investigate behavior and ultimately make recommendations about how choices or the settings in which those choices are made could be improved.

Facing the philosophical conundrum as to whether their behavioral models were positive or nominative, or possibly both, many economists took a pragmatic approach, suggesting that models have merit by existing per se, because some (even imperfect) model is better than no model. Surely human behavior was not as "perfect" as modeled, but as long as deviations were minor, models arguably offered a good approximation. At the same time, other economists adopted a more explicitly positivistic approach, claiming that the models that had been developed were based on reasonable principles of rationality that individuals were likely to respect. According to this view, with their models economists were describing the actual behavior of decision makers (Stigler & Becker, 1977).

To those outside of economics, the decision maker described by economics textbooks was strange and strikingly different from the person known to them through common experience. The economic decision maker knew what he wanted, did not doubt these preferences, was able to plan well ahead to reach his goals, could interpret complex incoming signals accurately to form accurate beliefs about his environment, and was able to engage in complex computations to arrive at the optimal solutions to his problems. This person was the perfect image of cold so-called "rationality".

In the second part of the 20th century, a growing amount of work by psychologists and experimental economists pointed to a range of problems with interpreting this model of human behavior as a description of what people actually do. Placed in controlled behavioral experiments, real humans did not act as predicted. They often misinterpreted noisy signals leading to distorted beliefs, and they failed to stick to their plans, leading to inconsistent choices over time. More worryingly, it seemed like even one of the most basic principles of existing economic models, namely the coherence and consistency of preferences, was not respected by experimental subjects (Kahneman, 2011).

These explorations, led by psychologists such as Kahneman and Tversky, eventually formed the foundations of the behavioral revolution in economics. A huge amount of empirical evidence was accumulated that painted a radically different picture of humans as imperfect decision makers. While *homo economicus* was the image of a perfect rational decision maker, *homo behavioralis* was—by the standards of *homo economicus*—a seriously impaired one (Binmore, 1994). His preferences were often incoherent, or just made up on the fly; his beliefs were distorted in many systematic ways; and his decision processes were slow and prone to error. However, paradoxically, this part of the behavioral revolution had retained something from the old economics textbooks. While it had rejected the *homo economicus* model as a positive theory describing how people actually make decisions, it still kept it as a normative theory of how people should behave if they want to make good decisions. In this behavioral approach, deviations from the standard model are caused by "biases" that lead people to make costly mistakes. The ability of humans to reason (so-called "System 2 thinking") is seen in this view as a tool we can use to correct mistakes to which our intuition would otherwise lead us (via "System 1 thinking") (Kahneman, 2003).

In this sense, at the heart of the new behavioral approach still stands the traditional figure of cold rationality as an ideal, notwithstanding the admission that it is an ideal that is not reached by real humans. Decision makers are seen as inherently flawed, and in need of supporting tools to help make better decisions.

The "heuristics and biases" approach of Kahneman and Tversky was not the only approach in psychology to advance a radically different view of human decision making from that assumed by conventional economic models. Gerd Gigerenzer argued that heuristics—psychological rules of thumb that humans use in their everyday lives (instead of the complex computations assumed by the *homo economicus* model)—make us smarter rather than dumber (Gigerenzer et al., 1999). In this view, what were seen as shortcomings in the Kahneman and Tversky framework were instead cognitive shortcuts that allow us to find quick and sufficient solutions to many of the complex situations we face every day.

At the heart of Gigerenzer's view is the idea that the problems we face and must solve in the real world are incredibly complex. So complex are they, runs the argument, that it is de facto out of bounds for a person of any reasonable computational abilities to arrive at a perfectly optimal solution within the limited time frame that is typically available to real human decision makers. In this light, the idea that decision makers could find the "optimal solution" is naïve. Many problems that economic decision makers face are demonstrably "computationally hard". The computational time required to solve these problems quickly becomes very large as the size of the problem increases. Problems as mundane as selecting the best basket of goods in a supermarket for a given budget limit can be shown to be computationally hard in this sense. While it may be easy to find a "good enough" solution, finding the optimal solution to such a problem can require enormous computational effort.

This approach pointed to a different lens through which humans' decision making techniques should be viewed. Rather than elevating the picture of a perfect Spock-like decision maker as a conceptual ideal, the behavioral scientist could try to understand how decision makers' traits helped them cope with a highly complex world. As our traits are the outcome of eons of evolution, humans cannot be entirely flawed as decision makers. Rather than hindering our ability to make good decisions, it is arguably more likely that the seemingly "irrational" features of our decision making processes represent adaptive solutions to the problems we have faced for generations in the real world.

A key aspect of this approach was its defense of aspects of human psychology that do not fit with the model of cold rationality. Gigerenzer contended that things such as emotions, intuitions, and gut feelings should be appraised positively for the role they play in human decision making. By providing readymade answers (using heuristics rather than perfect, cold calculations) in complex situations, our "irrational" side can help humans reach ecological rationality: making good decisions in the context of the real world.

The Role of Emotion

Emotions are generally considered to be cognitive or psychological states, brought about by experiential, behavioral, and/or visceral activity triggered by the stimulus of an object or event (Bechara & Damasio, 2005; Critchley & Harrison, 2013). The triggering event or stimulus may occur in the present, may have occurred in the past and be brought back in focus by a thought or memory, or may be anticipated to happen in the future. Emotions are useful to an organism in identifying the relevance of a stimulus and hence informing its behavior (Glimcher & Fehr, 2013). If stimuli cause unpleasant emotions then we will seek to remove ourselves from those stimuli, whereas the triggering of pleasant emotions by stimuli will cause us to seek them out.

Emotions can play a role in decision making through incidental or direct influence. In the case of incidental influence, the emotion has nothing to do with the actual decision being made, but it may nevertheless influence the decision making process in some way. In the case of direct influence, the need to make a decision invokes the emotion, which in turn may impact choice (Glimcher & Fehr, 2013).

The very influential research in neuroscience produced by Antonio Damasio has given further weight to such a view. He has shown that cold, i.e., emotion-free rationality, is not the optimal approach to take if one wishes to make good decisions. Instead, emotions are critical in decision making (Damasio, 1994). A huge amount of information about the surrounding world is processed automatically by the brain, producing positive and negative values as output in service our decision making. These internal signals are not brought to the fore of consciousness in many situations. Evidence suggests that they are however essential in enabling us to make even the simplest decisions. They give us a *warm* rationality.

At the heart of Bechara and Damasio (2005)'s neural theory of economic decision making is the somatic marker hypothesis. "Somatic marker" means "bodily signal", and this hypothesis provides useful scaffolding in understanding the various elements of our neurobiological system and how they inform economic decision making. According to this hypothesis, conscious awareness of a situation is neither a necessary nor a sufficient requirement for making advantageous economic decisions; in fact, only the emotional signaling informed by visceral or gut reactions to a given situation is required to make the most advantageous decision in that situation.

By providing a broad foundation for understanding the mind/body interaction, the somatic marker hypothesis paves the way for a possible role in decision making for interoception. The visceral sensations that inform our emotional state may be consciously perceived and interpreted, for example as pain or as nausea; they also may be unconsciously perceived in ways that influence our current emotions and decision making processes (Critchley & Harrison, 2013). The "feeling states" (emotions) arising from our visceral sensations may thereby play a role in influencing our decisions (Seth, 2013). These feeling states may be conscious or unconscious, with unconscious perception alone being enough to allow emotions to aid decision making (Bechara & Damasio, 2005).

Interoception encompasses both the unconscious perception of these feeling states and the conscious or unconscious perception of the intuition or "gut feeling" that evolves from them. Assuming interoceptive ability may differ across people, potentially explaining some of the variation in decision outcomes across individuals, a number of behavioral economic experiments have investigated a possible connection between interoceptive ability and decision making.

The Iowa gambling task (IGT) (Bechara, Damasio, Damasio, & Anderson, 1994) was developed to simulate real-life economic decision making through the incorporation of uncertainty of probability and uncertainty of economic reward and punishment into the decision making task. In the IGT, subjects are presented with four decks of cards turned face down, indistinguishable in attributes of size and shape. Players are asked to choose one of the decks of cards and turn over its top card. The front of each card tells the player how much money they have won or lost. Players are aware that their task is to accumulate as much money as possible and that they are free to switch between decks at any time. The players continue to turn over cards and their wins and losses are tallied. The players are not aware in advance of how many selections they are able to make, but usually they are allowed between 80 and 100 selections. The expected value of each of the four decks of cards will be dependent on the specific implementation of the IGT, but for a given experimental session, two decks have a high probability of a large gain but also a high probability of a large loss (and overall, choosing from only these two decks produce an expected net loss) and two decks have a high probability of a small loss or a small gain (and overall, choosing from only these two decks produce an expected net gain).

Werner, Jung, Duschek, and Schandry (2009) find that individuals with better interoception, measured as cardiac perception (described in more detail below), achieve a more advantageous outcome in the Iowa gambling task (IGT). In their study, participants with better interoception tended to choose the less risky decks of cards, and in doing so made more money. Their findings suggest that those who listen to their gut feelings may be better at assessing risks. In this experiment, the analysis controlled for anxiety, impulsiveness, sensation seeking, and the so-called Big Five personality traits of openness to experience, conscientiousness, extraversion, agreeableness, and neuroticism (Digman, 1990). However, as we only see correlation rather than causality in the results, it cannot be said that other factors, such as risk preference, may not also play a part.

Also using the IGT in the lab, Crone, Somsen, Beek, and Van Der Molen (2004) investigate how levels of heart rate and skin conductance change in high, moderate, and low performers in the task. Based on the somatic marker hypothesis, they predict that heart rate will slow and skin conductance will increase prior to making a disadvantageous decision. Both heart rate and skin conductance are considered somatic markers that should unconsciously inform the decision maker that the path he is about to go down is a bad idea, thereby encouraging him to choose a different path. The authors further suggest that this slowing heart rate and increase in skin conductance will be greater in those who perform better in the task overall. They use a modified version of the IGT in which participants, in each of 100 rounds, were asked to assist in feeding a donkey by repeatedly choosing one of four doors. Behind each door was a positive or negative quantity of apples. In keeping with the spirit of the IGT, two of the doors had a high variance with a negative average return, and two of the doors had a low variance with a positive average return. At the conclusion of the trial the subjects were divided into three groups: high performers, moderate performers, and poor performers, with performance gauged based on the number of apples collected for the donkey. Participants' levels of heart rate and skin conductance for advantageous and disadvantageous choices were compared across the three groups. The study found, that, as per the hypothesis, those who performed poorly showed no difference in either heart rate or skin conductance before making their choices, regardless of the quality of the choice. Conversely, those in the moderate and high performing groups displayed a slowed heart rate and increased skin conductance before making a poor choice. The authors use these observations to conclude that poor decision making in the poor performers was caused by a failure of autonomic functions to warn them that they were about to make a poor decision. While those in the moderate and high groups learned to make advantageous choices based on information from their autonomic nervous system.

Based on theories of emotion and decision making put forth by Damasio et al. (1996), Schachter and Singer (1962), and Lange and James (1922), Sokol-Hessner, Hartley, Hamilton, and Phelps (2015) conducted an experiment to test the hypothesis that heightened interoception predicts greater behavioral loss aversion. In this study, 25 individuals were asked to perform a cardiac perception task to measure their level of interoceptive ability. Participants then made 180 risky decisions in a lottery choice game. In 150 cases, the choices consisted of a gamble to win or lose with 50% probability of each outcome, or a certain null outcome. Specifically, subjects could choose lottery one with a 50% chance of winning $5 and a 50% chance of losing $3.50, or they could choose neither to win nor to lose anything at all. The remaining 30 choices tasks did not invoke the loss domain, offering instead only the choice to gamble and possibly win something, or the choice to receive something for sure. Specifically, in these 30 cases, subjects could choose a lottery with a 50% chance to win $5 and a 50% chance to win $0, or they could choose to receive $2.50 for certain. The overall finding of this study was that there is a correlation between interoceptive ability and loss aversion, but no correlation between interoceptive ability and either risk attitudes or choice consistency. In reviewing their findings, Sokol-Hessner et al. (2015) state that "individuals who show heightened interoception report greater subjective intensity of emotional feeling."

In an experiment on learning and unconscious perception, Katkin, Wiens, and Ohman (2001) hypothesize that individuals with good interoception will have an increased ability to predict electric shocks. Subjects were conditioned by pairing an electric shock and a backward masked picture of a snake or a spider. Backward masking is a process by which a picture is displayed for a very short amount, 10 milliseconds in this instance, which is too quick for the human brain to consciously perceive. They base their approach on the idea that this type of conditioning will cause the subjects to have a fear response when the picture is unconsciously perceived, and that those with better sensitivity to this subconscious fear response (i.e., heightened interoception) will then be able to better predict the electric shock that is to follow. The authors indeed found that subjects with good interoception, as measured by a heart rate detection task, were better at predicting the electric shocks, and they conclude that gut feelings and instincts may be based on visceral sensitivity. Although this experiment does not demonstrate causality, it does show a clear set of links between interoception, unconscious learning, and external stimuli.

DEFINITIONS AND MEASURES OF INTEROCEPTION

The physiology of interoception can best be understood in terms of the physiology of the nervous system. The summary that follows is based on modern scientific models of the nervous system, such as those presented in Bernstein, Penner, Clarke-Stewart, and Roy (2006). The human nervous system comprises the central nervous system (CNS) and the peripheral nervous system (PNS). The CNS is made up of the brain and the spinal cord. The spinal cord receives messages from the senses and sends them to the brain, which processes these messages and cascades them into thoughts, feelings, and actions. The spinal cord is also responsible for involuntary actions such as contracting the muscles required to pull your hand away from a hot flame after it has been burned. Involuntary actions such as these take place without involvement from the brain.

The PNS is comprised of the somatic nervous system and the autonomic nervous system. The somatic nervous system is responsible for communication back and forth between the senses, the muscles, and the CNS, and is ultimately responsible for biomechanical muscle movement. The autonomic nervous system, on the other hand, relays information to the major organs and is responsible for operations such as heart rate, blood pressure, and breathing. The information required to accomplish these functions is passed between these organs and the brain and occurs in a largely unconscious fashion.

Interoception is the ability to perceive (consciously or subconsciously) changes in the body's organs that are orchestrated by the autonomic nervous system. This system takes sensory input into the brain, for example in response to an external stimulus to the senses, and then implements changes to organs based upon that input. This interoceptive information is sent to the various brain structures responsible for interpreting this information through nerve signals and chemicals in the blood (Critchley & Harrison, 2013).

It is not exactly clear which areas of the brain process interoceptive signals, but neuroimaging studies suggest that the orbitofrontal cortex plays a key role in integrating signals from the viscera with the information processed in other brain regions (Bechara, Damasio, & Damasio, 2000), and the insular cortex (or insula) appears to aid in the perception of interoceptive signals and in converting them into emotions and feelings (Critchley & Harrison, 2013). The orbitofrontal cortex has also been linked to money, reward value, expected reward value, emotional processing, and decision making (Kringelbach, 2005). A number of studies on patients with damage to the orbitofrontal cortex have shown that such patients tend to make suboptimal decisions, and this has led to the hypothesis that interoception, emotions, and decision making are closely linked (Bechara et al., 2000; Hornak et al., 2003; Rolls, Hornak, Wade, & McGrath, 1994). The reader may find Fig. 2 of Chapter 8 in this book helpful to visualize where these cortices are located within the brain.

Given the possible role of interoceptive ability in decision making, researchers working in behavioral science have naturally tried to measure it. Garfinkel, Seth, Barrett, Suzuki, and Critchley (2015) proposed measuring individuals' interoceptive accuracy by their ability to objectively quantify some component of their autonomic nervous system. Measuring interoceptive accuracy in this way requires the identification of an autonomic function that is objectively quantifiable, and two components of the autonomic nervous system clearly meet this criterion: heartbeat and blood pressure. Heartbeat detection has been used as a proxy for interoception in numerous studies. The ability to detect one's heartbeat has also been found to correlate with the ability to detect other autonomic activity (Barrett, Quigley, Bliss-Moreau, & Aronson, 2004; Harver, Katkin, & Bloch, 1993; Whitehead & Drescher, 1980).

Due to its efficacy and ease of measurement, heartbeat detection accuracy tends to be the most common form of introspective measurement. This measurement has been approached using two forms of data capture: heart rate tracking and heartbeat discrimination. In a heart rate tracking task, subjects must guess the number of beats their heart makes over a given period of time. The period of time used is usually between 25 and 60 seconds, with the task repeated three to six times.

In a heartbeat discrimination task, participants must determine whether audible tones presented to them are synchronized with their heartbeat, with the experimenter controlling whether the tones in fact are synchronized or are instead played with a delay after the subject's heartbeat. Limits on the precision of human perception mean that delays in playing the tone of less than 200 milliseconds after the heartbeat go unnoticed, meaning that such tones are still perceived as synchronized (Sokol-Hessner et al., 2015). For this reason, the delay chosen by experimenters is usually between 300 milliseconds (Critchley, Wiens, Rotshtein, Ohman, & Dolan, 2004; Kandasamy et al., 2016) and 500 milliseconds (Barrett et al., 2004; Sokol-Hessner et al., 2015). The number of trials undertaken by subjects varies in the literature; Sokol-Hessner et al. (2015) used 25 trials each of synchronized and nonsynchronized tones, while Barrett et al. (2004) used 50 of each.

The two different measurement approaches differ in the type of mental processing required of subjects to complete the task. Heart rate tracking only requires the processing of internal information (i.e., counting beats), while heartbeat discrimination requires internal and external processing (i.e., listening to the external tone and perceiving beats). Accuracy seems to be greater with heart rate tracking, which may be due to this additional complexity of heartbeat discrimination (Garfinkel et al., 2015; Kandasamy et al., 2016; Knoll & Hodapp, 1992; Schulz, Lass-Hennemann, Sütterlin, Schächinger, & Vögele, 2013).

INTEROCEPTIVE ABILITY AND FINANCIAL PROFESSIONALS

We now describe the real-world implications of interoception by walking through a recent investigation by Kandasamy et al. (2016) of how traders in the financial markets benefit from their interoceptive ability.

Is it possible to beat the market?

Eugene Fama's efficient market hypothesis (EMH) (Fama, 1970) is a foundation of financial theory as it relates to making money on the financial markets. EMH states that, in the long term, it is not possible to "beat the market". That is, it is not possible for a single trader to make a return greater than the return of the market as a whole over an extended period. One year you may make more than the market, and in another you may make less, but over the longer term EMH contends that you will never beat it. To put it another way, it is not possible to earn above average returns without taking above average risks (Malkiel, 2003). While this may be profitable in the short term, in the long run, the increased risk would also lead to above average losses, which would equate to earning an overall return no better than the market.

Naturally, financial professionals who entered the game with the desire to make a lot of money want to believe that the market can be beaten. Two of the most common methods of trying to "beat the market" are known as technical analysis and fundamental analysis. Traders who undertake technical analysis use trends in historic stock price movements in an attempt to determine what the price of an asset will do next. Many technical analysts spend hours scrutinizing price graphs to identify technical indicators such as the "Moving average rule", and trend patterns such as "trading-range break", also known as "resistance" and "support" (Brock, Lakonishok, & LeBaron, 1992), and "the head and shoulders pattern" (Savin, Weller, & Zvingelis, 2006).

On the other hand, the fundamental analyst seeks reward through identifying financial instruments whose market prices are above or below where they should be. Fundamental analysts may look at the financial statements of a company in the context of fiscal policy and the wider macroeconomic setting, or they may look at the morning financial news to interpret how it may affect particular asset prices. One fundamental analysis technique that is commonly used is identifying stocks with a low price-earnings (PE) ratio. A PE ratio is simply the ratio of the company's current stock price to its earnings per share (EPS), where EPS is calculated as the company's net income divided by the number of outstanding shares. A lower PE ratio suggests a higher chance of earning a better-than-average return, as the investor will in theory recover an initial investment in a shorter-than-average amount of time.

According to the EMH, neither fundamental nor technical analysis should be useful in obtaining a better than average risk-adjusted return. This theoretical inability to beat the market is based on the idea that asset prices fully reflect all available information about the value of the assets in question, which implies that the changes in an asset's price from day to day are completely random in nature, rather than reflective of prior or current information that may give one trader an advantage over another.

Notwithstanding the debate around how to measure market efficiency, the EMH is generally held to be a reasonable theory of market behavior, and while anomalies have been identified, they have generally been explained as aberrations rather than indicative of a substantive flaw in the hypothesis. If this is true, then interoceptive ability should play no role in a trader's ability to derive profit above that of the market, nor in their longevity as a trader, because all information that would impact the value of an asset is already incorporated into its price. If this is the case, the results of the following study are striking.

Interoception on Wall Street

Kandasamy et al. (2016) investigate how interoceptive ability correlates with the professional ability of a group of London futures market traders. Futures are derivative contracts which have no inherent value themselves but derive their value from the expected future value of an underlying asset. The assets underlying futures contracts range from precious metals to stock indices to agricultural products. Futures may be used as a hedge for a product one wishes to buy or sell in the future, or they may be used to speculate. When used as tools of speculation, traders may use both fundamental and technical analysis in an attempt to make money.

Speculation is the purpose for which the 18 male traders in Kandasamy et al. (2016) trade futures, typically holding a given futures contract for only a few seconds to a few hours, and trading contracts at very high frequency. These traders are compensated based entirely on a percentage of the profit made on their trades. This type of trading requires very quick processing of a lot of information coming in from various sources, and tends to speedily weed out those traders who underperform. This was especially true at the time of the study, when the European sovereign debt crisis was coming to a close (late 2009 until 2012). During this crisis, a number of European countries, including Greece, Portugal, Ireland, and Spain, were unable to pay the large amount of debt they had incurred, requiring support from the European Central Bank and the International Monetary Fund. One consequence of this was that these countries were unable to support their sovereign financial institutions, many of which were in financial difficulties due to the global financial crisis (GFC). As such, there was a high level of market volatility, with many traders unable to fall back on their knowledge of market norms to inform their trading.

To measure the traders' interoceptive ability, Kandasamy et al. (2016) used both types of heart-related detection tasks described above. In the first instance, the authors used the heart rate tracking task over six different time periods of 25, 20, 35, 40, 45, and 50 seconds. Each subject undertook the tracking task for each time period, but the six tasks were presented to each trader in a random order. As is usual in these tasks, the subjects were not permitted to determine their heart rate manually by methods such as putting their fingers on their pulse. Each subject was then assigned a heartbeat detection score, as follows:

$$Score = 1 - \frac{|nbeats_{real} - nbeats_{reported}|}{(nbeats_{real} - nbeats_{reported})/2}$$

In the second interoceptive measurement task, each trader performed the tone synchronization task (described earlier) 15 times. In each of these 15 trials, the traders were asked whether the 10 tones they heard were played in synchronization with their own heartbeats. Traders' heartbeat detection scores were calculated as the percentage of answers (out of 15) that were correct. To assess each trader's level of interoceptive awareness (i.e., his/her degree of understanding of his own interoceptive ability), he/she was also asked to rate his/her confidence in his predictions in the two interoceptive measurement tasks. A control group of 48 students also undertook the two interoceptive measurement tasks. The students included both postgraduates and undergraduates, and were matched to the traders on the basis of age and sex.

Once the interoceptive measurement tasks were completed, the data gathered was matched to information about the traders' trading results and the length of time they had been in the business. The detection task results were also compared against the results of the control group.

In the first result of this study, Kandasamy et al. (2016) assessed the difference between the interoceptive ability of the traders and that of the student control group. Using the heart rate tracking task, the traders who participated in the experiment had statistically significantly better average interoceptive ability than the student control group. The mean score for traders was 78.2 compared to 66.9 for the student control group ($P = .011$). The traders' standard deviation for this measure was 11.5, and the controls' was 21.3. Both the difference in mean score and the large difference in standard deviation indicate that the traders, in general, had significantly better interoception than the student control group.

The second result of the study is that among traders, interoceptive ability is correlated with profitability. One year's average daily profit record, calculated as profit minus loss, for a trader was compared with his interoceptive ability based on the heartbeat discrimination task. There was a clear positive correlation between the two measures, with every 2.61% increase in heartbeat detection score predicting a one-pound increase in profit ($P = .007$). The traders were then ranked based on the amount of their net profit as calculated above. This ranking was regressed against interoception scores, and the relation between the two was found to be highly significant with each level of ranking indicating an increase of 17.84% in heartbeat detection score ($P = .01$).

Years of experience as a trader was also correlated with interoceptive skill among the group of traders, with every year of trading predicted by a 21.64% increase in heartbeat detection score ($P = .001$). This result was further analyzed to explore whether beginning traders' average heartbeat detection ability was the same as that of nontraders (the control group), and to explore the relationship between job tenure and interoceptive ability. Traders with between 1 and 4 years' experience were found to have a statistically equivalent mean and standard deviation of the distribution of interoceptive ability as the control group. However, for traders with between five and eight, or eight or more, years' trading experience, a statistically significant higher mean and lower standard deviation was found relative to the control subjects' distribution. Similarly, when the three groups of traders were compared against each other, increased experience was associated with a higher mean and a lower standard deviation of interoceptive ability.

The self-reported confidence of the traders' estimates in their heart rate tracking accuracy did not correlate at any statistically significant level with their actual heartbeat detection accuracy. The authors hypothesize that this divergence in objective performance and subjective assessment may have been caused by the interoception itself being undermined by the diversion of effort towards consciously assessing how well they were doing.

These results clearly demonstrate a correlation between the ability of traders to attend to their visceral feelings and both their profitability and longevity on the financial trading floor. As conjectured in Katkin et al. (2001)'s experiment that employed pictures of snakes and spiders, perhaps experienced traders are unconsciously conditioned to market conditions, such that their visceral responses have become informative (consciously or unconsciously) about perceived market conditions. This would suggest that traders' unconscious knowledge about market conditions develop over a period of time and that they learn about the nature of market signals through positive reinforcement, when they make money and negative reinforcement, when they lose money.

This reinforcement, or conditioning, can then be exploited by traders with better interoceptive ability to interpret the market signals their bodies pick up, and thereby make more money. While this study itself does not offer any conclusions about the efficiency of markets and the validity of the EMH, the biological mechanisms at work do lend weight to the idea that "gut feelings" impact how much money can be made in the market. If the EMH is correct, then the variation in traders' earnings over the long term should be purely a function of luck, as manifested in the random price changes of the assets that happened to be selected. Although we do not know whether the traders with the highest heartbeat detection scores were "beating the market", we do know that they had increased longevity in the profession and that they were earning more money than traders with lower heartbeat detection scores. From this we may infer, given the cut-throat nature of the business, that they were making enough profit to be considered valuable by their employer.

CONCLUSION

From the field of neurophysiology, there is evidence that enhanced perception of the viscera is linked with better decision making and that interoception can connect bodily states and decision making through unconscious learning or conditioning. This link has also been demonstrated in the field of behavioral finance and economics in financial decision making tasks, which suggests that it is financially beneficial to have good interoceptive ability.

The evidence is compatible with a causal effect of interoceptive ability on decision making, but it is primarily correlational. One could envisage other reasons for this correlation. For instance, interoceptive ability could be correlated with the ability for information to be encoded in the body. In that case, the heterogeneity in interoceptive ability across people would arise from heterogeneity in the ability of the body to learn, which would itself be the fundamental "cause" of better performance. One could easily envisage research studies where participants' interoceptive ability is fostered by training with biofeedback. Future research may examine whether such exogenously induced variation in interoception lead to different decision making, furthering our understanding of the role of the viscera in supporting good decisions.

REFERENCES

Barrett, L. F., Quigley, K. S., Bliss-Moreau, E., & Aronson, K. R. (2004). Interoceptive sensitivity and self-reports of emotional experience. *Journal of Personality and Social Psychology*, *87*(5), 684.

Bechara, A., & Damasio, A. R. (2005). The somatic marker hypothesis: a neural theory of economic decision. *Games and Economic Behavior*, *52*(2), 336–372.

Bechara, A., Damasio, A. R., Damasio, H., & Anderson, S. W. (1994). Insensitivity to future consequences following damage to human prefrontal cortex. *Cognition*, *50*(1–3), 7–15.

Bechara, A., Damasio, H., & Damasio, A. R. (2000). Emotion, decision making and the orbitofrontal cortex. *Cerebral Cortex, 10*(3), 295–307.

Bernstein, D. A., Penner, L. A., Clarke-Stewart, A., & Roy, E. J. (2006). *Psychology*. Boston, MA: Houghton Mifflin Company.

Binmore, K. G. (1994). *Game theory and the social contract: Playing fair*. Cambridge, MA: MIT Press.

Brock, W., Lakonishok, J., & LeBaron, B. (1992). Simple technical trading rules and the stochastic properties of stock returns. *The Journal of Finance, 47*(5), 1731–1764.

Bruni, L., & Sugden, R. (2007). The road not taken: how psychology was removed from economics, and how it might be brought back. *The Economic Journal, 117*(516), 146–173.

Butler, D., & Cheung, S. L. (2018). Mind, body, bubble! Psychological and biophysical dimensions of behavior in experimental asset markets. In G. Foster (Ed.), *Biophysical measurement in experimental social science research*. Oxford, UK: Elsevier.

Cameron, O. G. (2001). Interoception: the inside story—a model for psychosomatic processes. *Psychosomatic Medicine, 63*(5), 697–710.

Cannon, W. B. (1927). The James-Lange theory of emotions: a critical examination and an alternative theory. *The American Journal of Psychology, 39*(1/4), 106–124.

Critchley, H. D., & Harrison, N. A. (2013). Visceral influences on brain and behavior. *Neuron, 77* (4), 624–638.

Critchley, H. D., Wiens, S., Rotshtein, P., Ohman, A., & Dolan, R. J. (2004). Neural systems supporting interoceptive awareness. *Nature Neuroscience, 7*(2), 189–195.

Crone, E. A., Somsen, R. J., Beek, B. V., & Van Der Molen, M. W. (2004). Heart rate and skin conductance analysis of antecendents and consequences of decision making. *Psychophysiology, 41*(4), 531–540.

Damasio, A. R. (1994). *Descartes' error: emotion, reason, and the human brain*. New York: GP Putnam's Sons.

Damasio, A. R., Everitt, B. J., & Bishop, D. (1996). The somatic marker hypothesis and the possible functions of the prefrontal cortex [and discussion]. *Philosophical Transactions of the Royal Society, B: Biological Sciences, 351*(1346), 1413–1420.

Digman, J. M. (1990). Personality structure: emergence of the five-factor model. *Annual Review of Psychology, 41*(1), 417–440.

Dunn, B. D., Galton, H. C., Morgan, R., Evans, D., Oliver, C., Meyer, M., et al. (2010). Listening to your heart how interoception shapes emotion experience and intuitive decision making. *Psychological Science, 21*(12), 1835–1844.

Fama, E. (1970). Efficient capital markets: a review of theory and empirical work. *The Journal of Finance, 25*(2), 383–417.

Garfinkel, S. N., Seth, A. K., Barrett, A. B., Suzuki, K., & Critchley, H. D. (2015). Knowing your own heart: distinguishing interoceptive accuracy from interoceptive awareness. *Biological Psychology, 104*, 65–74.

Gigerenzer, G., Todd, P. M., & ABC Research Group (1999). *Simple heuristics that make us smart*. Oxford: Oxford University Press.

Gintis, H. (2007). Unifying the behavioral sciences ii. *Behavioral and Brain Sciences, 30*(1), 45–53.

Glimcher, P. W., & Fehr, E. (2013). *Neuroeconomics: Decision making and the brain*. London: Academic Press.

Hahn, H., Neurath, O., & Carnap, R. (1929). *The scientific conception of the world: The Vienna circle*.

Harver, A., Katkin, E. S., & Bloch, E. (1993). Signal-detection outcomes on heartbeat and respiratory resistance detection tasks in male and female subjects. *Psychophysiology, 30*(3), 223–230.

Hornak, J., Bramham, J., Rolls, E. T., Morris, R. G., O'Doherty, J., Bullock, P., et al. (2003). Changes in emotion after circumscribed surgical lesions of the orbitofrontal and cingulate cortices. *Brain*, *126*(7), 1691–1712.

Kahneman, D. (2003). A perspective on judgment and choice: mapping bounded rationality. *American Psychologist*, *58*(9), 697.

Kahneman, D. (2011). *Thinking, fast and slow*. New York: Farrar, Straus and Giroux.

Kandasamy, N., Garfinkel, S. N., Page, L., Hardy, B., Critchley, H. D., Gurnell, M., et al. (2016). Interoceptive ability predicts survival on a London trading floor. *Scientific Reports*, *6*, 32986.

Katkin, E. S., Wiens, S., & Ohman, A. (2001). Nonconscious fear conditioning, visceral perception, and the development of gut feelings. *Psychological Science*, *12*(5), 366–370.

Knoll, J. F., & Hodapp, V. (1992). A comparison between two methods for assessing heartbeat perception. *Psychophysiology*, *29*(2), 218–222.

Kringelbach, M. L. (2005). The human orbitofrontal cortex: linking reward to hedonic experience. *Nature Reviews Neuroscience*, *6*(9), 691–702.

Lange, C. G., & James, W. (1922). *The emotions* (Vol. 1). Philadelphia, PA: Williams & Wilkins.

Malkiel, B. G. (2003). The efficient market hypothesis and its critics. *Journal of Economic Perspectives*, *17*(1), 59–82.

Malkiel, B. G. (2007). *A random walk down wall street: The time-tested strategy for successful investing*. New York: WW Norton & Company.

Rolls, E. T., Hornak, J., Wade, D., & McGrath, J. (1994). Emotion related learning in patients with social and emotional changes associated with frontal lobe damage. *Journal of Neurology, Neurosurgery & Psychiatry*, *57*(12), 1518–1524.

Savin, G., Weller, P., & Zvingelis, J. (2006). The predictive power of "head-and-shoulders" price patterns in the US stock market. *Journal of Financial Econometrics*, *5*(2), 243–265.

Schachter, S., & Singer, J. (1962). Cognitive, social, and physiological determinants of emotional state. *Psychological Review*, *69*(5), 379.

Schulz, A., Lass-Hennemann, J., Sütterlin, S., Schächinger, H., & Vögele, C. (2013). Cold pressor stress induces opposite effects on cardioceptive accuracy dependent on assessment paradigm. *Biological Psychology*, *93*(1), 167–174.

Seth, A. K. (2013). Interoceptive inference, emotion, and the embodied self. *Trends in Cognitive Sciences*, *17*(11), 565–573.

Sokol-Hessner, P., Hartley, C. A., Hamilton, J. R., & Phelps, E. A. (2015). Interoceptive ability predicts aversion to losses. *Cognition and Emotion*, *29*(4), 695–701.

Stigler, G. J., & Becker, G. S. (1977). De gustibus non est disputandum. *The American Economic Review*, *67*(2), 76–90.

Werner, N. S., Jung, K., Duschek, S., & Schandry, R. (2009). Enhanced cardiac perception is associated with benefits in decision-making. *Psychophysiology*, *46*(6), 1123–1129.

Whitehead, W. E., & Drescher, V. M. (1980). Perception of gastric contractions and self-control of gastric motility. *Psychophysiology*, *17*(6), 552–558.

Chapter 7

Mind, Body, Bubble! Psychological and Biophysical Dimensions of Behavior in Experimental Asset Markets

David John Butler* **and Stephen L. Cheung**[†]
[*]Griffith Business School, Griffith University, Gold Coast, QLD, Australia, [†]*School of Economics, The University of Sydney, Sydney, NSW, Australia*

INTRODUCTION

The role of financial markets is to source capital for business investment and allocate risks to those best placed to bear it. The performance of these markets has profound implications for efficiency, stability, and the distribution of wealth in the economy. Yet the success of real-world markets in serving these functions has been hotly debated since the time of the Great Depression. On one side, the efficient markets hypothesis (EMH) of Fama (1970) asserts that asset prices fully reflect market fundamentals. However, others have argued that human psychology and emotions exercise an enormous influence over financial decision making, in a manner abstracted from in standard theory. Thus Keynes (1936) speaks of "animal spirits," and Shiller (2000) of "irrational exuberance," as distortionary influences upon asset prices. While both interpret such influences to be negative, emerging research suggests that our emotions may be an integral, even essential, component of human decision making in the face of risk. In this chapter, we review recent research that uses laboratory experimental methods to explore the influence of psychological and biophysical variables on decision making in financial markets.

Participation in financial markets exposes individuals to tradeoffs between risk and reward, and this is true not only for market professionals, but also for retail investors who face important choices involving their investment, borrowing, and retirement savings. Decision making in such settings is difficult and reflects a complex combination of forces. Factors that are emphasized in standard economics and finance include market institutions (such as access to

Biophysical Measurement in Experimental Social Science Research. https://doi.org/10.1016/B978-0-12-813092-6.00003-4

futures markets and constraints on short-selling); incentive and information structures; the risk, time and ambiguity preferences of market participants as well as their beliefs and expectations; and strategic uncertainty over the preferences and rationality of others. To this list, we can add features emphasized in behavioral finance and psychology such as cognitive limitations, self-control and emotions, as well as biophysical phenomena such as hormones and neural activity.

Under the EMH, asset prices fully reflect all available information; psychological and biophysical states of traders should not distort how that information is processed, and should have no direct predictive power. According to this standard view, a more rational trader could exploit a market participant who relied unduly upon emotions or "gut feelings," profiting at the latter's expense. In contradiction to the EMH, however, it is widely believed that asset prices at times deviate considerably from their fundamental value (FV, also known as intrinsic value), with market psychology implicated as a driving force behind such deviations. A bubble in asset prices is defined as "trade in high volume at prices that are considerably at variance from intrinsic value" (King, Smith, Williams, & van Boening, 1993, p. 183). Such a bubble, as well as its ensuing and ultimately inevitable crash, has tremendous societal implications including misallocation of capital, propagation of instability to the real economy, and redistribution of wealth.

Studying financial markets using observational data is difficult because the researcher cannot observe, let alone control, all relevant variables—most notably the FV of the assets that are bought and sold. When FV is unobservable, researchers may disagree over whether a bubble has occurred, even in hindsight (see Thompson, 2006, arguing that there was no Dutch tulip bubble, and Pástor & Veronesi, 2006, arguing that there was no dot-com bubble). This motivates a long tradition of using laboratory experiments to study the efficiency of market outcomes (Chamberlin, 1948; Smith, 1962; Smith, Suchanek, & Williams, 1988). These experiments allow a researcher to control key variables and generate repeated observations under identical conditions. As FV is under the control of the experimenter, price bubbles can be precisely quantified, and are in fact commonly observed. This is particularly the case in the paradigm introduced by Smith, Suchanek and Williams (Smith et al., 1988; SSW), described in more detail below, which is the focus of this chapter.

The literature using SSW experiments initially focused on evaluating the effects of market institutions, incentives, and information on market behavior (see Palan, 2013, for a review). This research proved somewhat unsatisfactory in that even after several decades of study, there remains considerable, indeed extraordinary, unexplained heterogeneity in behavior, both between markets under the same conditions and between individuals within a given market.

Experiments can be used not only to study traditional finance variables, but also to manipulate the mix of characteristics of market participants, and to measure their psychological and biophysical states. In this chapter, we review an emerging literature, almost all dating from the past 5 years, that shifts the focus of research onto the characteristics of the individuals who populate experimental markets. These characteristics include basic individual differences such as gender, traditional psychological variables such as cognitive ability, and other personality measures such as theory of mind (ToM, essentially the ability to attribute mental states to others). We also consider measures of changeable biophysical characteristics of a given individual, such as facial expression, levels of steroid hormones (e.g., testosterone and cortisol), measures of neural activity derived from fMRI techniques, and self-reported emotional states. Our review highlights how an array of tools to measure subjects' characteristics and emotional and biophysical states can be used, and can complement one another, in understanding the nucleation, expansion, and collapse of price bubbles.

THE ROLE OF THE BRAIN-BODY NEXUS IN FINANCIAL DECISION MAKING

Alongside the casino, asset markets are the classic environment in which substantial risks and rewards confront participants. Indeed, Coates and Gurnell (2017) assert that "financial markets present us with the largest and most intense competitive forum ever constructed." In economics and finance, the standard account of rational choice in financial markets is epitomized by the EMH that proposes that "security prices at any time 'fully reflect' all available information" (Fama, 1970, p. 383). Critics of this account suggest that it requires traders to routinely solve optimization problems that are computationally infeasible, even with unlimited processing capacity (see Chapter 2 and Bossaerts & Murawski, 2017). It also describes a world of "disembodied" traders, in which the rational mind makes decisions without input from the body in which, and with which, it evolved.

The Embodied Mind

Damasio's book *Descartes' Error* (1994) was the first to show how the anticipation of risk and reward activates and integrates the "soma," or body, in risky decisions. Patients with brain lesions preventing interoceptive access to somatic signals (our conscious and unconscious sensitivity to internal bodily sensations; see Chapter 6), but who were otherwise normal, experienced dramatic declines in decision quality, leading Damasio to develop the "somatic marker hypothesis." Somatic signals can assist fast and instinctive decision making of the type classified by Kahneman (2011) as "System 1 thinking," bypassing the types of deliberate cognitive engagement that standard theory takes to be our only method for choosing ("System 2 thinking"). While Kahneman emphasizes the potential bias that can arise from relying on System 1 alone, Damasio focuses instead on the visceral knowledge that System 1 can bring and he argues that it most often leads to improved decision making under risk. This new "risk as feelings" paradigm was further developed by Loewenstein, Weber, Hsee, and Welch (2001).

Without somatic signals, a trader will struggle to avoid high-variance but negative expected value alternatives (Bechara & Damasio, 2005). Although such traders would use "all available information" as the EMH presumes, they would be doing so without access to somatic or other emotional responses to the situation. Our emotional reactions are sensitive to a wider range of features of the decision environment than are System 2's cognitive evaluations alone; see the discussion of the Iowa Gambling Task in Chapter 6. This implies that efforts to "prime" traders with emotionally laden stimuli prior to trading can influence subsequent market outcomes in a manner inconsistent with standard theory.

The inevitable involvement of the soma in traders' decisions is vividly described by neuroscientist and former Wall Street trader John Coates, in his 2012 book *The Hour between Dog and Wolf: Risk Taking, Gut Feelings and the Biology of Boom and Bust.* He dramatizes the somatic effects on traders of an impending announcement by the US Federal Reserve as follows (p. 2):

> *Scott and Logan's bodies, largely unbeknownst to them, have also prepared for the event. Their metabolism speeds up, ready to break down existing energy stores in liver, muscle and fat cells should the situation demand it. Breathing accelerates, drawing in more oxygen, and their heart rates speed up … their nervous system, extending from the brain down into the abdomen, has begun redistributing blood throughout their bodies, constricting blood flow to the gut, giving them the butterflies.*
>
> *As the sheer potential for profit looms in their imaginations, Scott and Logan feel an unmistakable surge of energy as steroid hormones begin to turbo-charge the big engines of their bodies. These hormones take time to kick in, but once synthesized by their respective glands and injected into the bloodstream, they begin to change almost every detail of Scott and Logan's body and brain—their metabolism, growth rate, lean-muscle mass, mood, cognitive performance, even the memories they recall.*
>
> *Scott and Logan's testosterone levels have been steadily climbing. This steroid hormone, naturally produced by the testes, primes them for the challenge ahead, just as it does athletes preparing to compete and animals steeling for a fight. Rising levels of testosterone increase Scott and Logan's hemoglobin, and consequently their blood's capacity to carry oxygen; the testosterone also increases their state of confidence and, crucially, their appetite for risk. For Scott and Logan, this is a moment of transformation, what the French since the Middle Ages have called "the hour between dog and wolf."*
>
> *Another hormone, adrenalin, produced by the core of the adrenal glands located on top of the kidneys, surges into their blood. Adrenalin quickens physical reactions and speeds up the body's metabolism, tapping into glucose deposits, mostly in the liver, and flushing them into the blood so that Scott and Logan have back-up fuel supplies to support them in whatever trouble their testosterone gets*

> *them into. A third hormone, the steroid cortisol, commonly known as the stress hormone, trickles out of the rim of the adrenal glands and travels to the brain, where it stimulates the release of dopamine, a chemical operating along neural circuits known as the pleasure pathways ... An expectant hush descends on global markets.*

Somatic signals influence behavior by biasing the decision process toward or away from particular options (Bechara & Damasio, 2005). The brain's ventromedial prefrontal cortex (vmPFC), a center of rational thought, remains crucial for associating one's emotional state with any complex decision (Poppa & Bechara, 2018). The reader may find Fig. 1 helpful for a better picture of the neuroanatomy to which we are referring. However, numerous other brain regions, such as the amygdala, provide the visceral responses integrated by the vmPFC (Poppa & Bechara, 2018). The most critical conduit for these somatic signals is not the spinal cord but the vagus (or "wandering") nerve. The vagus nerve has "efferent" fibers to transmit messages from the brain stem to the body, including the enteric nervous system (also known as our "gut brain" or "second brain"), and "afferent" fibers carrying nerve signals from the body back to the brain stem, in a constant two-way chatter (Maniscalco & Rinaman, 2018). These signals to the lower brain stem (in particular, the caudal nucleus tractus solitarius, cNTS) stimulate the release of neurotransmitters such as dopamine, serotonin, noradrenaline (epinephrine), and acetylcholine that affect our central nervous system. Bechara and Damasio (2005) describe how these neurotransmitters then modulate the synaptic activity underpinning our choice behavior, until the dominant somatic state exerts its preferred biasing effect upon our decisions.

The cNTS is a key part of the brain's dorsal vagal complex, the central node for receiving interoceptive information from the soma, particularly the gut (Maniscalco & Rinaman, 2018). In a recent survey of this literature, Poppa and Bechara (2018) note that "the evidence strongly suggests that visceral processes mediated by afferent vagus nerve signaling participate in shaping higher-order cognition," indicating a central role for the vagus nerve in making advantageous decisions under risk. Vagal efferent effects on heart rate can occur within milliseconds, easily fast enough to impact traders' decisions.

If EMH holds true, biophysical measures of market participants cannot explain bubbles and crashes, nor can they predict the relative success of traders. However, contrary to EMH, human traders' interpretation of "all available information" can subconsciously skew toward *either* opportunity *or* risk, rather than a dispassionate assessment of both. Coates (2012) argues that excitement and fear manifest as shifts in confidence and risk preferences, caused by changes in circulating levels of testosterone (for reward) and cortisol (for risk). While testosterone sharpens responses, and boosts the confidence of male traders, a bear market may raise traders' levels of cortisol, exacerbating existing risk aversion that then deepens the downturn. The role of testosterone in female decisions has not been extensively studied to date; we return to this issue below.

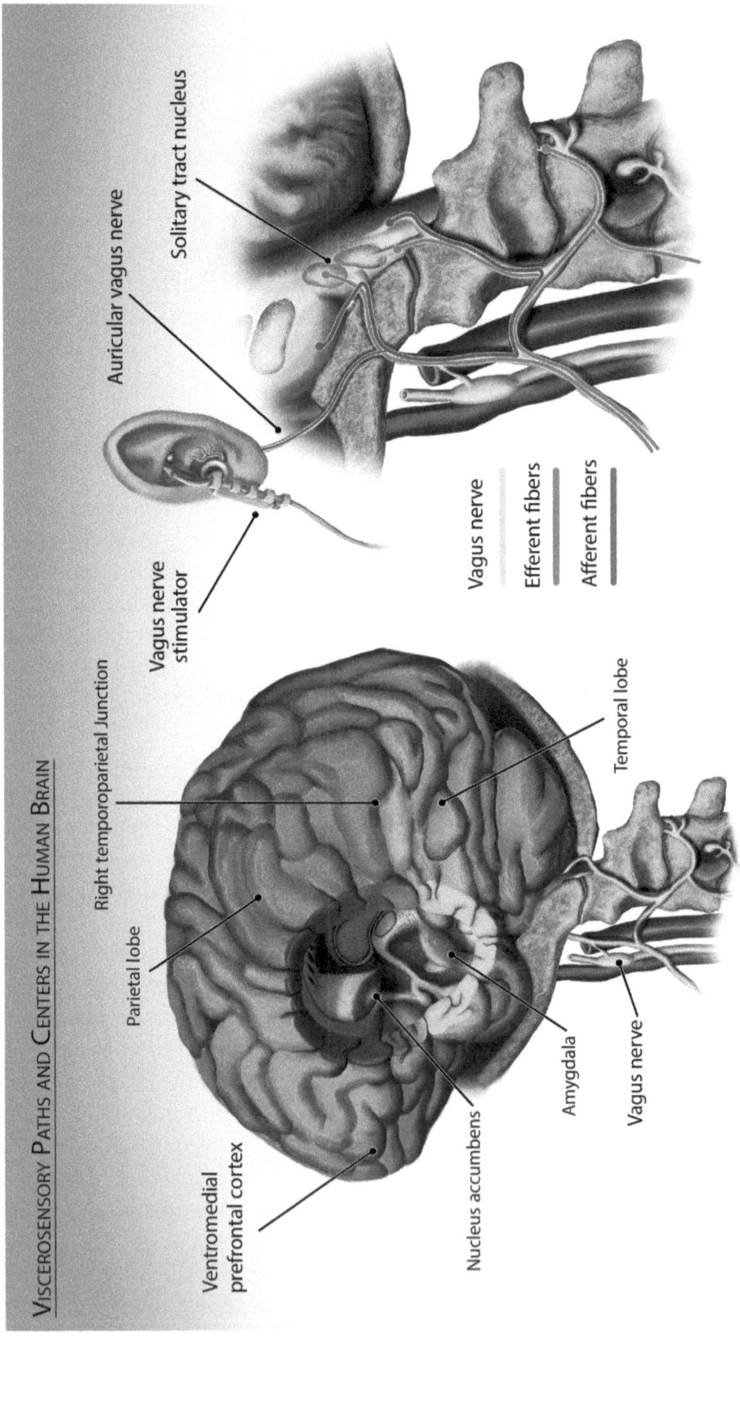

FIG. 1 Viscerosensory paths and centers in the human brain.

While serotonin influences our choices with conscious awareness, not all somatic signals accessible to us by interoception manifest consciously. The effects of other steroids, such as testosterone's effect on dopamine transmission in the nucleus accumbens (NAcc), manifest subconsciously. In this way, our choices can reflect the information content of these signals even before we can articulate why we choose as we do (Bechara & Damasio, 2005; also see Chapter 4).

We can measure the arousal triggered by risk and reward in many ways. These include skin conductance response (SCR), which measures changes in electrical conductance, heart rate, and heart rate variability (HRV; see Appendix 2). Some changes to our musculoskeletal system may be noticeable to others, such as our facial expressions, making them accessible to categorization (Colzato, Sellaro, & Beste, 2017; Darwin, 1872), most recently using face-reading software. Facial expressions do not cause behavior, but they are a convenient biomarker of the deeper visceral antecedents produced by the brain-body nexus when we face dynamic risk-reward environments. When our somatic responses to market conditions produce emotions, our facial expressions take on predictable patterns. For this reason, professional poker players go to great lengths to mask their reactions from other players as play unfolds.

Levenson (2014) reviews the evidence for coherence in how different parts of our autonomic nervous system react to emotion-laden stimuli. He describes one study that measured subjects' SCR, heart rate, and facial muscle movements in response to an image intended to provoke disgust. Each of the measures responded rapidly and coherently, despite exhibiting no correlation prior to the stimulus. Mauss, Levenson, McCarter, Wilhelm, and Gross (2005) also found strong evidence for coherence across very different response measures. For example, a film evoking sadness produced within-subject lagged correlation coefficients between facial expression and SCR of $r = -0.52$ and between facial expression and emotional self-reports of $r = 0.74$. This result is reassuring for researchers using emotional self-reports rather than, or in addition to, biophysical measures.

Interpersonal Differences

A growing number of psychological traits and capacities are now known to have specific and measurable biophysical manifestations. In an echo of nineteenth century phrenology, Riccelli, Toschi, Nigro, Terracciano, and Passamonti (2017) found the Big Five personality traits of a large sample of 507 subjects to have measurable correlates in the morphology of their prefrontal cortices. ToM (or "social intelligence") is also localized in the human brain. A recent meta-analysis of relevant fMRI studies found BOLD signals from the posterior region of the right temporal parietal junction (rTPJ) to be an independent region (distinct from the anterior rTPJ), isolated for this purpose (Krall et al., 2015). Deficits in social cognition (e.g., autism spectrum disorders) are associated with abnormal function of the posterior rTPJ (Pantelis, Byrge, Tyszka, Adolphs, & Kennedy, 2015). Luders, Narr, Thompson, and Toga (2009) and Menary et al. (2013), inter alia, find significant connections between measures of general intelligence and the size and structure of some brain areas. In particular, the size of the mid-saggital corpus callosum, which connects the two brain hemispheres, is positively associated with cognitive ability.

The effect of (changes in) hormone levels on decisions is not straightforward. For example, we can measure the organizational effects of prenatal androgen exposure using the ratio of lengths of our second and fourth fingers (2D:4D ratio), particularly of the right hand, which correlates with risk preference within, but not across, ethnicities (e.g., Brañas-Garza & Rustichini, 2011, and references therein). Interpersonal differences in biophysical characteristics, such as circulating steroid hormone levels and within-person shifts in these levels over time, can each induce systematic shifts in attitudes to the same information, contrary to EMH, leading to different actions. For example, some research suggests that both a "sufficiently male" brain structure (of a type possessed by only some males, and no females) *and* a sufficient amount of circulating testosterone are necessary for changes in testosterone levels to lead to shifts in utilities, confidence and risk preferences (Nadler, Jiao, Johnson, Alexander, & Zak, 2018; Coates, Gurnell, & Sarnyai, 2010).

Turning to gender differences, biophysical measures such as brain size and organization can be difficult to interpret, given the many kinds of sexual dimorphism in humans. For example, if investigating the effects of baseline circulating testosterone levels on trading behavior, it would be foolish to classify women as very low testosterone men and expect the results to be meaningful. Furthermore, the effects of testosterone and other hormones on differences in behavior between men and women is under-researched; again, see Chapter 4.

One explanation for this dearth of research is that female hormone levels differ pre- and post-menarche and menopause, and over the estrus cycle, making it less complicated to focus on males (see Chapter 4 and Maniscalco & Rinaman, 2018). For example, there are no experiments investigating the impact of the phase within the estrus cycle of female traders on asset price trajectories, even though such studies should be feasible. This lack of research examining biophysical measures of gender differences leaves us with few predictions for gender differences in behavior, even though gender differences are among the most profound of all inter-personal differences.

Damasio's early work comparing lesion patients with controls treated interoceptive ability as a characteristic that an individual either possesses or does not possess. The evidence today is that interoceptive abilities are distributed along a continuum, from Damasio's lesion patients at one extreme, to the most successful high-frequency traders at the other (Kandasamy et al., 2016; see also Chapter 6). By far the most common measure of interoceptive ability today is drawn from the heart rate detection task, following its successful generalization to the detection of other internal somatic responses (Critchley & Garfinkel, 2015).

Appendix 2 explains how electrocardiography can separate two bands of HRV: low frequency (LF) and high frequency (HF). The magnitude of the difference in HF HRV between systolic and diastolic phases is the best measure of how the ongoing activity of the vagus nerve (or "vagal tone") is instantiated. It provides our best measure of moment-to-moment emotional self-regulation, which operates primarily via the neurotransmitter acetylcholine (Fenton-O'Creevy et al., 2012). This HF HRV is arguably a key measurable biophysical characteristic that can identify one's position along the continuum of interoceptive ability; higher values indicating better emotional regulation and interoceptive ability, and low values associated with the opposite (Appelhans & Luecken, 2006).

It has recently become possible to stimulate the afferent fibers of the vagus nerve to enhance somatic signaling into the central nervous system, cheaply and noninvasively, using transcutaneous vagus nerve stimulation (tVNS) applied to the left ear (see Poppa & Bechara, 2018). Stimulation is known to produce BOLD signal changes detected by fMRI in several brain regions including the cNTS (Poppa & Bechara, 2018). New placebo-controlled research using tVNS to stimulate vagal tone shows the vagus nerve to be causally involved in creativity (Colzato, Ritter, & Steenbergen, 2018). By stimulating vagal afferent fibers, there is an increase in the steroid hormone epinephrine and the inhibitory neurotransmitter, gamma-amino butyric acid (GABA). These biophysical changes regulate our fear and anxiety response to a stimulus, such as falling stock prices: our ability to self-regulate our emotional responses diminishes if our GABA level is low (Colzato et al., 2018). Another possibility is to wear a device called a "doppel" on one's wrist that sends a constant heartbeat-like vibration to the inner wrist. Unlike the activity of the tVNS device, the wearer perceives the doppel's vibrations. Early placebo controlled research finds that this device successfully reduces the wearer's emotional reactivity in stressful environments (Azevedo et al., 2017).

In summary, and contrary to the EMH, what happens in vagus does not stay in vagus. By stimulating specific patterns of neurotransmitter release from the brain stem, the flow-on effects of vagal afferent signals ensure that markets are composed of "embodied," and not "disembodied," traders. In consequence, it is possible to measure, manipulate, and sort individuals by specific biophysical characteristics that we now know to influence decisions under risk. The studies that we review henceforth in this chapter focus on some pieces of the puzzle that help to further our understanding of the root causes of instability in financial markets.

EXPERIMENTAL ENVIRONMENT

We focus in this chapter on asset market experiments that build upon the paradigm introduced by Smith, Suchanek, and Williams (Smith et al., 1988; SSW), broadly interpreted. In these experiments, each participant receives an initial endowment of experimental money and "shares," which may be bought and sold in a market over several periods. Shares are assets that yield income in the form of dividends in each period. They have a finite lifetime, such that as the experiment progresses there are fewer dividends remaining, meaning that each share's risk-neutral fundamental value (FV, which is the expected dividend per period multiplied by the number of outstanding dividends) declines over time. As dividends have the same value to all traders, who are symmetrically informed, standard theory predicts that all trades should be priced at FV.

Because FV is induced by the experimenter, deviations from it can be precisely quantified, which is not the case in naturally occurring markets. We distinguish two broad forms of deviation. First, measures of *overvaluation* (such as the relative deviation, RD) capture the extent to which market prices tend to be above or below FV on average. In this type of measure, periods of positive and negative deviation cancel each other out. Second, measures of *mispricing* (such as the relative absolute deviation, RAD) capture the extent of absolute deviation from FV, without regard for sign. This type of measure penalizes all positive and negative deviations alike. In our review we focus primarily on market-level measures of overvaluation and mispricing, as well as comparisons of traders' final earnings where appropriate.

In the SSW environment, market bubbles and crashes are frequently observed, but there is also considerable heterogeneity between markets. For example, see the left panel of Fig. 2, from the data of Cheung, Hedegaard, and Palan (2014); these markets are on average overvalued by 8% and

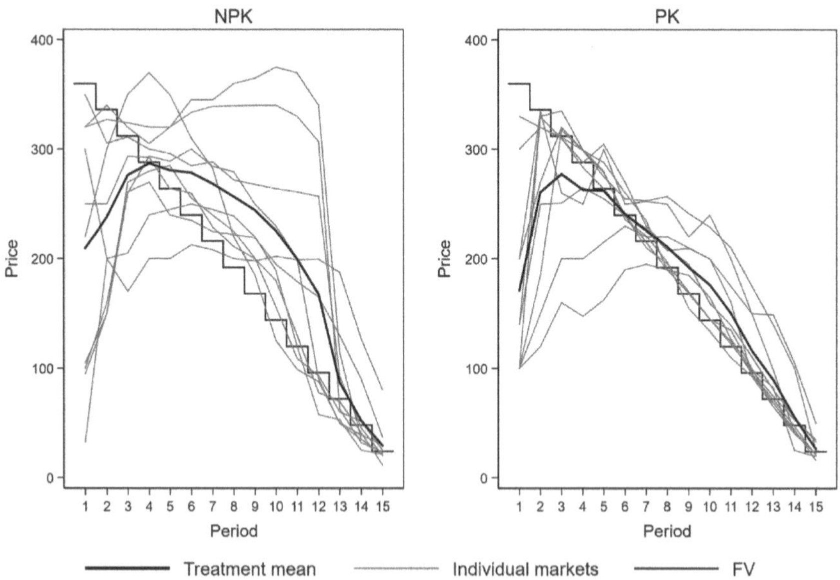

FIG. 2 Sample price paths in SSW markets, illustrating effect of knowledge of market composition. *(Source: Cheung, S. L., Hedegaard, M., & Palan, S. (2014). To see is to believe: Common expectations in experimental asset markets.* European Economic Review, 66, *84–96.)*

mispriced by 32% relative to FV, but there is clearly considerable variation around the mean.

Many studies have examined how market institutions (such as short-selling and futures markets) can improve the performance of SSW markets and have found the introduction of such institutions to have only limited success (see Palan, 2013, for a review). This motivates a shift toward studies of the psychological and biophysical characteristics and states of market participants, which we review here. However, it has also been claimed (Kirchler, Huber, & Stöckl, 2012) that mispricing in SSW markets may simply be an artifact of the fact that subjects—typically university students motivated by real monetary earnings—are "confused" by declining FV. This raises two issues, which we address in turn. The first is the role of subjects' beliefs regarding the rationality and behavior of others. The second is the scope for extensions of the SSW design to allow for nondeclining FV.

Recall the markets in the left panel of Fig. 2, which exhibit substantial mispricing and heterogeneity across markets. As it turns out, all subjects in each of these markets were thoroughly tested on their understanding of declining FV, but this was not made public knowledge (hence the acronym "NPK" appearing above this panel). Thus, while none of these subjects were themselves "confused," they may have believed that some others in the market might be confused, and so may have perceived an opportunity for profitable speculation. In the markets whose data are displayed in the right panel of Fig. 2, all subjects were similarly tested on their understanding that FV was declining, but this was made public knowledge ("PK") such that subjects in these markets should have no reason to doubt the rationality of others. The resulting markets are on average undervalued by 6% and mispriced by 20%, with both measures being significantly lower than in the NPK markets (Cheung et al., 2014). Given that many of the studies we review in this chapter manipulate the composition of the market with respect to characteristics such as cognitive ability or gender, this result highlights the importance of whether subjects are aware of such manipulations, as this knowledge may influence their expectations regarding the behavior of others and in turn affect their own actions.

While confusion alone cannot explain mispricing in SSW markets (see also Akiyama, Hanaki, & Ishikawa, 2017), it remains the case that declining FV may not be representative of naturally occurring markets. There are several ways to induce nondeclining FV in SSW style markets. One appealing approach is to introduce interest on cash (in conjunction with a terminal redemption value on shares; for details see, for example, Holt, Porzio, & Song, 2017). In this review, we interpret the SSW paradigm broadly to encompass extensions such as this. However, we note that even markets for assets with constant FV are characterized by considerable overvaluation and heterogeneity (Noussair, Robin, & Ruffieux, 2001), which again cannot be explained by features of the market environment alone. There is thus considerable scope for psychological and biophysical variables to enter the frame, despite their irrelevance under standard theory.

For our purposes, a key distinction can be drawn between variables that are fixed individual characteristics of market participants, such as gender and cognitive ability, and ones that are transitory states, such as emotions and phases in the circadian cycle. We review these separately in the following sections. In the case of fixed characteristics, a researcher may either measure these variables without making them a target of selection, or purposefully construct markets based upon them (for example, by comparing markets composed of males to ones composed of females). An advantage of the former approach is that it makes it straightforward to examine the effects of multiple characteristics; an advantage of the latter is that it makes it possible to identify causal effects of a single variable of interest. As illustrated by the discussion of Cheung et al. (2014) above, when markets are purposefully constructed it may also matter whether this is known to the participants; in other words, the knowledge of market composition may have important causal effects of its own. In the case of transitory states, a researcher may be able to measure the relevant variables repeatedly or even continuously over the life of the market, as well as to temporarily manipulate the levels of these states.

FIXED CHARACTERISTICS

Personality

Personality is a cornerstone of the psychology of individual differences, so it is perhaps surprising that its relation to economic behavior appears to be weak. Becker, Deckers, Dohmen, Falk, and Kosse (2012) examine associations of the so-called Big Five personality traits with experimental and survey measures of economic preferences. For risk and time preferences—these being the preference dimensions most relevant to financial decision making—the authors find that correlations with personality measures tend to be small, statistically insignificant, and not always consistent across datasets.

In the context of SSW markets, studies of personality have focused on its relation to the individual behavior of traders and have not used measures of personality as a basis to manipulate the composition of the market. Oehler, Wendt, Wedlich, and Horn (2018) find that more extroverted individuals are more prone to make purchases above the prevailing market price, while individuals who are more neurotic hold fewer shares. Cheung and Zhang (2018) classify traders' behavior for consistency with fundamental, momentum, and speculative strategies. They find that individuals who are more neurotic are more likely to follow fundamental value strategies and are less likely to be speculators. For the remaining Big Five traits, there are no significant effects.

While this literature finds few notable effects, those that are found are at least broadly compatible: the weight of evidence in Becker et al. (2012) indicates that extroverts tend to take more risks, while neurotic individuals take fewer risks. This is consistent with trading on fundamental value being a less risky strategy than speculation, where in the context of an overvalued market a fundamental value trader will also tend to hold fewer shares.

Cognitive Ability

The suggestion that mispricing in SSW markets may in part be an artifact of subjects' "confusion" (Kirchler et al., 2012) highlights the potential importance of cognitive ability in understanding behavior in these experiments. Moreover, as trading in a market involves strategic interaction with other market participants, a trader's beliefs regarding the skill and behavior of others may also come into play, as highlighted by the public knowledge manipulation in Cheung et al. (2014). An emerging literature links cognitive ability to a range of preferences, beliefs, and behaviors that are likely also to be relevant in a financial context. Thus Burks, Carpenter, Goette, and Rustichini (2009) and Dohmen, Falk, Huffman, and Sunde (2010) find that individuals with higher cognitive ability tend to be less risk averse and more patient, while Carpenter, Graham, and Wolf (2013) and Gill and Prowse (2016) find that such individuals also exhibit greater sophistication in strategic interactions.

Several SSW studies collect measures of cognitive ability—most commonly, the three-item Cognitive Reflection Test (CRT) of Frederick (2005)—and correlate traders' scores with their performance or behavior in the market. These studies typically find that higher-ability subjects also tend to attain larger earnings (e.g., Breaban & Noussair, 2015; Corgnet, Hernán-González, Kujal, & Porter, 2015; Cueva & Rustichini, 2015; Noussair, Tucker, & Xu, 2016). Breaban and Noussair (2015) also find that higher CRT scores are positively associated with the adoption of fundamental strategies, and negatively associated with momentum strategies. Cheung and Zhang (2018) examine multiple dimensions of cognitive ability, and find their relation to trading strategy to be complex and multifaceted. Fundamental strategies are associated with series reasoning (a task that requires identifying the next item in a sequence), speculation with Raven-style matrix reasoning (a task that involves identifying the geometric shape that best completes the stimulus), and momentum trading with verbal reasoning.

Hefti, Heinke, and Schneider (2016) argue that cognitive ability alone does not suffice to explain trading success, because ToM skills are also needed to infer the intentions and beliefs of other traders. The authors contend that both types of skill are necessary to trade successfully, and that deficiency in one cannot be compensated for by strength in the other. Hefti et al. (2016) conduct an SSW experiment in which traders' skills on both dimensions are measured (but not used to determine the composition of markets). The correlation between the two skills is found to be low, and traders who are strong in both enjoy the largest earnings. On the other hand, Cheung and Zhang (2018) find no significant effects of ToM or its interaction with cognitive ability on trading strategy. One explanation may be that Cheung and Zhang's verbal reasoning measure of cognitive ability partly captures the "nonanalytical" forms of intelligence that others have ascribed to ToM.

At an aggregate level, Breaban and Noussair (2015) and Cueva and Rustichini (2015) find that markets in which the average cognitive ability of traders is higher (through random variation, as opposed to purposeful assignment) tend to exhibit less mispricing. Going beyond correlational analyses of this type, two studies examine the effect of purposefully manipulating the composition of the market, with somewhat conflicting results. Bosch-Rosa, Meissner, and Bosch-Domènech (2018) compare markets composed solely of low- versus high-cognitive-ability subjects, finding that high-ability markets exhibit significantly less mispricing (with no significant difference in overvaluation). Hanaki, Akiyama, Funaki, and Ishikawa (2017) extend this approach by comparing homogeneous high- and low-ability markets with mixed ones, and systematically examining the effect of subjects' knowledge of the market composition. In contrast to Bosch-Rosa et al. (2018), Hanaki et al. (2017) find no significant difference in mispricing between homogeneous high- and low-ability markets, with both tracking FV similarly well. Instead, they find that mixed markets exhibit significantly greater mispricing than either high- or low-ability markets. Moreover, they find no significant effect of the knowledge of market composition, irrespective of whether that composition is high, low, or mixed.

Thus, to summarize the literature on cognitive ability in SSW markets, the evidence from correlational analyses generally indicates a positive association of cognitive ability with both individual and aggregate outcomes, although Hefti et al. (2016) suggest that cognitive ability alone may not be sufficient. To date, only two studies have examined the causal effect of constructing markets of different ability levels, with mixed results. Further research is needed to replicate and clarify these findings.

Gender

A large body of research examines the possibility of gender differences in behaviors potentially related to financial decision making. Much of this work is reviewed by Niederle (2016). It has been found that women and men perform differently under competitive incentives (Gneezy, Niederle, & Rustichini, 2003), and that women are less likely than men to select competitive environments (Niederle & Vesterlund, 2007). The latter finding has been attributed to a combination of gender differences in confidence, competitiveness, and risk preferences—all of which are relevant in financial settings. Women bid higher than men in first-price auctions (Chen, Katuščák, & Ozdenoren, 2013), consistent with women being more risk averse. However, Niederle (2016) cautions that gender differences in risk preference, while likely to be real, may be smaller and more heterogeneous than widely presumed.

For our purposes, two themes from this broader literature are worth highlighting. First, it has been found that gender differences in behavior vary between single-sex and mixed environments (Booth & Nolen, 2012). Second, while research has begun to investigate the biophysical underpinnings of gender differences in competitiveness and bidding behavior—for example, by examining how the behavior of women varies over the estrus cycle—results to date have been decidedly mixed, with Niederle (2016, p. 492) concluding that "clearly no obvious consensus has been reached."

Until recently, gender was not a variable of interest in research on SSW markets—Palan's 2013 review does not cite any papers or results about it. Eckel and Füllbrunn (2015, p. 914) assemble data on 35 markets from six studies in which the proportion of women in the market could be determined. They find this proportion to be significantly negatively correlated with the extent of overvaluation. In our own reanalysis of the same data, we find *no* significant correlation between gender composition and the severity of mispricing (Spearman rho $= -0.125$, $P = 0.473$). Taken together, these results indicate that prices in markets with more women tend to be lower, but not necessarily closer to the risk-neutral FV.

Four recent studies examine the effects of purposefully manipulating the composition of the market with respect to gender. They differ from each other in whether the gender manipulation is known to subjects, and whether FV follows a declining or constant path (as well as the methods used to induce constant FV). The picture that emerges from these studies is not at all clear. Fig. 3 and Table 1 report our own synthesis of this literature.

Eckel and Füllbrunn (2015) compare all-male, all-female, and mixed markets with declining FV. The gender composition was known because subjects could observe who would be in their market prior to the start of the experiment. As seen in the bar chart in the top left of Fig. 3, overvaluation declines monotonically when comparing male to mixed and female markets, with the male-mixed and male-female differences being statistically significant (Table 1, top panel). However, the line chart shows a nonmonotonic pattern for mispricing, which is lowest (with marginal significance) in mixed markets.

Two studies compare all-male and all-female markets with declining FV and *unknown* composition. We pool their data in the top right of Fig. 3 and the second panel of Table 1. Eckel and Füllbrunn (2017) are concerned with the extent to which their 2015 result is driven by stereotype-based expectations about the behavior of others, while Holt et al. (2017) are concerned with the robustness of their primary results, which are derived from a constant FV environment. Taken separately, the results of the two studies are contradictory: Eckel and Füllbrunn (2017) find that gender differences in overvaluation disappear when market composition is unknown (from which they conclude that their 2015 result is consistent with the hypothesis of stereotype-based expectations), while Holt et al. (2017) find that gender differences persist (from which they conclude that Eckel & Füllbrunn's, 2015 result is driven by declining FV). After pooling the

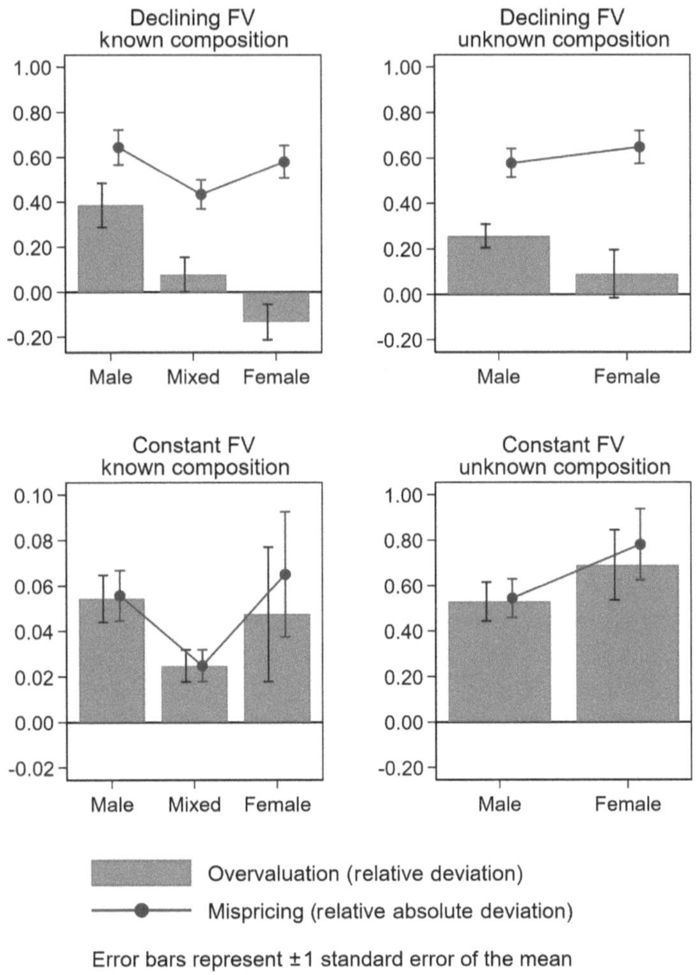

FIG. 3 Effects of gender composition on overvaluation and mispricing. *(Source: Authors' calculations, using data of studies cited in the text.)*

data of both studies (which employ identical parameters), we find the difference in overvaluation between male and female markets is smaller than when market composition is known but remains marginally significant; there is no significant difference in mispricing between markets of different genders.

Cueva and Rustichini (2015) and Holt et al. (2017) examine gender effects in markets with constant FV and known composition (depicted in the bottom left of Fig. 3)[1] or unknown composition (depicted in the bottom right of

1. We thank Carlos Cueva for sharing the data of Cueva and Rustichini (2015).

TABLE 1 Tests of Gender Effects of Market Composition (Mann-Whitney *P*-Values, Two-Sided)

Condition	Overvaluation (Relative Deviation)	Mispricing (Relative Absolute Deviation)
Declining value, known composition		
Male versus female	0.006***	0.522
Mixed versus male	0.032**	0.063*
Mixed versus female	0.116	0.199
Mixed versus homogeneous	0.735	0.063*
Declining value, unknown composition		
Male versus female	0.095*	0.469
Constant value, known composition		
Male versus female	0.174	0.597
Mixed versus male	0.059*	0.059*
Mixed versus female	0.821	0.174
Mixed versus homogeneous	0.218	0.059*
Constant value, unknown composition		
Male versus female	0.608	0.281

*P < *0.10.*
**P < *0.05.*
***P < *0.01.*
Source: Authors' calculations, using data of studies cited in the text.

Fig. 3),[2] respectively. However, these authors use different methods to induce constant FV, such that measures of overvaluation and mispricing are an order of magnitude smaller in the former study. In neither study are differences between male and female markets ever significant. Cueva and Rustichini also consider mixed-gender markets, which are found (as with the declining FV markets of Eckel & Füllbrunn, 2015) to exhibit the least mispricing.

Two conclusions are evident from our review of this literature on gender. First, where effects are found, they largely manifest as differences in

2. We pool the 15- and 25-period markets of Holt et al., because both support the same conclusion.

overvaluation rather than in mispricing. Markets composed of women generate prices that are lower but not necessarily closer to FV and are thus on average no more efficient than markets made up of men—if anything, mixed markets may be most efficient. Second, gender effects are more pronounced in a declining FV environment. Critics of that environment may dismiss those results on the basis that declining FV lacks ecological validity and is "confusing" to subjects. However, another interpretation is that because behavior under declining FV is inherently more variable, it may have greater power to identify factors that explain that variation. To observe gender differences reliably in constant-FV environments may simply require a much larger number of (rather costly) market observations. (See Niederle, 2016, for a related discussion of the role of the elicitation procedure in identifying gender differences in risk preferences).

TRANSITORY STATES

Hormones

When we confront risk and reward, our bodies react by modulating the levels of circulating steroids, including sex hormones. Cueva et al. (2015) measure endogenous levels of cortisol and testosterone in an SSW experiment. Sessions were all-male, all-female, or mixed, but otherwise not constituted according to baseline hormone levels. Measuring hormone levels at the start and end of each session, they find the market average pretrading cortisol level is positively associated with mispricing, but for male and mixed markets only. The market average testosterone level, separately averaged by gender, was not significantly associated with mispricing, nor was it correlated with trading profits of males or females.

As their first study could not establish causality, Cueva et al. conducted a second one in which they administered supplemental cortisol or testosterone, but to male subjects only. This second study focused on individual investment behavior and did not involve a market experiment. They found that hormone supplementation led to a decrease in risk aversion, either directly (for cortisol) or by inducing greater optimism regarding future asset prices (for testosterone). They also measured their subjects' 2D:4D ratio but found no evidence that this moderated the response of investment decisions to testosterone administration. This null result is notable given an earlier finding by Coates, Gurnell, and Rustichini (2009) that for high-frequency traders there is a significant interaction between the 2D:4D ratio and circulating testosterone levels. Coates et al. found that on high baseline testosterone days (relative to that trader's median), profitability increased, and that this effect interacted with 2D:4D ratio. Neither of these two studies involve an SSW experiment, however.

Nadler et al. (2018) address these contradictory findings with an SSW experiment consisting of 140 male subjects and the double-blind, placebo-controlled, exogenous administration of testosterone. They hypothesize that testosterone administration will shift subjects' thinking toward "System 1," with optimistic price expectations resulting in raised prices and inflated bubbles. The experiment was repeated several times, with the effects of testosterone administration—higher bids, asks and prices relative to placebo-treated sessions, leading to larger and longer bubbles—being most pronounced in the first market repetition. These results suggest that there is indeed a causal impact of testosterone administration on bubble inflation in men, at least temporarily. Both cortisol and testosterone have an inverted U-shaped dose-response curve for performance: too little and we do not trade, too much and irrational exuberance takes hold. Nadler et al. note that some male traders self-administer a testosterone gel before trading, and speculate that this may exacerbate financial market volatility. What effect testosterone gels would have in women, if any, is essentially unknown, and to find out might raise ethical as well as scientific concerns (see Chapter 4).

Systems 1 and 2

Nave, Nadler, Zava, and Camerer (2017) found that exogenous testosterone administration lowers performance on the Cognitive Reflection Test, suggesting a shift away from System 2 to System 1 reasoning. Some asset market studies focus more directly on the effects of nudging traders toward either System 1 or System 2 thinking. Dickinson, Chaudhuri, and Greenaway-McGrevy (2017) and Kocher, Lucks, and Schindler (in press) each investigate environments likely to promote System 1 thinking. The former study uses an online experiment to examine whether circadian-mismatched traders in a global market perform worse than traders in local markets composed solely of participants from a single time zone. The authors hypothesize that sleepy traders will be less able to anticipate others' actions, and so will hold more shares later in the experiment, thereby making less money. They also hypothesize that global markets (with sleepy traders) will produce larger bubbles than local markets. However, they find only modest evidence for greater mispricing and overvaluation in global markets, and no effect on earnings for their cognitively-strained sleepy subjects.

Kocher et al. (in press) compare markets where traders have depleted self-control with ones comprised of nondepleted traders. The experiment follows a "Stroop" task (Stroop, 1935) in which participants are presented with a series of word-color combinations and asked to identify the color of the font in which the word (itself the name of either the same or a different color) is displayed. In the difficult (self-control depleting) version of this task the name and color are always in conflict, whereas in the placebo version such conflict almost never occurs. Kocher et al. suspect that a lack of self-control contributes to more impulsive bidding. They find large effects of self-control depletion in the form of more aggressive bidding and greater overvaluation, and a particularly pronounced effect upon mispricing. As they also find that depleted traders experience stronger self-rated emotions, they suggest that depletion exerts its influence by enhancing traders' sensitivity to these emotions. A second experiment with mixed markets comprised of both depleted and nondepleted traders does not find any effect on traders' profits, corroborating the unexpected null result in Dickinson et al. (2017) for the profits of sleepy traders who presumably rely more on System 1 reasoning.

Two further studies take the opposite approach, aiming to enhance System 2 thinking to see whether doing so improves market outcomes. Ferri, Ploner, and Rizzolli (2016) mandate time for deliberation and reflection in an SSW experiment, using a ten-second "cooling off" period for each trade, compared with a no-time-delay treatment. They find that the time delay greatly reduces volatility and price dispersion. However, markets are undervalued in both treatments, and more so for time-delay markets, leading to worse mispricing in the delay treatment, assuming that traders are risk neutral. The authors then re-estimate FV using the measured risk aversion of their subjects and find that the time-delay treatment tracks this risk averse FV closely throughout the experiment. Finally, Cheung and Palan (2012) compare markets in which each decision making unit is a team of two, who must agree on each transaction they make, to conventional markets populated by individuals. They find that the teams treatment reduces bubbles, presumably because teams must deliberate to justify and agree on their decisions.

Taken together, these studies provide evidence that the decisions of traders relying on System 1 thinking, whether through sleepiness, high testosterone, or impulsivity, lead to greater market volatility than the decisions of traders relying more on System 2 thinking.

Emotions: Induced Through Priming

Background emotional states can influence our attitudes to risk and reward by changing the neuronal firing threshold in our brains (Kennedy, 2011), which may affect trading decisions. Several studies investigate how asset markets behave when traders in some markets are emotionally primed prior to the start of trade. Andrade, Odean, and Lin (2016) use video clips to induce excitement, fear, or calm, prior to an SSW experiment. All subjects in each market watch the same video; the authors do not consider mixed markets. Psychologists use the term "valence" (which may be positive or negative) to describe the intrinsic attractiveness or aversiveness of an emotion, and "arousal" (which may be high or low) to describe its intensity. Andrade et al. find that clips featuring high arousal and positive valence (intended to induce excitement) lead to significantly greater overvaluation than clips invoking high-arousal negative valence (fear) or low-arousal positive valence (calm). Other effects were marginal or insignificant. They argue that excitement has the strongest effect due to the congruence between contextual cues from a rising market and the stimulus, whereas the clip inducing fear has less effect as it lacks congruence with the context, such that the fear state is incidental and not reinforced. They do not proceed to investigate whether induced fear would enhance or dampen the downturn in crash-prone markets.

Newell and Page (2017) examine whether priming in boom or bust conditions (using a procedure developed by Cohn, Engelmann, Fehr, & Maréchal, 2015) affects subsequent trading behavior in an SSW experiment. Each market is comprised of traders who experience the same priming, in the form of a fictitious market price chart showing trajectories for strong gains (the "boom" condition) or strong losses (the "bust" condition). Subjects are then asked a series of questions designed to engage them with the economic realities of the scenario they are presented with, and thereby put them in the desired disposition. No control treatment is included for comparison.

The authors hypothesize that when traders are primed for boom conditions, bubbles will be larger, mispricing greater and price forecasts less accurate. They find overvaluation in both treatments, but significantly more so in the boom treatment. They also find less risk aversion, worse price predictions, and slightly greater mispricing in the boom condition. Newell and Page interpret their results in terms of countercyclical risk aversion, whereby self-reinforcing feedback loops exacerbate initial market movements away from FV. As they note, their results are consistent with those of Andrade et al. (2016) in that excitement is associated with boom times and fear is associated with busts.

Emotions: Repeated Measures

We previously noted evidence for strong coherence between different measures of fluctuating emotions (Levenson, 2014; Mauss et al., 2005), such as self-reports, skin conductance, and facial expressions. Hargreaves Heap and Zizzo (2011) elicit self-reported emotions during an SSW experiment, while Breaban and Noussair (2018) employ face-reading technology to assign emotional states to changes in facial expressions during trading. The former study uses a seven-point Likert scale to measure subjects' feelings of anger, anxiety, excitement, and joy. The authors find little effect of anger or joy, but significant and opposing effects of excitement and anxiety, the latter likely being a proxy for fear. Excitement is associated with overvaluation, and anxiety with trading close to FV. Emotional state is not related to traders' profits. The authors find evidence that a momentum effect arises endogenously via the effect of earlier price changes on excitement, raising current prices, and creating a self-reinforcing feedback loop away from FV.

Breaban and Noussair (2018) are also interested in the effect of emotional changes during trading in SSW markets. They use a novel face-reading software called Noldus Facereader to identify the "universal" expressions associated with happiness, surprise, anger, disgust, sadness, fear, "neutrality," and overall emotional valence (defined by Breaban and Noussair as "a composite measure of the positivity of emotional state"). The more highly cognitively-mediated emotions such as regret, which we assume to be specifically human, are not associated with a facial expression by Noldus Facereader. Breaban and Noussair (2018) find that the initial market average level of overall valence correlates positively with overvaluation, while initial fear (which is negative in valence) correlates with price decreases and selling. They find that the other emotions correlate with higher prices when positive, and lower prices when negative, but none are statistically significant. In general, the levels of different emotions can predict the direction but not the extent of price changes.

Breaban and Noussair (2018) also find that sales rise with *contemporaneous* fear, while purchases rise with *lagged* overall valence. They then assign each trader to one of three types: fundamental traders and speculators, both of whom are rational, and momentum traders, who are not, based on their buying and selling decisions while trading. Their strongest findings apply to momentum traders (34% of the sample), who buy more when market average valence is positive and sell more when it is negative. On average, these momentum traders earn less money than the other types. They also find that fear, anger, and surprise increase as a crash unfolds, but that just after the crash, surprise (which is neutral in valence) falls away and sadness (which is negative) rises instead. Finally, they find that traders who can maintain a relatively neutral emotional state during a crash earn greater profits overall, indicating that emotional self-regulation is important for trading success.

fMRI

Several studies use fMRI (see Chapter 8) to measure neural activity during an SSW experiment. This records the uptake of glucose in different brain regions known to be involved in specific neural processes, in the form of blood oxygenation level dependent (BOLD) signals, in near real time. The main limitations are small sample sizes, due to cost, and the need for a subject to lie in a scanner during the decision process, which restricts the types of tasks that can be measured.

De Martino, O'Doherty, Ray, Bossaerts, and Camerer (2013) compare fMRI BOLD signals in bubble markets with those in nonbubble markets for subjects with varying ToM abilities. They find that high ToM can be maladaptive when interacting with modern financial markets, even though the ability to infer the intentions of others is usually advantageous. A possible explanation is the interaction between cognitive ability and ToM as proposed by Hefti et al. (2016), discussed above, who argue that the most successful traders need both capabilities to judge the market correctly. Specifically, Hefti et al. find that "semiotic" traders, who have ToM above the median but cognitive ability below the median, perform poorly. These traders assign intentionality to the market itself and ride the bubble to its peak, but fail to sell out in time. De Martino et al. (2013) find greater activity in the ventromedial prefrontal cortex for those with a tendency to ride the bubble, interacting with stronger signals in the dorsomedial prefrontal cortex (a proxy for gauging intentionality), but only in sessions in which bubbles were present.

Smith, Lohrenz, King, Montague, and Camerer (2014) use fMRI to identify differential BOLD signals for those who ride the bubble up and sell out in time, compared with those who continue to buy or hold shares beyond the market peak. They find that in aggregate, neural activity in the nucleus accumbens (NAcc) tracks the expansion of the price bubble and can be used to predict future price trends. They also find that those traders who ride the bubble up but then fail to time their exit have particularly strong NAcc activity, which the authors interpret as a reinforcement and reward for buying. We noted earlier that testosterone affects dopamine transmission in the NAcc, but that this signal exerts its influence subconsciously. Smith et al. find that those who make the most money also exhibit a second BOLD signal, in their right anterior insula, that just precedes the peak of the bubble. The authors interpret this signal as an early warning indicator, perhaps reflecting discomforting somatic markers, which acts as the trigger to sell out to the bubble riders who do not experience this signal. The selling activity of those who experience this signal then precipitates the bursting of the bubble. The anterior insula is known to be associated with the processing of interoceptive signals, the experience of pain, and other emotional processing.

DISCUSSION AND CONCLUSION

Implications for Research

We have focused in this chapter on psychological and biophysical measures used in laboratory asset markets. We should be mindful of the limitations of such experiments, which include: greatly simplified environments; convenience samples of students (inexperienced and not representative of real-world traders); comparatively low-powered incentives that may not sufficiently engage the biophysical underpinnings of emotions; small numbers of participants within each market; and comparatively small samples of market observations (typically fewer than 10 observations per treatment condition). In their favor, we note that while not highly representative of professional traders, students may be more representative of retail investors making financial decisions, from those juggling retirement portfolios to those following the latest cryptocurrency craze. There is also a potential tradeoff between the external validity of experimental results and our ability to make causal inferences. In general, laboratory experiments emphasize the latter over the former. Given the limitations afflicting the experimental study of markets, one logical direction for future research is to bring psychometric and biophysical measurement into naturally occurring financial markets. We have referred above to some examples of this type of research.

We further caution that the effects of many variables are not always as clear cut—nor as eye catching—as a superficial reading of the most high-profile studies alone might suggest. For example, we have seen how the effects of variables such as cognitive ability and gender are complex and subtle, varying with factors such as the FV structure, knowledge of market composition, and the distinction between overvaluation and mispricing. Such nuances may be too arcane for nonspecialists, and are easily glossed over in an emerging field seeking to make a name for itself through headline-grabbing results. It is more reassuring to be able to fall back on simple certitudes such as "smart people are more rational," or that "women are less aggressive." Further, again taking cognitive ability and gender as examples, we have seen instances where near-contemporaneous studies, with very similar designs and research questions, have yielded nearly diametrically opposing results. Although not as professionally rewarding to researchers, we emphasize that null results, as well as efforts at replication, are essential for scientific progress in a relatively youthful field such as this. Of course, the above observations hold with equal force for studies of biophysical measurements and manipulations, such as fMRI or testosterone administration.

Implications for Our Understanding of Markets

Keynes (1936) referred to our "animal spirits" as a source of instability in financial markets and, more recently, Shiller (2000) refers to our tendency toward "irrational exuberance." On the other hand, Damasio (1994) has shown how access to our somatic reactions to risk and reward is essential for advantageous decisions. Optimal risky choices are impossible without somatic signals, but those same signals can also goad us to swing too far into optimism and pessimism (Coates & Page, 2016). So, are the emotions we experience at the time of decision essential, or at least helpful? Or are they disruptive to decision quality? If the latter, how can these emotions have remained so tightly interwoven with our choices over evolutionary time if they are not, on balance, advantageous to decision making?

The literature typically draws a distinction between emotions that are "integral," and so advantageous for decisions, and ones that are "incidental," and typically detrimental to decision making (Bechara & Damasio, 2005; Fenton-O'Creevy et al., 2012). While sensible as far as it goes, this distinction does not sufficiently capture the fine line between harnessing one's integral emotions and being a captive to them. Like fire, our emotions can be both a powerful servant to achieve our goals, and a dangerous master that can undermine them. Evidence suggests that emotional self-regulation can make a critical difference to which of these outcomes occurs (Fenton-O'Creevy et al., 2012, and references therein).

Further evidence suggests that emotional self-regulation manifests biophysically in our vagal tone. Experienced traders claim that emotional self-regulation when trading in volatile markets is a core skill they need to acquire: "for traders, low HF HRV is associated with greater susceptibility to incidental emotions and greater difficulty using integral emotions as a guide" (Fenton-O'Creevy et al., 2012). Indeed, Bechara and Damasio (2005) observe that lesion patients perform *better* than normal subjects do when the latter are suffering a wave of anxiety or fall in confidence. The lesion patient's decisions are not susceptible to somatic signals, whether helpful or disruptive alike, and so avoid the despair that can spread through markets.

Implications for Market Design, Regulation, and Policy

Human traders, in particular the young males who dominate the world's trading floors, face a maelstrom of emotions when facing risk and reward; not every trader is a very stable genius. We noted earlier that cortisol and testosterone have an inverted U-shaped dose-response curve for performance. Financial markets must thus navigate a tightrope of instability, seeking to avoid waves of optimism and pessimism that threaten to sweep away these young males with consequences for us all. To limit the damage caused by market instability, can we engineer the choice architecture of financial markets to be safer for human traders, as we design cars with myriad safety features to be robust to human drivers?

Coates et al. (2010, p. 340) and Eckel and Füllbrunn (2015, p. 919) both suggest that financial markets would be less volatile if they were more gender-balanced, raising obvious questions of how this might be achieved, and whether policy interventions are either necessary or appropriate. At the same time, and perhaps to contrary effect, there is growing anecdotal evidence that some financial professionals undergo pharmacological enhancement, for example by taking testosterone supplements in the belief that this will make them more competitive in the workplace (Wallace, 2012), or antidepressants that modulate serotonin pathways. The consequences of these (largely unregulated) actions for traders' performance, and for market stability more broadly, are to date for the most part unexplored.

Under the EMH, algorithmic trading can help to eliminate arbitrage opportunities and bring about greater stability and efficiency. Alternatively, as algorithms are created by humans, they may instead amplify human foibles and exacerbate market instability—as seen in so-called "flash crashes," where markets experience a rapid, but short-lived, plunge in prices. While not directly triggered by algorithms—in some cases, the root cause may be as simple as a "fat-fingered" human error—the amplitude and speed of these price swings may be exacerbated by the cascade of algorithmic orders they precipitate (Kirilenko, Kyle, Samadi, & Tuzun, 2017). Moreover, as Farjam and Kirchkamp (2018) demonstrate, the expectations and behavior of human traders may in turn be affected in unexpected ways by the knowledge that they may be interacting with algorithms.

If emotional and biophysical responses are essential for humans to make sound financial decisions, how do we incorporate such feedback into our computer algorithms? Alternatively, will the content of these algorithms render moot an inability to do so? We hope that this chapter will stimulate new approaches to these fundamental, and fundamentally human, questions.

REFERENCES

Akiyama, E., Hanaki, N., & Ishikawa, R. (2017). It is not just confusion! Strategic uncertainty in an experimental asset market. *Economic Journal, 127*(605), F563–F580.

Andrade, E. B., Odean, T., & Lin, S. (2016). Bubbling with excitement: An experiment. *Review of Finance, 20*(2), 447–466.

Appelhans, B. M., & Luecken, L. J. (2006). Heart rate variability as an index of regulated emotional responding. *Review of General Psychology, 10*(3), 229–240.

Azevedo, R., Bennett, N., Bilicki, A., Hooper, J., Markopoulou, F., & Tsakiris, M. (2017). The calming effect of a new wearable device during the anticipation of public speech. *Scientific Reports, 7*(1), 2285.

Bechara, A., & Damasio, A. R. (2005). The somatic marker hypothesis: A neural theory of economic decision. *Games and Economic Behavior, 52*(2), 336–372.

Becker, A., Deckers, T., Dohmen, T., Falk, A., & Kosse, F. (2012). The relationship between economic preferences and psychological personality measures. *Annual Review of Economics, 4*(1), 453–478.

Booth, A. L., & Nolen, P. (2012). Gender differences in risk behaviour: Does nurture matter? *Economic Journal, 122*(558), F56–F78.

Bosch-Rosa, C., Meissner, T., & Bosch-Domènech, A. (2018). Cognitive bubbles. *Experimental Economics, 21*(1), 132–153.

Bossaerts, P., & Murawski, C. (2017). Computational complexity and human decision making. *Trends in Cognitive Sciences, 21*(12), 917–929.

Brañas-Garza, P., & Rustichini, A. (2011). Organizing effects of testosterone and economic behavior: Not just risk taking. *PLoS One, 6*(12).

Breaban, A., & Noussair, C. N. (2015). Trader characteristics and fundamental value trajectories in an asset market experiment. *Journal of Behavioral and Experimental Finance, 8*, 1–17.

Breaban, A., & Noussair, C. N. (2018). Emotional state and market behavior. *Review of Finance, 22*(1), 279–309.

Burks, S. V., Carpenter, J. P., Goette, L., & Rustichini, A. (2009). Cognitive skills affect economic preferences, strategic behavior, and job attachment. *Proceedings of the National Academy of Sciences, 106*(19), 7745–7750.

Carpenter, J., Graham, M., & Wolf, J. (2013). Cognitive ability and strategic sophistication. *Games and Economic Behavior, 80*, 115–130.

Chamberlin, E. H. (1948). An experimental imperfect market. *Journal of Political Economy, 56*(2), 95–108.

Chen, Y., Katuščák, P., & Ozdenoren, E. (2013). Why can't a woman bid more like a man? *Games and Economic Behavior, 77*(1), 181–213.

Cheung, S. L., Hedegaard, M., & Palan, S. (2014). To see is to believe: Common expectations in experimental asset markets. *European Economic Review, 66*, 84–96.

Cheung, S. L., & Palan, S. (2012). Two heads are less bubbly than one: Team decision making in an experimental asset market. *Experimental Economics, 15*(3), 373–397.

Cheung, S. L., & Zhang, G. (2018). Effects of individuals' characteristics on trading strategies in an asset market experiment. The University of Sydney (in prepration).

Coates, J. (2012). *The hour between dog and wolf: Risk taking, gut feelings and the biology of boom and bust*. London: Fourth Estate.

Coates, J., & Gurnell, M. (2017). Combining field work and laboratory work in the study of financial risk-taking. *Hormones and Behavior*, *92*, 13–19.

Coates, J. M., Gurnell, M., & Rustichini, A. (2009). Second-to-fourth digit ratio predicts success among high-frequency financial traders. *Proceedings of the National Academy of Sciences*, *106*(2), 623–628.

Coates, J. M., Gurnell, M., & Sarnyai, Z. (2010). From molecule to market: Steroid hormones and financial risk-taking. *Philosophical Transactions of The Royal Society B: Biological Sciences*, *365*(1538), 331–343.

Coates, J., & Page, L. (2016). Biology of financial market instability. In *The new Palgrave dictionary of economics*. London: Palgrave Macmillan.

Cohn, A., Engelmann, J., Fehr, E., & Maréchal, M. A. (2015). Evidence for countercyclical risk aversion: An experiment with financial professionals. *American Economic Review*, *105*(2), 860–885.

Colzato, L. S., Ritter, S. M., & Steenbergen, L. (2018). Transcutaneous vagus nerve stimulation (tVNS) enhances divergent thinking. *Neuropsychologia*, *111*, 72–76.

Colzato, L. S., Sellaro, R., & Beste, C. (2017). Darwin revisited: The vagus nerve is a causal element in controlling recognition of other's emotions. *Cortex*, *92*, 95–102.

Corgnet, B., Hernán-González, R., Kujal, P., & Porter, D. (2015). The effect of earned versus house money on price bubble formation in experimental asset markets. *Review of Finance*, *19*(4), 1455–1488.

Critchley, H., & Garfinkel, S. (2015). Interactions between visceral afferent signaling and stimulus processing. *Frontiers in Neuroscience*, *9*, 286.

Cueva, C., Roberts, R. E., Spencer, T., Rani, N., Tempest, M., Tobler, P. N., et al. (2015). Cortisol and testosterone increase financial risk taking and may destabilize markets. *Scientific Reports*, *5*.

Cueva, C., & Rustichini, A. (2015). Is financial instability male-driven? Gender and cognitive skills in experimental asset markets. *Journal of Economic Behavior & Organization*, *119*, 330–344.

Damasio, A. R. (1994). *Descartes' error: Emotion, reason, and the human brain*. New York: G.P. Putnam.

Darwin, C. (1872). *The expression of the emotions in man and animals*. London: John Murray.

De Martino, B., O'Doherty, J. P., Ray, D., Bossaerts, P., & Camerer, C. (2013). In the mind of the market: Theory of mind biases value computation during financial bubbles. *Neuron*, *79*(6), 1222–1231.

Dickinson, D. L., Chaudhuri, A., & Greenaway-McGrevy, R. (2017). *Trading while sleepy? Circadian mismatch and excess volatility in a global experimental asset market*. Discussion paper 10984 IZA Institute of Labor Economics.

Dohmen, T., Falk, A., Huffman, D., & Sunde, U. (2010). Are risk aversion and impatience related to cognitive ability? *American Economic Review*, *100*(3), 1238–1260.

Eckel, C. C., & Füllbrunn, S. C. (2015). Thar SHE blows? Gender, competition, and bubbles in experimental asset markets. *American Economic Review*, *105*(2), 906–920.

Eckel, C. C., & Füllbrunn, S. C. (2017). Hidden vs. known gender effects in experimental asset markets. *Economics Letters*, *156*, 7–9.

Fama, E. F. (1970). Efficient capital markets: A review of theory and empirical work. *Journal of Finance*, *25*(2), 383–417.

Farjam, M., & Kirchkamp, O. (2018). Bubbles in hybrid markets: How expectations about algorithmic trading affect human trading. *Journal of Economic Behavior and Organization, 146*, 248–269.

Fenton-O'Creevy, M., Lins, J. T., Vohra, S., Richards, D. W., Davies, G., & Schaaff, K. (2012). Emotion regulation and trader expertise: Heart rate variability on the trading floor. *Journal of Neuroscience, Psychology, and Economics, 5*(4), 227–237.

Ferri, G., Ploner, M., & Rizzolli, M. (2016). *Count to ten before trading: Evidence on the role of deliberation in experimental financial markets.* Working paper 7, Center for Relationship Banking and Economics LUMSA University.

Frederick, S. (2005). Cognitive reflection and decision making. *Journal of Economic Perspectives, 19*(4), 25–42.

Gill, D., & Prowse, V. (2016). Cognitive ability, character skills, and learning to play equilibrium: A level-k analysis. *Journal of Political Economy, 124*(6), 1619–1676.

Gneezy, U., Niederle, M., & Rustichini, A. (2003). Performance in competitive environments: Gender differences. *Quarterly Journal of Economics, 118*(3), 1049–1074.

Hanaki, N., Akiyama, E., Funaki, Y., & Ishikawa, R. (2017). *Diversity in cognitive ability and mispricing in experimental asset markets.* Working paper 2017–08 GREDEG, Université de Nice Sophia Antipolis.

Hargreaves Heap, S., & Zizzo, D. J. (2011). *Emotions and chat in a financial markets experiment.* Working paper 11-11 Centre for Behavioural and Experimental Social Science, University of East Anglia.

Hefti, A., Heinke, S., & Schneider, F. (2016). *Mental capabilities, trading styles, and asset market bubbles: Theory and experiment.* Working paper 234 Department of Economics, University of Zurich.

Holt, C. A., Porzio, M., & Song, M. Y. (2017). Price bubbles, gender, and expectations in experimental asset markets. *European Economic Review, 100*, 72–94.

Kahneman, D. (2011). *Thinking, fast and slow.* New York: Farrar, Straus and Giroux.

Kandasamy, N., Garfinkel, S. N., Page, L., Hardy, B., Critchley, H. D., Gurnell, M., et al. (2016). Interoceptive ability predicts survival on a London trading floor. *Scientific Reports, 6*.

Kennedy, P. (2011). Changes in emotional state modulate neuronal firing rates of human speech motor cortex: A case study in long-term recording. *Neurocase, 17*(5), 381–393.

Keynes, J. M. (1936). *The general theory of employment, interest and money.* London: Macmillan.

King, R. R., Smith, V. L., Williams, A. W., & van Boening, M. V. (1993). The robustness of bubbles and crashes in experimental stock markets. In R. H. Day & P. Chen (Eds.), *Nonlinear dynamics and evolutionary economics* (pp. 183–200). Oxford: Oxford University Press.

Kirchler, M., Huber, J., & Stöckl, T. (2012). Thar she bursts: Reducing confusion reduces bubbles. *American Economic Review, 102*(2), 865–883.

Kirilenko, A., Kyle, A. S., Samadi, M., & Tuzun, T. (2017). The flash crash: High-frequency trading in an electronic market. *Journal of Finance, 72*(3), 967–998.

Kocher M.G., Lucks K.E. and Schindler D., Unleashing animal spirits: Self-control and overpricing in experimental asset markets, Review of Financial Studies (in press).

Krall, S. C., Rottschy, C., Oberwelland, E., Bzdok, D., Fox, P. T., Eickhoff, S. B., et al. (2015). The role of the right temporoparietal junction in attention and social interaction as revealed by ALE meta-analysis. *Brain Structure and Function, 220*(2), 587–604.

Levenson, R. W. (2014). The autonomic nervous system and emotion. *Emotion Review, 6*(2), 100–112.

Loewenstein, G., Weber, E., Hsee, C., & Welch, N. (2001). Risk as feelings. *Psychological Bulletin*, *127*(2), 267–286.

Luders, E., Narr, K. L., Thompson, P. M., & Toga, A. W. (2009). Neuroanatomical correlates of intelligence. *Intelligence*, *37*(2), 156–163.

Maniscalco, J. W., & Rinaman, L. (2018). Vagal interoceptive modulation of motivated behavior. *Physiology*, *33*(2), 151–167.

Mauss, I. B., Levenson, R. W., McCarter, L., Wilhelm, F. H., & Gross, J. J. (2005). The tie that binds? Coherence among emotion experience, behavior, and physiology. *Emotion*, *5*(2), 175–190.

Menary, K., Collins, P. F., Porter, J. N., Muetzel, R., Olson, E. A., Kumar, V., et al. (2013). Associations between cortical thickness and general intelligence in children, adolescents and young adults. *Intelligence*, *41*(5), 597–606.

Nadler, A., Jiao, P., Johnson, C. J., Alexander, V., & Zak, P. J. (2018). The bull of Wall Street: Experimental analysis of testosterone and asset trading. *Management Science*, *64*(9), 4032–4051.

Nave, G., Nadler, A., Zava, D., & Camerer, C. (2017). Single-dose testosterone administration impairs cognitive reflection in men. *Psychological Science*, *28*(10), 1398–1407.

Newell, A., & Page, L. (2017). *Countercyclical risk aversion and Self-reinforcing feedback loops in experimental asset markets*. Working paper 50 Queensland Behavioural Economics Group, Queensland University of Technology.

Niederle, M. (2016). Gender. In: J. H. Kagel & A. E. Roth (Eds.), *Vol. 2, The handbook of experimental economics* (pp. 481–562). Princeton: Princeton University Press.

Niederle, M., & Vesterlund, L. (2007). Do women shy away from competition? Do men compete too much? *Quarterly Journal of Economics*, *122*(3), 1067–1101.

Noussair, C. N., Robin, S., & Ruffieux, B. (2001). Price bubbles in laboratory asset markets with constant fundamental values. *Experimental Economics*, *4*(1), 87–105.

Noussair, C. N., Tucker, S., & Xu, Y. (2016). Futures markets, cognitive ability, and mispricing in experimental asset markets. *Journal of Economic Behavior & Organization*, *130*, 166–179.

Oehler, A., Wendt, S., Wedlich, F., & Horn, M. (2018). Investors' personality influences investment decisions: Experimental evidence on extraversion and neuroticism. *Journal of Behavioral Finance*, *19*(1), 30–48.

Palan, S. (2013). A review of bubbles and crashes in experimental asset markets. *Journal of Economic Surveys*, *27*(3), 570–588.

Pantelis, P. C., Byrge, L., Tyszka, J. M., Adolphs, R., & Kennedy, D. P. (2015). A specific hypoactivation of right temporo-parietal junction/posterior superior temporal sulcus in response to socially awkward situations in autism. *Social Cognitive and Affective Neuroscience*, *10*(10), 1348–1356.

Pástor, L., & Veronesi, P. (2006). Was there a Nasdaq bubble in the late 1990s? *Journal of Financial Economics*, *81*(1), 61–100.

Poppa, T., & Bechara, A. (2018). The somatic marker hypothesis: revisiting the role of the "body-loop" in decision making. *Current Opinion in Behavioral Sciences*, *19*, 61–66.

Riccelli, R., Toschi, N., Nigro, S., Terracciano, A., & Passamonti, L. (2017). Surface-based morphometry reveals the neuroanatomical basis of the five-factor model of personality. *Social Cognitive and Affective Neuroscience*, *12*(4), 671–684.

Shiller, R. J. (2000). *Irrational exuberance*. Princeton: Princeton University Press.

Smith, A., Lohrenz, T., King, J., Montague, P. R., & Camerer, C. F. (2014). Irrational exuberance and neural crash warning signals during endogenous experimental market bubbles. *Proceedings of the National Academy of Sciences, 111*(29), 10503–10508.

Smith, V. L. (1962). An experimental study of competitive market behavior. *Journal of Political Economy, 70*(2), 111–137.

Smith, V. L., Suchanek, G. L., & Williams, A. W. (1988). Bubbles, crashes, and endogenous expectations in experimental spot asset markets. *Econometrica, 56*(5), 1119–1151.

Stroop, J. R. (1935). Studies of interference in serial verbal reactions. *Journal of Experimental Psychology, 18*(6), 643–662.

Thompson, E. (2006). The tulipmania: Fact or artifact? *Public Choice, 130*(1), 99–114.

Wallace, C. (2012). *Keep taking the testosterone*. Financial Times.

Chapter 8

Opportunities and Challenges of Portable Biological, Social, and Behavioral Sensing Systems for the Social Sciences☆

Benno Torgler
Queensland University of Technology, Brisbane, QLD, Australia

---

Emotions move us.
Nobel laureate Charles Sherrington.

[W]e have feelings essentially all the time:
it is common to hear somebody say,
"Sorry, I wasn't thinking," but not "Sorry, I wasn't feeling."
Rosalind Picard (2003, p. 56).

INTRODUCTION

The increasing use of rigorous scientific methods to answer long-standing questions in the social sciences is producing an environment in which the boundaries between economics, social psychology, and sociology have become increasingly fluid, facilitating what Wilson (1998) called the mind's greatest enterprise: promoting the linkage between sciences and humanities. Technological advances in neuroscience in particular, such as wearable, nonintrusive, and noninvasive instruments, have opened fruitful new research avenues for the social sciences, on which they are likely in turn to have a major impact. Monitoring physiological processes through nonintrusive means, such as surface electrodes, is attractive for its potential to identify psychological or mental processes that are otherwise hard to measure. The dense continuous data such measurement

---

☆ I would like to thank the editor of this volume, Gigi Foster, and Brendan Wilson for their outstanding editorial work above and beyond their call of duty and therefore the parameters of their assignment. They substantially helped to improve the quality of this contribution.

Biophysical Measurement in Experimental Social Science Research. https://doi.org/10.1016/B978-0-12-813092-6.00004-6

produces described as a "second by second picture" by Pentland, Lazer, Brewer, and Heibeck (2009, p. 4) offers new ways of understanding human dynamics (Eagle & Pentland, 2006) and better equips social scientists to deal with the messiness and challenges encountered when studying the human mind or human behavior in the real world rather than the laboratory. Such messiness is exemplified in the following situation, adapted from Minsky (2006, pp. 97–99):

Gigi is starting to cross the street on her way to deliver her presentation at a conference. While thinking about what to say at the presentation, she hears a sound and turns her head—and sees a quickly oncoming car. Uncertain as to whether to cross or retreat, but uneasy about arriving late, Gigi decides to spring across the road. She later remembers her injured knee from too much long-distance running and reflects upon her impulsive decision. "If my knee had failed I could have been killed. Then what would my family and friends have thought of me?"

Although seemingly not out of the ordinary, this scenario reflects our constant confrontation in daily life with situations of comparable complexity. Any attempt to catalog Gigi's cognitive activities as the scenario unfolds quickly illustrates how far current neuroscience is from understanding how our cognitive processes work. The aspects of the mental work involved in the above everyday situation are in fact myriad: identification, specification, planning, attention, (in)decision, reaction, imagining, selection, reconsideration, reflection, self-reflection, empathy, reformulation, moral reflection, self-awareness, and self-imaging. Minsky's own attempt at analyzing human cognition led him to derive a six-level model of the mind (Minsky, 2006, pp. 130–131) that can be illustrated as follows, by application to the scenario above:

Inborn, instinctive reaction: Gigi hears a sound and turns her head because we are born with survival instincts.

Learned reaction: Gigi has learned since her childhood that certain conditions, such as seeing an oncoming car, demand specific ways to react.

Deliberative thinking: Gigi thinks about what to say at her presentation, considering, for example, several alternatives ways to begin the speech, and tries to decide which would be the best approach to take.

Reflective thinking: Gigi reflects on her decision, reacting to what is happening inside her brain.

Self-reflective thinking: Gigi is uneasy about arriving late so she thinks (fleetingly) about how she would deal with it.

Self-conscious emotions: Gigi thinks about higher values and ideals. In considering what her family and friends would think of her in case of an accident or death, she asks herself how well her actions agree with her ideals: "What would they have thought of me?"

Whether or not this particular multilayered model is an adequate representation of mental activities is not essential: six layers may be too many or perhaps too few. What matters is our need as scientists for ways in which to represent and explore sequential or parallel mental activities, a task for which such multilayer models offer potential. Rather than looking at the one-off decisions so widely studied in decision sciences and neuroeconomic studies (e.g., to buy a consumer good or not or to decide between lottery A and lottery B), if we are to develop a true theory of the mind, we must find ways to explore human nature and behavior in more complex and dynamic settings. The complexity of our environment means that a variety of (contextual) factors are active at any given moment in time and as illustrated in the excerpt below, our reactions to them, including our emotional responses, are affected by the situation itself:

Gigi's friends have always described her as a happy person. She likes to play tennis and finds great enjoyment in watching the top professionals play the game. One day, after watching her favorite player win the semifinal of a grand slam tennis tournament, Gigi contentedly stands in line under a hot August sun waiting to get a cool drink. As the glow of her vicarious victory fades, and the heat and humidity become more and more oppressive, Gigi suddenly feels a piercing pain from a blow to her lower back. She turns rapidly with an angry expression and clenched fist only to see that she has been hit by Rebecca, a woman with hemiplegia whose wheelchair went out of control and caused her to crash into Gigi and spill her drink on her dress. Gigi's understanding that the cause of her pain was an uncontrollable event that has embarrassed Rebecca immediately changes her anger to sadness and sympathy. Although still in pain, her happy nature surfaces, and she begins helping Rebecca recover from the accident (adapted from Izard, 1993, p. 68).

Research into how we mentally cope with the complexity that we face constantly in daily life is limited by existing technology and comes at a high price. For example, high resolution data derived from functional magnetic resonance imaging (fMRI) is extremely costly because of the sheer magnitude of the equipment and technology needed to retrieve it. Nor are such instruments wearable during daily activities. Research opportunities have received a boost, however, from the recent exponential growth in technological innovations (cf. Moore's law or the law of accelerating returns; see Kurzweil, 1999, 2012), including the production of an increasing array of wearable sensors that allow mapping of the behaviors and interactions of large numbers of individuals in their natural everyday environments. With more than 4.6 billion unique subscribers,[1] mobile phones offer clear potential in this area. Smart phones and wearable electronic badges with integrated sensors offer a variety of possibilities for simultaneously tracking the digital footprint of hundreds or thousands of individuals over days, months, or even years. For example, a phone with an emotion-sensing application can provide information on an individual's habits, movements, conversation patterns, health status, and social network, as well as

1. See https://www.gsmaintelligence.com/research/?file=9e927fd6896724e7b26f33f61db5b9d5&download.

contextual factors such as ambient sound (for an overview, see Eagle & Greene, 2014). Likewise, wearable biosensors can track heart rate variability, blood pressure, skin conductivity, and sleep patterns. Such technology seems less and less intrusive given how accustomed we are becoming to wearing fitness tracking gadgets such as Fitbits, TomTom, and Apple Watch.

The "reality mining" facilitated by such instruments has the power to increase the external validity of social science research orders of magnitude beyond what is possible using other methods of primary data collection. Wearable technologies will allow researchers to move beyond the artificiality of a subject lying in an fMRI scanner during an experiment, while also complementing the use of surveys, helping to compensate for their inherent problems of reporting biases, memory errors, and sparsity of continuous data (Eagle & Pentland, 2006; Pentland et al., 2009). Because reality mining allows what is measured to include the internal, environmental and situational realities of the individuals being observed (Eagle & Greene, 2014), we are increasingly likely to see studies that harness real time continuous biological data linked to both behavior and environmental conditions. If we are to gain realistic insights into complex phenomena such as human intentions, goals, wishes, conflicts, and values, we must not only combine sets of measurements and diverse tools but also pool the data derived from particular situations with randomized controlled trials and/or link them to historical natural experiments. Some scholars have coined the term "social fMRI" (Aharony, Pan, Ip, Khayal, & Pentland, 2011) to describe the collection of a multimodal and highly diverse range of signals through sources ranging from mobile phone sensing and social networking platforms to purchasing behavior and surveys. With more tools available, it may be possible to create what Watts (2013) terms a "social supercollider" (p. 7) and Helbing (2015) a "knowledge accelerator" (p. 3). The combination of multiple approaches and large scale integrated, overlapping data sources will help to produce a richer, more realistic portrait of human nature and social interactions.

To illustrate how smart sensing can be used to track our actions and outcomes, I describe below the appeal of three nonintrusive sensory instruments not yet fully explored in the social sciences: HRV measurement, sociometers, and emotional sense systems. All three instruments, whose common characteristic is the provision of real time feedback, complement self-reported data by offering better reliability (e.g., immunity from reporting or recall bias) and more timely information (Almaatouq, Radaelli, Pentland, & Shmueli, 2016; Leng, Rudolph, Pentland, Zhao, & Koutsopolous, 2016).

HEART RATE VARIABILITY MEASUREMENT, EMOTIONS, AND STRESS

Because HRV measurement has been described at length elsewhere (Dulleck et al., 2016; Dulleck, Ristl, Schaffner, & Torgler, 2011; Dulleck, Schaffner,

& Torgler, 2014) and in Appendix 1 of this volume (Fooken & Parker, 2018) with focus on the practical and technical dimensions of using HRV, I focus here more on what we can learn from applying it in research.[2] Although originally intended to identify medical conditions (Malik et al., 1996), HRV measures have been linked with psychological, mental, and emotional activities (Crone, Bunge, De Klerk, & Van der Molen, 2005; Crone, Somsen, Van Beek, & Van der Molen, 2004; Koelsch et al., 2007; Yang et al., 2007). This linkage is possible because emotions are not only cognitive but also physical (James, 1950). The brain and body interact during emotional experience. For example, chronically elevated levels of cortisol affect memory and various brain regions, killing neurons in the hippocampus, reducing hippocampal volume, and inducing a growth of branches in the amygdala, which makes thinking more emotional (Coates, 2012). Chronically high cortisol levels can also increase anxiety and suppress the production of testosterone, reducing confidence and suppressing risky behavior (Coates, 2012). Stuckler, Meissner, and King (2008) using international data from 1960 to 2002, provide empirical evidence in the form of increased heart disease mortality rates that bank crises can literally "break your heart."

From a technical standpoint, HRV provides information about the activity of two major parts of the autonomic nervous system (ANS): the sympathetic and the parasympathetic (see also Fooken & Parker, 2018). The sympathetic system, which is responsible for the fight-or-flight response, affects the heart rate indirectly through the sympathetic nerves and by releasing cell-stimulating hormones like adrenaline into the blood stream. The parasympathetic system, responsible for rest and relaxation responses, influences the heart directly through the vagal nerve's connection to the heart's specific "pacemaker" cells (Levy & Martin, 1979) (see Fig. 1). Because the changes in heart rate induced by the sympathetic system occur over a considerably longer time (with the maximum effect being reached after more than 5 s) than those induced by the parasympathetic system (where the maximum effect is reached after less than 5 s) (Levy, Martin, Iano, & Zieske, 1970), these timing differences can be used to identify separately the extent of sympathetic and parasympathetic activity. Activity in the sympathetic system is mainly reflected in an HRV machine's readings by high spectral power in the low frequency band (LF [0.033–0.15 Hz]), whereas activity in the parasympathetic system is reflected by high spectral power in the high frequency band (HF [0.15–0.4 Hz]) (Malik, 2008). HRV data are easy to collect in either the laboratory or the real world (e.g., via round-the-clock measurement as subjects go about their activities outside the laboratory) because a common heart rate monitor that records an individual electrocardiogram (ECG) with medical levels of accuracy is only about the size of a smartphone (see Fig. 1).

2. For those interested in reading more about data processing, I recommend Dulleck et al. (2016) and Fooken and Parker (2018), Appendix 2 in this book).

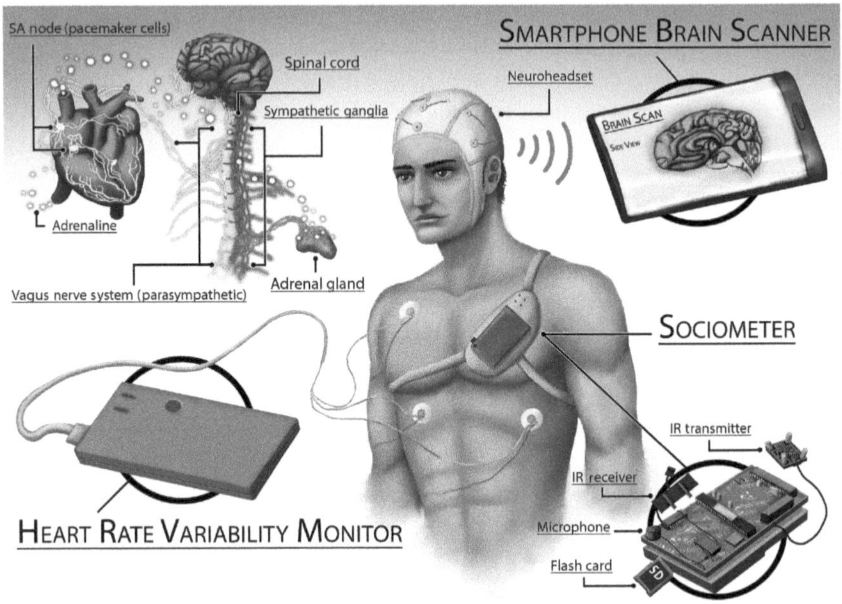

FIG. 1 Portable biological, social and behavioral sensing systems.

HRV data have been designated a "cardiac signature of emotionality" (Koelsch et al., 2007, p. 3331). Neuroimaging research has provided additional evidence that physiological measures such as HRV can detect emotional responses (Gardhouse & Anderson, 2013). For example, the sympathetic-to-parasympathetic ratio (LF/HF HRV ratio) has been shown to be correlated with levels of activation in particular brain regions during mental activity (Berntson & Cacioppo, 2008; Seong, Lee, Shin, Kim, & Yoon, 2004). Yang et al. (2007) also reported that during the presentation of fearful faces, heart rate is significantly correlated with activation in the right amygdala (Spearman's rho = 0.55), the organ that assigns emotional significance to events and is the seat of emotion, memory, and attention. As Coates (2012) put it, "without the amygdala, we would view the world as a collection of uninteresting objects. A charging grizzly bear would impress us as nothing more threatening than a large, moving object" (p. 50). HRV has also been connected with individual anxiety and emotional components of personality (Crone et al., 2004, 2005), with several studies showing its association with activation in a number of brain regions, including the amygdala and medial prefrontal cortex (Thayer, Åhs, Fredrikson, Sollers, & Wager, 2012).

Economists have rarely used HRV in their research, although Dulleck et al. (2011) discuss the method of HRV measurement and its application for experimental economics. One of the few exceptions is a study by Falk, Menrath, Verde, and Siegrist (2011), which evaluated data on 70 subjects to assess whether people's fairness perceptions are correlated with HRV. These authors identified a positive correlation between perceived of unfair pay and lower HRV (signifying higher stress). Another study by Van Lange, Finkenauer, Popma, and Van Vugt (2011) showed that introducing an experimental protocol measuring heart rate promoted behavioral trust in trust games and reciprocal giving, possibly because of interpersonal and intrapersonal mechanisms to do with the protocol itself. As the authors stress, positioning electrodes "typically involves interpersonal touch, interpersonal communication, as well as intrapersonal arousal, feeling of vulnerability, and perhaps even helplessness among participants" (p. 211) triggering processes that "serve as a social glue by promoting trust and trustworthiness between strangers" (p. 249). Brandts and Garofalo (2012) found no statistically significant effect of HRV on performance (measured as the number of correct answers out of six problems) when exploring how individuals respond to an audience which is composed of three people—either three women or three men. Males also exhibited a significant change in blood pressure, rather than HRV, in reaction to gender pairing between audience members and decision makers in the decision task. They are more stressed when they are paired with a female audience. For female participants, however, the gender audience does not matter for their blood pressure.

Some studies have used brain scanners to collect data while subjects play ultimatum bargaining games. The main goal is often to explore what happens in the responders' brain after they received the proposers' offers, neglecting therefore proposers' physiological reactions before or after their offer (for a discussion see Dulleck et al., 2014). Dulleck et al. (2014) used HRV to assess the physiological reactions of both responders and proposers in an ultimatum bargaining game, showing that low offers by a proposer cause signs of mental stress not only for the responder but also for the proposer. A key advantage of bringing HRV measurement into this setting is that it facilitates the exploration of all interacting individuals' behavior.

In related work, Dulleck et al. (2016) use HRV in a tax compliance setting, motivated by Erard and Feinstein's (1994) theory on the role of moral sentiments, which suggests that mere contemplation of noncompliance generates psychic costs and that this produces a desire to reduce this stress by reducing tax evasion. In other words, the intention to evade taxes induces guilt, which consequently reduces the utility of noncompliance and thus increases tax compliance. In their laboratory experiment, Dulleck et al. (2016) used HRV to measure psychic stress when subjects were offered the chance to cheat. They not only found, in line with Erard and Feinstein's theory, a positive correlation between psychic stress and tax compliance but identified three distinct types of individuals based on levels of psychic stress, tax morale, and tax compliance.[3] Following from this study, Macintyre, Schaffner, and Torgler (2017)

3. For a detailed discussion of how tax compliance research can profit from data delivered by such technology, see Torgler (2016).

used HRV to proxy emotional arousal in a study of national pride and tax compliance that employed several differently framed treatments to prime participants psychologically before the tax compliance decision. For example, one treatment video showed iconic images of Australia and another depicted memorable Australian sporting moments, with the images in the treatments accompanied by an orchestral version of the national anthem, "Advance Australia Fair." The control video, in contrast, showed random moving patterns accompanied by Mozart's neutrally themed "Adagio" (Oboe Quartet in F major, K.370). Such research complements both recent evidence from a field experiment on national priming and tax compliance (Gangl, Torgler, & Kirchler, 2016) and survey evidence on national pride and tax morale (Konrad & Qari, 2012; Torgler, 2004, 2007; Torgler & Schneider, 2005, 2007). According to Macintyre et al.'s (2017) study results, Australian participants experienced a decrease in stress during the treatments relative to the control group, while non-Australians experienced an increase. Moreover, while both the Australians who found the iconic images relaxing and the Australians who were emotionally aroused by the sports video showed higher levels of tax compliance than the non-Australians, the non-Australians in both the iconic images treatment group and (even more so) the sports treatment group had lower tax compliance than non-Australians in the control group. The authors conjecture that this pattern of results could be explained by an outgroup effect. As Tomasello (2016) points out, the "[m]odern human individual identified with their cultural group because everyone in the group needed everyone else—they were interdependent—for all kinds of life-sustaining help and support, including protection from the barbarians across the river" (p. 90). Finally, Fooken and Schaffner (2016), in exploring HRV's connection to risk attitudes, identified a tendency for individuals with lower physiological responses during a decision process to take higher risks, although they also observed some differences between their two risk elicitation methods (see p. 4) that could be driven by the measurement of different domains of risk taking.

Although measuring reactions in the real world may be the considered ideal, laboratory experiments are useful for isolating participants' psychological states because of the experimenter's ability to direct or prohibit physical activity, eating, and drinking by subjects (Berntson & Cacioppo, 2008). In particular, limiting participants' movements such as standing up or walking around reduces the physiological noise that could interfere with measuring the effect under exploration, which is particularly important when measuring the sympathetic-to-parasympathetic ratio to generate indicators of psychological state (for a more detailed discussion of context in which HRV is unlikely to capture emotional states, see Fooken & Parker, 2018). A recent study by Fooken (2017) compares stress magnitudes during a laboratory experiment with those outside the lab by using HRV data matched to activity diaries for the same group of students in three settings: during a normal (24 h) day (e.g., mental activities such as studying, attending a lecture or tutorial, or social activities), during a

(24 h) university exam day, and during an economic experiment (structure: public good game [stage 1], math task part 1 [stage 2], dictator game [stage 3], betting game and math task part 2 [stages 4 and 5], bidding game [stage 6], and ability test [stage 7]). This research design enables Fooken to test whether HRV differences are correlated with more or less stressful activities outside the lab (and to compare its magnitudes with the lab experiment [e.g., pro-social context]). Exams are significantly more stressful (higher HRV) than other mental activities. His results provide evidence underscoring the external validity of laboratory findings, indicating that HRV is connected to emotional states through reflecting psychologically induced physical stress (see p. 6). Dulleck, Ristl, Schaffner, and Torgler (2018) also employ a 24-h-measurement design to explore the correlation between self-reported subjective judgment about wellbeing and the objective measurement of HRV—which cannot be deliberately controlled—by measuring both the HRV and the self-reported feelings of 606 participants. Initial results indicate that a lower HRV (meaning lower stress) is correlated with self-reported positive affect (subjective well-being).

In general, controlled laboratory experiments increase our understanding of aspects of emotional experience such as arousal (i.e., intensity) and valence (i.e., relative pleasantness). These differentiated aspects often function and interact jointly during emotional experiences (Gardhouse & Anderson, 2013). Future experimental and field studies can provide more insights into how positive and negative arousal are linked to HRV and behavioral responses. The evaluation of HRV data is particularly valuable in settings prone to emotional response, which for economists might be situations of social dilemma in which there is a conflict between individual and collective interests, scenarios where self-control and will power are central (Baumeister & Tierney, 2012), or settings featuring social comparisons, teamwork involving cooperation and the exchange of information hierarchical relations between leaders and subordinates, or the centrality of reputation and trust. HRV could also be useful in exploring mental and physical resilience, an area that Coates (2012) covers in the last part of his book (Part IV, this chapter and Chapter 9).

Apart from HRV, other physiological indicators used in laboratory experiments to measure emotional arousal and stress, respectively, include skin conductance responses (e.g.Buser, Dreber, & Mollerstrom, 2017; Coricelli, Joffily, Montmarquette, & Villeval, 2010) and salivary cortisol (Buser et al., 2017) (see also Soroka (2018) on skin conductance in Chapter 3 and Hardy (2018) on steroid hormones in Chapter 8). For example, in an experiment involving decks of cards with specific properties (some that offer participants a low initial amount of money with higher gains over time, and others with the opposite characteristics which leads to an overall loss), Bechara, Damasio, Tranel, and Damasio (1997) found that skin conductance began to spike when participants contemplated playing from the money-losing decks before being consciously aware of such a risky choice. Coates (2012), after concluding that increased familiarity (i.e., low novelty of stimuli) and rest reduce physiological load opine that: "Instead of traveling, we may be better off remaining on home turf, surrounding ourselves with family and friends, listening to familiar music, watching old films" (p. 256). With respect to familiarity, he made the following comment about the vagus nerve that structurally and functionally links the heart and brain (Thayer et al., 2012, p. 754):

> *Besides dampening physiological arousal, familiarity ... can convince our vagus nerve, that angel of mercy, to become maximally involved in our problems, take charge of our shattered body and calm things down. The vagus has in its hands the power to slow our stressed heart, ease our breathing, settle our stomach. It can save our life (Coates, 2012, pp. 256–257).*

Coates also cited research on rats indicating that predicable, acute, short-lived stress followed by recovery—required in order to avoid depletion of amine-producing cells—can increase immunity to the damaging effects of stressors, and can build endurance (p. 241), an effect comparable to that observed from time-interval training in physiology (Gibala, 2017). After noting that physiological coping and emotional distress are alternatives, he then reported his own experimental findings that (i) the most experienced and profitable traders showed high and volatile steroid hormone levels of testosterone and cortisol and that (ii) toughened individuals had lower amine levels that increased more significantly under stress but also shut off more quickly.

SOCIOMETERS AND EMOTIONAL SENSE SYSTEMS

Today's widely adopted and pervasive electronic technologies enable human tracking like never before. Smart phones, GPS traces, credit card transactions, and webpage visits create digital human footprints or "digital bread-crumbs" of digital traces of our activities (Almaatouq et al., 2016, p. 407). Mobile phones in particular are so ubiquitous and nonintrusive that people using them quickly forget that they are being measured, which increases the likelihood of observing spontaneous behavior (Rachuri et al., 2010). Recognizing the opportunity for research that our modern electronic habits present, a group of scholars at Massachusetts Institute of Technology (MIT) in the USA (see Pentland, 2008, 2014) developed a sociometer designed to quantify human social behavior in the context of social networks (see Fig. 1). A core interest for this research group was to explore and quantify nonlinguistic social signals like body language, facial expression, voice tone, and aspects of speech such as energy, pitch, and speaking rate (Gatica-Perez, McCowan, Zhang, & Bengio, 2005). Unlike traditional neuroscientific technologies, the sociometer allows researchers to focus on social interactions such as individual turn taking (Choudhury & Pentland, 2004), while also measuring stress via variation in prosodic emphasis (i.e., tone of voice, or the way people vary pitch and volume while speaking; see Pentland,

2005, 2008). Pentland (2014) explains that the sociometer can "accurately predict outcomes of dating situations, job interviews, and even salary negotiations" (p. xi), with the sociometer's sensors able to extract information on both the users' behavior and their environment (for example, location, ambiance, and the presence of others involved in the conversation). According to Choudhury and Pentland (2004), individuals show individually idiosyncratic patterns of activity and sound signaling. To measure these variables, the sociometer takes into account conversational dynamics. It stores the sociometer wearer's identity in an infrared sensor and a person's speech information via an 8 KHz microphone, discriminating between verbalizations that take the form of speech and those that are nonspeech. According to Choudhury and Pentland (2004), these measures work very well for conversations of at least 1 min in duration (to increase the accuracy numbers of detecting conversations). Pentland et al. (2009) refer to "reality mining" via sociometers as a "sort of low-resolution brain scanning technology" (p. 4). Pentland (2014) identified four aspects of human action and interaction that appeared central to the use of sociometers, each of which is explained in more detail below.

Influence

The level of influence that person A has on person B may be measurable by the extent to which, in interaction with A, B's speaking pattern changes to match A's speaking pattern. In support of this conjecture, Gregory and Webster (1996) showed that Larry King, who hosted the nightly TV interview program *Larry King Live* between 1985 and 2010, shifted his vocal frequencies to match the pattern of his higher-status guests but retained his own frequency with lower status individuals. Dominance and high status have also been operationalized by observing speaking time. Those with higher dominance/status tend to talk more than those with lower dominance/status (Schmid Mast, 2002). Body position and movement also reveal emotions, and research into the neurobiology of emotional body language is rapidly growing (see, for example, De Gelder, 2006).

Mimicry

Humans have an automatic tendency to imitate other people (Van Baaren, Holland, Steenaert, & van Knippenberg, 2003, p. 394) through reflective copying in the form of smiles, interjections, head nodding, and other movement (Bailenson & Yee, 2005), a response that has been dubbed the "chameleon effect" (Chartrand & Bargh, 1999). Thus, as Pentland (2008) pointed out, "when one person laughs, our reflex to copy the laughter is so automatic that often it is hard to not laugh, even when it is inappropriate" (p. 6). Thought possibly to have an evolutionary adaptive function of enhancing interpersonal closeness and liking ("benevolence toward the imitator" as put by Van Baaren et al., 2003), mimicry may even be an unconscious signal of empathy (Chartrand & Bargh, 1999; Pentland, 2004). Evolutionarily, copied actions or patterns have been argued to be an essential part of cultural learning (Henrich, 2016), and the greater the challenge or uncertainty present in a situation, the more inclined humans are to copy successful others to augment their own chances of survival (i.e., they use the heuristic of "if in doubt, copy," p. 120). As a simplistic yet clear example, it is better to gather nuts and fruits that have previously been safely collected and eaten by others than to experiment with unfamiliar ones that could be poisonous.

Activity Level

Activity levels are related to the ANS. Excitement leads to a general arousal within the ANS which results in a higher level of motor activity: "[E]xcited adults still fidget more, talk more, and talk more quickly ... it is hard to pay attention to the arousal level of our ANS, and even harder to accurately control its effects. The result is that our activity level, even when suppressed and visible only as fidgets and nervousness, is an honest signal of interest" (Pentland, 2014, p. 13). Movement or motor activity data can also be supplemented with geolocation data that enables the mapping of human mobility patterns (Fan, Leng, & Yang, 2016). Demonstrating the research applicability of such data, Dong, Lepri, and Pentland (2011) tracked the spatio-temporal patterns of residents in an MIT student dormitory for over 9 months to understand how social relationships and individual behaviors coevolve in time and space. They find that by modeling the dynamics in sensor data, they are able to predict friendships.

Consistency

As humans experience different thoughts and emotions, their speech and movements become jerky and unevenly accented and paced. Pentland (2014, p. 16) provides a useful example: "Imagine, for instance, that you are in the middle of a salary negotiation and the other person has just thrown you off balance by proposing something completely unexpected. Somehow you have to quickly figure out what to do without letting on that this has left you flailing about for the right response. Here's what is likely to happen next with your behavior: your speaking pace, emphasis, and even hand and body movements become uneven as your mental resources strive to work on the new problem and at the same time carry on the conversation as if nothing happened. It is this variability in emphasis and rhythm that people are really unable to control. Consequently, the consistency of one's emphasis and timing is an honest signal of a focused and smoothly functioning mind."

Capturing Nonverbal Dynamics: The Current Frontier

In the area of group dynamics and decision making, sociometric analysis has revealed that team performance can be predicted by such social signals as turn taking, response patterns, and conversational balance (Pentland, 2008). Sociometric data thus complement information from linguistic studies of the content of verbal communication (see, for example, Pennebaker, Chung, Ireland, Gonzales, & Booth, 2007; Strapparava & Mihalcea, 2007; Whissell, 2009; and other literature on text content analysis). One readily accessible sociometric tool, the Emotion Sense mood-tracking application[4] (Rachuri et al., 2010), allows researchers to supplement recorded linguistic speech data with information on speakers' emotions. Rachuri et al. (2010) extract data from audio samples and compare these data against a set of preloaded emotion and speaker-dependent models, and against information collected offline during system setup to derive a mood tracker. Using equipment like this, individuals' emotions can be automatically detected by means of off the shelf mobile phone devices rather than purpose-built devices such as sociometers.

Currently, the MIT Media Lab Human Dynamics group led by Alex "Sandy" Pentland is using open source platforms to develop new, inexpensive ways to measure face to face group communication via smart phones or badges (Lederman et al., 2017). Stopczynski et al. (2014) have developed a "smartphone brain scanner" that uses open source software and provides low density but real time imaging of brain activities using neuroheadsets based on 16 electrodes placed on the scalp, producing a portable 3D EEG imaging system (see Fig. 1). To avoid delays in signal processing these authors suggest that in future work, parts of the processing could be offloaded to an external server unencumbered by the limited computational power of mobile devices. The application of sensory data in real world settings is likely to be useful to social scientists wishing to assess many hours' worth of interactions, drawn from the workplace, during leisure time, or before, after, and during the various developmental and transitional phases of the lifecycle, such as partnership, parenthood, midlife, and retirement. Sensory data can also help organizations to improve their collective intelligence (Olguín & Pentland, 2010) and may even provide health benefits to individuals under observation (Pentland et al., 2009), as self-motoring or self-tracking devices can assist in the early recognition of symptoms such as those of depression (Olguın & Pentland, 2007). The major challenge to the use of large scale sensory data is that it requires informed consent from the participants. For a discussion this and other "big data" challenges, see Helbing (2015).[5]

---

4. For more details on the Emotion Sense app, see http://www.cam.ac.uk/research/news/mood-tracking-app-paves-way-for-pocket-therapy.

5. See Pentland et al. (2009) for consideration of questions relating to privacy and data ownership. It is important that such behavior-tracking technologies are not forced on anyone, providing safeguards to maintain individual privacy. The authors suggest that discussions are also advisable to clarify how the technology will and should be used.

FUTURE OPPORTUNITIES

Toward a Better Micro-Foundation of Human Behavior

The above discussion raises the central question of what type of research agendas could benefit from a better biological micro-foundation for our understanding of the behavior of individual humans, as well as from the ability to observe, track, and map individuals' interactions with one another. Despite Wilson's (1998) promotion of a science-humanities link, we are still in the process of deriving the analytical techniques required to successfully explain human behavior using biological measures (Bouchaud, 2008). In addition, many social scientists, particularly economists, do not see the value of a biological microfoundation, believing that behavioral observation is adequate—for example, that the knowledge that loss aversion exists obviates the need for a biological explanation of it. Others, like Cambridge neuroscientist, physiologist, and former Wall Street trader Coates believe that "economics needs to put the body back into the economy. Rather than assuming rationality and an efficient market—the unfortunate upshot of which has been a trading community gone feral—we should study the behavior of actual traders and investors, much as the behavioral economists do, only we should include in that study the influence of their biology" (2012, p. 36). To this end, Coates and Herbert (2008), by taking saliva samples from traders, showed that male traders whose testosterone levels were higher than average made above-average profits later that day (for an extended discussion of hormones, see Chapter 8). They also showed a positive association between mean cortisol levels or their variance with the variance in a trader's posted returns (i.e., a higher level of volatility in outcomes). In fact, the levels of cortisol in some of their subjects increased by as much as 500%, a number usually only observed in a pathological clinical setting. In a follow-up laboratory study, artificially raising volunteer participants' cortisol levels was shown to lead to an increase in their risk aversion (Kandasamy et al., 2014).

In recent years, neuroscientists and scientists studying artificial intelligence have both embraced the goal of understanding the experience and processes of emotions or feelings. They have pondered, for example, whether it is possible to explain the mechanisms of love, attachment, pain, suffering, or consciousness to a degree sufficient to enable the construction of an emotion machine. The investigation of questions related to this goal has been facilitated by the dramatic growth over the past decade of such fields as affective neuroscience and the neuroeconomics of prosocial behavior, which have made affective processes more visible and amenable to experimental research (Armony & Vuilleumier, 2013; Declerck & Boone, 2016). Emotional arousal can now be monitored physiologically in various ways that go beyond neurological perturbations, including through the heart, skin, respiration, muscle and gland fluctuations, facial expressions, and pupil dilation (for a detailed discussion, see Gardhouse & Anderson, 2013 and various chapters in this book). Individuals can either be constrained (Kahneman, 2011) by intuitive, emotional, and physiological factors, or can profit (Simon, 1983; Gigerenzer, 2007) from them. Nonintrusive or noninvasive instruments offer another path toward delivering insight into these issues.

Whichever the research paradigm adopted, because both brain and body interact in the generation of emotions, any realistic theory of thinking, acting, and problem solving must incorporate the influence of emotion (Simon, 1983). Hence, one urgent research task is to understand how emotions interact with other motivations to produce behavior (Elster, 1998, p. 73). One potentially major determinant of choice, for example, is emotionally guided attentional focus (Simon, 1983), a phenomenon highlighted by the substantial (and growing) evidence of emotions' essential role as an intelligent mechanism (Picard, 2000). The emotions of fear and anxiety serve to narrow attention to better equip the individual to meet threats and challenges, and thus survive dangerous situations. More broadly, Simon (1983, p. 32) contends that "most humans are able to attend to issues longer, to think harder about them, to receive deeper impressions that last longer, if information is presented in a context of emotion."

Scientific Philosophy and Method

If our brains' depictions of events are more complex than currently recognized by most practicing social scientists (as hinted by the catalog provided at the start of this chapter of Gigi's cognitive activities when crossing the road), researchers wishing to push their theories toward physiological realism would benefit from creative use of technological instruments, while remaining aware of what they can or cannot achieve. As a general principle, we should avoid rejecting or neglecting theories just because we do not yet have the tools to test them. For example, scientists working in the artificial intelligence (AI) arena have developed interesting theories about representation and resourcefulness that neuroscientists have completely ignored because they cannot be tested with the current available technological possibilities. One early cognitive model suggested by Minsky (1986) revolves around the creation of knowledge which he calls "K lines": "Whenever you "get a good idea," solve a problem, or have a memorable experience, you activate a K-line to "represent" it. A K-line is a wire-like structure that attaches itself to whichever mental agents are active when you solve a problem or have a good idea" (p. 82). This activation to a specific mental state requires agents to be aroused or activated, which one of Minsky's students illustrated as follows:

> *You want to repair a bicycle. Before you start, smear your hands with red paint. Then every tool you need to use will end up with red marks on it. When you're done, just remember that red means "good for fixing bicycles." Next time you fix a bicycle, you can save time by taking out all the red-marked tools in advance*

... Later, when there's a job to do, just activate the proper K-line for that kind of job and all the tools used in the past for similar jobs will automatically become available (p. 82).

Just because we cannot identify whether K-lines actually exist in the brain, which would require better imaging resolution, we should not disregard such a theory. Having an extra arsenal of theories to draw on, even including ones perceived as obscure, vague, or ill-defined, is always useful. As Minsky (2006) himself advised, "when you *know* that your theory is incomplete, then you ought to leave some room for other ideas that you later might need. Otherwise, you will take the risk of adopting a model so clean and neat that new ideas won't fit into it" (p. 147).

Maslow (1966) suggests that the first attempt to research a new problem should not be criticized as inelegant, imprecise, and crude (p. 14). Why, for example, should one criticize the K-line theory (Restak, 2006) while remaining open to the theory of "qualia" (alternatively expressed as "sentience" [Pinker, 2009] or "phenomenal awareness" [Dehaene, 2014]), a somewhat obscure idea that is dominant among philosophers of the mind and some neuroscientists?[6] Minsky (2006) emphasizes that the "apparent 'directness of experience' is an illusion that comes because our higher mental levels have such limited access to the systems we use to recognize, represent, and react to our external and internal conditions" (p. 329).[7] Qualia, like K-line, belong to the set of theoretical but not empirically functional concepts but K-line, contrary to qualia, has the functional strength of mapping the discovery and identification process of mental representations and states.

It may therefore be useful to consider the scholarly motto of "What needs doing is worth doing, even *not* very well" (Maslow, 1966, p. 14) as an alternative to dictum religiously followed by economists that "If it's worth doing, it's worth doing well." Following the latter doctrine, economists proudly zero in on effect sizes in their interpretations rather than attempting to improve the classification of such factors as the level of uncertainty about the estimates. Thus, Manski (2013), after criticizing the incredible certitude of economists as "wish

6. Qualia are proposed as the raw feelings, the internal or sentient experiences, that make up the conscious experience—such as the colors of yellow, red, or green, or composites such as smell or touch. We cannot know whether these phenomena are experienced identically by all individuals—how, for example, can I explain the redness of red or the painfulness of pain that I perceive vividly if this quality cannot be precisely communicated to others (Crick, 1994)? Nonetheless, scholars like Koch (2012) view qualia as properties of the world and the consequences of unknown laws still needing to be uncovered (pp. 27–28). Crick (1994) emphasized that even if the redness of red is unexplainable, it is impossible to be sure that everyone sees red differently (pp. 9–10). That is, the neural correlate of red might be exactly the same in the brains of different individuals. The problem is the exact definition of "exactly" and how precise the likeness must be to satisfy its definition, given that individuals' past experiences affect their perceptions.

7. For a discussion on the "fuzziness of qualia," see the interview with Marvin Minsky available at: https://www.youtube.com/watch?v=jSOXlKjk6pg.

extrapolation" (p. 31), advocated reporting bounds instead of point estimates, which would make transparency and openness preconditions in the messy environment in which economists work.

Over recent years, neuroscience too has faced considerable methodological attack for its low average statistical power, which has led not only to failure to detect true effects, but to overestimation of effect size and low reproducibility of results (Button et al., 2013). For instance, close reexamination of such questionably high correlations as the 0.8 association between brain activation and personality measures has determined such results to be inflated (Vul, Harris, Winkielman, & Pashler, 2009). Likewise, because fMRI data are noisy, neuroimaging studies have unintentionally produced biased data/results, including many false voxels (three-dimensional pixels) (Abbott, 2009). According to Kriegeskorte, Simmons, Bellgowan, and Baker (2009), such distorted results and invalid statistical inferences have been generated when the same dataset is used for both selection and analysis (i.e., when the results are not inherently independent of the selection criteria under the null hypothesis). In other words, a nonindependence error occurs by selecting data using a statistical test (selecting the small volumes of the brain [voxels] on the basis of their high correlation with a psychological response) and then applying a second nonindependent statistical test to those data (report the magnitude of that correlation) (Abbott, 2009). These criticisms are supported by Nieuwenhuis, Forstmann, and Wagenmakers (2011) review of numerous behavioral, systems, and cognitive neuroscience articles in five top-ranked journals (*Science*, *Nature*, *Nature Neuroscience*, *Neuron*, and *Journal of Neuroscience*). This review identified at least one error in around 50% of the cases in which interactive effects (e.g., the effect of the interaction of time and group in repeated measurements) should have been analyzed. Instead of applying a difference-in-difference approach, some studies were found to point to just the posttest differences on the tacit assumption that they are not required to consider the corresponding pretest scores.

From a theoretical viewpoint, vagueness about effect size should not be a problem per se as long as the researcher has a general idea of a phenomenon. For example, the very fact that anyone trying to explain consciousness quickly runs into problems may suggest that pursuing a precise definition of consciousness may not be fruitful, as it might prompt scholars to stop pondering the phenomenon. Nonetheless, failing to define a concept is still a sign that we do not have a good theory of it. Hence, many challenging phenomena, including consciousness, might best be treated as "suitcase phenomena" of which full understanding requires exploration of different subelements and their interactions. Emotion is another good example of this.

Without knowing what they are looking for, scholars must derive diverse theories, approach problems from different angles, and be inventive in the tools used and experiments run, while also being open minded and willing to create and test drive new theoretical and empirical ways of answering questions. The simultaneous use of a number of different tools and instruments is particularly important because, as Maslow (1966) pointed out, "it is tempting, if the only tool you have is a hammer, to treat everything as if it were a nail" (pp. 15–16). To illustrate this point, he recalled having seen once "an elaborate and complicated automatic machine for automobiles that did a wonderful job washing them. But it could do only that, and everything else that got into its clutches was treated as if it were an automobile to be washed" (p. 15). To avoid this problem, research efforts that draw on biophysical measures, such as fMRI studies of how different neurons are structurally connected (Declerck & Boone, 2016), will need theory as a guide. Without such guidance, endeavors such as the neuroscientific quest to map the brain become mere grunt work that, although pragmatically important, risks losing coherence due to the absence of theoretical scholars suggesting where and how to look for answers. Progress is further hampered by the fact that inferences about underlying physiological mechanisms based on the activity levels of particular brain regions are limited to the correlational rather than the causal (Gardhouse & Anderson, 2013). Progress in the area of wearable sensors, in contrast, is so impressive that even minds as great as William Stanley Jevons' (1871) could not have foreseen what they might allow us to measure:

> *I hesitate to say that men will ever have the means of measuring directly the feelings of the human heart. A unit of pleasure or of pain is difficult even to conceive; but it is the amount of these feelings which is continually prompting us to buying and selling, borrowing and lending, laboring and resting, producing and consuming; and it is from the quantitative effects of the feelings that we must estimate their comparative amounts. We can no more know nor measure gravity in its own nature than we can measure a feeling; but, just as we measure gravity by its effects in the motion of a pendulum, so we may estimate the equality or inequality of feelings by the decisions of the human mind.*

From Micro to Macro

The environment in which humans act is complex. Any realistic model of human behavior must be able to handle interdependencies between underlying model assumptions, observed social communications, and the resulting individual behavior. The new technical tools discussed in this chapter can be used to develop and test increasingly sophisticated theories about how social systems emerge from the interactions among their constituent individuals (i.e., "social intelligence"; Pentland, Choudhury, Eagle, & Singh, 2005), thus connecting the micro and macro levels of analysis.

These tools also enable better empirical testing of theories and concepts developed many decades ago in such areas as cybernetics, systems theory, and nonlinear science (see, for example, Nicolis, 1995), as well as emerging approaches like integral biomathics (Simeonov, Matsuno, & Root-Bernstein, 2013). Whereas cybernetics, systems theory, and nonlinear science produced myriad models of complex behavior (see, for example, Holland, 1995; Mitchell, 2009; Page, 2011; Miller & Page, 2007, for an overview), integral biomathics was developed as part of the European FP7[8] Framework INBIOSA initiative (www.inbiosa.eu) to model the complex phenomena of living systems.

Micro-level sensory data in particular can guide both micro- and macro-oriented research endeavors such as agent based modeling (Bonabeau, 2002; Miller & Page, 2007), feedback loops (as learning is an interactive feedback-based process [Sterman, 1994]), and network theory (Newman, 2010; Newman, Barabási, & Watts, 2006), catalyzing efforts from the exploration of heuristics that guide individuals' behavior to the identification of emergent behavior patterns in society (Epstein & Axtell, 1996) that integrate contextual forces (Axelrod & Cohen, 2000). Information gathered by sensing devices could also potentially be used to improve the functioning of teams, work groups, organizations, and even society in general as they may further illuminate the structure of decision making and interpersonal processes.[9] Nonetheless, the fact that complex emergent patterns are notoriously difficult to identify (Kitto, 2008) and even more difficult to simulate mathematically, presents a major challenge, even for researchers armed with sensing devices. Modeling the ways in which a set of individuals form an emergent society that in turn affects them could require the treatment of groups, organizations, and societies as if they were organisms or open,[10] complex and adaptive living systems. Economies are organic structures, always discovering, creating, and in process (Arthur, 2006), in which knowledge, and creativity can be viewed as key resources and possibilities and problems are created and resolved as ecological interactions proceed. In such an environment, entities are not always stable and events not always repeatable, presenting significant challenges for the empiricist. Hence, understanding change in these settings requires comprehending the dynamic communication and feedback channels within the system, as well as the architecture and design of social institutions. The use of continuous, fine-grained data rather than coarse cross-sectional data can greatly advance our ability to understand these dynamics. As Altshuler, Fire, Aharony, Elovici, and Pentland (2012) point out, fine-grained data provide scientists with "an unprecedented window into the lives of individuals and entire communities" (p. 2). The sensing tools discussed above show great potential for achieving these goals, especially in terms of the following research questions.[11]

8. FP7 (7th Framework Programme for Research and Technology) was a European Union research and innovation funding program that lasted for 7 years (from 2007 to 2013) and had a budget of over €50 billion.

9. For a discussion on groups, power, and the development of institutions, see Frijters & Foster, 2013.

10. An open system is a system with external interactions (see https://en.wikipedia.org/wiki/Open_system_(systems_theory).

11. The four research probes were developed in collaboration with Kirsty Kitto and Markus Schaffner.

Problem 1. How do humans interact and coordinate?

Given the wide variety of human interactions in response to which individuals form their preferences (Simon, 1993), classical definitions of communication as pure information transmission (Shannon & Weaver, 1949) are arguably incomplete. Models are needed that treat communication as a process of establishing common meaning among human individuals (Mitchell, 2009), a common meaning necessary to the very definition of human social systems. Without knowledge about the mental models and norms held by certain individuals and shared with other individuals via communication, the social system simply cannot be fully understood. Hence, communication and information processes, mediated through social interactions, are essential to the development of organizations, something as true in the biological world as it is in the social world (Boulding, 1968). In social systems, information, rather than being auxiliary to the system, is often the key commodity because adaptation, lifecycle, and developmental processes rely on information, including feedback mechanisms. Our understanding of how humans perceive and think about a particular situation can also be improved by accommodating both verbal and nonverbal communication, and by seeking the patterns in a dynamic exchange rather than simple behavioral endpoints of social processes.

Problem 2. What underlying mechanism(s) should be used to model human social interaction?

Humans are biological, psychological, social, emotional, and (boundedly) rational beings who have developed basic behavioral programs (e.g., acquiring, bonding, learning, and defending) that have genetically evolved to increase inclusive fitness and guide human reasoning and decision making (Lawrence & Nohria, 2002). An individual's behavior can depend on the individual's image of the world, which is itself formed by learning and knowledge generation, and is ever-changing: "A hundred and one things may happen. As each event occurs, however, it alters my knowledge structure or my image. And as it alters my image, I behave accordingly" (Boulding, 1961, p. 6). Hence, understanding social interactions requires recognition not only of the roles played by history, conventions, and social norms or culture (Durlauf & Young, 2001; Henrich, 2016), defined here as information acquired from other individuals via social transmission mechanisms such as language, teaching, or imitation (Mesoudi, 2011, pp. 2–3). Culture is so important as to persuade Henrich (2016) that "addiction to culture" is the secret to the success of the human species (p. 3). Individuals may prefer to learn from others similar to themselves (Henrich, 2016; Mesoudi, 2011), copying ideas, beliefs, skills, and knowledge but changing the information content based on their own experiences and ideas. These observations raise questions about the conditions in which learning occurs and from whom,[12] elements that are particularly affected by the social fabric and sensing systems can help mapping such elements. During information transmission, for example, individuals who participate in communication networks may care about how others perceive them and communicate their personality accordingly (although personality is not the only dimension of someone's social image), in which case learning may be impeded by ideology (see, for example, Boulding, 1964).

Problem 3. How does the social fabric affect human decision making?

Interaction between individuals produces the social fabric (Morin, 2001): "Interaction between individuals produce society, and society, which testifies to the emergence of culture, retroacts on individuals by culture" (p. 44). Thus, new organizational arrangements create new opportunities for individuals. Hence, just as living systems coevolve with their environment, human behavior coevolves within the social fabric, and both social and individual factors determine the interactions that influence individual preferences, beliefs, and opportunities (Durlauf & Young, 2001). Human culture is based on symbols transmitted by learning and tradition, channels through which humans determine and communicate future goals. Our nature as a cultural species is reflected in the large bodies of human practices, techniques, heuristics, tools, motivations, values, and beliefs (Henrich, 2016). Human learning is a key source of social change, and humans are in no way the "robots" envisioned in many behavioral models, reacting in a predictable manner to a stimulus response program (von Bertalanffy, 1967). Rather, the decision maker is embedded within a social fabric, which is the sphere of direct personal interactions and all other socializing influences upon the individual which sociometric sensing systems can help identifying and quantifying.

Problem 4. What drives creativity and innovation?

The ongoing advance of human thought (including, but not only in, scientific enterprise, where new theories compete with existing ones based on coherence, generality, and agreement [Kuhn, 2012]) proceeds in a fashion similar to that of biological evolution in the sense that it exhibits cumulative, adaptive, open-ended change (Gabora, 2013). Humans have a remarkable capacity to actualize

12. Henrich (2016): "Aspiring young hunters first glean as much as they can from those to whom they have ready access, like their brothers, fathers, and uncles. Later, perhaps during adolescence, learners update and improve their earlier efforts by focusing on and learning from the older, most successful, and most prestigious hunters in their community. That is, learners should use three cultural learning cues to target their learning: age, success, and prestige ... More broadly, evolutionary reasoning suggests that learners should use a wide range of cues to figure out whom to selectively pay attention to and learn from. Such cues allow them to target those people most likely to possess information that will increase the learner's survival and reproduction" (p. 37).

ideas that previously existed in a state of potentiality, thereby generating innovations that fuel change (Gabora, 2013; Gabora & Kitto, 2013; Gell-Mann, 1994). The development of human thought is also characterized by periods of relative stability followed by innovative periods of rapid change, which evolutionary biologists refer to as punctuated equilibrium (Eldredge & Gould, 1972). According to Smith and Szathmary (1997), such punctuations are seen in several transitional points in the history of life on Earth, from the emergence of protocells up to the origins of societies and language, a claim that has generated the suggestion that ideas may be comparable to genotypes (for an overview see Gabora, 2013). Gabora (2013), however, showed that acquiring new ideas in a culture is not subject to selective pressures but that communal exchange is instead the source of cultural evolution—i.e., that the information transmission occurs due to interactions with the environment rather than as the consequence of information transfer from parent to offspring (Lamarckian instead of Darwinian process). This would imply a pivotal role for the ways in which people share information and ideas. Yet the generation of ideas and adjacent possibilities is also constrained by the current environment (Kauffman, 1993). This fertile body of work raises many important questions: What steps are involved in the mechanism of innovation? Which mixture of competition and cooperation would produce high versus low levels of creativity and innovation in a society? Can progress be hastened, so that the wait for new ideas is reduced? Could an explosion of niches in the form of self-maintaining structures be manufactured, providing an opportunity for society, scientists, or the modern world in general to escape from what Gell-Mann (1994) calls the "intellectual rut in which we are trapped" (p. 265)? Do principles exist that can be exploited to enhance the capacity of ideas to complement one another in mutual interactions? To begin answering these questions, one could model major transition points as markers in the natural evolution of a social system (Smith & Szathmary, 1997), with the goal of revealing how new characteristics emerge that promote innovation and novel behavior.

What is not in question is that the social fabric inherently affects decision makers' learning and cognition, with this influence frequently going unrecognized by decision makers themselves. Conscious learning can be distinguished from other less deliberate cognitive processes such as attitude change, internalization, or imitation. Because the context surrounding the decision maker implicitly affects his or her decisions (Helbing, 2012), scientists wishing to study the interaction between person and society require whole system analysis over long periods of time (cf. Sterman, 2006). Large-scale sensory data can assist in such endeavors by helping to map the system and the feedback loops that characterize it over time, creating strong path dependence. Continuous, fine-grained data streams prevent the loss of information like "footprints in the sand." Better data may also allow the testing of sophisticated new mathematical approaches that model the social context in which individuals act (Gabora & Kitto, 2013; Kitto & Boschetti, 2013). Which patterns of gradual change over time trigger a gateway of (radical) change, innovation, or creativity

(Gell-Mann, 1994; Morowitz, 1999)? These and related questions may be addressed in the near future with the assistance of sociometric sensing systems, illuminating the mechanisms of human progress and creativity.

REFERENCES

Abbott, A. (2009). Brain imaging studies under fire. *Nature*, *457*(15), 245.

Aharony, N., Pan, W., Ip, C., Khayal, I., & Pentland, A. (2011). Social fMRI: Investigating and shaping social mechanisms in the real world. *Pervasive and Mobile Computing*, *7*(6), 643–659.

Almaatouq, A., Radaelli, L., Pentland, A., & Shmueli, E. (2016). Are you your friends' friend? Poor perception of friendship ties limits the ability to promote behavioral change. *PLoS One*, *11*(3).

Altshuler, Y., Fire, M., Aharony, N., Elovici, Y., & Pentland, A. (2012). How many makes a crowd? On the evolution of learning as a factor of community coverage. In *SBP* (pp. 43–52).

Armony, J., & Vuilleumier, P. (Eds.), (2013). *The Cambridge handbook of human affective neuroscience*. Cambridge: Cambridge University Press.

Arthur, W. B. (2006). *The nature of technology: What it is and how it evolves*. New York: Free Press.

Axelrod, R., & Cohen, M. D. (2000). *Harnessing complexity: Organizational implications of a scientific frontier*. New York: Basic Books.

Bailenson, J. N., & Yee, N. (2005). Digital chameleons: Automatic assimilation of nonverbal gestures in immersive virtual environments. *Psychological Science*, *16*(10), 814–819.

Baumeister, R. F., & Tierney, J. (2012). *Willpower: Rediscovering the greatest human strength*. New York: Penguin Books.

Bechara, A., Damasio, H., Tranel, D., & Damasio, A. R. (1997). Deciding advantageously before knowing the advantageous strategy. *Science*, *275*(5304), 1293–1295.

Berntson, G. G., & Cacioppo, J. T. (2008). Heart rate variability: Stress and psychiatric conditions. In J. A. Camm & M. Malik (Eds.), *Dynamic electrocardiography*. Oxford: John Wiley & Sons, Ltd.

Bonabeau, E. (2002). Agent-based modeling: Methods and techniques for simulating human systems. *Proceedings of the National Academy of Sciences*, *99*(Suppl 3), 7280.

Bouchaud, J. P. (2008). Economics needs a scientific revolution. *Nature*, *455*(7217), 1181.

Boulding, K. E. (1961). *The image: Knowledge in life and society*. Ann Arbor: University of Michigan Press.

Boulding, K. E. (1964). *The meaning of the 20th century: The great transition*. New York: Harper Colophon.

Boulding, K. E. (1968). *Beyond economics: Essays on society, religion, and ethics*. Ann Arbor: University of Michigan Press.

Brandts, J., & Garofalo, O. (2012). Gender pairings and accountability effects. *Journal of Economic Behavior & Organization*, *83*(1), 31–41.

Buser, T., Dreber, A., & Mollerstrom, J. (2017). The impact of stress on tournament entry. *Experimental Economics*, *20*(2), 506–530.

Button, K. S., Ioannidis, J. P., Mokrysz, C., Nosek, B. A., Flint, J., Robinson, E. S., et al. (2013). Power failure: Why small sample size undermines the reliability of neuroscience. *Nature Reviews Neuroscience*, *14*(5), 365–376.

Chartrand, T. L., & Bargh, J. A. (1999). The chameleon effect: The perception-behavior link and social interaction. *Journal of Personality and Social Psychology*, *76*(6), 893–910.

Choudhury, T., & Pentland, A. (2004). Characterizing social networks using the sociometer. In: *Proceedings of the North American Association of Computational Social and Organizational Science (NAACSOS)*.

Coates, J. (2012). *The hour between dog and wolf: Risk-taking, gut feelings and the biology of boom and bust*. New York: The Penguin Press.

Coates, J. M., & Herbert, J. (2008). Endogenous steroids and financial risk taking on a London trading floor. *Proceedings of the National Academy of Sciences, 105*(16), 6167–6172.

Coricelli, G., Joffily, M., Montmarquette, C., & Villeval, M. C. (2010). Cheating, emotions, and rationality: An experiment on tax evasion. *Experimental Economics, 13*(2), 226–247.

Crick, F. (1994). *The astonishing hypothesis: The scientific search for the soul*. New York: A Touchstone Book.

Crone, E. A., Somsen, R. J., Van Beek, B., & Van der Molen, M. W. (2004). Heart rate and skin conductance analysis of antecendents and consequences of decision making. *Psychophysiology, 41*, 531–540.

Crone, E. A., Bunge, S. A., De Klerk, P., & Van der Molen, M. W. (2005). Cardiac concomitants of performance monitoring: Context dependence and individual differences. *Cognitive Brain Research, 23*(1), 93–106.

Declerck, C., & Boone, C. (2016). *Neuroeconomics of prosocial behavior: The compassionate egoist*. Amsterdam: Academic Press.

De Gelder, B. (2006). Towards the neurobiology of emotional body language. *Nature Reviews Neuroscience, 7*(3), 242–249.

Dehaene, S. (2014). *Consciousness and the brain: Deciphering how the brain codes our thoughts*. New York: Viking.

Dong, W., Lepri, B., & Pentland, A. S. (2011). Modeling the co-evolution of behaviors and social relationships using mobile phone data. In *Proceedings of the 10th international conference on mobile and ubiquitous multimedia*, (pp. 134–143): ACM.

Dulleck, U., Schaffner, M., & Torgler, B. (2014). Heartbeat and economic decisions: Observing mental stress among proposers and responders in the ultimatum bargaining game. *PLoS One, 9*(9).

Dulleck, U., Ristl, A., Schaffner, M., & Torgler, B. (2011). Heart rate variability, the autonomic nervous system, and neuroeconomic experiments. *Journal of Neuroscience, Psychology, and Economics, 4*(2), 117–124.

Dulleck, U., Ristl, A., Schaffner, M., & Torgler, B. (2018). *Positive affect and heart rate variability: A verification of large scale subjective data with objective physiological data, mimeo*. Queensland University of Technology.

Dulleck, U., Fooken, J., Newton, C., Ristl, A., Schaffner, M., & Torgler, B. (2016). Tax compliance and psychic costs: Behavioral experimental evidence using a physiological marker. *Journal of Public Economics, 134*, 9–18.

Durlauf, S. N., & Young, H. P. (Eds.), (2001). *Social dynamics*. Cambridge, MA: MIT Press.

Eagle, N., & Greene, K. (2014). *Reality mining: Using big data to engineer a better world*. Cambridge: MIT Press.

Eagle, N., & Pentland, A. S. (2006). Reality mining: Sensing complex social systems. *Personal and Ubiquitous Computing, 10*(4), 255–268.

Eldredge, N., & Gould, S. J. (1972). Punctuated equilibria: An alternative to phyletic gradualism. In T. J. M. Schopf (Ed.), *Models in Paleobiology* (pp. 82–115). San Francisco: Freeman Cooper.

Elster, J. (1998). Emotions and economic theory. *Journal of Economic Literature, 36*(1), 47–74.

Epstein, J. M., & Axtell, R. (1996). *Growing artificial societies: Social science from the bottom up*. Washington, DC: Brookings Institution Press.

Erard, B., & Feinstein, J. (1994). The role of moral sentiments and audit perceptions in tax compliance. *Public Finance, 49*, 70–89.

Fan, B., Leng, S., & Yang, K. (2016). A dynamic bandwidth allocation algorithm in mobile networks with big data of users and networks. *IEEE Network, 30*(1), 6–10.

Falk, A., Menrath, I., Verde, P.E., & Siegrist, J. (2011). Cardiovascular consequences of unfair pay. IZA Discussion Paper Series No. 5720.

Fooken, J. (2017). Heart rate variability indicates emotional value during pro-social economic laboratory decisions with large external validity. *Scientific Reports*, *7*(44471), 1–11.

Fooken, J., & Parker, S. L. (2018). Using heart rate variability measures in social science research. In G. Foster (Ed.), *Biophysical measurement in experimental social science research*. Oxford, UK: Elsevier.

Fooken, J., & Schaffner, M. (2016). The role of psychological and physiological factors in decision making under risk and in a dilemma. *Frontiers in Behavioral Neuroscience*, *10*(2), 1–10.

Frijters, P., & Foster, G. (2013). *Economic theory of greed, love, groups, and networks*. Cambridge: Cambridge University Press.

Gabora, L. (2013). An evolutionary framework for culture: Selectionism versus communal exchange. *Physics of Life Reviews*, *10*(2), 117–145.

Gabora, L., & Kitto, K. (2013). Concept combination and the origins of complex cognition. In L. Swan (Ed.), *Origins of mind* (pp. 361–381). Dordrecht: Springer.

Gangl, K., Torgler, B., & Kirchler, E. (2016). Patriotism's impact on cooperation with the state: An experimental study on tax compliance. *Political Psychology*, *37*(6), 867–881.

Gardhouse, K., & Anderson, A. K. (2013). Affective science: The objective measurement of subjective experience. In P. Vuilleumier & J. Armony (Eds.), *The Cambridge handbook of human affective neuroscience* (pp. 57–81): Cambridge University Press.

Gatica-Perez, D., McCowan, L., Zhang, D., & Bengio, S. (2005). Detecting group interest-level in meetings. In *Vol. 1. IEEE international conference on acoustics, speech, and signal processing, 2005. Proceedings (ICASSP'05)* (pp. 1–489): IEEE.

Gigerenzer, G. (2007). *Gut feelings: The intelligence of the unconscious*. New York: Penguin Books.

Gell-Mann, M. (1994). *The quark and the jaguar: Adventures in the simple and the complex*. New York: A W. H. Freeman.

Gibala, M. (2017). *The one-minute workout*. New York: Avery.

Gregory, S. W., Jr., & Webster, S. (1996). A nonverbal signal in voices of interview partners effectively predicts communication accommodation and social status perceptions. *Journal of Personality and Social Psychology*, *70*(6), 1231–1240.

Hardy, B. (2018). Steroid hormones in social research. In G. Foster (Ed.), *Biophysical measurement in experimental social science research*. Oxford, UK: Elsevier.

Helbing, D. (2012). *Social self-organization: Agent-based simulations and experiments to study emergent social behavior*. Heidelberg: Springer.

Helbing, D. (2015). *Thinking ahead-essays on big data, digital revolution, and participatory market society*. Heidelberg: Springer.

Henrich, J. (2016). *The secret of our success: How learning from others drove human evolution, domesticated our species, and made us smart*. Princeton: Princeton University Press.

Holland, J. H. (1995). *Hidden order: How adaptation builds complexity*. New York: Basic Books.

Izard, C. E. (1993). Four systems for emotion activation: Cognitive and noncognitive processes. *Psychological Review*, *100*(1), 68–90.

Jevons, W. S. (1871). *The theory of political economy*. London: Macmillan.

James, W. (1950). *The principles of psychology*. New York: Dover Publication.

Kahneman, D. (2011). *Thinking, fast and slow*. New York: Farrar, Straus and Giroux.

Kandasamy, N., Hardy, B., Page, L., Schaffner, M., Graggaber, J., Powlson, A. S., et al. (2014). Cortisol shifts financial risk preferences. *Proceedings of the National Academy of Sciences*, *111*(9), 3608–3613.

Kauffman, S. A. (1993). *The origins of order. Self-organization and selection in evolution*. Oxford: Oxford University Press.

Kitto, K. (2008). High end complexity. *International Journal of General Systems*, *37*, 689–714.

Kitto, K., & Boschetti, F. (2013). Attitudes, ideologies and self-organisation: Information load minimisation in multi-agent decision making. *Advances in Complex Systems*, *16*(2–3), 1–37.

Koch, C. (2012). *Consciousness: Confessions of a romantic reductionist*. Cambridge: MIT Press.

Koelsch, S., Remppis, A., Sammler, D., Jentschke, S., Mietchen, D., Fritz, T., et al. (2007). A cardiac signature of emotionality. *European Journal of Neuroscience*, *26*(11), 3328–3338.

Konrad, K. A., & Qari, S. (2012). The last refuge of a scoundrel? Patriotism and tax compliance. *Economica*, *79*(315), 516–533.

Kriegeskorte, N., Simmons, W. K., Bellgowan, P. S., & Baker, C. I. (2009). Circular analysis in systems neuroscience: The dangers of double dipping. *Nature Neuroscience*, *12*(5), 535–540.

Kuhn, T. S. (2012). *The structure of scientific revolutions*. Chicago: University of Chicago press.

Kurzweil, R. (1999). *The age of spiritual machine: When computers exceed human intelligence*. New York: Penguin Books.

Kurzweil, R. (2012). *How to create a mind: The secret of human thought revealed*. New York: Penguin Books.

Lawrence, P. R., & Nohria, N. (2002). *Driven: How human nature shapes our choices*. San Francisco: Jossey-Bass.

Lederman, O., Calacci, D., MacMullen, A., Fehder, D. C., Murray, F. E., & Pentland, A. S. (2017). Open badges: A low-cost toolkit for measuring team communication and dynamics. *arXiv preprint arXiv:1710.01842*.

Leng, Y., Rudolph, L., Pentland, A. S., Zhao, J., & Koutsopolous, H. N. (2016). Managing travel demand: Location recommendation for system efficiency based on mobile phone data. In: *Proceedings of data for good exchange (D4GX), New York*.

Levy, M. N., Martin, P. J., Iano, T., & Zieske, H. (1970). Effects of single vagal stimuli on heart rate and atrioventricular conduction. *American Journal of Physiology*, *218*(5), 1256–1262.

Levy, M. N., & Martin, P. J. (1979). Neural control of the heart. In: R. M. Berne (Ed.), Vol. 2. *Handbook of physiology* (pp. 582–620). Washington, DC: American Physiological Society.

Macintyre, A., Schaffner, M., & Torgler, B. (2017). *Tax compliance and national pride: An experimental investigation using a physiological marker*. Queensland University of Technology.

Malik, M. (2008). Standard measurement of heart rate variability. In J. A. Camm & M. Malik (Eds.), *Dynamic electrocardiography* (pp. 13–21). New York: John Wiley & Sons.

Malik, M., Bigger, T. J., Camm, J. A., Kleiger, R. E., Malliani, A., Moss, A. J., et al. (1996). Heart rate variability: Standards of measurement, physiological interpretation, and clinical use. *Circulation*, *93*(5), 1043–1065.

Manski, C. F. (2013). *Public policy in an uncertain world: Analysis and decisions*. Cambridge: Harvard University Press.

Maslow, A. H. (1966). *The psychology of science: A reconnaissance*. Chicago: Henry Regnery.

Mesoudi, A. (2011). *Cultural evolution: How Darwinian theory can explain human culture and synthesize the social sciences*. Chicago: Chicago University Press.

Miller, J. H., & Page, S. E. (2007). *Complex adaptive systems: An introduction to computational models of social life*. Princeton: Princeton University Press.

Minsky, M. (1986). *The society of mind*. New York: Simon & Schuster.

Minsky, M. (2006). *The emotion machine: Commonsense thinking, artificial intelligence, and the future of the human mind*. New York: Simon & Schuster.

Mitchell, M. (2009). *Complexity: A guided tour*. Oxford: Oxford University Press.

Morin, E. (2001). *Seven complex lessons in education for the future*. Paris: UNESCO.

Morowitz, H. J. (1999). A theory of biochemical organization, metabolic pathways, and evolution. *Complexity*, *4*(6), 39–53.

Newman, M. E. J. (2010). *Networks: An introduction.* Oxford: Oxford University Press.

Newman, M. E. J., Barabási, A. -L., & Watts, D. J. (2006). *The structure and dynamics of networks.* Princeton: Princeton University Press.

Nicolis, G. (1995). *Introduction to nonlinear science.* Cambridge University Press.

Nieuwenhuis, S., Forstmann, B. U., & Wagenmakers, E. J. (2011). Erroneous analyses of interactions in neuroscience: A problem of significance. *Nature Neuroscience*, *14*(9), 1105–1107.

Olguín, D. O., & Pentland, A. (2010). Assessing group performance from collective behavior. In *Vol. 10. Proc. of the CSCW.*

Olguın, D. O., & Pentland, A. S. (2007). Sociometric badges: State of the art and future applications. In: *Doctoral colloquium presented at IEEE 11th international symposium on wearable computers, Boston, MA.*

Page, S. E. (2011). *Diversity and complexity.* Princeton: Princeton University Press.

Pennebaker, J. W., Chung, C. K., Ireland, M., Gonzales, A., & Booth, R. J. (2007). *The development and psychometric properties of LIWC.* Austin, TX: LIWC.net.

Pentland, A. (2004). Social dynamics: Signals and behavior. In *International conference on developmental learning.* San Diego: Salk Institute.

Pentland, A. (2005). Socially aware, computation and communication. *Computer*, *38*(3), 33–40.

Pentland, A. (2008). *Honest signals: How they shape our world.* Cambridge: MIT Press.

Pentland, A. (2014). *Social physics: How good ideas spread: The lessons from a new science.* New York: Penguin Press.

Pentland, A., Choudhury, T., Eagle, N., & Singh, P. (2005). Human dynamics: Computation for organizations. *Pattern Recognition Letters*, *26*(4), 503–511.

Pentland, A., Lazer, D., Brewer, D., & Heibeck, T. (2009). *Improving public health and medicine by use of reality mining.* Whitepaper for the Robert Wood Johnson Foundation.

Picard, R. W. (2000). *Affective computing.* Cambridge: MIT Press.

Picard, R. W. (2003). Affective computing: Challenges. *International Journal of Human-Computer Studies*, *59*(1), 55–64.

Pinker, S. (2009). *How the mind works.* New York: W. W. Norton & Company.

Rachuri, K. K., Musolesi, M., Mascolo, C., Rentfrow, P. J., Longworth, C., & Aucinas, A. (2010). EmotionSense: a mobile phones based adaptive platform for experimental social psychology research. In Proceedings of the 12th ACM international conference on Ubiquitous computing, pp. 281–290. ACM.

Restak, R. (2006). *Mind over matter.* Washington Post.*http://www.washingtonpost.com/wp-dyn/content/article/2006/12/14/AR2006121401554.html?noredirect=on.*

Shannon, C. E., & Weaver, W. (1949). *The mathematical theory of communication.* Urbana, IL: University of Illinois Press.

Simeonov, P. L., Matsuno, K., & Root-Bernstein, R. S. (Eds.), (2013). Can biology create a profoundly new mathematics and computation? In *113(1). Progress in Biophysics and Molecular Biology (Special Issue)* (pp. 1–230).

Schmid Mast, M. (2002). Dominance as expressed and inferred through speaking time. *Human Communication Research*, *28*(3), 420–450.

Seong, H., Lee, J., Shin, T., Kim, W., & Yoon, Y. (2004). The analysis of mental stress using time-frequency distribution of heart rate variability signal. In *The 26th annual international conference of the IEEE on engineering in medicine and biology, (1)* (pp. 283–285).

Simon, H. A. (1983). *Reason in human affairs.* Stanford: Stanford University Press.

Simon, H. A. (1993). Altruism and economics. *American Economic Review*, *83*, 156–161.

Smith, J. M., & Szathmary, E. (1997). *The major transitions in evolution.* Oxford: Oxford University Press.

Soroka, S. N. (2018). Skin conductance in the study of politics and communication. In G. Foster (Ed.), *Biophysical measurement in experimental social science research.* Oxford, UK: Elsevier.

Stopczynski, A., Sekara, V., Sapiezynski, P., Cuttone, A., Madsen, M. M., Larsen, J. E., et al. (2014). Measuring large-scale social networks with high resolution. *PLoS One*, *9*(4).

Sterman, J. D. (1994). Learning in and about complex systems. *System Dynamics Review*, *10*, 291–330.

Sterman, J. D. (2006). Learning from evidence in a complex world. *American Journal of Public Health*, *96*(3), 505–514.

Strapparava, C., & Mihalcea, R. (2007). SemEval-2007 Task 14: Affective Text.

Stuckler, D., Meissner, C. M., & King, L. P. (2008). Can a bank crisis break your heart? *Globalization and Health*, *4*(1), 1–4.

Thayer, J. F., Åhs, F., Fredrikson, M., Sollers, J. J., & Wager, T. D. (2012). A meta-analysis of heart rate variability and neuroimaging studies: Implications for heart rate variability as a marker of stress and health. *Neuroscience & Biobehavioral Reviews*, *36*(2), 747–756.

Tomasello, M. (2016). *A natural history of human morality.* Harvard University Press.

Torgler, B. (2004). Tax morale in Asian countries. *Journal of Asian Economics*, *15*(2), 237–266.

Torgler, B. (2007). *Tax compliance and tax morale: A theoretical and empirical analysis.* Cheltenham: Edward Elgar Publishing.

Torgler, B. (2016). Can tax compliance research profit from biology? *Review of Behavioral Economics*, *3*, 113–144.

Torgler, B., & Schneider, F. (2005). Attitudes towards paying taxes in Austria: An empirical analysis. *Empirica*, *32*(2), 231–250.

Torgler, B., & Schneider, F. (2007). What shapes attitudes toward paying taxes? Evidence from multicultural European countries. *Social Science Quarterly*, *88*(2), 443–470.

Van Baaren, R. B., Holland, R. W., Steenaert, B., & van Knippenberg, A. (2003). Mimicry for money: Behavioral consequences of imitation. *Journal of Experimental Social Psychology*, *39*(4), 393–398.

Van Lange, P. A., Finkenauer, C., Popma, A., & Van Vugt, M. (2011). Electrodes as social glue: Measuring heart rate promotes giving in the trust game. *International Journal of Psychophysiology*, *80*(3), 246–250.

von Bertalanffy, L. (1967). *Robots, men and minds: Psychology in the modern world.* New York: George Brazilier.

Vul, E., Harris, C., Winkielman, P., & Pashler, H. (2009). Puzzlingly high correlations in fMRI studies of emotion, personality, and social cognition. *Perspectives on Psychological Science*, *4*(3), 274–290.

Watts, D. (2013). Computational social science: Exciting progress and future directions. *The Bridge on Frontiers of Engineering*, *43*, 5–10.

Whissell, C. (2009). Using the revised dictionary of affect in language to quantify the emotional undertones of samples of natural language. *Psychological Reports*, *105*(2), 509–521.

Wilson, E. O. (1998). *Consilience: The unity of knowledge.* New York: Vintage Books.

Yang, T. T., Simmons, A. N., Matthews, S. C., Tapert, S. F., Bischoff-Grethe, A., Frank, G. K. W., et al. (2007). Increased amygdala activation is related to heart rate during emotion process in adolescent subjects. *Neuroscience Letters*, *428*, 109–114.

Chapter 9

Can Social Scientists Use Molecular Genetic Data to Explain Individual Differences and Inform Public Policy?

Steven F. Lehrer[*,†,‡] **and Weili Ding**[*,†]
[*]*Queen's University, Kingston, ON, Canada,* [†]*NYU-Shanghai, Shanghai, China,* [‡]*National Bureau of Economic Research, Cambridge, MA, United States*

INTRODUCTION

Heritability is generally defined as the proportion of variation in a population's observable characteristics or outcomes that is accounted for by genetic factors. The role of heredity in most socioeconomic outcomes ranging from income to educational attainment is not in itself a new revelation. However, until the human genome was decoded in 2001, it was considered unlikely that much could be done with this knowledge.

With the availability and sheer volume of datasets containing individual molecular genetic information growing at a rapid pace in recent years, the tantalizing possibility now exists to identify specific genes and the pathways through which they operate to drive important socioeconomic outcomes. More generally, Conley (2009) argues that this new information can be deployed to (1) assess the direct impact of specific genetic phenomena on socioeconomic and behavioral outcomes, (2) explore genetic-environmental interactions, and (3) trace genealogies across time and space. This knowledge may have substantial policy implications and may also be of use in refining social science theories to improve their realism and predictive accuracy.

This chapter focuses primarily on the findings of studies that fall under the umbrella of molecular genetics. These studies examine whether and how

☆ We are grateful to both Gigi Foster and Brendan Wilson for their patience and detailed comments on earlier drafts, that both markedly improved the exposition and clarified many concepts in this chapter. We also wish to thank Pietro Biroli for initial encouragement to undertake this chapter. Lehrer also wishes to thank SSHRC for research support.

Biophysical Measurement in Experimental Social Science Research. https://doi.org/10.1016/B978-0-12-813092-6.00009-5

variation at specific locations in the individual genetic code is associated with individual socioeconomic or health outcomes. This approach differs from the main approach, drawn from behavioral genetics, that social scientists have historically employed to understand the role of genetic factors in explaining outcomes. Studies taking this more traditional behavioral genetics approach typically use data collected from family-based samples, such as twins or siblings. In this literature, researchers often assume that the driver of all variation in the outcome being investigated could be decomposed into additively separable genetic and environmental sources: the nature (genetic) effect and the nurture (environment) effect. Research using a behavioral genetics approach was recently surveyed in Behrman (2016) and first entered the economics literature in Taubman (1976). This approach has also been used with a sample of adopted children to understand the role of "nurture" in producing outcomes (see, for example, Sacerdote, 2007).

Findings from studies that use molecular genetic data have already produced profound implications for diagnostics, preventive medicine, and therapeutics. As our knowledge about the links between genes and complex socioeconomic outcomes such as educational attainment or behavioral traits continues to grow, societies will face critical questions, such as: Should molecular genetic information be considered in the design of social and economic policies? Should genes come to play a central role in society's thinking about socioeconomic issues? In parallel, researchers are faced with the question of whether they wish to use these exciting new sources of data that allow them to enter the black box of what were previously known as individual-fixed effects, or in other words, individual-specific permanent unobserved heterogeneity. Genetic markers may be truly what past researchers meant by permanent unobserved heterogeneity, because such markers are assigned at conception and, with the sole exception of monozygotic twins, differ markedly (potentially, according to 1000 Genomes Project Consortium (2015), on average at over 4.1 million locations on our DNA) across individuals. Social science researchers have historically employed fixed effects to capture permanent productivity characteristics of each individual, and data on the genetic markers themselves allows us to examine the nature and dimensions of these individual effects. Entering this black box, while tempting, may expose researchers to the accusation that their research endeavors or results implicitly promote social eugenics.

This chapter first updates the comprehensive reviews presented in Benjamin et al. (2007, 2012), Lehrer (2016), and Lehrer and Ding (2017) that explore the use of genetic markers in studies within economics, discussing the most recent findings. Second, this chapter contains a discussion of how genetic markers are influencing drug development, including consideration of the unintended consequences of policies that promote personalized medicine. With this chapter we aim to help social scientists interested in integrating genetic factors within their studies while being cognizant of the broader social and philosophical implications of such an effort. The chapter's sectioning is organized around the following questions: how is genetic data collected?; how is genetic data used by social scientists?; what policy implications arise from genetic evidence and the data collection methods that support it?; and finally, where might or should we go next?

In the next section, we provide a brief scientific primer on what genetic data is and how it is collected. We then summarize how social scientists, and particularly economists, have used this information in their empirical analyses. We draw distinctions between descriptive work, research that aims to establish evidence of causation in one primary direction, and studies that seek to identify gene-environment interactions in producing outcomes. Understanding how genetic markers associate with health and socioeconomic outcomes may have implications for public policy, a subject we then discuss with a heavy focus on innovation policy as it impacts the pharmaceutical industry, because genetic markers can be targeted in the delivery of specific treatment regimens (popularly referred to as "personalized medicine"). We conclude the chapter by discussing promising directions for future research that continues economists' disciplinary tradition of simultaneously developing new tools and new models that incorporate the data drawn from those tools, so we can better understand how outcomes develop and—based on this knowledge—enrich both policy and academic discussions.

SCIENTIFIC PRIMER

As background, research on heredity dates back over 1000 years, but the mechanism of heredity that ignited the modern field of genetics did not receive widespread scientific attention until long after Gregor Mendel first published the fundamental laws of inheritance in 1866. Mendel's research was conducted with pea plants and led him to the insights that genes come in pairs and are inherited as distinct units, one from each parent. These insights were drawn from tracking the patterns of inheritance of seven different features between parental and offspring pea plants. As Mendel was not an academic but rather a little-known Central European monk, his work largely went unrecognized until 1900. Only recently has knowledge about the genetic factors that contribute to health and socioeconomic outcomes begun to emerge, and much of this knowledge has been generated in the last 15 years. To assist the reader who may be unfamiliar with the terms and jargon in the molecular genetics literature that we draw on in this section, a glossary of scientific terms is offered at the end of this chapter.

A Brief Review of the Development of Molecular Genetics Over the Last Century

Readers interested in an accessible review, designed for nonacademic audiences, of the historical study of human heredity and its main findings related to the modern field of genetics that has developed since Mendel (1866) are referred to Mukherjee (2017). The first half of the twentieth century saw the blossoming of what is now known as classical genetics. Many recent breakthroughs in our knowledge are due to a combination of important findings made in the second half of the twentieth century and recent technological advances. Perhaps one of the best known and most important findings in genetics that led to the development of molecular genetics as a field was published in 1953, when James Watson and Francis Crick described the double helix structure of deoxyribonucleic acid (DNA). DNA is composed of two strands of "nucleotides" coiled around each other and can be viewed as an immensely long ladder twisted into a helix, or coil, where the nucleotides are linked together (like rungs on a ladder) by hydrogen bonds. Each strand is composed of multiple instances of four complementary nucleotides. A nucleotide consists of a base (one of four chemicals: adenine (A), thymine (T), guanine (G), or cytosine (C)) plus a molecule of sugar and one of phosphoric acid. These nucleotides are often referred to as the building blocks of DNA. A complementarity between the two strands of DNA arises because adenine on one strand always bonds with thymine on the other, and similarly, cytosine is always paired with guanine. The DNA "base-pairs"—i.e., the pairs of nucleotides that can be found at any cross-sectional slice of the two complementary DNA strands—are thus guanine-cytosine ("GC") and adenine-thymine ("AT").

DNA is hereditary material that contains detailed instructions, in the form of a set of biological messages, for how an organism needs to develop, live, and reproduce. DNA is located on 23 pairs of chromosomes in every cell of an organism that has a nucleus. To provide some additional intuitive understanding of the genome, we employ here the analogy provided in Lehrer and Ding (2017). Our DNA can be understood as an instruction manual composed of 23 chapters (chromosomes) that in total contain over 3.2 billion letters (DNA base pairs). The length of each chapter varies from 48 to 250 million letters (A, C, G, T) without any spaces. Although there are no spaces, a gene can be viewed as a paragraph in the chapter. Each gene is a segment of DNA that can vary in size from a few hundred letters (i.e., DNA bases) to more than 2 million letters. Thus, a single chromosome (chapter) can have hundreds or even thousands of genes (paragraphs) containing millions of letters.

The structure of DNA is formed at conception, when one member of each pair of chromosomes is inherited from the mother and the other from the father. Homologous chromosomes have the same genes arranged in the same order, but slightly different DNA base-pair sequences within these genes across individuals. Our DNA is able to produce variation in our individual outcomes insofar as part of the human genome—less than 2% of it, according to modern measurement and classification techniques—encodes information to make proteins through the order, or sequence, of the nucleotides along each DNA strand.[1]

1. The remaining 98% of the human genome is often referred to as "non-coding DNA". While it does support a large variety of functions that are crucial to the survival of an organism (e.g., regulating when proteins are made, and controlling the packaging of DNA within the cell), the exact role of this remaining 98% remains less understood than that of the 2% of our DNA that encodes protein-production instructions.

In other words, one of the reasons that individuals differ from one another is that their DNA consists of different nucleotide sequences and, consequently, carry different biological messages regarding protein production. As we will shortly discuss, knowing that the base-pair sequence of a gene determines the amino acid sequence of the resulting protein is crucial for the development of technologies to sequence our individual genetic code.

Proteins are complex molecules involved in many critical functions of the body's tissues and organs ranging from the production of antibodies to the transportation of substances, the creation of structures, regulation, and sending messages. Hormones and enzymes that cause chemical changes and control all body processes are made of *proteins*. For example, antibodies, also known as immunoglobulins, consist of proteins produced by white blood cells and play a critical role in the body's immune response by specifically recognizing and binding to particular antigens, such as bacteria or viruses, and aiding in their destruction. Thus, if different amounts of proteins are produced in different people due to differences in the nucleotide sequences in their DNA, some individuals may produce lower levels of immunoglobulins than others and will be more likely to become ill when they encounter a virus. As another example, growth hormone is a protein produced by somatotropic cells that acts as a messenger to coordinate processes between different cells and organs to stimulate growth, which occurs at different times and rates across individuals.

Beginning in the mid-1970s, methods were developed to determine the sequence of the nucleotides in a given sample of DNA to help uncover the genetic components of individual difference. To complete this goal, the United States Department of Energy and National Institutes of Health joined with numerous international partners in October 1990 to provide funding for and start the Human Genome Project. The Human Genome Project's goal was to sequence all 3.2 billion base pairs, which is the complete set of DNA in the human body.[2] Human beings are all 99.9% the same, DNA-wise, and human DNA is about 99% the same as that of chimpanzees, our closest relatives. It has been suggested that if two individuals were selected at random they would only differ at about one in every 1200–1500 DNA base pairs. Most genome variations between a given pair of individuals are relatively small and simple, such as an A substituted for a T at a specific location on one strand. These single-base-pair differences across individuals are known as single nucleotide polymorphisms (SNPs).

The complete human genome sequence that was announced in June 2000 is a "representative" genome sequence based on the DNA of only a few individuals. To accelerate the pace of medical discovery worldwide, all data generated by

2. The size of the human genome is quite large relative to the genome for either *Escherichia coli* (a bacterium that lives in the human gut) and a fruit fly that are, respectively, approximately five million and 123 million base pairs in length. However, the human genome is much shorter than the genome for other living things, such as the loblolly pine tree, which is roughly 23 billion base pairs in length.

the Human Genome Project was made freely and rapidly available on the internet. In April 2003, researchers successfully completed the Human Genome Project.[3]

Once the human genome was decoded, researchers in multiple disciplines strove to conduct studies that would elucidate how each of the many parts of our chromosomes works with the others in generating individual outcomes. Motivating much of this research is the goal of understanding individual outcomes that are hypothesized to be polygenic, i.e., due to multiple genes where each gene may play a small role. Unlike outcomes such as sickle cell disease and cystic fibrosis that can generally be explained by alterations in a single gene, many outcomes of research interest are the product of numerous genes, each with a small effect and often interplaying with the environment. The susceptibility of individual genes to contribute to certain outcomes may vary with environmental factors. Central to informing research objectives in this area, the National Institutes of Health began in 2005 to produce a catalog of common genetic patterns, referred to as the HapMap (http://hapmap.ncbi.nlm.nih.gov/ (web archive link)).

The HapMap can help to identify the locations on the human genome of outcome-relevant genetic variation, which aids researchers in developing hypotheses and new types of tests that measure genetic variation. In the first HapMap published in 2005, approximately one million SNPs were genotyped (i.e., produced from a process of determining whether there are differences, and of what type, in the genetic sequence of an individual relative to the DNA sequence of a reference individual). In 2007, the second HapMap was published, containing descriptions of over three million SNPs. Updated versions of the HapMap continue to be issued, rapidly expanding our knowledge of SNPs, in turn improving the accuracy of the unique individual-specific genetic fingerprints used in identity testing and other applications. It has been estimated that there are roughly 10 million SNPs on the human genome—on average, about one instance per 300 base pairs—on which a mutation (i.e., a variation in one single nucleotide) commonly occurs in humans. Thus, only at every 300 base pairs on average, as we move along a DNA strand, is there a genetic difference between two random individuals.

Genetic researchers use terminology such as "rs15260(A;C)" to indicate someone with a sequence of A and then C, at location rs15260 of the genome, which is a specific position on a chromosome at which a particular SNP appears. At this location, most people might have the nucleotide "A" on one strand and

3. A draft of the entire human genome sequence was first made available in 2001, but it was only finalized on April 14, 2003. A major quality assessment in Schmutz et al. (2004) of the human genome sequence was published on May 27, 2004, indicating that in over 92% of samples taken, the sequence exceeded 99.99% accuracy, which was within the intended goal. A "Gold Standard" version of the human genome sequence excluding one chromosome was then released in October 2004. The full sequence of the last chromosome was published in the journal *Nature* in May 2006.

"A" on the other, and a small subgroup might have an alternative base pair (such as CC or AC). No distinction is made between AC or CA, and researchers do not distinguish whether a person inherited the A from the mother or the father. Each variant of a SNP that has been observed in humans is called an "allele." Hence, alleles code variant forms of given gene that are found at the same place on a homologous chromosome. The most common allele on a given SNP is known as the major allele, and a less common allele is sometimes called a minor allele or risky allele. For example, a frequently studied SNP is called "TaqI DRD2" and is located at chromosomal position rs1800497. This SNP was originally believed to play a role in determining the density of dopamine receptors in the brain. These receptors play a key role in transmitting signals across regions of the brain, and fewer receptors meant signals would take longer to be received. Across individuals, there are genetic variants in this SNP known as A1A1, A1A2, and A2A2, where A1 is the risky allele. That is, carriers of the Taql DRD2 A1 allele have significant loss of dopamine receptor density in the brain, and this is often hypothesized to be linked to poor outcomes.

In practice, researchers often refer to the number of possible genetic variants of a given SNP by the number of risky (i.e., minor or low-frequency) alleles that the SNP contains. For example, rather than referring to someone as having variant "rs1800497(A1;A1)," researchers will often refer to this person as having "two risky alleles for the Taq1 DRD2 gene." At present, it is believed that only a very small minority of all the known SNPs play important roles in influencing the function and structure of the human body. These roles could be selectively advantageous or disadvantageous (of which the latter possibility is the source of the term "risky"), and the genetic material accounting for these SNPs takes up less than 0.1% of the human genome. It is this genetic material that is most frequently targeted by current research aiming to explain the genetic underpinnings of observed differences across human individuals in socioeconomic outcomes.

Collecting Molecular Genetic Data

To obtain genetic data, most academic data collections as well as commercial direct-to-consumer companies that provide genetic reports use a procedure called a buccal smear. The survey participant or consumer is provided with a vial and a small brush or cotton swab that is used to collect a sample of cells from the inside surface of the cheek. These cells are then placed into the vial and sent to a laboratory for sequencing. While buccal smears are popular, genetic tests can also be performed on samples of blood, hair, skin, and amniotic fluid, among other tissues.

While there are many potential SNPs, researchers' ability to measure genetic factors is constrained by the type of test being used by the laboratory. Most tests used take measures not of the whole genome, but of just a targeted section. As a matter of terminology, a "genetic test" examines a targeted section of DNA whose genes have a known function such as producing a protein, whereas a "genomic test" investigates large sections of genetic material and information where there is often no specific genetic target.[4] Often the target of a genetic test is a region of the genome, often called an "exon," that codes for the production of a specific protein. Every sequence of three nucleotides on the genome, called a "codon," relates to the production of one amino acid that itself is an input to protein production. To identify gene variants, genetic tests use the links from nucleotide to codon to amino acid to the protein produced, based on what appears in a particular exon.

To illustrate, suppose the area of a specific exon contains 600 nucleotides. This exon would contain $600/3 = 200$ codons, and the protein produced with reference to this exon would contain 200 amino acids. The size of a protein can be expressed as its molecular mass, and genetic tests use this fact to measure the amino acids produced based on instructions in the codons, which helps to identify the SNP variant present in the tested subject's DNA, as the exact sequence of nucleotides in a gene determines the amino acid sequence of the resulting protein. Sequencing that targets exons is necessarily limited to examining the roughly 1% of a person's genome in which exons are present, corresponding to only roughly 2% of human genes that code for proteins. While methods to undertake whole genome sequencing are also available, they are both more costly and more time consuming than tests targeted to particular protein-encoding exons. Most techniques used to measure SNPs in datasets that social scientists employ focus exclusively on exons.

In general, the quality of a given genetic test depends on the average number of times each base pair in the genome is read during the test's sequencing process. The goal of sequencing is to determine the precise order of nucleotides, so testing methods must identify which of the four nucleotides (A, C, G or T) is located at a specific point in a strand of DNA. As reading each base pair in every chromosome of a subject can become quite expensive in terms of time and resources, many datasets used to produce research published in both scientific and social science disciplines report an imputed SNP. To impute a SNP, geneticists rely on what is known as "linkage disequilibrium." Two SNPs on the genome are said to be in linkage disequilibrium when the patterns observed in their alleles are related in a population. High linkage disequilibrium—perhaps counterintuitively to the ears of economists—means that the SNPs' particular allele patterns are almost always inherited together. High linkage disequilibrium thus means that by having accurate information on the alleles present in neighboring SNPs, one can take a well-informed guess of the alleles on a given SNP an individual has inherited.

4. Indeed, at present the most common routine for sequencing an individual human's genome involves generating a "draft" sequence for the tested individual and comparing it to the representative human genome, viewed as a "reference" human genome sequence.

The fact that many SNPs are imputed is generally ignored in subsequent empirical analyses (i.e., researchers typically treat the data as if it were measured without any error). The genetic data available to researchers is a product of the type of sequences that have been assessed (whether the whole genome or particular SNPs) that determine the content of the data, and the number of steps and activities involved in the data collection process, which determines the overall quality level of the data. Decisions about the type and quality level of the genetic sequencing conducted in laboratories are often influenced by budgetary and other considerations not directly related to a social scientist's likely research agenda, and these decisions jointly affect which SNPs are available for analysis and the potential degree of estimation error that afflicts the data provided.

In the next section, we briefly summarize the molecular genetic research conducted by social scientists, primarily utilizing data on SNPs, that has generated important new empirical and theoretical insights. These insights are limited at the moment but will likely grow at a rapid rate as the declining cost of genetic sequencing will enable more social scientists to augment their data collections with genetic information.

New insights from social science research using genetic information may have substantial economic value, potentially delivering a second wave of innovation and windfall gains on the heels of the first. The Human Genome project spurred a revolution in biotechnology spending and innovation around the world. Results from the Human Genome project are claimed by Battelle Technology Partnership Practice (2011) to have generated US$796 billion in economic activity in the US alone. Revolutionary advances in DNA sequencing technologies have enabled rapid, low cost determination of individuals' DNA sequences, increasingly marketed direct to consumers (e.g., by companies such as ancestry.com and 23andme). The growing field of pharmacogenomics examines how genetic variation affects an individual's response to a drug, and scientists have been able to leverage findings from this field, together with techniques founded in molecular biology and genetics, spawning the creation of new goods such as new crop varieties. The continued application of genomics in this area could lead to agricultural products with specific nutritional content, or products of a specific size or texture that could yield economic benefits by lowering the cost of shipping. However, some envisioned applications have raised ethical concerns in the scientific community about the control of access to data on genetic markers, as well as public concerns about the appropriate use of genomic information.

SOCIAL SCIENCE RESEARCH USING GENETIC DATA

Social scientists who utilize molecular genetic data as a source of explanatory variables in their analyses must decide how these measures should be introduced. Some researchers create a single measure, such as the count of risky alleles for a SNP. This formulation imposes the assumption of linearity in the effects of risky alleles on the outcome under consideration, while having the advantage of leading to a sparser set of covariates than many alternative formulations. Other researchers create a set of indicator variables, each of which flags a particular variant of the risky allele relative to the base category. To illustrate, let us return to the Taq1DRD2 gene that has variants A1A1, A1A2, and A2A2, where A1 is the risky allele. Using the first approach mentioned above, an individual's genetic material present on the Taq1 DRD2 SNP is coded as zero (for A2A2 individuals), one (for A1A2 individuals), or two (for A1A1 individuals). Using the second approach, this same variation is captured with a vector of dummy variables for having the A1A1 variant and the A1A2 variant, with the effects of each variant being estimated relative to the most common (A2A2) variant that serves as the base category.

One advantage of the second approach is that there is no need to make a functional form assumption about the way that the genetic information affects the outcome of interest. A simple statistical test can be employed to determine whether the estimated effects indicate that the linear restriction implied by the first approach is warranted. A second advantage of the indicator variable approach relates to the interpretation of genetic effects. Genetic markers are immutable characteristics that are fixed at conception. Greiner and Rubin (2011) point out that immutable characteristics can be viewed as treatments, as many outcomes are determined through the mediation of perception rather than directly from those immutable characteristics, and perceptions are not immutable. In this "potential outcome" framework, a specific SNP variant could be viewed as a legitimate treatment: any difference in outcomes between two individuals who are identical in all other characteristics except for their genetic sequence on that specific SNP could be attributed to that genetic difference—with the exact mechanism generating the difference in outcomes remaining unspecified and open to further inquiry. In contrast, using the number of risky alleles as the approach to capturing the genetic information would not only restrict the mechanism to operate solely through the count of risky alleles, but would also require maintaining the assumption of continuous treatment effects: the (single) estimated marginal effect on the outcome would be identical when moving from zero to one risky alleles as when moving from one to two risky alleles. On balance, discretizing genetic information in empirical work through the creation of large dummy variable arrays may be preferable, at least at this stage in our understanding of the link between genetic information and socioeconomic outcomes.

Existing work by social scientists falls under one of the following three areas: reporting associations; recovering causal effects; and exploring the interactions of genes with the environment that are relevant to outcome generation. We next summarize some of the key developments in each of these areas.

From Candidate Genes to Genome-Wide Studies

Initially, social scientists who incorporated molecular genetic data into their research programs focused on a handful of genetic markers. These markers, called "candidate genes," were generally those occupying specific pre-selected regions of our DNA. These locations were not selected randomly, but rather were chosen as the target of genotyping either due to being suspected of being directly involved in generating the outcome, or because the types of protein encoded by the candidate gene(s) located there may logically suggest that those genes could influence the outcome being investigated. A candidate gene study ex ante selects one or more specific genetic markers—essentially a set of tested SNPs—to investigate. Candidate gene studies address the question of whether the specific SNPs studied are associated with outcomes of interest to social scientists. These associations may arise if the test SNP is directly associated with the outcome, or if it is indirectly associated with the outcome because of linkage disequilibrium, whereby another SNP whose occurrence is correlated with the test SNP is the one that directly affects outcomes. Most researchers producing candidate gene studies assume they are identifying a direct association, and further work would be required to rule out indirect channels. As an example, some early work (e.g., Zhong, Israel, Xue, Ebstein, and Chew (2009) and Dreber et al. (2009)) tried to provide a biological microfoundation to utility maximization by examining the associations across people with patterns on particular SNPs with measures of economic primitives collected in the laboratory, such as risk aversion and time discounting. Indirect effects may arise in this case if intergenerationally-transmitted traits affecting risk aversion and time discounting result in part from schooling decisions made by parents and not from predetermined characteristics inherited from one's parents.

Candidate gene studies were easy and quick to undertake, making them seductive to researchers. Numerous researchers generating these early studies do not explicitly explain how their putative candidate genes were chosen. Many studies appear to have been carried out mainly due to data availability, with ex post justification rather than a clear theoretical rationale provided for the exercise. Further, concerns regarding proper scientific practice in this area have emerged. Many early studies lack statistical power, yielding potentially false-positive results. As the number of studies using this approach increased, it became apparent that many of the early results could not be replicated in analyses undertaken with other samples. For example, Chabris et al. (2013) illustrate several points about the limits of candidate gene studies by trying to replicate previously identified candidate genes using data from three independent longitudinal studies. Their results are disappointing from a replication perspective, as they found fewer significant associations than a traditional power analyses would have predicted ex ante.

To help ensure that evidence generated using the method of candidate genes would be credible, in 2012 the academic journal *Behavior Genetics* adopted strict standards for the publication of candidate gene studies (Hewitt, 2012). To be considered for publication, any candidate gene study must be well powered and make corrections in statistical inference for multiple testing, and any new finding must be accompanied by a replication. These higher publication standards have meant that conducting candidate gene studies is relatively less appealing today than undertaking research that seeks to identify the associations of characteristics or behavior with measures of SNP variation across the full genome.

Studies using information on SNPs across the genome are typically designed as a data mining exercise, requiring no prior knowledge, imperfect as it might be, of which genes are likely to be related to the outcome of interest. Over the last decade, these studies have involved increasingly larger sample sizes that are generally constructed by combining multiple datasets. Each of the data sets being combined is required to have measures of the same set of common SNPs as well as the target outcome measure. The sampling criteria across the pooled data sets are often not identical, with social science surveys that have well developed sampling frames being pooled with voluntary response samples such as those from 23andMe (where participants must elect to send a sample to 23andMe for genotyping) and case-control studies, in which data is collected separately on groups who differ in some outcome. Despite the reduction in external validity of any findings that this may produce, proponents argue that drawing genetic information about narrow demographic groups from large pooled datasets can better support the detection of robust evidence linking outcomes to genetic variation, even when the associations are modest in practical terms.

The standard approach taken in a large-scale genome-wide association (GWA) study begins with estimating a model on a "training sample." The training sample utilizes all the observations contained in most, but not all, of the assembled datasets. To convince the research community that a given GWA study has detected a true association, it is now standard that researchers examine whether the results using the training sample replicate using data from the datasets that were held out from the initial analysis. These additional datasets are then referred to collectively as an "evaluation" (or "test") dataset. In spirit, this approach is in line with that of time-series econometricians comparing the accuracy of alternative strategies used to calculate an economic forecast, as illustrated in the box office revenue prediction exercise discussed in Lehrer and Xie (2017).

The implementation of this type of design is supported by recent data-sharing initiatives, such as the pooling of databases collected by individual research teams under the stewardship of the Wellcome Trust Case Control Consortium (https://www.wtccc.org.uk), with the stated aim of improving the understanding of the etiological basis of several major causes of global disease.

GWA studies can appear complicated to those familiar with conventional social science research, as the method relies on understanding work conducted in the statistical genetics literature in which scientists use different terminology than what is used in the econometrics literature. However, the development of off-the-shelf software designed to implement a GWA study promises a dramatic reduction in the barriers to entry. Not only does off-the-shelf software obviate the need to fully comprehend the underlying statistical genetics literature, HapMap-based genotyping platforms further facilitate the genome-wide approach by enabling theory-blind data mining across the genome in search of possible sources of variation relevant to a particular outcome.[5]

In practice, an important ingredient in any GWA study is how to choose focal SNPs optimally, based on HapMap data, to maximize the regional genomic variation that the researcher will subsequently be able to use in identifying genetic effects. Intuitively, because markers located near each other are often inherited jointly, increasing the independent variation available in the data drawn from each SNP, thereby avoiding the covariance produced by linkage disequilibrium, means selecting SNPs that are reasonably far apart on the genome. Researchers often select one SNP among a highly correlated set of SNPs to include in a specification. While this may sound promising, there is a trade-off: in order to make a valid claim about the source of the genetic effects found, the researcher must choose from among the SNPs located in a particular chromosomal region the one that is in fact responsible for the outcome, either on its own or through interaction with the environment. If the wrong SNP is selected, the researcher may falsely attribute an association between the included SNP and the outcome to the influence of genes located on the included SNP, rather than to genes located on an omitted SNP whose genetic information is strongly associated with that appearing on the included SNP, due to linkage disequilibrium. This can be viewed as a particular form of omitted variable bias. The challenge posed by linkage disequilibrium varies across racial and ethnic groups due to both their population size and their migration history. For example, there are differences across population subgroups in the mean size of regions of strongly associated SNPs, sometimes called haplotype blocks, that are defined algorithmically in units of measurement called kilobases where 1 kilobase is equal to 1000 base pairs of DNA. For populations of European or Asian ancestry, a haplotype block is estimated to be 22 kilobases, while in populations of recent African ancestry, a haplotype block is estimated to be 11 kilobases. Because of such differences, in a GWA study, researchers only consider individuals of a specific ancestry.

Perhaps the best-known example of GWA is illustrated in a sequence of papers carried out by The Social Science Genetic Association Consortium (www.thessgac.org) that seeks to understand the associations between genetic markers and educational attainment. This outcome was selected partly because

5. An important but often overlooked weakness of much of the off-the-shelf GWA software available today is that its measurement of the variation in each SNP is strictly in the form of counts of the number of risky alleles.

it appears in a multitude of datasets. The most recent project, Lee et al. (2018), uses data on 1.1 million individuals and identifies 1271 independent genome-wide-significant SNPs. Genome-wide-significant SNPs are those whose associations with the focal outcome have *p*-values below a specific threshold for statistical significance, a distinction critical to control the number of false-positive associations. Currently, standard practice is to use a genome-wide significance p-value threshold of 5*10E-8 to judge whether a SNP is significantly associated with the outcome under consideration. However, since there are more possible hypotheses of significant association than data points (the authors could potentially include data on 7.1 million SNPs), one must make corrections for multiple testing. In Lee et al. (2018), a Bonferroni corrected p-value threshold needed to hold the overall type 1 error rate at the desired level would be 1.25*10E-8. The Bonferroni procedure is often viewed as being quite conservative in the multiple testing literature because it divides the overall significance level by the number of hypotheses undertaken in the study. If the Bonferroni threshold were applied to the Lee et al. (2018) results, only 1024 of the 1271 SNPs would have been judged statistically significant.[6]

Lee et al. (2018) presents a marked extension of an earlier GWA study of educational attainment conducted by the SSGA consortium. Prior work in this stream of research investigating the genetic basis of educational attainment appeared in Rietveld et al. (2013), who combined data on 42 cohorts consisting of over 100,000 individuals, and Rietveld et al. (2014) who further expanded that dataset. Okbay et al. (2016) was the third study, conducting a GWA of roughly 300,000 people, and finding 74 SNPs associated with educational attainment. Akin to prior GWA of educational attainment, in Okbay et al. (2016) only one trait/outcome was considered, whereas Lee et al. (2018) use a recent methodological extension to classical GWA to examine how the same set of genetic markers is associated with multiple cognitive traits. The most striking finding from the series of papers completed by the SSGA consortium appears in the portion of Okbay et al. (2016) that conducted a replication with a test dataset involving 110,000 individuals from the UK Biobank, showing that 72 of the initially identified 74 SNPs remain significantly associated with educational attainment. The authors conduct numerous robustness checks of their main analyses where they ensure common support is imposed across samples by excluding dissimilar individuals, and consider alternative sets of control variables to capture any potentially unobserved confounding genetic differences across the samples used in the main analysis. Further, they utilize the latest quality control protocols being applied in the medical genetics literature (Winkler et al., 2014) and carefully account for population stratification, defined formally in the next section, to ensure that similar people are being compared across the combined datasets. This line of research holds the potential to help

6. Note that in most of the GWA reported in Lee et al. (2018) each specification included up to 10,000 SNPs if data from 23andMe was utilized.

us map the molecular basis for educational attainment, although the economic significance of each of the individual 74 SNPs is found to be quite small. Further, in aggregate, the 74 SNPs identified in Okbay et al. (2016) explain only 0.43% of the variation in educational attainment across individuals in the sample.

The idea of using larger sample sizes to detect the true association between genetic variation and a disease, assuming such an association exists, is motivated by statistical power considerations. To retain power, sample sizes must increase with the following: higher odds of a type one error emerging, as more SNPs are included and more association tests performed; higher odds of measurement error in either the outcome or the explanatory variables; smaller magnitude of the genetic effect; lower frequency of the risky allele; and increased importance of omitted factors, including heterogeneity in the underlying association being estimated, caused for example by multiple genes that contribute to the disease, ancestry differences across population subsets, or gene-gene or gene-environment interactions.

One of the main outputs from GWA studies that proponents suggest could be useful for social scientists is what is known as a polygenic score. A polygenic score is constructed as a weighted sum of the individual risky alleles for each SNP used in a GWA study that is reliably related to a particular trait or outcome, where each allele is weighted by its effect size as estimated in the study (Dudbridge, 2013). In practice, different methods are used in different studies to construct polygenic scores and there does not appear to be a consensus emerging on the most appropriate way. The alternative methods primarily differ in terms of the weighting schemes and which SNPs are included in the calculation. In all methods, the underlying idea is that based on GWA study results, we can apply weights that indicate the relative importance in generating the focal outcome of the genetic information present on each SNP. The resulting polygenic score can be used by researchers to exploit the joint predictive power of many SNPs within an estimating equation to predict a focal outcome.

As an explanatory variable, a polygenic score will explain more variation in outcomes than any set of individual SNPs, and can also accommodate the possibility of combined genetic influence. From an econometric perspective the score is a generated regressor, an issue that most analysts using polygenic scores in their models ignore. From a behavioral perspective, the score is just a linear combination of different candidate causal factors, and implicitly makes assumptions about the relative substitutability of those factors (i.e., of the genetic variation present in different SNPs) within the total effect-generation mechanism. From a more policy-oriented or therapeutic standpoint, polygenic scores provide a way of identifying individuals at high risk for certain outcomes.

GWA studies have given rise over time to polygenic scores that can predict a significant amount of variation in important outcomes. For example, the polygenic score constructed in Lee et al. (2018) from their GWA can explain 11% of the variation in educational attainment of participants of The National Longitudinal Study of Adolescent to Adult Health (http://www.cpc.unc.edu/projects/

addhealth), *and* 13% of the variation in educational attainment using data from The Health and Retirement Study (http://hrsonline.isr.umich.edu/). These figures represent marked increases in the predictive power of generated polygenic scores relative to those calculated from earlier GWA studies, including Okbay et al. (2016). To provide more context for how well their score can predict educational attainment, Lee et al. (2018) show that their constructed score does a better job of predicting educational attainment than household income but is a worse predictor than either mother's or father's education. More concretely, in specifications that control for all demographic variables jointly, the score's incremental R-squared is 4.6%.

Papageorge and Thom (2017) and Barth, Papageorge, and Thom (2018) each present an early application of polygenic scores in labor economics. The former study, using the Health and Retirement Study (HRS), presents evidence that the polygenic score that predicts educational attainment is also associated with higher wages, but only among individuals with a college education. Further, suggestive evidence is provided that the genetic gradient in wages has steepened in more recent birth cohorts, which the authors suggest is consistent with interactions between technological change and labor market ability (what might be termed good-gene-biased technological change). In the latter study, evidence is presented using the same dataset that the polygenic score from Lee et al. (2018) to predict wealth at retirement. The authors suggest that the polygenic score is a proxy variable for one's ability to navigate complex financial choices.

At present, research using GWA is more favored within the research community than that using the candidate gene approach. On the one hand, without strong prior hypotheses, the agnosticism of a GWA study regarding theories of outcome determination, and its survey of the entire genome, hold appeal. It is a pure empirical exercise. On the other hand, the specific empirical specification used in a GWA study is not innocent: any specification imposes strong assumptions on how genetic factors are linked to the outcome under consideration, including the absence of gene-by-environment interactions. In practice, these assumptions are often implicit and not well justified as being reasonable in the empirical application. This runs counter to standard practice in most social science research using conventional methods. Hence, we predict that as the methodology becomes better understood, more criticism will emerge from social scientists about this aspect of GWA research.

More generally, it is hard to see how evidence from GWA studies contributes to existing literatures in the social sciences that are informed by an underlying behavioral model. For example, consider the earlier GWA of educational attainment. A voluminous literature in multiple disciplines examines how individuals make a sequence of education choices (e.g., what courses to choose in high school, whether to apply to college, which college to attend, what major to select, whether to persist in higher education, and so on) and generally postulates that faced with imperfect information about their options, individuals trade-off the expected costs and benefits of each potential choice. In most situations, individuals themselves have imperfect (if any) knowledge of their own genetic code when making these decisions. If individuals differ in terms of the genetic markers that can explain educational attainment, do these differences change how benefits or costs are assessed in ways that should be accommodated in our behavioral models—or is genetic information already encapsulated implicitly in these models, through what is presently known as preference-based heterogeneity? Making this distinction is important for social science modelers. Put differently, does the belief that one possesses the genes for education and success as calculated by the polygenic score of Lee et al. (2018) influence effort on studying, hiring a tutor, or persisting in education? Do genes affect constraints, and if so which ones?; or does their influence directly affect utility, as speculated in several candidate gene studies?

Further, studies in the social sciences often seek to understand the scenarios, such as particular environments or types of samples, in which significant effects emerge. In the case of a large scale GWA study, the odds of finding a significant effect are higher when a specific genetic variant has a similar effect in all samples, which themselves likely differ in terms of environmental and sample characteristics. This means that the variation in environment and sample type that the social scientist would normally use to identify effect strength across the whole population does not play a role in effect identification in a GWA study. Indeed, the method is likely to mask effects that are highly heterogeneous across context or sample. Second, genetic researchers in the scientific literature are generally interested mainly in gauging the total amount of variance in outcomes that the included genetic information explains (e.g., in calculating the R^2 statistic for the full set of genetic factors included in the specification), and point estimates are generally not the focus. This differs from the orientation of most studies in the social sciences, where researchers often examine the sign, magnitude, and statistical significance of key explanatory covariates included in a baseline preferred specification and complement their baseline results by investigating their sensitivity to alternative specifications. In summary, while GWA techniques transplanted into social science from the scientific literature hold the potential to uncover associations between genetics and traits and behaviors of interest to social scientists, there are dimensions of methodological tension between GWA and more conventional approaches that will take time to resolve.

Moving Beyond Association: Using Genetic Markers to Estimate Causal Effects

Angrist and Pischke (2010) recently argued that what they term the credibility revolution in empirical economics has spawned many research studies over the last 30 years that increasingly exploit plausibly exogeneous variation to identify causal effects that are of interest to both academic and policy audiences. Whatever its source, this undeniable trend has spurred significant controversy within the profession as to whether causal effects (as opposed to structural parameters that can be tied to an underlying behavioral model) are of prime interest, and whether researchers are choosing projects based on the availability and plausibility of identifying variation, irrespective of the importance of the research question being addressed.[7] Parallel debates have occurred within economics and epidemiology regarding whether studies that use genetic data are thereby capitalizing on a source of exogenous variation with which to identify the impact of specific health conditions on socioeconomic outcomes. Using genetic information as a source of exogenous identifying variation was first introduced in economics by Ding, Lehrer, Rosenquist, and Audrain-McGovern (2009), who essentially used candidate genes as instruments to understand the impact of health outcomes on academic performance using instrumental-variable techniques.[8] This empirical approach requires the researcher to assume that the genetic instruments are not only correlated with health outcomes,[9] but that they only influence academic outcomes through their influence on health.

The main empirical finding from this study is that depression and obesity each lead to approximately a one standard deviation reduction in academic performance. This deterioration is shown to differ by gender: young women's academic performance is found to be more adversely affected than that of young men by negative physical and mental health conditions. Additionally, using genetic instruments, the separate estimated impacts of inattention and hyperactivity on academic performance differ sharply in magnitude and sign from effects estimated conventionally, with the instrumental variables estimates substantially larger in magnitude relative to ordinary least squares estimates that ignore the endogeneity of health. The differential effects of inattention and hyperactivity are not observed if one does not decompose the diagnosis of ADHD into being clinically inattentive (AD) or clinically hyperactive/impulsive (HD). These results indicate that there are poor health consequences only from AD, and the authors speculate that this may arise because parents, peers, and teachers may be more likely to respond with extra investments to a child with HD than to a child with AD.

---

7. See Angrist and Pischke (2010) for more discussion, and comments by Keane (2010) and Sims (2010) that provide a critique of this shift.
8. This paper was first presented at a conference in 2003, and an early version appears as a NBER working paper (Ding, Lehrer, Rosenquist, & Audrain-McGovern, 2006).
9. As discussed earlier, there are likely significant advantages of using arrays of binary indicators for different genetic variations as instruments, relative to using variables that count the number of alleles. The results of models using binary indicator arrays are more flexible, easier to interpret, and enable the researcher to more easily investigate which particular variants are driving the identification. While using arrays that comprehensively dummy out all observed genetic variations will increase the number of instruments and could lead to a many-instrument problem (Hausman, Newey, Woutersen, Chao, & Swanson, 2012), new strategies have been proposed in Belloni, Chen, Chernozhukov, and Hansen (2012) that use the least absolute selection and shrinkage operator ("Lasso") to reduce the number of instruments.

Concerns regarding the plausible exogeneity of the genetic instrument used in Ding et al. (2009) have emerged. These concerns have focused on population stratification, pleitropy, and dynastic effects. We expand on these concerns in the next two paragraphs.

The concern about population stratification is based on the existence of subtle genetic differences between groups of individuals that are not accounted for in the model, and the resultant possibility that the gene being used as the source of exogenous variation is correlated with a missing genetic marker related to group membership that is itself driving the results. Pleiotropy is the phenomenon of a single genetic variant influencing multiple traits. Pleiotropy is likely to be widespread in the human genome and was first pointed out as a concern in Conley (2009). More recent work has shown that if pleiotropy arises because the SNP instrument(s) influences one trait, which in turn influences another (known as "vertical pleiotropy"), then instrumental variables strategies can still be used. However, if pleiotropy arises due to the SNP instruments influencing two traits through independent pathways ("horizontal pleitropy") then there is a greater chance that the instrument is invalid due to violation of the exclusion restriction (meaning in the context of Ding et al. (2009) that the genetic marker in fact belongs in the outcome equation itself, rather than only influencing outcomes via health). Hemani, Bowden, and Davey Smith (2018) present a recent review of methods that researchers can employ to assess whether horizontal pleiotropic associations are a concern, and many of these tools nicely complement the work of Conley, Hansen, and Rossi (2012) that Ding et al. (2009) encourage researchers to use as a form of sensitivity analysis in studies using genetic instruments.

Dynastic effects relating to the line of heredity present obvious challenges to the use of genetic information as instrumental variables, because, where unobserved, such effects may confound the estimates. For example, consider using a genetic marker for a particular poor health condition in children as an instrument to identify the effect of that health condition on children's academic performance. Without more detailed data on parental diagnoses as well as parental genes, we cannot use the intended instrument to separate out the portion of academic performance that is uniquely due to the child's condition. The instrumental variables effect estimated may include the impact of family environments provided by the parents whose own poor health, which partly fed into those environments, can be explained by the same genes that were chosen as instruments for the children. Despite this concern that the instrument in such a case violates the exclusion restriction, in fact impacting academic performance through channels other than child health, we suggest that recovered estimates are still of policy relevance as individuals are in general not randomly assigned to families, and policymakers are generally interested in the total impact of these disorders.

At a fundamental level, one will never know whether a specific candidate gene is a valid instrument, as one cannot randomly assign genes to humans or create human equivalents to knock-out mice. A knock-out mouse is a genetically-modified mouse in which researchers have inactivated, or "knocked out," an existing gene by replacing it or disrupting it with an artificial piece of DNA. By causing a specific gene to be inactive in the mouse and observing differences in the mouse from normal behavior or physiology, researchers can infer the probable function of that gene. Considering that such experiments are impossible to conduct in humans due to ethical concerns, Ding et al. (2009) suggest that researchers using genes as instruments should apply Conley et al. (2012)'s proposed "local to zero approximation" method that methodically tests the sensitivity of the results obtained to the degree of plausibility of the identifying assumptions.

The analysis in Ding et al. (2009) points out an additional concern that applies more broadly to many studies seeking to understand the causal effect of poor health on academic and labor market outcomes—including those that do not use genetic instruments. Comorbid health conditions, defined as conditions in which two or more disorders or illnesses occur in the same person (whether simultaneously or sequentially), are frequently observed in humans. Ding et al. (2009) show that failing to account for comorbid diagnoses would result in biased estimates of the causal effect of specific health diagnoses on socioeconomic outcomes. The authors also suggest that comorbidity can strongly influence whether genetic instruments satisfy the exclusion restriction criteria that must be satisfied to justify their use as instruments.

The issue of comorbidity has broad implications for genetic studies in many subfields. Recently, Brickell et al. (2018) provide evidence of a strong association between a polygenic score predictive of a diagnosis of ADHD ($R^2 = 0.83\%$–1.69%) and a broad range of childhood psychiatric symptoms among children aged nine to twelve in Sweden. This suggests that common genetic risk variants associated with ADHD also influence a general genetic liability towards broad psychopathology in childhood, hinting strongly at common genetic bases for multiple co-occurring psychiatric conditions. This type of finding reinforces the challenge that comorbidity poses in disentangling the underlying genetic basis of disease and reinforces the need to consider carefully the justification for particular specifications of empirical models in studies that use genetic data.

The challenge of comorbidity is also a motivation for calculating polygenic scores. Most definitions of health are based strictly on the presence or absence of symptoms, and when similar symptoms are shared by multiple health conditions, diagnosis of the true underlying condition may be delayed. However, by comparing a patient's polygenic scores for different conditions, doctors may be better able to judge the relative likelihood of multiple candidate comorbid conditions underlying the presenting patient's symptoms. As the predictive accuracy of polygenic scores continues to increase, genetic markers could not only increase the palette of options for pursuing instrumental variable strategies, but also help solve both econometric and diagnostic challenges created by comorbidity.

In the epidemiological literature, the use of genetic information as a source of identifying variation is termed Mendelian randomization. Mendelian randomization was first proposed in Katan (1986) and applied empirically in Smith and Ebrahim (2003). To fully merit the term "randomization," Mendelian randomization would require the absence of dynastic effects. However, genes are inherited by design from one's parents, and those parents also transmit environmental and behavioral traits across generations. Lehrer and Ding (2017) suggest that epidemiological studies relying on what is claimed as Mendelian randomization would be more accurately described as following a "Mendelian encouragement" design. Even in the presence of dynastic effects, genetic markers still encourage certain traits and behaviors, and their influence on outcomes at the population level may still be significant despite obvious ways for individuals not to comply behaviorally with their genetic assignments.

Within the epidemiological literature, important methodological developments have addressed a variety of concerns relating to the use of SNP variations as instruments. One set of extensions, proposed in Bowden, Davey Smith, and Burgess (2015), uses Egger regression analysis, a tool initially developed in Egger, Davey Smith, Schneider, and Minder (1997) to detect small study bias in meta-analyses. Bowden et al. (2015) demonstrate that this alternative estimator can recover consistent parameter estimates even if all genetic instrumental variables are invalid by invoking an assumption about the strength of the instruments in the first-stage independent of their direct effects on the outcome. While this approach can mitigate problems owing to weak instruments, it does not deliver an estimate interpretable as a local average treatment effect (cf. Imbens and Angrist (1994) for the assumptions required to merit this interpretation), and it is unclear how exactly how to interpret the estimates recovered. While these alternative strategies developed in the epidemiological literature can recover a consistent parameter estimate under certain assumptions, the recovered estimate does not have a direct causal interpretation akin to that of the conventional instrumental variables estimate if there is treatment effect heterogeneity. Other recent innovations face similar challenges related to interpretation. Examples include Gage et al. (2017)'s "bidirectional Mendelian randomization," proposed to deal with potential reverse causation (i.e., causal effects of the outcome on the endogenous regressor) and Rees, Wood, and Burgess (2017)'s "multivariable Mendelian randomization," designed to deal with a finite set of ex ante known possible pleiotropic characteristics of the SNP-based genetic instruments.

A final emerging approach to recovering causal effects involves using polygenic scores as instruments. As noted above, these scores can explain far more variation in the variable being instrumented than can variations in individual SNPs. However, because polygenic scores contain information drawn from multiple SNPs, some of which may independently affect the focal outcome, the likelihood of violating of the exclusion restriction assumption is increased. Further, many of the gene variants used to construct the polygenic score could have pleiotropic effects that lead to indirect influence on the focal outcome. Conley and Zhang (2018) elucidates further concerns with recent proposed extensions to instrumental variable methods that involve polygenic scores as the source of identifying variation. Debates about polygenic scores extend beyond considerations of their validity as instruments in support of causal identification. Purcell et al. (2009) list concerns about their usefulness, whereas Belsky et al. (2012, 2013) provide empirical examples illustrating their potential benefits.

Within economics, a final variant of the instrumental variable strategy that exploits genetic inheritance within full biological siblings was introduced by Fletcher and Lehrer (2009a, 2009b, 2011). Fletcher and Lehrer coin the term "genetic lottery" to motivate the use of an instrumental variable estimator for family fixed effects based on genetic information. Assuming a genetic lottery operates on humans is intuitively what is meant by the term "Mendelian randomization." Controlling for family fixed effects as instrumented by genetic information removes any (fixed) dynastic effects on outcomes that are shared between full biological siblings.

This strategy exploits variation in genetic inheritance within families and can also be used to test an important empirical model known as the family fixed effects estimator.[10] Researchers using this estimator to estimate a casual effect essentially compare siblings (or twins) with different exposure to a particular treatment. This estimator is popular because it allows researchers to eliminate all family-level correlates of treatment likelihood and can be carried out when there is no quasi-experiment to exploit. However, researchers must assume that all within-family decisions related to treatment take-up are exogenous. The genetic lottery approach of Fletcher and Lehrer relaxes that assumption, allowing for endogenous take-up decisions within families. The estimates recovered through their approach also enable a formal specification test of the assumption that the family fixed effects estimator on its own fully solved the endogeneity problems in a given study employing that estimator. Researchers interested in conducting such a specification test are strongly encouraged to use a bootstrapped Hausman test in place of the traditional Hausman test used in Fletcher and Lehrer (2011), as neither the conventional family fixed effects estimator nor the Fletcher and Lehrer (2011) genetic lottery instrumental variables estimator is efficient under the null hypothesis of the Hausman test. In each of the applications they examine, with the traditional test Fletcher and Lehrer reject that the family fixed effects estimator does not fully solve the endogeneity

10. The family fixed effects estimator is a workhorse estimator used in behavioral genetics as well as in family and population economics. For example, this strategy has been used to examine the longer-run effects of early childhood education programs (see, for example, Currie and Thomas (1995), Deming (2009)) and the causes and consequences of early-life health indicators (see, for example, Almond, Chay, and Lee (2005), Figlio, Guryan, Karbownik, and Roth (2014)), among other research questions.

problem in health when estimating its effects on academic and early labor market outcomes. The genetic lottery approach offers a new research design for researchers in the social sciences.

In summary, there is a rich and growing toolbox of genetically informed methods being developed in the epidemiological literature for estimating how outcomes of interest to social scientists are generated. Each new tool relies on a different set of identifying assumptions to support its use in causal inference. These methods are becoming increasingly available to research communities across the biomedical and social sciences and have potential applications beyond estimating causal effects including in testing the validity of the assumptions maintained when conducting conventional analysis. Genetic data can also help us understand new dimensions of individual difference, and its causes and effects.

Gene-Environment Interactions

Genetic markers can be used to explore the possibility of heterogeneous responses, both to policies and to (economic or therapeutic) treatments. Heterogeneous responses often imply an interaction of genetic and environmental influences (henceforth "G*E") in producing outcomes. Researchers across a multitude of disciplines champion the importance of G*E effects, particularly for early childhood education. The consensus view is that it is highly unlikely that genes are destiny: environmental exposure appears to change how genes are expressed and therefore their scope for influencing outcomes.[11]

At present, studies in the social sciences that estimate G*E effects are mainly confined to examining the effects of adding genetic interaction terms to existing research designs. A subset of these research designs exploits plausibly exogenous variation in environments; a second subset follows Fletcher and Lehrer (2011) in exploiting variation in genes within families; and a third subset is more exploratory in nature, aiming to elucidate which possible channels of influence may be most promising to investigate in further research. We discuss each of these strategies, in reverse order.

Pinning down causal G*E effects requires either exogenous variation in environmental factors or an econometric strategy that can discover breakpoints

---

11. A fascinating recent study by Huber, Donnelly, Rokem, and Yeatman (2018) shows that altering a child's educational environment through a targeted intervention program can induce rapid, large-scale changes in the properties of the brain's white matter tissue. This is relevant to policy, because white matter properties are often held to underlie variation in performance and to causally influence individual learning trajectories. Individual differences in white matter properties likely reflect the joint influence of genetics and environment. If underlying genetic differences predestine certain individuals to struggle with learning, then understanding the way these genetic differences translate into different effects of learning interventions may suggest optimal ways to allocate different interventions across students to ensure that all children have the opportunity to start schooling with an equal level of (genetically customized) preparation.

in the relationships between genetic factors and outcomes which, in turn, can be exploited for the identification of causal effects. Rosenquist et al. (2015) follow the latter approach. Motivating their study is the observation that many gene-environment interaction studies examine within-birth-cohort differences among individuals with varying environmental exposures occurring within a similar time period of data collection. This research design, while valuable, relies upon the assumption that the environmental variation of interest is not linked with any other genetic and/or environmental factors that also affect the outcome. Using between-birth-cohort differences, on the other hand, allows for the testing of hypotheses related to time varying changes in the whole of the environment affecting the population. The authors use the longitudinal offspring sample of the Framingham Heart Study collected between 1971 and 2008. This study collected data for people in one small geographic area, thereby reducing any biases due to unobservables that might explain sorting across regions based on environmental conditions. They restrict the individuals in the sample to be between the ages of 30 and 63 to ensure there are no differences in the age support across birth cohorts which might lead them to confound age and cohort effects. The main analysis applies the threshold regression estimator of Hansen (1999) to determine whether there is a structural break, of unknown timing, in the relation between genes and body mass index (BMI) using variation in both genes and outcomes across cohorts. The selected breakpoint is based on the model that best fits the data, using a grid-search algorithm.

Specifically, Rosenquist et al. (2015) test whether the well-documented association between a particular SNP variant (located at rs993609) and BMI varies across birth cohorts, the time period in which the data was collected, and/or the lifecycle. The analysis can be viewed as an examination of how trajectories of obesity across the lifecycle vary across birth cohorts in ways that are explained by genetic inheritance. Put differently, the analysis is designed to disentangle the extent to which historical versus contemporaneous environmental factors interact with genetic features. The SNP variant studied is known as the FTO gene, first christened drily by Peters, Ansmeier, and Ruther (1999) as "the fatso gene." This gene has been well studied. Frayling et al. (2007) present evidence that on average, one copy of the risky variant of this SNP produces up to three and a half extra pounds of weight. Two copies of the gene lead to seven extra pounds—and increase a person's risk of becoming obese by 50%. Yet, there is a great deal of variation in the magnitude of this association as estimated in different studies.

The main finding of Rosenquist et al. (2015) is that there is a robust change in the relationship between the FTO risky allele and BMI across birth cohorts, with an observed inflection point for those born after 1942. This result is robust to the inclusion of family fixed effects. The threshold regression estimator allows Rosenquist et al. (2015) to statistically test for the presence of a structural break in the relationship of genes to obesity. Their result suggests that in samples containing individuals born prior to 1942, having one or two copies of the risky allele would not lead to the addition of a statistically significant amount of weight. This statement can be made with confidence based on specification tests of the unrestricted model that controls for gene*cohort, gene*time, and gene*age effects. These tests provide evidence that gene*time effects are not statistically significant once the other two sources of variation are accounted for. Only if one were to ignore gene*cohort effects would it seem that G*E effects are due to chronological timing (i.e., to events unfolding through time that affected the strength of the relationship between FTO variations and BMI, regardless of cohort or age). Upon reflection, this result is unsurprising because environments are highly correlated over the lifecycle for most individuals and so, once cohort and age effects are controlled, there is limited variation remaining in experienced environmental conditions that might affect the strength of genetic influences on outcomes.

Understanding which specific historical influences alter the impact of genetic variants on outcomes across cohorts is not considered in the study. There are many environmental changes between birth cohorts hypothesized to be responsible for the modern rise in obesity, including rates of change in the likelihood of sedentary lifestyles, urban design, occupational shifts, dietary modifications (e.g., the growth of fast food restaurants), and social effects, among others. The authors suggest that their finding may explain the low replication rates of the findings produced in many GWA studies, as GWA studies often pool together different datasets that are collected in different periods of time, failing to account for the possibility that genetic associations may differ across birth cohorts due to variation across cohorts in prevailing environmental factors. The authors suggest that GWA researchers may wish to counter this problem by controlling for environmental stratification in addition to the more commonly employed population stratification across the pooled datasets.

Rosenquist et al. (2015)'s control for gene*age effects may also help to explain the low replicability of GWA results concerning other outcomes. For example, Oliynyk (2018) examines how the age of the sample can influence the findings of a GWA study concerning late onset human diseases that have a large genetic component. Many common diseases, such as dementia, fit into this category and a better understanding of them is critical to policy making as the population in many developed countries continues to age. The evidence suggests that for diseases that show high cumulative incidence together with high initial heritability, samples that balance the age and birth cohorts of case and control observations may be inferior to samples that combine the youngest possible cases with the oldest possible controls, if our objective is to use these samples to gain the maximum discovery power available from GWA studies. Such studies show the importance of understanding heterogeneity in G*E effects across both age and birth cohort dimensions for improving the potency of the GWA method in detecting and correctly interpreting genetic associations.

Beyond generating methodological insights of benefit to researchers applying GWA approaches, G*E studies conducted through a social scientific lens can help determine whether policies, such as sin taxes, have different impacts on people according to their genetic predisposition to risky behaviors. If this is the case, then some policies may place a disproportionate burden on individuals with specific genetic dispositions.

Social scientists exploring G*E effects can also improve our ability to gauge human progress. An interesting example of a G*E study of this type exploits an experiment due to history. Rimfield et al. (2018) use the independence of Estonia following the fall of the Soviet Union to ask whether there was a difference in the genetic determinants (based on SNPs and polygenic scores) of educational attainment and occupation before versus after the collapse of the USSR. DNA differences are found to explain twice as much variation in educational attainment and occupational status in the post-Soviet era compared with the Soviet era. This change in the extent of genetic influence in the Estonian population is interpreted by the authors as illustrating an increased importance of the meritocratic dimension of selection into both education and occupation following the shift from a communist to a capitalist society.

Another example of a study that compares the genetic component of response to a policy across cohorts is found in Okbay et al. (2016). These authors compare cohorts before and after a suite of schooling reforms in Sweden that, most importantly, extended mandatory schooling from 7 to 9 years. The authors find that the association between educational attainment and the polygenic score they constructed from their own GWA study is roughly half as large among Swedish individuals in the later cohort compared to the earlier cohort, suggesting that the Swedish reforms reduced the importance, in terms of educational attainment, of having won the "genetic lottery."

Much other work by social scientists evaluating G*E effects does not explicitly consider the endogeneity of the environmental variables that are to at least some extent selected by the individual. Some of this work is more structural in nature, intending to shed new light on an underlying behavioral model. For example, Biroli (2015) integrates genetic factors into the canonical model of health production due to Grossman (1972), allowing genetic variants to differentially affect both the health production function and preferences related to the incentives surrounding health investment faced by individuals. Using data from both the Framingham Heart Study and Avon Longitudinal Study of Parents and Children, he finds evidence that genetic factors do change both the production function of BMI and the level of investments in health that are optimal for an individual.

The unbiasedness of the coefficients estimated in the empirical analysis of Biroli (2015) requires the assumption that caloric intake is an exogenous environmental factor, and not a behavioral choice. The endogeneity of environmental variables is also not considered in Hatemi's (2013) exploration of G*E effects from proximate events such as losing a job, suffering a major financial loss, or getting a divorce, on the short-term change in attitudes towards economic policy. The underlying logic is that such events should change attitudes towards policy such that they stay aligned with the maximization of self-interest, and that the degree of adjustment in their attitudes that individuals experience when such events occur may be moderated by genetic factors. The analysis presents associations that are suggestive of different responses by those with different genetic markers, with individuals who lost a job more likely to oppose policies that may have caused the change in their economic situation when they have specific genetic markers. Future work exploring G*E effects flowing from environmental shocks would clearly be more credible if the identifying variation in the environmental variables were plausibly exogenous.

Rather than exploiting variation in environmental variables, Thompson (2014) exploits within-family variation in genetic inheritance (i.e., in an individual's draw from the genetic lottery) to explore differences in the relation between household income and children's educational outcomes across households with different variants of the *MAOA* (monoamine-oxidase A) *gene*, located at rs1465108, that encodes an enzyme partially responsible for the metabolism of several neurotransmitters. Results indicate that the impact of income on outcomes is stronger for those with rarer variants. Conley and Rauscher (2013) advise caution on the back of implementing a research design that aims to capture G*E effects by exploiting within-family variation. They explore how genetic traits moderate the relationship between birthweight and several outcomes, including high school GPA, by exploiting birthweight differences within twins. The sole statistically significant G*E effect reported has a sign that is the opposite of what had been suggested by prior scientific research.

Credible evidence of G*E effects may help policymakers target the delivery of policies to those who would benefit most. However, as we discuss in the next section, genetic data will also pose challenges for policymakers who have been slow to develop regulatory policies related to how genetic data can be used.

CAN GENETIC RESEARCH FINDINGS INFORM PUBLIC POLICY?

With a growing evidence base emerging, it is natural to ask how policymakers should leverage many of the important genetic discoveries surveyed above. Answers to this question depend upon what type of policy is being considered. For example, as an increasing number of studies connect DNA variation with individual-specific predictors of socioeconomic status such as intelligence and personality traits, the ethical, legal, and social implications of using the findings produced in scientific studies are likely to loom large.

Ding and Lehrer (2017) argue that when discussing genetics and public policy, attention should not be focused upon the question of whether a specific outcome or trait is primarily a function of genes that are immutable. As with many policies that target environmental influences, the question that policymakers must continue to ask is whether the available evidence suggests that a proposed policy would pass a conventional cost-benefit test. To illustrate this argument, they draw on an example in Goldberger (1979) that clearly points out that there is an ethically defensible role for public policy when a problem has its root in genetic factors. Goldberger uses the example of poor eyesight: even if poor eyesight were strictly a result of genetic inheritance, policymakers could provide glasses to those afflicted. Not doing so would be inefficient and even arguably less ethically sound than doing so.

Genetic factors, while themselves immutable, offer policymakers the ability to personalize how policies are delivered to individuals. This personalization also opens a new set of challenges to designing effective policy, as issues related to privacy and discriminatory treatment based on genetic characteristics may emerge. Any cost-benefit test applied to the use of genetic markers in designing public policy should weigh the consequences of issuing a broad mandate (a one-size-fits-all policy approach) versus targeting policy to those with specific characteristics.

There is perhaps no area where genetic data is currently playing a larger role than personalized medicine and the pharmaceutical industry. Pharmacogenomic tests can already identify whether a breast cancer patient will respond to the drug Herceptin, whether an AIDS patient should take the drug Abacavir, or what the correct dose of the blood-thinner Warfarin should be for a person with a specific genetic marker profile. Proponents of using genetic data in health policy suggest that by tailoring recommendations to each person's DNA, health care professionals will be able to work with individuals to focus efforts on the specific strategies—from diet to high-tech medical surveillance—that are most likely to maintain health for each individual.

The potential of precision medicines that create a better match between patients and medications is tantalizing for policymakers. In early 2015, the US White House announced a "bold new research effort to revolutionize how we improve health and treat disease," and launched a Precision Medicine Initiative with a US$215 million initial investment in 2016. The United States is not alone in its interest in this space. Other countries, including France and China, have recently announced major public investments ranging from the equivalent of several hundreds of millions to several billions of US dollars over the coming years. While this funding promotes innovation in the biotechnology and pharmaceutical industries, Stern, Alexander, and Chandra (2017) point out that it also changes many of the economic incentives that pharmaceutical manufacturers face in the drug development process. These changes may have important unintended consequences.

First, studies aiming to develop precision medicine approaches will mechanically target smaller patient populations than more traditional approaches to health research. The products discovered are likely to include those with large expected clinical benefits to small patient populations selected on specific genetic dimensions, with these benefits unlikely to be as significant, or present at all, in the population at large. For example, in January 2018, the US Food and Drug Administration (FDA) approved Luxturna to treat Leber congenital amaurosis (LCA), an inherited eye disorder. Targeting a variant of the RPE65 gene, this is the first gene therapy to gain FDA approval, and the one-off treatment is priced in the United States at slightly over US$400000 per eye. This high price arises because the marginal customer is expected to have a greater willingness to pay for Luxturna than for a more conventional therapy, as the drug has been proven to be more efficacious than conventional therapies within a smaller patient population. The higher price also helps to justify the fixed costs of drug development. The increase in funding for personalized medicine may cause drug manufacturers to shift their attention to subsets of products that are effective for smaller populations and are able to command high(er) prices.

Drug price and market size are naturally related. For example, Acemoglu and Linn (2004), Kyle and McGahan (2012) and Dubois, de Mouzon, Morton, and Seabright (2015) each present evidence that market size for a particular drug is associated with the number of firms conducting research in the area of that drug. Further, targeting patient subpopulations with particular biomarkers often allows manufacturers to more easily qualify for an "orphan drug" designation through the Orphan Drug Act of 1983. To receive this designation, a company must argue that it is focusing on developing a therapy for a disease subpopulation of fewer than 200,000 patients. Being awarded this designation has been found to deliver powerful financial incentives for pharmaceutical firms. If the FDA approves a new molecular entity (i.e., a drug) to treat an "orphan condition," the innovating firm receives tax credits equaling 50% of clinical trial expenses and an extra 2 years of marketing exclusivity. These benefits appear to be enticing: in 2015, 47% of new drugs approved by the FDA were orphan drugs.

Not only does this policy environment for orphan drugs support higher prices for longer, but because the market for precision medicines is small, price competition through follow-on entry (i.e., by firms producing generic or biosimilar drugs) may not develop. Existing evidence from the European Union in Scott Morton, Stern, and Stern (2018) and Berndt and Trusheim (2015) shows that even after the exclusivity periods granted to orphan drugs end, there may not be a large enough market to stimulate the development of biosimilar follow-on drugs, weakening the potential for price competition. The consequences of a decline in price competition for health treatments will arguably be more severe in single-payer health systems that face a balanced budget requirement, in which the increased funding that is required to provide precision medical treatments is often financed via reductions in government expenditures on other programs.

Perhaps of greater concern is that biomarkers may lead pharmaceutical companies to engage in genetically informed price discrimination. For example, a second gene therapy drug approved by the FDA in May 2018 is known as Kymriah. The pharmaceutical company that developed the drug is following a practice that they term "indication-based pricing." This means that the price varies according to the therapeutic application. In this case, for those with large B-cell lymphoma, the price is US$373000 for the one-time treatment, while the price for using the treatment to treat pediatric leukemia is US$475000. Identifiable biomarkers which include but are not limited to specific SNP variants can become an important tool for facilitating price discrimination, as they can be used to segment the drug market into identifiable subgroups that differ based on not only the expected efficacy of the product, but (and because of that) by willingness to pay for the product.

Aligning the price of a drug to its clinical value in each approved indication is a profit-maximizing strategy that proponents suggest helps ensure social benefits from drug development. However, it could also increase health spending, that society would have to cover either through taxes or insurance costs.

Beyond pricing, the FDA noted in 2016 that a shift in focus towards precision medicines will likely result in targeting only a subset of genetic markers. Specifically, the FDA-NIH (2016) speculate that attention will be paid to developing drugs that are tied to markers that are either predictive of therapeutic sensitivity or could be used for diagnosis and prognosis. They write that markers can be "used to identify individuals who are more likely than similar individuals without the biomarker to experience a favorable or unfavorable effect from exposure to a medical product." This could shift attention away from markers that were not previously investigated for association, perhaps due to being omitted due to linkage disequilibrium or not being measured for other reasons, as well as from developing drugs that have small genetic components.

On a more positive note, Budish, Roin, and Williams (2015) suggest that increases in the speed of clinical trials, for example due to larger expected effect sizes, may provide an incentive for pharmaceutical manufacturers to target drugs for different conditions, thus potentially bringing more innovations to the market. This could counteract some of the drawbacks of creating drugs that target smaller patient populations. Chandra, Garthwaite, and Stern (2018) provide evidence that genetic markers are associated with the length of clinical trials for cancer drugs. Precision-based medicines are found to be developed from trials that are on average 6–7 months shorter in duration than those designed to test nonprecision medicines. The authors speculate that this decrease in trial duration occurs because a therapeutic effect is easier to detect due to the greater putative efficacy of genetically-targeted drugs in the targeted subpopulation.

Despite the great potential of developing precision treatments, the above examples show that this new direction in medical research is not a free lunch. There are unintended consequences of shifting the attention of pharmaceutical companies towards precision medicines newly conceivable in part based on scientific findings from molecular genetic discoveries. These consequences relate to companies' decisions about which therapies to develop, how to price new drugs, and how to design and implement clinical trials. More policy attention is needed to reduce the negative consequences that may develop in response to the growing body of evidence documenting the genetic determinants of health and disease outcomes.

A second important policy area relates to the possible misuse of genetic data. This includes not just the potential promotion of eugenics-style initiatives, but also the potential for genetic data on inherited predispositions to influence decisions in the workplace or in relation to insurance coverage. For example, genetic data and research findings based on it may lead to differential treatment, or genetic discrimination, by health insurers. The most obvious possibility in this space would be an insurer's refusal to give coverage to an individual who has a genetic variation that raises his odds of developing a specific health disorder.

In the United States, the 2008 Genetic Information Nondiscrimination Act (GINA) attempts to address the need to regulate how genetic information is used, most notably protecting against discrimination in health insurance provision and employment. However, GINA does not apply to either life insurance or long-term care insurance, or to employers of fewer than 15 employees. More challenging is that GINA places the burden on victims of genetic discrimination to prove that their information was misused.

Last, policy that more carefully considers privacy is likely needed to regulate how genetic testing is undertaken. Two important facets of privacy relate to the scope of parties to whom and context in which genetic test results should be returned, and to the question of whether direct-to-consumer genealogic testing companies should be required to undertake a subject verification process before proceeding with testing. On the latter, there are currently few hurdles (if any) to companies proceeding with testing once a request has been made and money has changed hands. It would be quite possible to send someone else's tissue sample for testing and receive a full report on that person's genetic profile. Variants of this idea appear in numerous TV shows and films in scenes where characters try to creatively obtain DNA information from materials a person may have touched. One popular example on detective shows is collecting a water bottle from a suspect being interrogated.

Results from genetic tests are often difficult to interpret. Many individual genetic factors have very small effects, and arming people with knowledge of these predispositions without providing the appropriate context and qualifiers could worsen outcomes. Adverse reactions by individuals to poorly communicated test results may lead to unintended consequences, e.g., due to an over-response to the presence of a genetic predisposition (which is merely correlational), possibly leading to patient-demanded medical care that may be unnecessary and ineffective. As an example in the area of education and social policy, suppose parents have knowledge of the polygenic scores for educational attainment of their two children, and that there is a marked difference in these genetic scores, such as 35%. As discussed above, the available evidence suggests that the effect on outcomes of each risky allele used in the calculation of the polygenic score is very small in magnitude. However, not understanding the small effect that corresponds to weeks (and not years) of education, the parents may make investment decisions about how to assign inputs such as tutoring or time helping with homework that can accentuate rather than mitigate this genetic difference.

On a more positive note, consider the following example. Suppose that genetic screening can reliably predict complex learning disorders that are a function of many genes, each with a very small effect. If a single polygenic score is calculated from an ensemble of markers that have well validated significant (if individually small) effects, this score can be interpreted as a measure of an individual's risk for a specific disorder or trait, which, in many situations, may take psychologists years to diagnose. Armed with knowledge of whether their child or employee is at an elevated risk for poor learning outcomes, parents and employers will be able to make different investments years prior to receiving a formal diagnosis through conventional means. As these investments may affect how the underlying genes are expressed and thereby alter the risk of observing the outcome, regulations that effectively support this type of communication and limit unintended consequences may assist in raising welfare.

Ding and Lehrer (2017) point out that beginning in April 2017, the US Food and Drug Administration allowed the genetic testing firm 23andMe to sell reports with qualifiers showing customers whether they have an increased genetic risk of developing certain diseases and conditions. The number of conditions is limited, and this policy reversed a decision in 2013 that forced 23andMe to stop communicating the results of health-related traits. The authors also suggest that the Stanford Cancer Institute's decision support information web-based interface, available at http://brcatool.stanford.edu/, is an example of an effective mechanism that communicates sensitive personal information with appropriate safeguards. Regulations may be needed in these areas, particularly in light of our current limited understanding of how genetic markers operate.

Developing regulations regarding how test results are returned, to whom they are returned, and for what purposes they are returned may also aid social scientists wishing to collect molecular genetic data from participants in research studies. Higher compliance rates may result if participants are given information at point of consent about the purpose of data collection and how the data will be shared within the research community. Without such disclosure, the use of molecular genetic data by other researchers for reasons that were not apparent at the time of data collection—something quite likely given the data sharing infrastructure in this area—may constitute a violation of individual privacy, on top of the usual data security concerns. As an example of this issue, consider how law enforcement in Sacramento, California were able to track down and arrest the "Golden State Killer," Joseph James DeAngelo. The lead investigator submitted DNA collected years ago from one of the crime scenes to an open source genealogy website called GEDmatch, thereby narrowing the field to a small pool of potential suspects. As the site is open source, no court records were needed to access the DNA records on the GEDmatch web site, but privacy advocates argue that most individuals who submit their DNA to these companies are unaware that they are effectively sharing their DNA with law enforcement.

In summary, policy making in the brave new world of genetic information does not require a wholesale transformation of how policies are developed. The speed at which concerns regarding genetic data can be effectively integrated into policy design is tied partly to improvements in scientific understanding of how genetic markers operate, but even more strongly to the speed with which this developing knowledge is conveyed to stakeholders so that a social consensus on optimal policy can emerge.

CONCLUSIONS AND FUTURE DIRECTIONS

Heritability plays a role in generating nearly every socioeconomic and health outcome. This feature has long been ignored by social scientists due in part to data availability, and by policymakers who often fall victim to thinking that the fixity of one's genetic code at conception implies that there is nothing we can do to improve outcomes, even if we knew an individual's complete genetic code. However, heredity is not destiny, and much work is needed to clarify what is meant by a genetic predisposition and what policy levers are revealed by knowing in which people such predispositions lie. Social scientists can contribute to this work by translating the revolutionary advances in genetics and genomics to reach both policy audiences and the broader academic community. Great care must be taken in these translations to elucidate the assumptions imposed in the underlying analyses, to ensure that our developing knowledge is used appropriately to develop effective policy.

Genes influence not only health and disease, but also human traits and behaviors. Science is only beginning to unravel the complicated pathways leading from genes through the environment to outcomes, and there are numerous avenues via which social scientists can enter this area to generate new insights.

Much of the current research in the social sciences that uses genetic data draws heavily on the literature from molecular genetics and other nonsocial sciences. Knowledge and protocols from the social sciences can assist in expanding the evidence base. For example, researchers in population studies and sister fields have substantial experience with data collection and issues related to pooling data from different sources. Much of the current literature in genetics reviewed above does not consider sampling issues or explicitly discuss the external validity of findings. Social scientists familiar with data manipulation and imputation would also be well placed to advise upon the consequences of using imputed versus actual SNP data, and other matters relating to data quality. Further, methodologists may be able to develop methods to improve the efficiency of estimation based on data collected in alternative manners.

From a more theoretical perspective, many scientific studies that draw on genetic data are silent on the topic of underlying behavioral models, yet many outcomes including those in health and education are likely a function of a sequence of individual decisions, genetic factors, and the interactions of the two. For example, conventional GWA protocols ignore the interaction of the environment with genetic factors, frequently assuming linear effects on outcomes of the simple count of alleles. The calculation of polygenic scores from GWA estimates and the subsequent use of these scores in outcome prediction ignore issues related to uncertainty and estimation error. By incorporating an underlying behavioral model, researchers could be explicit about the assumptions being imposed in such exercises, and the evidence from integrating genetic markers into an existing conventional analysis could then be used to further refine the behavioral model. Work in this direction holds the potential to advance our understanding of genetic mechanisms in a logically consistent and statistically valid framework.

There is also considerable scope for methodological developments driven by social scientists to take the analysis of genetic data far beyond the use of off-the-shelf software. For example, applying new econometric tools to uncover and understand heterogeneity in genetic effects holds much promise. These tools can draw from the expanding literature on treatment effect heterogeneity and may be quite useful in particular for G*E analyses. Lehrer (2016) also points out that there may be a serious identification challenge in current G*E analysis wherein the same data is used to describe both situations where exposure to an environmental factor that predicts a behavior is conditional upon a person's genotype, and situations when the genotype's direct effect on the behavior is moderated by some environmental effect. For example, suppose that a gene affects a risky health behavior that is also cue-conditioned (i.e., faced with a given environment, an individual is more likely to engage in the behavior—e.g., smoking in a night club is more likely than in other locations). It may be the case that in addition to interacting with smoking to produce disease, the gene also directly leads those who possess it to visit night clubs. While statistically separating these pathways is desirable, better communication protocols are also required to help policy audiences understand what is being identified in any given analysis. Lehrer (2016) suggests that researchers use the terminology "G*E responses" to refer to situations where exposure to an environmental factor that in turn predicts behavior is conditional upon a person's genotype, and the term "G*E modifications" to refer to differential genetic reactions to environmental factors. Personalized medicine and many policies that would target individuals by genotype may be best guided by information about G*E modifications, whereas G*E responses may be more interesting for researchers to study if they are interested in the underlying behavioral reasons for observed heterogeneity in estimated environmental effects on outcomes across the population.

With improved methodological tools, more credible evidence from rigorous G*E studies may lead to the reshaping of social science theories. Many policies and programs have been observed to have heterogeneous effects on individuals with different demographic and socioeconomic characteristics that are consistent with an underlying theory. For example, with information on genetic markers that associate with addiction, there is the possibility to better understand why changes in sin taxes affect decisions on the intensive and extensive margins of substance use differently for different individuals. Rather than characterizing individuals as simply being "rational" or "impulsive" or "behavioral," researchers may be able to pinpoint individual biological characteristics that can explain the underlying heterogeneity in choice behavior. Similarly, as Biroli (2015) illustrates, one can ask whether heterogeneity due to genetic inheritance affects calories burnt and/or calories consumed, thereby helping to shape future theories about the development of obesity by explaining why behavioral heterogeneity may arise. Many simple economic models predict treatment effect heterogeneity based on individual characteristics (see Lehrer, Pohl, and Song (2016) for an illustration of this using a static labor supply model) and treat genetic influence as predetermined at conception. Future theoretical work could relax these assumptions by exploring whether arming individuals with knowledge of their genetic make-up, e.g., through receiving results from genetic testing companies, shapes decisions in various realms, including insurance coverage up-take or risky behaviors. The existence of direct-to-consumer genetic testing introduces a new source of an information asymmetry, known to the individual but unknown to insurers, that may affect individual decisions and thereby expand the scope of treatment effect heterogeneity.

Beyond statistical issues and theoretical modeling, perhaps the area where social scientists' increased involvement with genetic data may prove to be most valuable relates to knowledge translation activities for the benefit of policy audiences. We argue that the social benefits of using genetic information are tied to how that information is communicated. Findings from research that is well designed and robust should be clearly communicated in a way that neither oversimplifies nor overstates the role of genetic factors. The problematic consequences of inadequate communication are well known. Findings from previous research in behavioral genetics have not always been well communicated, with the unfortunate example of the analysis of Herrnstein and Murray (1994), whose book *The Bell Curve* (1994) led to significant controversy. Given this history and the real potential for recurrence as new findings emerge from genetic studies, it is of the utmost importance not only to gather sufficient scientifically valid information about the genetic factors underpinning outcomes, yielding more definitive scientific insight, but to communicate these insights in a way that avoids misunderstanding and stigmatization when considering the implications of such research for individuals and society.

REFERENCES

1000 Genomes Project Consortium (2015). A global reference for human genetic variation. *Nature*, *526*, 68–74.

Acemoglu, D., & Linn, J. (2004). Market size in innovation: theory and evidence from the pharmaceutical industry. *The Quarterly Journal of Economics*, *119*(3), 1049–1090.

Almond, D., Chay, K. Y., & Lee, D. S. (2005). The costs of low birth weight. *The Quarterly Journal of Economics, 120*(3), 1031–1083.

Angrist, J. D., & Pischke, J. -S. (2010). The credibility revolution in empirical economics: how better research design is taking the con out of econometrics. *Journal of Economic Perspectives, 2* (1), 3–30.

Barth, D. J., Papageorge, N., & Thom, K. (2018). *Genetic endowments and wealth inequality.* NBER Working paper w24642.

Battelle Technology Partnership Practice (2011). *The U.S. Biopharmaceuticals Sector: Economic Contribution to the Nation. Available athttp://phrma-docs.phrma.org/sites/default/files/pdf/ 2011_battelle_report_on_economic_impact.pdf.*

Behrman, J. R. (2016). Twin studies in economics. In J. Komlos & I. Rashad (Eds.), *The Oxford handbook of economics and human biology* (pp. 385–404). Oxford University Press, New York ISBN 978-0-19-93829-2.

Belloni, A., Chen, D., Chernozhukov, V., & Hansen, C. (2012). Sparse models and methods for optimal instruments with an application to eminent domain. *Econometrica, 80*(6), 2369–2429.

Belsky, D. W., Moffitt, T. E., Baker, T. B., Biddle, A. K., Evans, J. P., Harrington, H., et al. (2013). Polygenic risk and the developmental progression to heavy, persistent smoking and nicotine dependence: evidence from a 4-decade longitudinal study. *JAMA Psychiatry, 70*(5), 534–542.

Belsky, D. W., Moffitt, T. E., Houts, R., Bennett, G. G., Biddle, A. K., Blumenthal, J. A., et al. (2012). Polygenic risk, rapid childhood growth, and the development of obesity: evidence from a 4-decade longitudinal study. *Archives of Pediatrics & Adolescent Medicine, 166*(6), 515–521.

Benjamin, D. J., Cesarini, D., Chabris, C. F., Glaeser, E. L., Laibson, D. I., Guðnason, V., et al. (2012). The promises and pitfalls of genoeconomics. *Annual Review of Economics, 4*, 627–662.

Benjamin, D. J., Chabris, C. F., Glaeser, E. L., Gudnason, V., Harris, T. B., Laibson, D. I., et al. (2007). Genoeconomics. In M. Weinstein, J. W. Vaupel, & K. W. Wachter (Eds.), *Biosocial surveys, committee on population, division of behavioral and social sciences and education.* Washington: The National Academies Press.

Berndt, E. R., & Trusheim, M. R. (2015). Biosimilar and biobetter scenarios for the US and Europe: what should we expect? In *Biobetters* (pp. 315–360). New York: Springer.

Biroli, P. (2015). Genetic and economic interaction in the formation of human capital: the case of obesity. In *Mimeo.* University of Zurich.

Bowden, J., Davey Smith, G., & Burgess, S. (2015). Mendelian randomization with invalid instruments: effect estimation and bias detection through Egger regression. *International Journal of Epidemiology, 44*(2), 512–525.

Brickell, I., Larsson, H., Lu, Y., Pettersson, E., Chen, Q., Kuja-Halkola, R., et al. (2018). The contribution of common genetic risk variants for ADHD to a general factor of childhood psychopathology. *Molecular Psychiatry.* https://doi.org/10.1038/s41380-018-0109-2in press.

Budish, E., Roin, B. N., & Williams, H. (2015). Do firms underinvest in long-term research? Evidence from cancer clinical trials. *The American Economic Review, 105*(7), 2044–2085.

Chabris, C. F., Lee, J. J., Benjamin, D. J., Beauchamp, J. P., Glaeser, E. L., Borst, G., et al. (2013). Why is it hard to find genes that are associated with social science traits? Theoretical and empirical considerations. *American Journal of Public Health, 103*(S1), S152–S166.

Chandra, A., Garthwaite, C., & Stern, A. D. (2018). Characterizing the drug development pipeline for precision medicines forthcoming. In E. Berndt, D. Goldman, & J. Rowe (Eds.), *Economic Dimensions of Personalized and Precision Medicine.* University of Chicago Press, Chicago.

Conley, D. (2009). The promise and challenges of incorporating genetic data into longitudinal social science surveys and research. *Biodemography and Social Biology, 55*(2), 238–251. https://doi.org/10.1080/19485560903415807.

Conley, D., & Rauscher, E. (2013). Genetic interactions with prenatal social environment: effects on academic and behavioral outcomes. *Journal of Health and Social Behavior, 54*(1), 109–127. https://doi.org/10.1177/0022146512473758.

Conley, D., & Zhang, S. (2018). The promise of genes for understanding cause and effect. *Proceedings of the National Academy of Sciences, 115*(2), 5626–5628. https://doi.org/10.1073/pnas.1805585115.

Conley, T. G., Hansen, C. B., & Rossi, P. E. (2012). Plausibly exogenous. *The Review of Economics and Statistics, 94*(2), 260–272.

Currie, J., & Thomas, D. (1995). Does head start make a difference? *American Economic* Review, *85* (3), 341–364.

Deming, D. (2009). Early childhood intervention and life-cycle skill development: evidence from head start. *American Economic Journal: Applied Economics, 1*(3), 111–134.

Ding, W., & Lehrer, S. F. (2017). What is the role for molecular genetic data in public policy? *IZA World of Labor, 395*, Available athttps://wol.iza.org/articles/what-is-the-role-for-molecular-genetic-data-in-public-policy/long.

Ding, W., Lehrer, S. F., Rosenquist, J. N., & Audrain-McGovern, J. (2009). The impact of poor health on academic performance: new evidence using genetic markers. *Journal of Health Economics, 28*(3), 578–597.

Ding, W., Lehrer, S. F., Rosenquist, N. J., & Audrain-McGovern, J. (2006). *The impact of poor health on education: new evidence using genetic markers.* National Bureau of Economic Research Working Paper Series No. 12304.

Dreber, A., Apicella, C. L., Eisenberg, D. T. A., Garcia, J. R., Zamore, R. S., Lum, J. K., et al. (2009). The 7R polymorphism in the dopamine receptor D4 gene (DRD4) is associated with financial risk taking in men. *Evolution and Human Behavior, 30*(2), 85–92.

Dubois, P., de Mouzon, O., Morton, F. M. S., & Seabright, P. (2015). Market size and pharmaceutical innovation. *The Rand Journal of Economics, 46*(4), 844–871.

Dudbridge, F. (2013). Power and predictive accuracy of polygenic risk scores. *PLoS Genetics. 9*(3) https://doi.org/10.1371/journal.pgen.1003348.

Egger, M., Davey Smith, G., Schneider, M., & Minder, C. (1997). Bias in meta-analysis detected by a simple, graphical test. *British Medical Journal, 315*, 629–634.

FDA-NIH Biomarker Working Group (2016). *BEST (biomarkers, EndpointS, and other tools) resource.* Silver Spring, MD: Food and Drug Administration (US). Bethesda, MD: National Institutes of Health. Available at*https://www.ncbi.nlm.nih.gov/books/NBK326791/*.

Figlio, D., Guryan, J., Karbownik, K., & Roth, J. (2014). The effects of poor neonatal health on Children's cognitive development. *American Economic Review, 104*(12), 3921–3955.

Fletcher, J. M., & Lehrer, S. F. (2009a). *Using genetic lotteries within families to examine the causal impact of poor health on academic achievement.* National Bureau of Economic Research Working Paper Series No. 15148.

Fletcher, J. M., & Lehrer, S. F. (2009b). The effects of adolescent health on educational outcomes: causal evidence using genetic lotteries between siblings. *Forum for Health Economics & Policy 12*(2)https://doi.org/10.2202/1558-9544.1180Article 8.

Fletcher, J. M., & Lehrer, S. F. (2011). Genetic lotteries within families. *Journal of Health Economics, 30*(4), 647–659.

Frayling, T. M., Timpson, N. J., Weedon, M. N., Zeggini, E., Freathy, R. M., Lindgren, C. M., et al. (2007). A common variant in the FTO gene is associated with body mass index and predisposes to childhood and adult obesity. *Science, 316*(5826), 889–894.

Gage, S. H., Jones, H. J., Burgess, S., Bowden, J., Davey-Smith, G., Zammit, S., et al. (2017). Assessing causality in associations between cannabis use and schizophrenia risk: a two-sample Mendelian randomization study. *Psychological Medicine, 47*(5), 971–980.

Goldberger, A. S. (1979). Heritability. *Economica, 46*(184), 327–347.

Greiner, J., & Rubin, D. (2011). Causal effects of perceived immutable characteristics. *The Review of Economics and Statistics, 93*(3), 775–785.

Grossman, M. (1972). On the concept of health capital and the demand for health. *Journal of Political Economy, 80*(2), 223–255.

Hansen, B. E. (1999). Threshold effects in non-dynamic panels: estimation, testing, and inference. *Journal of Econometrics, 93*(2), 345–368.

Hatemi, P. K. (2013). The influence of major life events on economic attitudes in a world of gene-environment interplay. *American Journal of Political Science, 57*(4), 987–1000.

Hausman, J. A., Newey, W. K., Woutersen, T., Chao, J. C., & Swanson, N. R. (2012). Instrumental variables estimation with heteroskedasticity and many instruments. *Quantitative Economics, 3* (2), 211–255.

Hemani, G., Bowden, J., & Davey Smith, G. (2018). Evaluating the potential role of pleiotropy in Mendelian randomization studies. *Human Molecular Genetics, 27*(R2), R195–R208. https://doi.org/10.1093/hmg/ddy163.

Herrnstein, R. J., & Murray, C. (1994). *The bell curve.* New York: The Free Press.

Hewitt, J. K. (2012). Editorial policy on candidate gene association and candidate gene-by-environment interaction studies of complex traits. *Behavior Genetics, 42*(1), 1–2.

Huber, E., Donnelly, P. M., Rokem, A., & Yeatman, J. D. (2018). Rapid and widespread white matter plasticity during an intensive reading intervention. *Nature Communications, 9*, 2260. https://doi.org/10.1038/s41467-018-04627-5.

Imbens, G. W., & Angrist, J. D. (1994). Identification and estimation of local average treatment effects. *Econometrica, 62*(2), 467–475.

Katan, M. B. (1986). Apolipoprotein E isoforms, serum cholesterol and cancer. *Lancet, 327*, 507–508.

Keane, M. (2010). A structural perspective on the experimentalist school. *Journal of Economic Perspectives, 24*(1), 47–58.

Kyle, M. K., & McGahan, A. M. (2012). Investments in pharmaceuticals before and after TRIPS. *The Review of Economics and Statistics, 94*(4), 1157–1172.

Lee, J. J., Wedow, R., Okbay, A., Kong, E., Maghzian, O., Zacher, M., et al. (2018). Gene discovery and polygenic prediction from a 1.1-million-person GWAS of educational attainment. *Nature Genetics, 50*(8), 1112–1121. https://doi.org/10.1038/s41588-018-0147-3in press.

Lehrer, S. F. (2016). Biomarkers as inputs. In J. Komlos & I. Rashad (Eds.), *The Oxford handbook of economics and human biology* (pp. 339–365). Oxford University Press, New York.

Lehrer, S. F., & Ding, W. (2017). Are genetic markers of interest for economic research? *IZA Journal of Labor Policy. 6*(2)https://doi.org/10.1186/s40173-017-0080-6.

Lehrer, S. F., Pohl, V. R., & Song, K. (2016). *Targeting policies: multiple testing and distributional treatment effects.* National Bureau of Economic Research Working Paper Series No. 22950.

Lehrer, S. F., & Xie, T. (2017). Box office buzz: does social media data steal the show from model uncertainty when forecasting for Hollywood? *The Review of Economics and Statistics, 99*(5), 749–755.

Mendel, G. J. (1866). Versuche über Pflanzen-Hybriden [experiments concerning plant hybrids]. *Verhandlungen des naturforschenden Vereines in Brünn [Proceedings of the Natural History Society of Brünn]* (pp. 3–47). Vol. IV, 1865, (pp. 3–47). .

Mukherjee, S. (2017). *The gene: An intimate history.* Scribner Press, New York.

Okbay, A., Beauchamp, J. P., Fontana, M. A., Lee, J. J., Pers, T. H., Rietveld, C. A., et al. (2016). Genome-wide association study identifies 74 loci associated with educational attainment. *Nature, 533*, 539–542. https://doi.org/10.1038/nature17671.

Oliynyk, R. T. (2018). Age-related late-onset disease heritability patterns and implications for genome-wide association studies. *biorxiv*. https://doi.org/10.1101/349019.

Papageorge, N. W., & Thom, K. (2017). *Genes, education, and labor market outcomes: evidence from the health and retirement study*. IZA Discussion Paper dp10200.

Peters, T., Ansmeier, K., & Ruther, U. (1999). Cloning of Fatso (Fto), a novel gene deleted by the Fused toes (Ft) mouse mutation. *Mammalian Genome*, *10*(10), 983–986.

Purcell, S. M., Wray, N. R., Stone, J. L., Visscher, P. M., O'Donovan, M. C., Sullivan, P. F., et al. (2009). Common polygenic variation contributes to risk of schizophrenia and bipolar disorder. *Nature*, *460*(7256), 748–752.

Rees, J. M. B., Wood, A. M., & Burgess, S. (2017). Extending the MR-Egger method for multivariable Mendelian randomization to correct for both measured and unmeasured pleiotropy. *Statistics in Medicine*, *36*, 4705–4718.

Rietveld, C. A., Esko, T., Davies, G., Pers, T. H., Turley, P. A., Beben, B., et al. (2014). Common genetic variants associated with cognitive performance identified using proxy-phenotype method. *Proceedings of the National Academy of Sciences*, *111*(38), 13790–13794. https://doi.org/10.1073/pnas.1404623111.

Rietveld, C. A., Medland, S. E., Derringer, J., Yang, J., Esko, T., Martin, N. W., et al. (2013). GWAS of 126,559 individuals identifies genetic variants associated with educational attainment. *Science*, *340*(6139), 1467–1471. https://doi.org/10.1126/science.1235488.

Rimfield, K., Krapohl, E., Trzaskowski, M., Coleman, J. R. I., Selzam, S., Dale, P. S., et al. (2018). Genetic influence on social outcomes during and after the soviet era in Estonia. *Nature Human Behaviour*, *2*, 269–275.

Rosenquist, J. N., Lehrer, S. F., Malley, A. J. O., Zaslavsky, A. M., Smoller, J. W., & Christakis, N. A. (2015). Cohort of birth modifies the association between FTO genotype and BMI. *Proceedings of the National Academy of Sciences*, *112*(2), 354–359.

Sacerdote, B. (2007). How large are the effects from changes in family environment? A study of Korean American adoptees. *The Quarterly Journal of Economics*, *122*(1), 119–157.

Schmutz, J., Wheeler, J., Grimwood, J., Dickson, M., Yang, J., Caoile, C., et al. (2004). Quality assessment of the human genome sequence. *Nature*, *429*(6990), 365–368.

Scott Morton, F. M., Stern, A. D., & Stern, S. (2018). The impact of the entry of biosimilars: evidence from Europe. *Review of Industrial Organization*, *53*(1), 173–210.

Sims, C. A. (2010). But economics is not an experimental science. *Journal of Economic Perspectives*, *24*(1), 47–58.

Smith, G. D., & Ebrahim, S. (2003). Mendelian randomization': can genetic epidemiology contribute to understanding environmental determinants of disease? *International Journal of Epidemiology*, *32*(1), 1–22.

Stern, A. D., Alexander, B. M., & Chandra, A. (2017). Innovation incentives and biomarkers. *Clinical Pharmacology & Therapeutics*, *103*(1), 34–36. https://doi.org/10.1002/cpt.876.

Taubman, P. (1976). The determinants of earnings: genetics, family, and other environments: a study of white male twins. *American Economic Review*, *66*(5), 858–870.

Thompson, O. (2014). Economic background and educational attainment the role of gene-environment interactions. *Journal of Human Resources*, *49*(2), 263–294.

Winkler, T. W., Day, F. R., Croteau-Chonka, D. C., Wood, A. R., Locke, A. E., Mägi, R., et al. (2014). Quality control and conduct of genome-wide association meta-analyses. *Nature Protocols*, *9*(5), 1192–1212.

Zhong, S., Israel, S., Xue, H., Ebstein, R. P., & Chew, S. H. (2009). Monoamine oxidase a gene (maoa) associated with attitude towards longshot risks. *PLoS One*. *4*(12)https://doi.org/10.1371/journal.pone.0008516.

GLOSSARY

Allele Allele is used to describe variant forms (i.e., where the base pairs differ) of a given gene. Each person inherits two alleles for each gene, one from each parent. If the two alleles are the same, the individual is homozygous for that gene. If the alleles are different, the individual is heterozygous.

Amino acid Amino acids are a set of 20 different molecules used to build protein. In exome sequencing, microarrays provide information on the amino acid sequence of proteins and by using this information one can learn the sequence of genes.

Base Each unit of DNA is made up of one of four different bases (Adenine (A), Cytosine (C), Thymine (T), and Guanine (G)) that are attached to sugar (deoxyribose).

Base pair The strands of DNA inherited from each parent are joined together in a specific manner (A base pairs with T and C base pairs with G) by hydrogen bonds. Knowledge of one side of DNA gives information of the base on the other side.

Chromosome The chromosome located in the nucleus of each cell is how DNA is stored. Humans have 23 pairs of chromosome and the length of each of these strands of DNA varies between 48 million to 250 million bases.

Codon A codon is a trinucleotide sequence of DNA that corresponds to a specific amino acid. The genetic code describes the relationship between the sequence of DNA bases (A, C, G, and T) in a gene and the corresponding protein sequence that it encodes.

DNA DNA stands for deoxyribonucleic acid and it is made up of the four bases. The DNA molecule consists of two strands that wind around one another to form a shape known as a double helix. The sequence of the bases in DNA influence how proteins are assembled and numerous outcomes.

DNA sequencing Techniques used by laboratories to determine the exact sequence of bases (A, C, G, and T) in a DNA molecule.

Double helix DNA is made up of two strands that are twisted together in a shape that is known as the double helix. The structure was discovered by Watson and Crick (1953).

Exome The genome can be simplified into two components: parts that code for protein and parts that do not. The part that codes for protein ($\sim$2% of the total genome), is also known as the exome.

Exon Just like the genome is broken into parts that code for protein (exome) and the parts that do not, genes are broken into parts that code for protein and parts that do not. Exon refers to the part of a gene that codes for amino acids that subsequently combine to make proteins.

Gene A gene is a piece of DNA that generally varies between a few hundred base pairs to many thousand base pairs. Genes are arranged on the chromosome and provide instructions to build proteins.

Genetic Map This provides the relative locations of genes on each chromosome. The map uses the concept of linkage disequilibrium because the closer two genes are to each other on the chromosome, the greater the probability that they will be inherited together.

Genetic Marker A DNA sequence with a known physical location on a chromosome.

Genome In humans, the genome consists of 23 pairs of chromosomes, found in the nucleus, as well as a small chromosome found in the cells' mitochondria. Each set of 23 chromosomes contains approximately 3.2 billion bases of DNA sequence.

Genotype A term used to refer to the two alleles inherited for a particular gene. This is the version of a DNA sequence an individual has.

HapMap A map describing common patterns of genetic variation among individuals. It provides information on the location of DNA variations from combinations of alleles or to a set of single nucleotide polymorphisms (SNPs) on each chromosome.

Imputation A statistical method to predict which of the four bases (A, C, G, or T) is located at a position that was not sequenced by using information on bases located close by on the chromosome.

Linkage This provides information on how associated DNA sequences are on the same chromosome. Two genes that tend to be transmitted together we say are linked to each other.

Nucleotide A building block of RNA and DNA. The bases used in DNA adenine (A), cytosine (C), guanine (G), and thymine (T).

Polygenic Trait A characteristic or outcome that is affected by many, many different genes.

Protein Proteins are complex molecules involved in many critical functions of the body ranging from the production of antibodies to the transportation of substances, structure and sending messages. Each protein is composed of a chain of amino acids.

Polymorphism A term indicating the location of variation in a DNA sequence across individuals.

Sequencing The process of reading the bases in DNA. Whole genome sequencing is comprehensive, whereas other methods may only sequence a few bases. The sequence of bases along DNA provides instructions to assemble protein and RNA molecules.

Single Nucleotide Polymorphisms (SNPs) A polymorphism involving variation in a single base pair.

Variant A single difference in the DNA between two people and is also known as single nucleotide polymorphism (SNP) and, on occasion, as an allele.

Whole Genome Sequencing (WGS) The process of reading every single of the 3.2 billion bases in the DNA of an individual.

Chapter 10

Conclusion

Gigi Foster
School of Economics, University of New South Wales, Sydney, NSW, Australia

INTRODUCTION

At the dawn of modern social science, the machines whose wide-scale use and output are examined in this volume were only twinkles in the eyes of the most forward-thinking students of human behavior. The building blocks of modern social science were derived from scientists' intuition and critical examination of externally evident phenomena, rather than from proven internal and outwardly hidden attributes of the human machine. As Camerer, Loewenstein, and Prelec (2005) state (p. 9), "[t]he foundations of economic theory were constructed assuming that details about the functioning of the brain's black box would not be known."

This is not to say that external observation cannot betray internal processes. For centuries, people have read others' inner states based on outward signals such as posture, facial expression, and even the color of the cheeks. However, the machinery did not exist to measure internal states with sufficient precision or on a scale wide enough for these states to become centerpieces in our models of human behavior. Far safer for the early social scientist was to focus on uncontestably observable and measurable phenomena, and to reduce our complex inner workings to broad, ill-defined constructs such as "utility" and "animal spirits," rather than to base his theories in more specific dimensions of the slippery land of the signaled but unseen and poorly measured.

With the advent of modern biophysical measurement technology, social science today has a new lens through which to examine the likelihood or otherwise of its initial guesses. Did the founders of our disciplines fix upon core features of choice makers and choice making that correspond to biophysical realities, as we are only now privileged to perceive them? Is there modern machine-readable evidence about our inner workings to support the assumptions that lie at the base of our most (in)famous models of the drivers of outward behavior?

The evidence reviewed in this volume points to substantial gulfs between what we thought we knew, because it was baked into our theories of individual behavior, and what machines have told us about ourselves. We have

Biophysical Measurement in Experimental Social Science Research. https://doi.org/10.1016/B978-0-12-813092-6.00010-1

seen evidence that people respond differently to news, perceived probabilities of events, and alternatives in a choice set depending on facets of themselves and the situation that play no role in the founding theories of economics. Not only are phenomena like hormones, genes, interoception, and emotion unaccounted for explicitly in economic models, but the axiomatically well-behaved preferences that underpin a huge literature in microeconomics cannot be matched to any direct measurement taken by an fMRI scanner. What does this mean for our theories?

Peering inward on a wide scale carries further implications for the science of human behavior, in the realm of individual rights and responsibilities. No longer protected by the technological infeasibility of direct monitoring, our bodies can now be examined by machines in detail in orders of magnitude greater than what we ourselves can perceive as residents within them. This is a sobering truth, carrying the prospect of potential violations of individuals' rights to privacy and self-determination. How will social scientists and those we work with, including policy makers, negotiate the ethical dimensions of our newfound technology-enabled measurement and knowledge?

I do not attempt a satisfactory answer to these three crucial questions here, but rather state them plainly in the hope of encouraging others, including those who directly use biophysical measures, to ponder them. Rather than rush headlong and unthinking into the brave new world of wide-scale biophysical measurement, impressing editorial teams by applying novel measurement techniques to large samples because that capability is now within reach, social scientists would be wise to consider how to use biophysical data to deeply enhance both the science that has come before them and the ultimate maximand: the human experience.

I begin this brief chapter by discussing the ethical dimensions of biophysical measurement, and how such measurement relates to the historical position of social science. I then briefly review the fields of pupillometry, facial musculature analysis, and gait analysis to complement the discussions of other techniques throughout this volume. I conclude with some observations about the interface between biophysical measurement and social science theories and practice going forward. While acknowledging the relevance of biophysical measurement to other social sciences (including small subfields of them, an example of which is noted in Floyd, 2004), I place the strongest emphasis in this chapter as in the book as a whole on economics, its theories, and its interface with ethics and policy.

While most economic models of choice assume that decision makers have unlimited computational ability to evaluate and choose from the available choice sets, in reality people's ability to process information has limitations. Our brains consist of a limited number of cells that have a bounded capacity for conveying information. This implies that many seemingly irrational behaviors may be, in fact, due to the limitations of otherwise rationally-acting human nervous systems. The idea that behavioral biases can be explained by the features of the nervous system dates back to Herbert Simon (1955), in writings that long preceded the development of tools to study the structural and functional properties of living brains. In this chapter, I first briefly review the theoretical literature from economics that derives optimal behavior given biological constraints. I point out that various modeling approaches arrive at the following similar insights: (1) capacity limitations on the nervous system should affect choice, and (2) widely observed behaviors, such as those identified in the famous prospect theory of Kahneman and Tversky (1979), are the direct consequence of the limits of human cognition. Then I briefly describe the techniques and equipment used to estimate gray matter volume in the living brain and summarize the empirical evidence that neuroeconomists have accumulated so far about the relationship between the limited neural capacities and economic decision making.

ETHICAL MATTERS

The image of a human subject hooked up to electrodes is powerful. For those who came of age in the post-World War II period, this image may recall to mind experiments of the Stanley Milgram variety (Milgram, 1963), conducted with what by the standards of human ethics boards in many countries would be viewed as perilous casualness towards the possible psychological effects of participation as a laboratory subject in a study of sensitive dimensions of behavior. For those of a slightly older generation, the image may pair with a very different affective response: a sense of wonder at frontier machinery and the new worlds of learning that it might offer to us as social scientists. Like today's developments and debates around artificial intelligence, the advent of new machines in the twentieth century and in other eras of human history have elicited a combination of those two responses: wonder and caution.

Moving beyond the first-blush emotional reactions to new measurement machinery, whether of shock, awe, or a combination of the two, what new substantive ethical questions arise from the modern availability of biophysical technology at scale to social scientists?

I see three such questions. The first relates to rights and permissions in respect of the access that the human subject can now give researchers to data about his own body. The second relates to the arena of information sharing, and the third relates to the use of these new data in decision making—both for the individual researcher, and for others who may be granted access to the data, such as individuals, families, or governments.

On the first question, a subject today can enter a laboratory and sign a consent form that provides access to data about his body to a researcher. Yet the consent he provides is in some ways artificial because neither he, nor in many cases the researcher, knows what the biophysical data might reveal and thus the full gamut of implications of the consent he is providing. This is generally not true in the case of measures of external behavior, where the subject and the researcher are fully aware of what is being tracked (e.g., the selection of option A or option B) and where individual choice data are anonymized by convention before feeding into whole-sample analysis. A study that tracks heart rate variation might incidentally reveal a heart abnormality, for example, a genomic study may reveal an inherited disorder, or an fMRI scan may show unexpected cognitive degradation, for a particular experimental subject whose identity could in principle be tracked at least until the point of that discovery. Is the researcher ethically obliged, given his privileged access, to check the data he obtains in all technologically feasible ways for anything that looks out of the ordinary? What should subjects be told in advance about what might or might not be revealed in the data about their bodies, and about what actions might or might not result from those revelations?

Second, if a researcher does come across something unusual in the biophysical data he collects, whether by design or by accident, is he ethically obliged to inform the subject from whom it came? More generally, once biophysical data are obtained, with whom (subjects, families, other scientists, employers, insurers, governments) should it be shared, and how?

Third, how should biophysical data be used in choice making by individuals, groups, and societies? Choices of all sorts could plausibly be influenced by biophysical data, and in some cases this influence has the potential to be welfare-enhancing. The example in Ding and Lehrer's chapter of the child who is identified as genetically predisposed to learning difficulties provides an interesting case study of how biophysical data could be used to help the person from whom it was drawn. If we think about the implications of this type of use for the broader society, however, the situation becomes cloudier. Does the whole society benefit when extra resources are provided to particular individuals based on their genetic data, rather than based on their outward behaviors and stated desires, and/or on phenomena observable not at the micro but at the *meso* or macro levels (i.e., about groups, markets, nations, and so on)? Would the redirection of extra resources to children ear-marked with particular genetic predispositions and away from others give rise to gaming by families, and even to the birth of companies designed to provide genetically-argued routes to special treatment, available to those who can afford to pay the testing company?

One might most obviously look to the ethical dimensions of the practice of medical science and health policy for guidance in these areas. Another promising area is law, with its weighty consideration of intent versus effect. Intent is interior, whereas effect is exterior, yet both play a role in sentencing, as do many aspects of the context in which a crime was committed. In parallel, it may be that the most ethical way to use biophysical data is not on its own, but rather in close combination with observed choices, stated preferences, and other aspects of the micro, *meso*, and macro situations in which the measured subject is operating.

CURRENT PRACTICE IN HISTORICAL CONTEXT

Experimental psychologists were employing modern machinery by the middle of the past century to probe the physiological covariates of affect and behavior.

The technique of biofeedback (e.g., King & Montgomery, 1980; Lang, Sroufe, & Hastings, 1967; Omizo, 1980) retained the subject's agency and involvement in such exercises, implicitly promising heightened personal mastery, made possible through technology, over the chaos of physical and emotional dimensions of human response.

Economics was several decades behind psychology in its adoption of experimental methods, and also in its use of biophysical measurement tools. This was arguably a natural consequence of the very different orientations of the two disciplines during the era when technology that could be used to safely and reliably measure the biophysical signals of large numbers of subjects was starting to develop. While psychology as a discipline acknowledged generations ago the inextricable influence of physiological dimensions of response on outward behavior—an influence that could potentially be controlled, it was reasoned, given enough understanding of it—economics went down a different path. The stylized model of man used in economic models in the mid 1900s was devoid of emotion and essentially noncorporeal. The sole signal that anything apart from mindful rationalization drove his behavior was the claimed existence of (fixed) preference maps, springing like a deus-ex-machina from deep in a scientifically unplombed well to which only he had direct access. The very notion that an economic scientist might wish to plomb that well was deemed by some indecent and/or not acceptable for the discipline to support.

With this blinkered view of individual choice making as a backdrop, it is little wonder that the breakthrough of what we now term behavioral economics brought such upheaval and fractiousness to the economics discipline. Those researchers who managed to insert some echoes, however faint, of a corporeal existence into standard economic models were elevated far beyond what their achievements might have merited in a world where economics had not been starting from such a low base. Prospect theory (Kahneman & Tversky, 1979) and search theory (Albrecht, 2011) are two cases of successful marriages by economists of some notion of "irrationality" together with canonical economic modeling, producing hybrids that appeared to substantially advance the discipline. Yet while good bait for luring economists away from hyper-unrealistic models of behavior, our advances in these areas have proven so far to be scientifically unsatisfying inasmuch as they lack a deeper incorporation of the body and soul of decision making. What is it that makes people more sensitive to losses than to gains, and when (and why) does this factor create that difference in sensitivity? What ultimately drives how people choose to search, thereby selectively feeding themselves information that, counter to the assumptions of mainstream economic models, was not initially available to them at zero cost?

Modern biophysical measurement tools promise a path towards answering questions such as these. For every canonical economic assumption that might be challenged, there is the promise that a biophysical explanation might account for the difference between the behavior it predicts and the behavior we observe. This is partly why biophysical measurement has seemed so appealing to social scientists, although not all might admit it: the image of incontrovertible, clearly interpretable biophysical realities offers the prospect of reconciliation between theory and observation, where previously there was only frustrating dissonance. As Camerer et al. (2005) state, "New tools ... define new scientific fields and erase old boundaries" (p. 11). The promise of biophysical measurement, as-yet unfulfilled, is the erasure of the boundary between the social scientific models of behavior whose building blocks we nominated generations ago, and how our brains and bodies actually function.

FRONTIERS

This book has reviewed the most common types of biophysical measurement presently used in social science research. Three other techniques with a history of use in social science but without their own dedicated chapters in the volume are described briefly below for completeness.

Pupillometry

Since at least the middle of the past century, we have had machine-generated evidence that the pupils widen when we are looking at something interesting or challenging (e.g., Hess & Polt, 1960; Hess & Polt, 1964). This observation has been used in examinations of learning (Kahneman & Beatty, 1966; Kahneman & Peavler, 1969) and, more recently, of deceitful behavior (Wang, Spezio, & Camerer, 2010). Other early work using pupillometry in psychology, following the approach alluded to above, focused on training individuals to improve their understanding of and/or performance in situations using bio-feedback about pupillary response (e.g., King, 1979). Modern pupillometric work in psychology more frequently aims at translating pupils' signals into a common meaning than is facilitating choice makers' interpretation of those signals in situ (see, for example, Laeng, Sirois, & Gredeback, 2012, which also contains a review of 50 years of research in pupillometry within the discipline of psychology).

Human-mediated observation of pupil dilation patterns, at least in the important sphere of sexual attraction, long predates the machine's confirmation of it. Apart from a more formal (because of being machine-mediated and hence "objectively" verified) entry into modern scientists' already long list of behavioral correlates, what does social science then gain from wide-scale pupillometric studies using modern measurement machinery?

The promise of pupillometry, as of many of the tools reviewed in this book, is to affirm the relevance to choice of our corporeal nature. To affirm this is to reject the disembodiment of choice makers implicit in the first principles of economics. Whether these principles can be edited to accommodate the body in an explicit way, while retaining sufficient simplicity to be useful—and what marginal gains to understanding or policy making can be achieved from theories built on assumptions that have been edited in this way—are questions yet to be answered.

Emotion Recognition Based on Facial Musculature or Gait Analysis

As with our perceptions of others' eye movements, our perceptions of others' whole faces have been an input into humans' interpersonal exchanges for eons. Most of us also feel we instinctively know when someone walking into a room or across the street is particularly happy, stressed, or in pain, through observing how they move. The advent of modern machinery promises that our instinctive knowledge about how to read one another might be captured and used to code algorithms that read facial expressions or gait patterns without the need for human mediation.

Adolphs (2002) illustrates the complexity of humans' internal mechanisms for decoding facial expressions, stating in his review of the psychological investigations of these mechanisms that "recognizing facial emotion draws on multiple strategies subserved by a large array of different brain structures" (p. 21). Our understanding of this complexity at the moment is developed far less than what would be required to program a machine via mimicry of the human perceptual response, following what Skinner (1963) termed with some denigration a "mentalization" approach. By contrast, Skinner's "behavioral" approach would seem plausible: to instead focus on and capture what people do, or what they conclude, when they see and internally process different signals sent by the face.

Montepare, Goldstein, and Clausen's (1987) study examines how accurately people can identify the emotional state of a person based on how they are walking, revealing that we can do this identification, although with varying accuracy depending on the emotion. In particular, pride seems harder to identify than more basic emotions like anger and happiness. Another paper in this vein, Weisfeld and Beresford (1982), documents a correlation between social dominance and erect posture. As in the case of decoding facial musculature patterns, however, how humans' internal mechanism works to decipher the social or emotional meaning of body position and movement is not well understood.

In light of this state of science, and given the ubiquitous capture of millions of people's faces and gaits on surveillance cameras throughout the modern world, one might imagine an artificial intelligence programming initiative based on these biophysical dimensions that could deliver readings of the moods and/or self-perceived social positions of large numbers of people—even whole populations of countries. Unlike in the case of many biophysical methods discussed in the other chapters of this volume, facial and gait analysis is arguably not heavily contaminated by ambient context, at least when the subject is in a familiar setting; it can be observed at low levels of granularity, such as that delivered by CCTV cameras; and it is highly noninvasive. With input from humans to program and calibrate the machines, we could use the mass-scale face and gait readings they produce for many purposes. We might for example identify people who may be depressed or in pain, and use that information to target interventions; or we might gauge the variation in mood present in different populations, creating another potentially internationally comparable measure of inequality.

RELEVANCE OF BIOPHYSICAL METHODS TO THE FUTURE DEVELOPMENT OF THEORIES AND POLICY RECOMMENDATIONS

Of all the techniques covered in this book, eye tracking is perhaps the one most commonly applied in research, which may be in part because to obtain the path of someone's gaze does not appear to immediately suggest that any particular existing social scientific theory is erroneous. No one contests that humans have eyes, and the notion that eye movements might betray the type of thinking that occurs behind those eyes seems at face value not to threaten even standard economic models of rational choice. Hence the use of eye tracking seems reasonably innocuous.

Yet the very idea that tracking the eye might provide insight into the determinants of choice unavoidably implies the potential importance for behavior of something about our physiology, which presently plays no role in the theories of behavior that we teach students of economics. Acknowledging the potential usefulness of eye tracking implies one of two things that are both inconsistent with mainstream economic theory. If eye tracking reveals heterogeneity across people, which presumably is part of the expectation that drives an eye-tracking study, then either (a) people are thinking about different things, as betrayed by their eye movements, when making the same decision; and/or (b) people are being exposed to different visual stimuli in the course of making that decision. If it is useful for a behavioral scientist to know more about either of these phenomena, which is the implication of running a study that tracks the eyes, then it follows that even when exposed to identical situations containing identical information, people will be influenced internally or externally (or both) to process the information in different ways that are meaningful for their ultimate decisions. The influence flows through physiology—through the brain, or the eyes, or both—and the mediation of physiology between environment and action is simply not accommodated in conventional economic theories of choice.

Only recently have theorists in economics begun to acknowledge in their models that attention, like mental effort of any sort, is finite (Koszegi & Szeidl, 2013; Marković, Gläscher, Bossaerts, O'Doherty, & Kiebel, 2015; Sims, 2003; Woodford, 2012). This implies inevitably that no human is omniscient, such that no choice is made based on perfect information, irrespective of many mainstream models' implicit claim to the contrary. The barrier to reconciliation here has been not so much that economists refuse to see biophysical realities, but that no alternative exists that could replace economists' present model of choice while retaining simplicity and tractability. In the absence of such an alternative, the discipline has been vulnerable to fragmentation, pitching those who defend existing models as stylized yet useful and able to accommodate new insights via cleverly designed tweaks, against those who point relentlessly to the incompleteness of these models and to the shallowness of these tweaks. This fragmentation leaves those who have used eye tracking yet still acknowledge the usefulness of standard economic models in an inconvenient position: they belong to neither camp, with no third way yet lighted. A similar story can be told for users of many other technologies reviewed in this volume, the very usefulness of which at some level threatens the assumptions of conventional models.

In the presence of this dilemma, and until such a third way becomes available, how best can the individual researcher who uses biophysical data serve the goal of advancing science? I have argued elsewhere (Foster, 2018) that any science stalls without continued rejuvenation of its theoretical spine, and that economics—like other social sciences—is no exception to this rule. Economics is exceptional in one dimension, however: the very generality and broad applicability of its core theoretical structures make it appear able to accommodate a sea of novelty, including whatever novel insights come to us through biophysical measurement. While seductive and even helpful in thinking about new insights in the short run, this appearance of infinite theoretical flexibility is illusory in the long run, for the simple reason that any theory that can be anything to anyone is ultimately useless. Economists will need to decide over the next generation which aspects of the models formalized in the mid-1900s to retain, and which aspects to cross out and rewrite based on new information about how our brains and bodies actually function, in order to take the discipline forward. Individual researchers can assist in this effort by recognizing this longer-run problem and selecting questions to investigate that assist in separating the theoretical wheat from the chaff, being mindful of the danger that Paul Frijters warns us of in his Foreword: the crowding out of the big picture and the massive gains in understanding that picture made by prior generations of scientists by a laser focus on some small aspect of the problem, whose importance for understanding and guiding our societies then looms in our minds to be larger than it really is.

Finally, as the ultimate goal of economics is to promote social welfare, what opportunities does mass biophysical data afford us to do that, in ways that were previously unavailable?

Tymula points to the derivation of an actionable policy to improve adult mathematics ability—specifically, finger differentiation exercises for children—based on evidence from brain scanning. Cheung and Butler cite the suggestion of other researchers that information about the association of testosterone and trading behaviors should lead us to place more financial decisions into the hands of women, but do not themselves take a specific position on how best to apply our burgeoning understanding of the relation of hormones to market bubbles and crashes to the design of marketplaces. Soroka is even more cautious, explicitly citing the limitation of our understanding of what skin conductance measures actually indicate as reason to see any specific call to policy action based on skin conductance data as premature. Lehrer and Ding suggest that we should use information about genetics to direct health policy optimally by exploiting a core, and arguably often overlooked, comparative strength of social scientists relative to other scientists: our ability to communicate research results effectively.

As stewards of the role that social science has come to play in shaping policy, we should evaluate these and other suggestions about how to use biophysical data in policy setting with a long-run view of their possible consequences in what economists term general equilibrium: the state of the world that would pertain if the suggested policy were implemented and known to all members of society and its constituent groups. I hope social scientists will take this perspective and apply our growing understanding of humanity to the problem of predicting what big biophysical data will mean for the full gamut of human choices—including those of us scientists—and for our larger societies, proceeding along the frontiers of scientific innovation and policy making with a firm grip on both wonder and caution.

REFERENCES

Adolphs, R. (2002). Recognizing emotion from facial expressions: psychological and neurological mechanisms. *Behavioral and Cognitive Neuroscience Reviews*, *1*(1), 21–62.

Albrecht, J. (2011). Search theory: the 2010 Nobel memorial prize in economic sciences. *Scandinavian Journal of Economics*, *113*(2), 237–259.

Camerer, C., Loewenstein, G., & Prelec, D. (2005). Neuroeconomics: how neuroscience can inform economics. *Journal of Economic Literature*, *43*(1), 9–64.

Floyd, K. (2004). An introduction to the uses and potential uses of physiological measurement in the study of family communication. *Journal of Family Communication*, *4*(3–4), 295–317.

Foster, G. (2018). Towards a living theoretical spine for (behavioural) economics. *Journal of Behavioral Economics for Policy*, *2*(1), 75–81.

Hess, E. H., & Polt, J. M. (1960). Pupil size as related to interest value of visual stimuli. *Science*, *32*, 349–350.

Hess, E. H., & Polt, J. M. (1964). Pupil size in relation to mental activity during simple problem solving. *Science*, *140*, 1190–1192.

Kahneman, D., & Beatty, J. (1966). Pupil diameter and load on memory. *Science*, *154*, 1583–1585.

Kahneman, D., & Peavler, W. S. (1969). Incentive effects and pupillary changes in association learning. *Journal of Experimental Psychology*, *79*(2), 312–318.

Kahneman, D., & Tversky, A. (1979). Prospect theory: an analysis of decision under risk. *Econometrica*, *47*(2), 263–292.

King, A. (1979). Pygmalion and pupillometry: development of expectations in managers. *Human Organization*, *38*(3), 248.

King, N. J., & Montgomery, R. B. (1980). Biofeedback-induced control of human peripheral temperature: a critical review of the literature. *Psychological Bulletin*, *88*(3), 738–752.

Koszegi, B., & Szeidl, Á. (2013). A model of focusing in economic choice. *Quarterly Journal of Economics*, *128*(1), 53–107.

Laeng, B., Sirois, S., & Gredeback, G. (2012). Pupillometry: a window to the preconscious? *Perspectives on Psychological Science*, *7*(1), 18–27.

Lang, P. J., Sroufe, A., & Hastings, J. E. (1967). Effects of feedback and instructional set on the control of cardiac-rate variability. *Journal of Experimental Psychology*, *75*(4), 425–431.

Marković, D., Gläscher, J., Bossaerts, P., O'Doherty, J., & Kiebel, S. J. (2015). Modeling the evolution of beliefs using an attentional focus mechanism. *PLoS Computational Biology*, *11*(10).

Milgram, S. (1963). Behavioral study of obedience. *Journal of Abnormal and Social Psychology*, *67*, 371–378.

Montepare, J. M., Goldstein, S. B., & Clausen, A. (1987). The identification of emotions from gait information. *Journal of Nonverbal Behavior*, *11*(1), 33–42.
Omizo, M. M. (1980). The effects of biofeedback-induced relaxation training in hyperactive adolescent boys. *The Journal of Psychology*, *105*(1), 131–138.
Simon, H. (1955). A behavioral model of rational choice. *The Quarterly Journal of Economics*, *69*(1), 99–118.
Sims, C. A. (2003). Implications of rational inattention. *Journal of Monetary Economics*, *50*(3), 665–669.
Skinner, B. F. (1963). Behaviorism at 50. *Science*, *140*(3570), 951–958.
Wang, J. T., Spezio, M., & Camerer, C. F. (2010). Pinocchio's pupil: using eyetracking and pupil dilation to understand truth telling and deception in sender-receiver games. *American Economic Review*, *100*, 984–1007.
Weisfeld, G. E., & Beresford, J. M. (1982). Erectness of posture as an indicator of dominance or success in humans. *Motivation and Emotion*, *6*(2), 113–131.
Woodford, M. (2012). Prospect theory as efficient perceptual distortion. *American Economic Review: Papers and Proceedings*, *102*(3), 41–46.

Appendix 1

Getting Started With Eye Tracking

Daniel Pearson[1], Mike Le Pelley[1] and Tom Beesley[2]
[1]*School of Psychology, UNSW Sydney, Sydney, NSW, Australia,* [2]*Department of Psychology, Lancaster University, Lancaster, United Kingdom*

A (VERY) BRIEF EXPLANATION OF VIDEO-BASED EYE TRACKING

Throughout the history of eye movement research, multiple techniques have been developed to track the orientation of the eye and thereby determine the location of gaze (for a review, see Duchowski, 2017). While some of these techniques remain in use to varying degrees today (e.g., Agrawal et al., 2014; Bulling, Ward, Gellersen, & Tröster, 2011), the vast majority of eye tracking systems currently used in academic and consumer research are what are commonly known as "video-based eye trackers". These systems use a combination of infrared illumination and video recording to noninvasively track the eye and estimate gaze location. While a detailed technical description of this technique is beyond the scope of this chapter, we briefly cover the fundamentals of how these systems operate below (for a more detailed explanation, see Duchowski, 2017; Hansen & Ji, 2010; Holmqvist et al., 2011).

In the context of video-based eye tracking, the two most important structures of the eye are the pupil and the cornea (see Fig. 1). The pupil is the opening in the center of the eye that allows light to pass through to the retina, where it activates photoreceptors and is changed—or "transduced"—into electrical signals that are sent to the brain's visual cortex for further processing. The pupil appears black when viewed externally, as the light that passes through it is mostly absorbed by the tissue inside the eye. The cornea, on the other hand, is the mostly transparent layer that covers the front part of the eye (i.e., the pupil, iris, and anterior chamber). Importantly, the cornea does not allow all light to enter the eye, but instead reflects some light, creating the reflection that you can see when you look into someone's eyes. The cornea reflects light from multiple

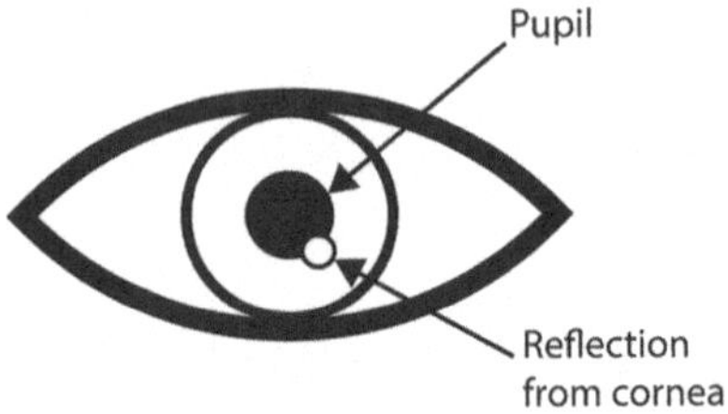

FIG. 1 Diagram of the eye illustrating the pupil and the reflection from the cornea. Both features are commonly used by video-based eye tracking systems.

different light sources at any one time (e.g., overhead lighting, sunlight, and a computer monitor). This minimizes any confusion of signals due to the different positions of these natural reflections. Video-based eye tracking systems illuminate the eye with one or more infrared light sources and record images of the eye using an infrared camera. The use of infrared light allows the eye tracker to know for certain that the reflection it is analyzing comes from a known location (i.e., the location of the infrared light source(s)). The eye tracker analyzes the images that it records and estimates the gaze location, typically by using the relative position of the pupil and the infrared reflection from the cornea in combination with information gained through a prior calibration procedure that provides a baseline measurement of what the subject's eyes look like when gazing at various known locations.

By tracking the relative positions of the pupil and the corneal reflection, the eye tracker can distinguish between eye movements and head movements. This is because the relative position of the pupil and the corneal reflection will remain mostly constant during head movements, but will shift during eye movements (Holmqvist et al., 2011). The exact method used to estimate the gaze location varies depending on the brand of eye tracker that is being used, and the specific details of the gaze-estimation algorithm are often proprietary and hidden from the user.

CHOOSING THE EYE TRACKING SYSTEM THAT IS RIGHT FOR YOU

There are many different brands and types of eye tracking systems available for purchase. Each of these different models will have been designed with a specific purpose and/or user group in mind, and so each has its own unique set of advantages and disadvantages. As we (the authors) do not have experience using all these different eye tracking systems, and we have not done any formal comparison of their features, we cannot make specific recommendations for brands or models that will be most suitable to a particular application. However, there are many important features to consider when purchasing an eye tracking system, and we briefly review these later in this chapter.

TYPES OF EYE MOVEMENTS TARGETED IN EYE TRACKING RESEARCH

Before we cover the different types of eye tracking systems and their relative pros and cons, we first describe the different types of eye movements that you may want to measure with your eye tracker. As discussed in Chapter 2, a variety of different eye movements are analyzed in the eye tracking literature, the two most common of which are:

- Fixations: periods where the eye remains relatively still, focused on one location, and information about the visual world is processed.
- Saccades: periods where the eye is rapidly moving from fixation to fixation, and visual information is not processed.

The majority of eye tracking research is limited to the analysis of one or both features of gaze, and most eye tracking systems will usually be accompanied by software that parses the eye-gaze data into these different features. There are also third-party eye-movement parsing algorithms that are freely available from other eye tracking researchers (e.g., Nyström & Holmqvist, 2010; Saez de Urabain, Johnson, & Smith, 2015), or an experienced programmer could write one from scratch (for descriptions of such algorithms, see Salvucci & Goldberg, 2000).

While most of the eye tracking literature focuses on fixations and saccades, a range of other eye movements may be of interest to would-be eye tracking researchers, depending on their research question. Examples include:

- Smooth pursuit movements: slow movements of the eyes that keep a moving stimulus in the center of the field of vision, e.g., when tracking a tennis ball across the court.
- Vergence movements: small inward or outward movements of the eyes that keep objects at different distances from the observer in the center of the field of vision, e.g., as an object moves closer to an observer, the eyes must make a vergence movement inwards towards the nose in order to keep the object centered and in focus.
- Microsaccades: small involuntary saccades that are made during periods of fixation. The function of microsaccades is still debated, but they appear to be important for perception (Martinez-Conde, Otero-Millan, & Macknik, 2013).
- Glissades: small corrective eye movements that are made when a saccade overshoots (or undershoots) a target location (Nyström & Holmqvist, 2010).

The software that comes with some eye tracking systems may have the capability to parse these less-frequently analyzed eye movements from gaze data;

however, this is uncommon. Usually, the analysis of these eye movements is restricted to more specialized psychophysiology research, and requires the use of independently developed event-detection algorithms (for examples, see Larsson, Nyström, Andersson, & Stridh, 2015; Nyström & Holmqvist, 2010; Vidal, Bulling, & Gellersen, 2012).

For researchers without extensive experience with eye tracking and/or programming, converting the raw eye-gaze data into eye movement events can seem overwhelming. Thankfully, as we will discuss later in this chapter, it is possible to answer many common eye tracking research questions without parsing the data into discrete eye movements at all.

TYPES OF EYE TRACKERS

The essential components of a video-based eye tracker are a source of infrared illumination and an infrared video camera. These components can be positioned in several different configurations. There are three main types of video-based eye tracker, which differ in terms of the position of the camera and illumination source, the data that they produce, and the types of research for which they are most suitable.

Tower-Mounted Trackers

Tower-mounted eye trackers immobilize the participant's head, typically via forehead and chin rests that restrict the extent to which the head can move. The infrared illumination source and camera are located inside a box at the top of the tower, above the forehead and chin rests. The camera and illumination source are angled downwards and reflected up into the eye from below using a mirror (see Fig. 2A).

Tower-mounted systems have several advantages over other types of eye trackers. In particular, these systems typically have the highest sampling frequency, accuracy, and precision (discussed in detail later). This is largely due to the consistent location of the eyes relative to the camera, which allows the eye to be recorded close-up with high resolution. However, there are some disadvantages to these systems. For example, the participant may become

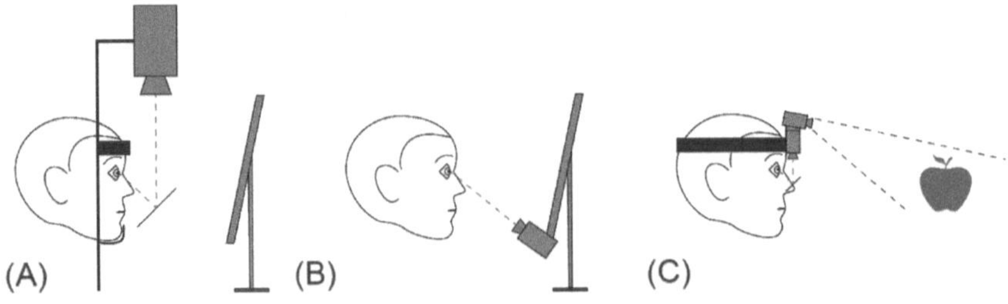

FIG. 2 Three different types of eye tracker: (A) a tower-mounted eye tracker, (B) a remote eye tracker, and (C) a head-mounted eye tracker.

uncomfortable sitting in the chin and forehead rest for an extended period. Furthermore, the experience of using a tower-mounted eye tracker is rather unlike the more common experience of viewing a standard computer monitor. It might be argued that this may lead the participant to behave less naturalistically, though to our knowledge this possibility and its resulting effect on behavior have not been formally tested. It is certainly true, however, that the design of tower-mounted systems means that it is very clear to the subject that their eyes are being tracked. This precludes the use of these systems for applications in which we might want to track a participant's eyes covertly. For example in experiments using "implicit" procedures that rely on the participant being unaware of the eye tracking manipulation (e.g., Beesley, Pearson, & Le Pelley, 2015).

Remote Trackers

Remote eye tracking systems have the illumination source and the camera positioned separately from the participant, typically attached to the computer monitor that is also used to present the stimuli in the experiment (Fig. 2B). If the participant's head is somewhere within a limited three-dimensional space in front of the camera (known as the head box), the eye tracker will record his or her eye movements. This means that the participant's head does not need to be immobilized. Remote systems have several advantages over other types of eye trackers. For example, participants may be more comfortable, and therefore behave more naturalistically. These systems may also be better suited to testing populations that struggle to sit still for extended periods (e.g., infants, or certain psychiatric populations). They also allow for other experimental equipment to be attached to the head (e.g., electroencephalography electrodes). Finally, implicit experimental manipulations in which the eyes are tracked surreptitiously can be implemented using remote systems.

On the other hand, remote systems have their disadvantages. Most importantly, the data produced by remote eye tracking systems is generally of a lower quality than that from tower-mounted systems. This is because of imperfections in gaze estimation models during head movements, which are typically uncontrolled in these systems, as well as the lower resolution recording of the eye in remote systems (a consequence of the wider camera angle needed to allow for more varied positioning of the eye relative to the camera). Another disadvantage of remote eye tracking systems is that the system needs to determine afresh where the eyes are in three-dimensional space whenever the participant blinks, closes the eyes for an extended period, or briefly moves the eyes out of the head box. The calculations required to determine the location of the eyes take time to process (known as recovery time), and so remote systems will have longer periods in which gaze location cannot be determined following these events. The effect of these limitations can be reduced to some extent by combining a remote eye tracking system with a head restriction, for example, by using a chin rest.

Head-Mounted Trackers

Head-mounted eye tracking systems have both the illumination source and the camera attached to the head of the participant, typically with another camera (the "scene camera") facing outwards to record the environment around the participant, which acts as the stimulus; see Fig. 2C. These systems allow for maximum mobility, and thus make it possible to track a participant's gaze while in a natural environment (e.g., moving around in a shopping center or driving a car). However, many head-mounted systems are generally not recommended for research involving nonnaturalistic stimuli. The reason for this is that the gaze coordinates outputted by the eye tracker often do not correspond to a fixed location in the environment. Rather, they correspond to a region on the video output of the scene camera, which changes over time depending on the orientation of the participant's head. Therefore, data analysis becomes more difficult to automate. A particular set of gaze coordinates may correspond to an object of interest at time A, but not at time B. This means that commonly-used eye tracking measures, such as gaze dwell time or fixation time on an area of interest (AOI), cannot be easily derived. Some manufacturers have developed solutions to this problem that involve attaching sensors to either the objects of interest in the environment (e.g., a computer monitor or a print advertisement) and/or to the participant's head, thereby allowing for easier coregistration of gaze coordinates with objects in the testing environment.

SAMPLING FREQUENCY

Sampling frequency refers to the speed at which the eye tracking system takes images (samples) of the eyes and analyzes them to determine gaze location. Sampling frequency is measured in Hertz (Hz), which corresponds to the number of samples taken per second: a system with a sampling frequency of 250 Hz takes 250 images of the eye each second (i.e., one image every four milliseconds [ms]). The sampling frequency of an eye tracking system is typically the feature most publicized by the manufacturer, with common sampling frequencies ranging from 25 Hz to >1000 Hz. Faster systems are necessary for the accurate measurement of fast eye movements (e.g., finding the peak velocity of small saccades and microsaccades; see Inchingolo & Spanio, 1985; Juhola, Jäntti, & Pyykkö, 1985; Martinez-Conde, Macknik, Troncoso, & Hubel, 2009), but are more expensive, bulkier, and produce larger data files than their lower sample-rate counterparts. Therefore, when looking to purchase an eye tracker, it is important to consider what speed you will need to answer your research question most appropriately, and to factor in the increased cost and size associated with higher-frequency measurement systems.

How Sampling Frequency Affects Measurement Error

In a 250 Hz system, it is not the case that each sample lasts for 4 ms, but rather that the gap between each of the samples is 4 ms. This introduces some error into the measurement of eye movements. For example, if gaze is detected at a certain location (e.g., on a particular stimulus that has been presented on the screen) in one sample, the eyes could have arrived on that location at the exact time that the sample was taken, or at any time during the 4 ms window before the sample was taken. For a 25 Hz system, the eyes could have arrived on the location at any time during the 40 ms window prior to the sample. Thus, the higher the sampling frequency, the more precisely we can measure the onset and offset of eye movement events.

The error introduced by these gaps between samples has different implications depending on whether the measure of interest is an event duration (i.e., the time between two gaze-related events, such as the time between a set of eyes arriving on a stimulus and the time at which they move away from that stimulus) or an event latency (i.e., the time between some nongaze-related event, such as the start of a trial, and a gaze-related event). When measuring event durations, the distribution of the sampling error has been shown to be centered around zero (Andersson, Nyström, & Holmqvist, 2010). This is because both the onset and offset of the event should be overestimated to an equivalent degree (as shown in Fig. 3), and so these errors will cancel each other out on average. However, given the same number of data points, the variance of this error will be larger for a low-frequency system than for a high-frequency system. Importantly, simulation studies (e.g., Andersson et al., 2010) have demonstrated that it is possible to reduce the variance in the error by increasing the number of data points (e.g., by increasing the number of participants, or the number of trials). In this way, it is possible to achieve the same level of error variance in the estimation of an average fixation duration with a 25 Hz system and 250 Hz system by collecting 100 times more data points with the 25 Hz system.

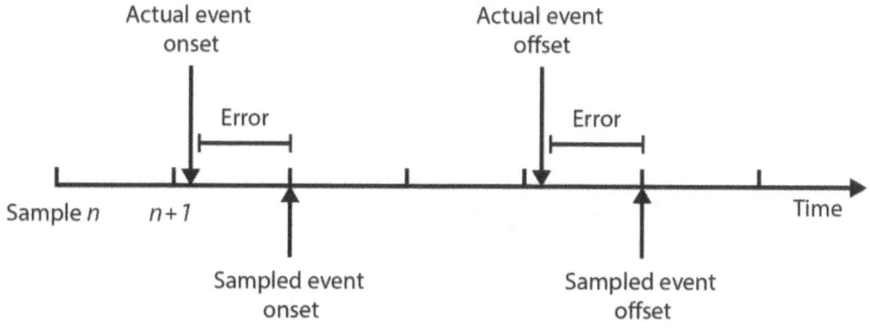

FIG. 3 An illustration of the overestimation of eye movement event onsets and offsets by eye tracking systems due to the gaps between each successive sample.

In contrast, event latencies are calculated from a single gaze-related event and so the timing of the event will be consistently overestimated. It can be shown that the distribution of the sampling error will not be centered around zero but will instead be centered around half of the time lag between samples (e.g., for a 250 Hz tracker, the average error is expected to be (1000/250)/2 = 2 ms). Increasing the number of data points will reduce the variance of the error around this value, to the point that the average error value can be either added to, or subtracted from, the average event latency across subjects as a constant to yield a more accurate estimate of the true event latency.

Sampling Frequency and Gaze Contingency

Gaze-contingent experiments involve changing the stimuli presented to the participant in some way because of how the eyes move. For example, an experiment might register a correct response and advance to the next trial only after a certain dwell time has been recorded on a target stimulus (e.g., Le Pelley, Pearson, Griffiths, & Beesley, 2015). In some cases, these gaze-contingent manipulations rely on high-speed identification of eye movements. For example, the location of a target might change after the participant has initiated a saccade towards that location, but before the eyes have landed on the location (e.g., Godijn & Theeuwes, 2002). The steps involved in such a manipulation would be as follows: (1) the participant begins to saccade towards the target location; (2) the eye tracker records a series of gaze location samples during this movement, the speed of which is directly related to the eye tracker's sampling frequency; (3) the eye tracking software parses the raw gaze location data and determines that a saccade has been initiated; (4) the software controlling the presentation of the stimuli in the experiment calculates the new target location; (5) the target is presented in the new location on the computer monitor. All of these steps must occur before the participant's eyes land on the original target location, which may take anywhere from 20 to 200 ms depending on how far the eyes have to move. Given the limited time available for these steps, a system with a high sampling frequency, and therefore minimal delay between samples, would be desired.

What Sampling Frequency do You Need?

As discussed above, the sampling frequency of your eye tracking system has implications for the types of measures and effect sizes that you can reliably detect. If you wish to estimate the properties of short saccades or microsaccades, detect small differences in latencies and durations of eye-movement events with a reasonable number of data points, or use rapid gaze-contingent manipulations in your research, you would likely need an eye tracking system with a relatively high sampling frequency ($\geq$250 Hz). However, if you are interested in relatively large differences in dwell time, fixation time, or event latency, you may be able to get by with a lower frequency system. In general, there are no strict rules about what sampling frequency is necessary for a particular research question or eye movement measure. So, the short answer is to survey other research in the field and purchase a system with similar specifications to that being used by other research groups investigating research questions similar to yours.

ACCURACY AND PRECISION

In addition to advertising the sampling frequency of their eye trackers, manufacturers will also typically make claims about accuracy and precision. Accuracy refers to how well the recorded gaze position captures the true gaze position, measured by the angular distance between the recorded line of sight and the true line of sight. Precision is the reliability, or "tightness," of the eye tracker's measurements. These two concepts are illustrated in Fig. 4.

High accuracy is critical for research that uses an area of interest (AOI) approach, in which AOIs are defined and eye movements/dwell times are calculated relative to that AOI. Suppose, for example, that we wish to measure the amount of time that participants spend looking at a button before clicking on it. We would need to be sure that the data output by the eye tracker is an accurate reflection of where the participant is looking. In contrast, accuracy is of relatively little importance for studies that do not measure eye movements relative to a particular AOI. For example, if we want to measure the peak velocity of the first saccade that is initiated following a cue, then knowing exactly where the participant is looking on the screen is less important. Accuracy is influenced by a variety of factors, including the type of system used (tower-mounted systems typically have the highest accuracy, with remote systems having the lowest); the quality of the calibration; the shape, size, color, and positioning of the participant's eyes (e.g., eyes that are less obscured by low eyelids and long eyelashes are generally easier to track); and other environmental factors (e.g., ambient light level).

The average accuracy reported by the manufacturers of some of the most commonly used eye tracking systems is <0.5° (SensoMotoric Instruments,

FIG. 4 An illustration of the different combinations of high and low precision and accuracy.

2009; SR Research Inc., 2007; Tobii Technology, 2011). However, independent tests conducted by researchers have shown that accuracy in real-world set-ups can be considerably worse than what is reported by manufacturers (e.g., Nyström, Andersson, Holmqvist, & van de Weijer, 2013). Recently, methods have been developed for post hoc processing of eye-gaze data to correct for systematic error caused by environmental factors (e.g., Vadillo, Street, Beesley, & Shanks, 2015).

Precision is usually measured as the square root of the average squared error, where the error is defined as the angular distance between successive data samples when the eye is in a fixed location. Precision relates strongly to the ability to accurately calculate fixation duration and saccade measures, as a high degree of variability in samples can lead a true fixation to be classified as an eye movement. A general rule of thumb that has been recommended is to ensure that any eye tracker used for the calculation of fixation durations or saccadic measures has a precision value of $<0.05°$ (Holmqvist et al., 2011).

Eye Tracker Latency

Eye tracker latency[1] refers to the average end-to-end delay from the time a participant's eye moves to the time that the computer registers that a movement has taken place. Having a low latency system is particularly important for gaze-contingent research, as discussed above, as it allows for maximal time for the presentation software to update the stimuli presented to the monitor after the participant's eye-movement triggers the change.

In general, eye tracker latency is less important for research based on offline analysis of eye movements (typically measuring whether gaze falls in certain areas of interest, as we discuss later), as long as it is relatively consistent. However, on lower-end systems this may not necessarily be the case. If both the images collected by the eye tracker and the presentation of the stimuli are processed by the same central processing unit (CPU), competition for CPU time can lead to spikes in the latency between samples. Higher-end systems typically overcome this problem by having a separate CPU that is either built into the tracker or sits apart from it and is solely responsible for processing the images collected by the eye tracker and outputting the processed data.

BINOCULAR VERSUS MONOCULAR TRACKING

Binocular eye trackers record data from both eyes, whereas monocular eye trackers record data from only one. The vast majority of eye tracking research is done using monocular data. This is because it is generally assumed that both eyes are doing similar things at the same point in time, so analyzing the data

1. The meaning of the term "eye tracker latency" used here is different from that of the term "event latency" defined previously in this chapter.

from the other eye is unlikely to provide any additional utility. Furthermore, it is considerably easier to process and analyze a single stream of data than two streams. The majority of eye tracker systems are monocular, and it is relatively easy to convert the binocular data that some systems produce into a single stream. For instance, some researchers will average the X and Y coordinates from the two streams of a binocular system, which can considerably increase the accuracy and precision of the data (Cui & Hondzinski, 2006). Others will select a single stream of data based on the quality of the two streams, comparing the proportion of missing samples from each of the streams on each trial and selecting the stream that has the lower proportion of missing data.

ANALYSIS SOFTWARE

The gaze recording and analysis software provided by the various manufacturers of eye tracking systems generally reflect their different customer bases. The increase in the use of eye trackers in more applied domains (e.g., user experience design) means that many manufacturers' analysis programs are primarily focused on producing simple statistics and visualizations (e.g., heat maps) which may be suitable for presentations and figures in publications but may not support the sorts of statistical analyses required for publication in academic journals. However, most eye trackers will let you extract the raw *X* and *Y* coordinate data, amongst other measures, which you can then analyze in other free or commercially available data analysis programs (e.g., R, Python, MATLAB).

A SIMPLE EYE TRACKING EXPERIMENT FROM DESIGN TO DATA ANALYSIS

As discussed in Chapter 2, researchers have used eye tracking methods to gain insight into many interesting psychological processes, ranging from the processing of words during reading to the allocation of attention to reward signaling stimuli. Across these different research areas, many different eye-gaze measures have been developed and analyzed in a nearly limitless variety of experimental designs. As an introduction to the process of developing your own eye tracking tasks, we present below a very basic experiment that uses one of the simplest eye-gaze measures—dwell time—and discuss the factors to consider in all stages of the experimental process, ranging from design and programming, to data collection, through to data analysis.

Design

Imagine that we have been asked to design a new advertising poster for a major art gallery and have been instructed that the poster should contain a picture of one of the gallery's paintings. But which one? To answer this question, we decide to run an experiment to see which of two paintings—say, a Renaissance

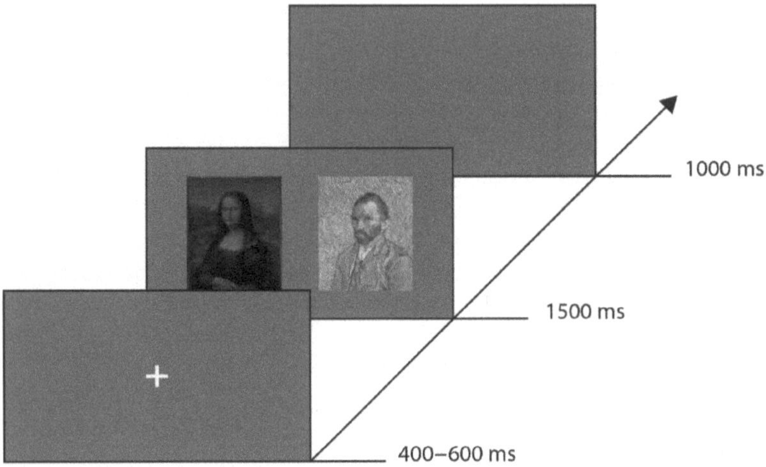

FIG. 5 The sequence of events in each trial of the experiment.

piece or an Impressionist piece—is more eye-catching (i.e., which of them a typical person will look at for a longer period of time).

Fig. 5 shows the sequence of events for each trial of our experiment. First, a white fixation cross will appear in the center of the display and remain on screen for a period that varies randomly between 400 and 600 ms. The purpose of the fixation cross is to draw participants' gaze to the center of the screen at the start of each trial, thereby preventing any carryover effects from the end position of the gaze on the previous trial. The variable period of time that the fixation cross is displayed is to ensure that participants are not able to predict the specific time at which the stimuli will be presented on the screen, preventing participants from starting to move their eyes in anticipation before the stimuli are presented. Following this, the two images—one Renaissance painting and one Impressionist painting—will be presented on the screen, one on the left side of the display and the other on the right side. These images will remain on screen for a period of 1500 ms before being replaced with a blank screen for a period of 1000 ms.

When designing an eye tracking task such as the one we have just described, there are a number of factors to consider to ensure that the conclusions drawn are valid. We want to be sure that the data says something interesting about the research question that motivated the experiment, and that our findings are not confounded by other methodological explanations which would be considerably less interesting. Many of these considerations are the same as those that would apply in any behavioral experiment. Examples of design features intended to mitigate such problems include:

(1) Varying the side of the screen on which each class of stimulus is presented. In this case, we would want to ensure that in half of the trials the Renaissance painting is shown on the left and the Impressionist painting on the right, and in the other half of the trials the Renaissance painting is shown on the right and the Impressionist painting on the left—with these different trial types randomly intermixed throughout the experiment. This avoids confoundment with any systematic bias that participants might have towards one side of the display. For example, participants from English-speaking backgrounds might be more likely to look at objects on the left side of the screen before they look at objects on the right side of the screen.

(2) Varying the order of stimulus presentation across participants. For each participant, the sequence of trials that they receive would be randomly generated (e.g., trial one: Renaissance left—Impressionist right, trial two: Impressionist left—Renaissance right, trial three: Impressionist left—Renaissance right, etc.). Across subjects, this prevents systematic differences in dwell time on the two classes of stimuli arising because of order or learning effects.

(3) Ensuring that the task is sufficiently interesting that participants remain engaged and focused. This is particularly important for eye tracking experiments, as participants who are not engaged in the task may stop looking at the screen in front of them and instead start looking around the room (or scrolling through social media on their smartphones). Such disengagement would considerably reduce the amount of eye-gaze data available for analysis. In the case of this experiment, we might introduce a manipulation where participants are periodically shown an array of different paintings, one of which was not presented on the previous trials, and their task is to select the painting that they have not previously seen. This active component would likely make the experiment more engaging than an alternative experiment in which participants simply view the stimuli passively.

(4) Presenting a convincing "cover story" for the task so that the participants are less likely to guess the design of the experiment and respond according to what they believe the experimenter wants them to do. Following on from the above manipulation, we might tell participants in our task that we are examining memory for images, rather than preference for different types of art. Of course, whether or not such a cover story would be appropriate would also depend on discipline-specific norms regarding the acceptability of deception.

There are also several other design questions to consider that are more specific to eye tracking as opposed to other types of experiments. For example:

(1) Should stimuli be presented for a fixed period or until the participant makes a response (e.g., a button press, or mouse click)? Tethering stimulus presentation time to participant response time can be potentially problematic for eye tracking experiments that use dwell time or fixation time on different stimuli as a dependent variable. For example, if participants need to make different responses to the different stimuli, and the response to one stimulus is associated with a longer response time (either because determining the correct response to that stimulus is more difficult and therefore requires more "thinking" time, or because it takes longer to physically make the correct response), it might not be surprising to find that participants spend longer (in terms of absolute time) looking at that stimulus. The easiest way to overcome this problem would be to present the stimuli on screen for a fixed period, with responses available only after the stimuli have been removed from the screen. Another option would be to represent the time spent looking at each stimulus as a proportion of the total trial time rather than as an absolute measure (e.g., Beesley, Nguyen, Pearson, & Le Pelley, 2015).

(2) Stimuli should ideally be matched according to physical characteristics such as size, brightness, and contrast, differing only along the dimension of research interest. If stimulus A takes up 60% of the on-screen "real estate" in the display, and stimulus B takes up only 30%, it may not be particularly surprising to find that participants spend more time looking at stimulus A. Indeed, if participants were fixating at random points on the screen, we would expect them to spend approximately twice as much time gazing at stimulus A than at stimulus B. Similarly, if stimulus A is bright and has high contrast with its background, making it physically salient, and stimulus B is dull and barely distinguishable, then any difference in gaze directed towards these stimuli could easily be explained by the physical differences between them rather than by the psychological process into which the researcher is trying to gain insight.

Programming

The software that comes with some eye tracking systems may allow for a simple experiment such as the one we have described to be programmed relatively easily. However, the process of programming and analyzing the data will likely be different for each company's software. Therefore, we present below the general form of experiment and data analysis programs that we have used in our labs. We typically use MATLAB, in combination with the Psychophysics Toolbox (Brainard, 1997) for the presentation of stimuli and data analysis, as well as functions from the Tobii Software Development Kit (SDK) to interface with Tobii TX-300 remote eye trackers. The general principles outlined here could be applied to experiments programmed in other languages and that use different eye tracking systems.

Fig. 6 presents pseudocode for the task in the experiment outlined above. Initially, a start signal is sent to the eye tracker to commence tracking of the participant's eyes. Then a loop through all the trials in the experiment is started. On each of these trials, the fixation cross is presented on the display and remains on screen for a random period of time between 400 and 600 ms. Then, the stimuli (i.e., images of paintings) are presented on the display. At this point, the presentation software saves a timestamp that indicates the time at which the stimuli

```
- send start signal to eye tracker
- FOR each trial in the experiment:
        - present fixation cross on screen
        - wait random amount of time between 400 and 600 ms
        - present stimuli on screen
        - save timestamp for start of trial
        - wait 1500 ms
        - present blank screen
        - save timestamp for end of trial
        - wait 1000 ms
- THEN send stop signal to eye tracker
```

FIG. 6 Pseudocode for the eye tracking experiment.

are presented. This timestamp will be used during data analysis to trim the continuous gaze data to the epoch of interest (i.e., the time that the stimuli were on screen). After the stimuli have remained on screen for 1500 ms, a blank screen is presented, and another timestamp is saved indicating the point at which the stimuli are no longer on the screen. The blank screen remains on for a period of 1000 ms, after which the program reads the gaze data for the trial from the eye tracker and saves it to a file. At this point, the trial has ended, and the trial loop begins again, continuing until all trials of the experiment have been completed. At the end of the experiment, a stop signal is sent to the eye tracker to signal that the experiment is finished and that the participant's eyes should no longer be tracked.

DATA COLLECTION

In eye tracking research, as with many other psychophysiological methods, it can be said that "there is no substitute for clean data" (Luck, 2014). Here we will describe some of the processes involved in data collection, and the ways in which common problems that arise when collecting data can be overcome.

Calibration

The shape and size of people's eyes vary considerably (e.g., in diameter; see Bekerman, Gottlieb, & Vaiman, 2014). It is for this reason that the starting point of any eye tracking experiment is the calibration. The calibration process allows the eye tracker to gather images of a subject's eye when gaze is assumed to rest on predefined points. The eye tracking system will then analyze these images and alter the variables in its gaze-estimation algorithm to try to fit its estimated gaze points accurately to the calibration locations that were presented to the participant.

Calibration is typically done by presenting participants with a number of calibration points, such as 5, 9, or 13 points, that are positioned around the area where the relevant stimuli will be presented. Typically, one of these points corresponds to the center of the computer monitor, and the remaining points are positioned at equal distances from the center in the four quadrants of the screen. These points should be small and highly salient, to ensure that participants look at them as accurately as possible. This can be achieved by animating the calibration points (e.g., having them shrink from a large dot to a small dot), or by requiring the participants to make a response to them (e.g., clicking on the points with a mouse to indicate that they are looking at them). When calibrating to the eyes of special populations, such as children, it might be even more important to make the calibration points as engaging as possible, for example, by using cartoon images. Most if not all eye trackers come with some sort of built-in calibration procedure that can either be used out-of-the-box or modified to better suit the specific needs of your research. For example, you may be positioning your stimuli in only one quadrant of the computer screen, so you may wish to increase the number of calibration points in that quadrant to increase the accuracy of tracking in that area.

When positioning the eye camera for calibration, it is important that neither the pupil nor the reflection from the cornea is obscured or mistaken for other objects as the eye moves around in its socket. A camera angle that looks up into the eye from below will minimize the possibility of these problems. The extent to which the camera angle can be adjusted will depend on the type and brand of eye tracking system that you are using. Some eye tracking systems do not allow for much experimenter control over the angle of the camera, so it may be necessary to adjust the position of the participant's head instead. Of those eye tracking systems that do allow for control over the camera angle, some allow the experimenter to see an image of the eye as filmed by the eye-camera while the camera position is being adjusted. This is ideal, as it allows for direct feedback about how the camera's position affects the detection of the pupil and the cornea. Other systems do not provide this full information, but instead use a simplified representation of the eye, such as a dot that changes color depending on how accurately the features of the eye are being detected. While such a system does not give the same wealth of information to the experimenter as an actual image of the eye, the experimenter can try various camera positions using a trial-and-error approach until the simplified representation indicates that the eye is being accurately tracked.

Once the calibration process has completed, it is important to validate the calibration and confirm that the participant was looking at the appropriate locations throughout. That is, even though the calibration has completed, it may be the case that the participant was not looking at one or more of the calibration points (e.g., due to blinking or moving the eyes) when the image of the eye was taken. Depending on the model of eye tracker that is used, this validation process will vary. For example, some systems give a numeric accuracy value representing the average deviation between the calibration points and the estimated gaze positions. It has been suggested that a maximum average deviation of 0.5° should be required for most studies (Holmqvist et al., 2011). Other studies will simply provide an image overlaying the estimated gaze positions on the calibration points. This makes validation more difficult to keep consistent, as it relies on a qualitative, rather than quantitative, judgement. However, with sufficient experience and training a researcher can learn to identify when a calibration is sufficiently accurate.

Troubleshooting Common Problems in Data Collection

When setting up the eye tracker and calibrating it for each participant, a number of common problems may arise that can lead to poor quality data. Table 1 presents some of these problems and suggested solutions for each.

Some participants have "droopy" eyelids that may partially cover the pupil from certain camera angles, preventing the eye tracker from being able to calculate the pupil's position relative to the corneal reflection and thereby

TABLE 1 Common Problems Encountered in Eye-Gaze Data Collection and Suggested Solutions

Common Problems	Suggested Solutions
Droopy eyelids partially covering pupil	- Position camera so that it views eye from below
	- Test in a well-lit room, so that the pupil remains relatively small
	- Encourage participants to keep eyes open wide
	- Use adhesive tape to lift upper eyelid
Long hair covering eyes	- Have hair ties and/or pins available to participants
Mascara causing eyelashes to partially cover pupil	- Instruct participants not to wear mascara
	- Have eye makeup removal kit available to participants
Eye-glasses reflecting infrared light	- Position camera so that reflection is positioned further away from the pupil - Ask participant whether they are comfortable viewing the stimuli without their glasses
Bubbles under contact lenses interfering with corneal reflection	- Reduce focus of eye camera
Infrared illumination and shadows from external light sources	- Conduct testing in an artificially lit room with good shades or without windows

interfering with the estimation of gaze position. Droopy eyelids can be due to a variety of factors including the participant's age, genetics, level of tiredness, and degree of engagement with the task. Several solutions to this problem have been suggested, the most important of which is to ensure that the eye camera is viewing the eye from below, as this reduces the likelihood that the eyelid will occlude the pupil and/or corneal reflection for most positions of the eye. Another useful solution is to ensure that the testing room is well illuminated, so that the pupil is relatively small; this reduces the extent to which droopy eyelids will occlude the pupil. Other options include instructing the participant to keep the eyes open wide while completing the task, or even using small pieces of adhesive tape to gently lift the participant's upper eyelid (Holmqvist et al., 2011). However, the lattermost option may be considered too intrusive or uncomfortable for some participants.

Another common issue is that participants will arrive to a testing session wearing mascara. This can also lead to problems in pupil detection, as the eye tracker can become confused between the dark spot that corresponds to the location of the pupil, and the dark patch of mascara-coated eyelashes that may be partially covering the eye. Solutions to this problem include having clear instructions to participants that they should not wear mascara on the day of testing, and to have an eye makeup removal kit available for participants who may disregard these instructions.

Glasses and contact lenses can also be a potential source of frustration for eye tracking researchers. In the case of glasses, the problem is usually that infrared illumination reflects off the glass and is confused by the eye tracker for the corneal reflection, or in some cases that shadows from the frame of the glasses interfere with the detection of the pupil. These problems can typically be addressed by adjusting the angle of the eye camera so that any reflection and/or shadow from the glasses is not projected over the eye and is therefore easier for the eye tracker to distinguish from the critical features of the eye. However, in some cases, such as when the participant wears bifocal lenses, which introduce a border into the image of the eye, adjusting the position of the camera may not be sufficient. In these cases, the experimenter may wish to raise the possibility of the participant completing the experiment without wearing glasses. Obviously, whether this is an appropriate approach will depend on the demands of the task and the quality of the participant's vision without glasses. If the participant needs to focus on fine-grained detail (e.g., the orientation of lines, details of photographic images, or text), then asking participants to remove their glasses may lead to participant discomfort as well as poor quality data. On the other hand, if the task involves looking at simple stimuli like geometric shapes, then this may be a workable solution. In the case of contact lenses, small bubbles that get trapped under soft contact lenses can interfere with the detection of the corneal reflection. It has been suggested that a potential solution to this problem would be to reduce the focus of the eye camera (Holmqvist et al., 2011). However, it is not always possible for the researcher to adjust the focus of the camera, especially when using remote eye tracking systems, as many of these systems automatically adjust their focus to allow the participant's head to be positioned at different distances from the eye tracker.

Another major concern is reflections and/or shadows that are caused by external sources of infrared light. Sunlight contains significant levels of infrared light that can be reflected off the cornea, outshining the reflection from the eye tracker's infrared illumination source and causing problems for the gaze-estimation algorithm. This can be addressed by conducting all testing in a room that either has high-quality shades installed or is free of windows entirely. However, as mentioned above, this does not mean that the testing should be conducted in a dark room, as that may lead to problems with pupil detection. Rather, a room that is well-lit by a single artificial light source will typically produce the highest quality data.

Despite the experimenter's best efforts, there are likely going to be some participants who will arrive at a testing session and are simply too difficult to track with sufficient quality. What to do in these cases will vary depending on whether the study that you are running will analyze the eye-gaze data offline, or if instead there are online gaze-contingent manipulations in the task (i.e., situations in which the participant's gaze determines the events that occur in the experiment). If gaze data are to be analyzed offline, it would be advisable to continue with testing and collect the participant's data. It will always be possible to exclude a subset of subjects' eye-gaze data during analysis, and there may end up being some salvageable data, such as any behavioral measures that might be taken. In the case of gaze-contingent designs, it may be more appropriate to send the participant away after giving appropriate reimbursement, as trying to complete the task may become too frustrating—for both participant and experimenter!

DATA ANALYSIS

Data Preprocessing

When first getting started with eye tracking research, it can be easy to feel overwhelmed by all the data made available to you. Some systems output >1000 samples per second across many different variables, such as the timestamp of each sample, two-dimensional gaze coordinates, three-dimensional gaze coordinates, eye position coordinates, validity/event codes, and pupil size. If you are using a binocular eye tracking system, all this information may be provided for both eyes, effectively doubling the amount of data to work through. Therefore, the first step in any data analysis procedure is to process and condense the data into a more manageable form, by selecting the time period of interest—in our art gallery advertising study, this will be the time that the images of paintings were on the screen—and the variables of interest, namely:

- Timestamp: a high precision record (e.g., in microseconds) of the exact time at which each sample of gaze location was recorded by the eye tracker relative to the time that the eye tracking hardware was started. This is sometimes referred to as the remote timestamp. It can be analyzed with respect to comparable timestamp data from the computer (the local timestamp), which will mark when stimulus events or responses occurred.
- Horizontal and vertical (*X* and *Y*) two-dimensional gaze coordinates, that record the location on the screen at which gaze was estimated to fall at that time.
- Validity/event codes: sometimes the eye tracker fails to record gaze at a particular sample time, perhaps because the participant was blinking, or because the tracker could not estimate pupil position due to one of the problems listed in Table 1. At other times, the tracker may be able to estimate pupil position, but with a low degree of confidence. Some eye tracking systems will output a validity code that records whether, for a particular gaze sample, the tracker has been able to estimate gaze with high confidence, low confidence, or not at all. Other systems may parse the data into eye-movement events, giving an event code for each sample indicating whether it is thought to be part of a blink, failure to detect gaze, fixation, or saccade.

The first part of the data analysis process is relatively simple when using a monocular eye tracking system: it simply involves loading the data, which is usually saved as a text file, into a data analysis program like R or MATLAB and selecting the relevant variables from the data matrix. However, when working with a binocular eye tracking system, the dual streams of data make analysis somewhat more complicated. In order to keep the data analysis workflow as simple as possible, it is usually preferable to condense the streams of data from each eye into a single stream. There are several different methods that researchers have used to do this. One common option is to average across the estimated gaze coordinates for the left and right eye. This has the added advantage of substantially improving the precision and accuracy of the gaze data (Cui & Hondzinski, 2006). However, it relies on the assumption that the left and right eye are moving in similar ways at similar points in time. Depending on the design and variables of interest in your experiment, this may not necessarily be the case (for example, when studying vergence movements, you would expect the eyes to move in opposite directions as a stimulus moves closer to or further away from the participant). Other options for condensing binocular data include examining the quality of the data for each eye (e.g., by looking at the proportion of the samples in which gaze was validly estimated, as indicated by validity codes) and either picking the eye that has the higher proportion of valid samples across the whole experiment or picking the eye that has the higher proportion of valid samples on each trial. Both of these options condense the binocular data down to a single stream but depending on the design of the experiment it may not always be appropriate to analyze a different eye for each participant or each trial.

After the continuous data for each trial have been condensed into a simplified form, the next step is to trim these data down to a time window, or epoch, that contains only the data from the critical period of the trial. In the art gallery advertising experiment described earlier, the critical period would be the 1500 ms when both painting stimuli were presented on the screen. This trimming process is done by using the local timestamp data that was collected by the software that controlled the presentation of the stimuli in the experiment. Depending on the eye tracking system that you are using, these timestamps may need to be converted into the same format as the remote timestamps from the eye tracker itself. In the case of the Tobii systems that we have used in our lab, the manufacturer's software provides a function that can be used to easily convert local timestamps into remote timestamps, or vice versa. After all timestamps are in a consistent format, it is simply a matter of programming a function to select the samples with timestamps greater than some designated "start time" (e.g., when stimuli appear) and less than or equal to a designated "stop time" (e.g., when the stimuli are removed from the display).

Once the data have been condensed to the variables and time periods of interest, the final preprocessing step is determining what to do with the periods in which the system could not estimate the gaze position. These segments of blank data usually correspond to times in which the participant was blinking but may also represent periods where the participant was looking away from the screen, or in which the eye tracker could not determine the location of the pupil and corneal reflection due to interference from droopy eyelids or other problems. As noted above, some eye tracking systems, such as the Tobii systems that we typically use, provide validity codes to assist with identifying these periods. In this case, it is simply a matter of finding the samples in the stream of data that have validity codes indicating that neither eye was validly tracked. However, in systems that do not provide these validity codes, it may be necessary to look through the X and Y coordinate data for brief segments in which the gaze coordinates suddenly change to zeros. What to do with these periods will once again depend on the design of your experiment and the variables that you are using. If it is essential to have a constant stream of valid gaze data throughout the critical period of the trial, then you may want to discard entirely any trials that contain blinks. However, in most simple dwell time designs, it is usually more practical to simply remove the periods of these blinks and analyze the data surrounding them. It is also possible to approximate the missing data by using linear interpolation. For example, if we know that a participant's eyes were on coordinates $[X_{n-1}, Y_{n-1}]$ at Time_{n-1} and on $[X_{n+1}, Y_{n+1}]$ at Time_{n+1}, we could interpolate the missing data point $[X_n, Y_n]$ at $Time_n$ using the following formulas:

$$X_n = \frac{(Time_n - Time_{n-1})(X_{n+1} - X_{n-1})}{(Time_{n+1} - Time_{n-1})} + X_{n-1}$$

$$Y_n = \frac{(Time_n - Time_{n-1})(Y_{n+1} - Y_{n-1})}{(Time_{n+1} - Time_{n-1})} + Y_{n-1}$$

This approach may seem like a useful way of "recovering" the missing data. However, it is important to be wary when interpolating data in this way. While it is possible that the participant was looking at the screen during the period of missing data, and thus that the interpolation provides a "good enough" estimate of gaze location, it is also possible that the participant may not have been looking at the screen at all during this period. This could be problematic if you are interested in determining whether the participant looked at a particular stimulus on the screen, in that your analysis might indicate that the participant's gaze was on that stimulus, but in reality, the participant's eyes were closed. For this reason, it is advisable to use interpolation to estimate gaze location only for short sections of missing data, such as $<$50 ms, which are likely to represent sporadic problems with tracking rather than changes in the participant's behavior.

Defining Areas of Interest

To determine whether participants were looking at certain locations on the screen, how long they were looking at these locations, and perhaps even the order in which they looked at them, we first need to define the AOIs in the display that we want to know about. In the art gallery advertising experiment, this is straightforward: the AOIs are defined by the borders of the rectangular stimuli that are presented on the screen (see Fig. 7A). However, such a clear definition of AOIs may not necessarily be possible in all experiments. For instance, you may wish to know about how participants distributed gaze around the different features of the stimulus, perhaps defining rectangular AOIs around elements of the stimulus (for example, the eyes, mouth, and hands in the paintings we have used in this experiment; see Fig. 7B). Alternatively, you may wish to define your AOI as a circle or ellipse around some feature of the stimulus, for example as shown in Fig. 7C.

Defining rectangular AOIs using data analysis software such as MATLAB is quite easy. It is simply a matter of creating a vector of X and Y coordinates for the top-left and bottom-right vertices of the rectangle, e.g., $[X_1, Y_1, X_2, Y_2]$. Circular AOIs can be defined by a vector containing the center point of the AOI as well as the radius, e.g., $[X_C, Y_C, r]$. See Fig. 8 for an illustration of these definitions.

A Simple Method for Calculating Dwell Time

One of the simplest units of analysis for AOI-based eye tracking designs is dwell time. A dwell is defined as a single visit to the AOI, from the point that the eyes first enter the AOI until they exit. Dwell time is simply the amount of total time across the entire trial in which the eyes were dwelling on one of the AOIs. Calculating dwell time involves stepping through the samples one by

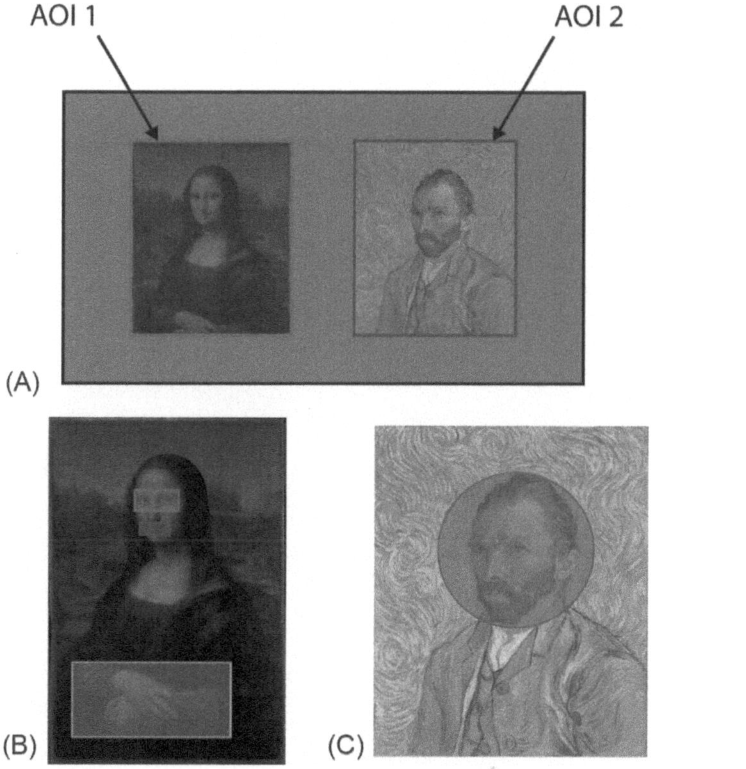

FIG. 7 Examples of different types of AOIs: (A) the AOIs are defined by the borders of the stimuli used in the experiment, (B) rectangular AOIs centered around various features of the stimulus, and (C) a circular AOI centered around a feature of the stimulus.

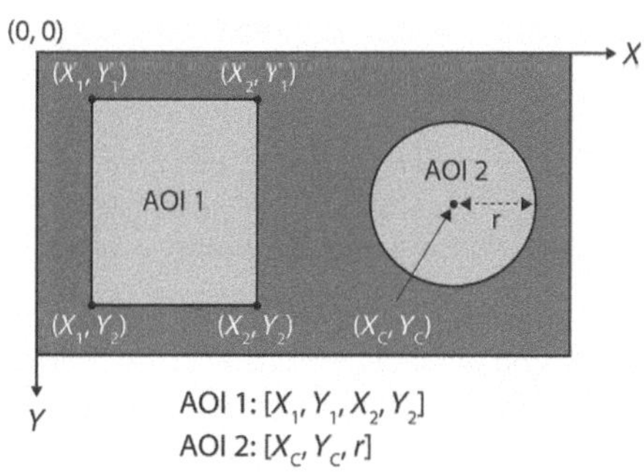

FIG. 8 Definitions of rectangular and circular AOIs.

one, determining whether each is located within one of the AOIs, keeping a running total of the number of samples per AOI, and then finally multiplying the number of samples in each AOI by the sampling frequency of the eye tracking system that was used. Pseudocode for two basic dwell time analysis programs, one for rectangular AOIs and one for circular AOIs, is presented in Fig. 9.

```
Dwell time analysis for rectangular AOIs

- define AOIs as [X1, Y1, X2, Y2]
- FOR each participant:
        - FOR each trial in the experiment:
                - determine which stimulus was presented in each AOI
                - FOR each data sample in the trial:
                        - extract Gaze_X and Gaze_Y co-ordinates
                        - FOR each AOI:
                                - IF Gaze_X is greater than X1 AND
                                  Gaze_X is less than X2 AND
                                  Gaze_Y is greater than Y1 AND
                                  Gaze_Y is less than Y2 THEN:
                                        - add 1 to store of samples on current
                                          AOI for current participant
- multiply stores of samples by interval between samples to obtain total
  dwell time on each AOI
- divide total time with gaze on each AOI by number of trials to obtain
  mean dwell time per trial
```

```
Dwell time analysis for circular AOIs

- define AOIs as [XC, YC, r]
- FOR each participant:
        - FOR each trial in the experiment:
                - determine which stimulus was presented in each AOI
                - FOR each data sample in the trial:
                        - extract Gaze_X and Gaze_Y co-ordinates
                        - FOR each AOI:
                                - IF (Gaze_X-XC)^2 + (Gaze_Y-YC)^2 < r^2
                                        - add 1 to store of samples on current
                                          AOI for current participant
- multiply stores of samples by interval between samples to obtain total
  dwell time on each AOI
- divide total time with gaze on each AOI by number of trials to obtain
  mean dwell time per trial
```

FIG. 9 Pseudocode for determining dwell time on rectangular and circular AOIs.

After the total dwell time on each AOI has been calculated across each trial, means can be calculated for each participant, and quantitative data analysis techniques such as analysis of variance (ANOVA) and/or *t*-tests can be conducted to compare the average dwell time across the different types of stimuli.

SUMMARY

Eye tracking is rapidly becoming a widely-adopted experimental technique in the social sciences due to its ability to provide insight into a range of otherwise covert cognitive processes. However, for those researchers interested in delving into the world of eye tracking, understanding how and where to start can be overwhelming. Here we have presented a simple introduction to the technical aspects of video-based eye tracking, including an explanation of the advantages and disadvantages of the various different types of eye tracking systems, tips for calibrating and recording eye gaze data, and simple methods for analyzing eye tracking experiments that can be used as a starting point for would-be eye tracking researchers. It is worth noting that the field of eye tracking is well-established, with a number of highly detailed methodological texts covering all sorts of different techniques and eye-movement measures (e.g., Duchowski, 2017; Holmqvist et al., 2011). What we have provided here should be enough to get you started, but as you further exploit the potential of eye tracking in your research, you will likely want to consult some of these more advanced texts.

References

Agrawal, Y., Schubert, M. C., Migliaccio, A. A., Zee, D. S., Schneider, E., Lehnen, N., et al. (2014). Evaluation of quantitative head impulse testing using search coils versus video-oculography in older individuals. *Otology & Neurotology*, *35*, 283–288.

Andersson, R., Nyström, M., & Holmqvist, K. (2010). Sampling frequency and eye tracking measures: How speed affects durations, latencies, and more. *Journal of Eye Movement Research*, 3.

Beesley, T., Nguyen, K. P., Pearson, D., & Le Pelley, M. E. (2015). Uncertainty and predictiveness determine attention to cues during human associative learning. *The Quarterly Journal of Experimental Psychology*, *68*, 2175–2199.

Beesley, T., Pearson, D., & Le Pelley, M. (2015). Implicit learning of gaze-contingent events. *Psychonomic Bulletin & Review*, *22*, 800–807.

Bekerman, I., Gottlieb, P., & Vaiman, M. (2014). Variations in eyeball diameters of the healthy adults. *Journal of Ophthalmology*, *2014*.

Brainard, D. H. (1997). The psychophysics toolbox. *Spatial Vision*, *10*, 433–436.

Bulling, A., Ward, J. A., Gellersen, H., & Tröster, G. (2011). Eye movement analysis for activity recognition using electrooculography. *IEEE Transactions on Pattern Analysis and Machine Intelligence*, *33*, 741–753.

Cui, Y., & Hondzinski, J. M. (2006). Gaze tracking accuracy in humans: Two eyes are better than one. *Neuroscience Letters*, *396*, 257–262.

Duchowski, A. T. (2017). Eye tracking techniques. In *Eye tracking methodology: Theory and practice* (2nd ed.). Cham: Springer International Publishing.

Godijn, R., & Theeuwes, J. (2002). Programming of endogenous and exogenous saccades: Evidence for a competitive integration model. *Journal of Experimental Psychology: Human Perception and Performance*, *28*, 1039–1054.

Hansen, D. W., & Ji, Q. (2010). In the eye of the beholder: A survey of models for eyes and gaze. *IEEE Transactions on Pattern Analysis and Machine Intelligence*, *32*, 478–500.

Holmqvist, K., Nyström, M., Andersson, R., Dewhurst, R., Jarodzka, H., & Weijer, J. V. D. (2011). *Eye tracking: A comprehensive guide to methods and measures*. Oxford, UK: Oxford University Press.

Inchingolo, P., & Spanio, M. (1985). On the identification and analysis of saccadic eye movements-a quantitative study of the processing procedures. *IEEE Transactions on Biomedical Engineering*, 683–695.

SensoMotoric Instruments (2009). *iView X system manual (Version 2.)*. Berlin, Germany: SensoMotoric Instruments.

Juhola, M., Jäntti, V., & Pyykkö, I. (1985). Effect of sampling frequencies on computation of the maximum velocity of saccadic eye movements. *Biological Cybernetics*, *53*, 67–72.

Larsson, L., Nyström, M., Andersson, R., & Stridh, M. (2015). Detection of fixations and smooth pursuit movements in high-speed eye tracking data. *Biomedical Signal Processing and Control*, *18*, 145–152.

Le Pelley, M. E., Pearson, D., Griffiths, O., & Beesley, T. (2015). When goals conflict with values: Counterproductive attentional and oculomotor capture by reward-related stimuli. *Journal of Experimental Psychology: General*, *144*, 158–171.

Luck, S. J. (2014). *An introduction to the event-related potential technique*. Cambridge, MA: MIT Press.

Martinez-Conde, S., Macknik, S. L., Troncoso, X. G., & Hubel, D. H. (2009). Microsaccades: A neurophysiological analysis. *Trends in Neurosciences*, *32*, 463–475.

Martinez-Conde, S., Otero-Millan, J., & Macknik, S. L. (2013). The impact of microsaccades on vision: Towards a unified theory of saccadic function. *Nature Reviews Neuroscience*, *14*, 83–96.

Nyström, M., Andersson, R., Holmqvist, K., & van de Weijer, J. (2013). The influence of calibration method and eye physiology on eyetracking data quality. *Behavior Research Methods*, *45*, 272–288.

Nyström, M., & Holmqvist, K. (2010). An adaptive algorithm for fixation, saccade, and glissade detection in eyetracking data. *Behavior Research Methods*, *42*, 188–204.

Saez de Urabain, I. R., Johnson, M. H., & Smith, T. J. (2015). GraFIX: A semiautomatic approach for parsing low- and high-quality eye tracking data. *Behavior Research Methods*, *47*, 53–72.

Salvucci, D. D., & Goldberg, J. H. (2000). Identifying fixations and saccades in eye tracking protocols. In *Proceedings of the symposium on eye tracking research & applications—ETRA'00* (pp. 71–78). New York, NY: ACM Press.

SR Research Inc (2007). *EyeLink user manual (version 1)*. Mississauga, Ontario, Canada: Author.

Tobii Technology (2011). *Tobii TX300 eye tracker user manual (version 1)*. Danderyd, Sweden: Tobii Technology.

Vadillo, M. A., Street, C. N. H., Beesley, T., & Shanks, D. R. (2015). A simple algorithm for the offline recalibration of eye tracking data through best-fitting linear transformation. *Behavior Research Methods*, *47*, 1365–1376.

Vidal, M., Bulling, A., & Gellersen, H. (2012). Detection of smooth pursuits using eye movement shape features. In *Proceedings of the symposium on eye tracking research and applications*, (pp. 177–180).

Appendix 2

Using Heart Rate Variability Measures in Social Science Research

Jonas Fooken[1] and Stacey L. Parker[2]
[1]Centre for the Business and Economics of Health, The University of Queensland, Brisbane, QLD, Australia, [2]School of Psychology, The University of Queensland, Brisbane, QLD, Australia

INTRODUCTION

This chapter offers practical advice and shares experience on using heart rate variability (HRV) data in social science experiments, complementing the earlier chapter by Torgler (2018) in this book. Central to this chapter is the notion that using HRV can be valuable in certain research contexts but also has limitations and may not always be the best tool at hand. As the focus is on practical issues, we also describe the time horizon required to make effective use of HRV data, which is relevant to research workflow considerations involving grant application writing, the hiring of PhD students, and related issues. We aim to help the reader new to HRV consider whether using HRV in a study is promising, achievable, and overall a good choice vis-à-vis alternatives. We also offer advice about central questions to ask when preparing an HRV study.

There are three main questions to ask when contemplating the use of HRV data in a research project. The first is the consideration of what type of information HRV data can provide. What—and how much—can HRV data reveal about the target research question? The second consideration concerns the nature of HRV data. That is, what type of data is created in HRV measurements and at what level of precision? The answer to this question will depend on the type of recording device used and the data processing software the researcher relies on. The choice of precision also impacts the feasibility of integrating HRV measurements with other research data to address a particular research question, as HRV does not itself contain information apart from being a physiological indicator. Third, when is HRV data better than other data? We suggest that for the purpose of measuring emotional reactions, HRV data lies somewhere on a scale between the data available from a brain scanner and that available from administering a questionnaire. This chapter is organized around these three questions.

As a set of guidelines, the information in this chapter is far from comprehensive. Rather, it is mainly based on the authors' research experience and discussions with colleagues, including personal conversations, seminars, conferences, and interactions with peer reviewers. Our studies have investigated the relationship of HRV with risk preferences (Fooken & Schaffner, 2016), social preferences (Fooken, 2017), tax compliance decisions (Dulleck et al., 2016), voting decisions (Fooken, Morton, & Torgler, 2018), stressful work events and their regulation (Parker, Jimmieson, & Newton, 2015), and evening recovery from work stress (Parker, Sonnentag, Jimmieson, & Newton, 2018). These studies documented connections between HRV measures and emotionally costly deviations from social norms (Dulleck et al., 2016; Fooken, 2017) and risk taking (Fooken, 2017; Fooken & Schaffner, 2016). They also examined the correspondence of emotional value as measured in the laboratory to that occurring in the real world, documenting the external validity of HRV, by relating laboratory based pro-social decisions to stressful events outside of the laboratory (Fooken, 2017) and relating emotions (as measured by HRV) with voting decisions in a real-world voting booth (Fooken et al., 2018). However, we also have observed in laboratory research that HRV measurement can suggest relationships that are absent in survey data (Parker, Laurie, Newton, & Jimmieson, 2014). Unlike survey data, HRV is measured continuously during performance of a task, allowing it to capture the emotional experience of that task while it is occurring, rather than only after it has been completed and a survey is administered.

This chapter draws together selected insights we have learned in the process of planning and conducting these studies, focusing particularly on practical issues. The goal is to provide field-tested advice for researchers contemplating or carrying out research projects using HRV in economics, psychology, political science, or other social science disciplines.

HRV: WHAT TYPE OF INFORMATION IS PROVIDED?

Heart Rate Variability Versus Heart Rate

HRV measures, as the name suggests, the variability of the heart rate. New users of HRV often intuitively start at an even more basic level, the heart rate. The heart rate, typically measured as the number of heart beats per minute, is not

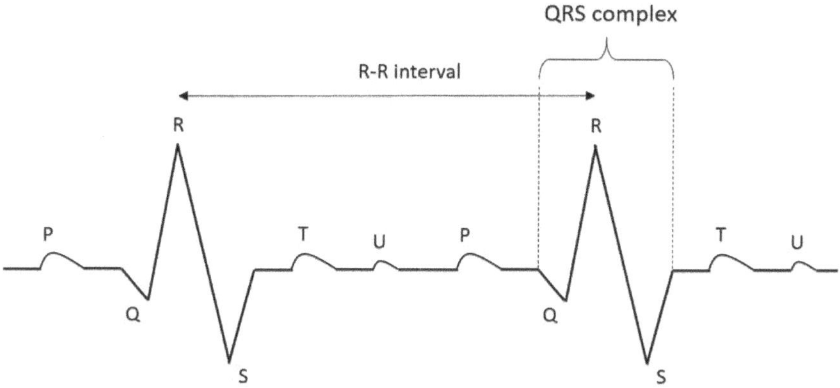

FIG. 1 Illustration of the ECG trace, highlighting R-R intervals and the QRS complex.

the target quantity when HRV is measured. This is not to say the heart rate is uninformative or uninteresting for researchers, but information provided by the heart rate and information provided by HRV are quite different. Simply speaking, the heart rate provides information about the level of physical activity of an individual—for example, our heart rate is typically higher when we are (or have just been) running. HRV, by contrast, is a measure of the change in the lag between two (or more) heart beats over time, and hence it can capture changes in the rhythm of the heart rate, including acceleration and deceleration as well as the strength of changes. The lag between beats that underpins HRV measures is illustrated in Fig. 1. Not only does HRV change when we start or stop running, but it constantly adjusts all the time. Its continual change is part of what makes it interesting from a research point of view.

But what does HRV reflect? The truth is that we as a research community do not know exactly what it tells us, but we can empirically observe it. It is seen as an output of the autonomous nervous system and is interpreted in this context as informing us about unconscious and uncontrollable bodily reactions such as fight-and-flight responses versus rest-and-relaxation responses. Relevantly for social science researchers, it has also been found to correlate with mental activity, particularly when we are experiencing emotions and when we are under psychological stress or pressure. For example, research has found HRV to be a sensitive index of mental workload (Hoover, Singh, Fishel-Brown, & Muth, 2012; Jorna, 1992), stress and emotion regulation processes (Appelhans & Luecken, 2006; Geisler, Vennewald, Kubiak, & Weber, 2010; Segerstrom & Nes, 2007; Thayer, Åhs, Fredrikson, Sollers III, & Wager, 2012), and even self-control/willpower (see Zahn et al., 2016, for a meta-analysis). See also Massaro and Pecchia (2016) for a review of HRV in the organizational neuroscience literature and a methodological overview.

Hence, in contrast to the heart rate, HRV tells us more about mental activity or stressors, and the regulation of this emotion, than about physical activity.

Nonetheless, HRV is influenced by the level of physical activity, and the patterns of HRV during physical activity are also interesting from a research point of view. However, the interesting feature about HRV from a social science perspective is that it can tell us something about mental processes, which can help us interpret certain behavioral and self-reported measures.

Deciding on a Measurement Approach

While the measurement of HRV may appear simple, acquiring the measure—i.e., a number to use for later analysis—is quite a complicated task, as it necessarily involves understanding the different possible measurement approaches, selecting and implementing the right one, estimating the target number, and data cleaning. These decisions and steps in the data preparation process can take up a considerable amount of time before a researcher can move to writing up results, for example in an academic paper or thesis. Not only are there several measurement methods, but there are conflicting views about which method is appropriate.

There are two types of approaches to the measurement of HRV: time-domain methods and frequency-domain methods. In our research we have a general preference for frequency-domain methods. However, depending on the context and research question, time-domain methods may be more appropriate, and they are usually understood to be simpler estimation approaches. Massaro and Pecchia (2016) provide more detail on the two methods, what problems may lead to data leakage, and which method is best to address resulting problems. From the same raw data, usually all methods can be calculated, and Massaro and Pecchia (2016) suggest using multiple indicators as a robustness check of results. The different measures are all essentially based on the time between beats, but this information is processed in slightly different ways. We find in our own data that different time-based and frequency-based measures of HRV are highly correlated (with Pearson correlations of between 0.80 and 0.90). Based on the publication trends in psychology, we would recommend the use of HF, a frequency-based measure, or RMSSD, a time based measure (see below). Indeed, in a recent meta-analysis on the link between HRV and self-control (Zahn et al., 2016), 21 papers used HF, while 12 used RMSSD, and some papers used both. We recommend researchers be aware of what is normative in a particular area, which is usually best discovered via targeted literature reviews.

Time-domain methods follow the very basic logic with which HRV has been introduced above—essentially determining the time-based (i.e., millisecond) changes in the heart rate pattern, meaning the lag between successive heart beats. Here the first question to consider is the point in time at which a single heart beat occurs. The so-called QRS complex is usually used to conceptualize the idea of a heart beat, although not all heart beats adhere to this pattern. Fig. 1 illustrates the QRS complex using the electrocardiogram (ECG) trace of two successive heart beats. Each heart beat is described by a sequence of waves, denoted by P, Q, R, S, T, and (sometimes) U. Most basic estimation methods using the change in inter-beat intervals (IBIs) to determine the rate of R-R (or RR or NN) changes, again as illustrated in Fig. 1. In practice, however, it is common to use other measures, including the standard deviation between RR intervals (SDNN). Even more common is to use the root mean square of successive RR interval differences (rMSSR/RMSSD). There are further measures considered in a dynamic literature revisiting the reliability of measures, and which particular measure may be preferred at which point. A good starting point may be to read Porges (2007) and Berntson et al. (1997), and to research further into this literature as required. Massaro and Pecchia (2016) provide further guidance on the advantages and disadvantages of the available methods (particularly when deciding between time- and frequency-domain methods), depending on a given research question and design.

Frequency-domain methods follow a slightly different logic. These methods view HRV patterns as best explained by overlapping signals, which have different frequencies. Intuitively, one may think of different waves that lie on top of each other, creating varying patterns of heart rates over discrete periods of time. The basic idea of these methods is that an entire heart rate pattern can be decomposed into distinct underlying frequencies. These frequencies of the heart rate can be classified into different domains: the high frequency (HF), the low frequency (LF), the very low frequency (VLF), and the ultra-low frequency (ULF). The commonly-used respiratory sinus arrhythmia (RSA) is understood as a component of HF, or closely related to it (Massaro & Pecchia, 2016). RSA is understood as part of the synchronization of breathing and heart rate, with the R-R interval being shortened during inspiration and prolonged during expiration, and changes in breathing consequently influencing HRV.

Each frequency domain has a particular importance (or "power") at a particular point in time for determining the heart rate, and its power relative to the other frequency domains changes over time. This power can in turn be estimated using a number of methods, for example via fast-Fourier transformation (FFT). See, for example, Fooken and Schaffner (2016) or Fooken (2017), who both use so-called wavelet methods, or Parker et al. (2014), who use FFT. While being relatively complicated and based upon computation-intensive estimation, frequency-domain-based HRV measures are usually provided by ready-made software delivered together with heart rate (variability) recording devices. Such tools are convenient, and make the generation of the HRV measure essentially a black box from the researcher's perspective. We encourage researchers who find themselves using such software to contact the software developers directly if they wish to gain a better understanding of the program settings that define the estimations, which is what Parker et al. (2014) were able to do.

Alternatively, other custom-designed software can be used to implement HRV estimation, such as Matlab programs like ANSLAB or HRVAS. Both programs include open source elements, allowing relatively easy use and closer oversight of the estimation process. Another option is the program Kubios (https://www.kubios.com/; Tarvainen, Niskanen, Lipponen, Ranta-Aho, & Karjalainen, 2014), a popular and freely downloadable HRV analysis software designed for use by researchers. Kubios is in its third edition now and provides good processing power along with flexibility in determining the analysis settings. Researchers interested in the RSA measure of HRV might also consider using the software developed by the research group headed by Stephen W. Porges, Cardio Edit and Cardio Batch, accessible by contacting the research team directly. Finally, researchers may design an estimation program themselves, as done for Dulleck et al. (2016), Fooken and Schaffner (2016), and Fooken (2017). However, this requires some degree of programming skill and time investment. Furthermore, the calculation of HRV measures, particularly for longer durations (of several hours), can be time consuming and may require enhanced computing power.

Not only do frequency-domain methods produce measures of HRV, but the power of certain frequency domains can be interpreted, although there is some controversy about what exactly each frequency tells us. Usually, the LF and the HF are deemed to be the most interesting measures in the context of social science research as they appear to inform about the psychological or emotional activity of decision makers. HF is theorized to be a measure of parasympathetic cardiac control (Thayer et al., 2012). LF is sometimes considered a measure of sympathetic nervous system activity, but this is contested, and many researchers are more comfortable saying that we do not know what exactly LF measures (Berntson, Norman, Hawkley, & Cacioppo, 2008; Porges, 2007). VLF and ULF, although calculated by many available HRV analysis programs, are not usually interpreted by social science researchers. The importance of HF is also reflected in literature using RSA as an HRV indicator, which is highly similar to HF measures. Some researchers also use the ratio of the LF and the HF (i.e., LF/HF, or "LFHF"), which is said to inform about the "sympathovagal balance" of a decision maker (see also Berntson et al., 2008). The term "sympothovagal balance" refers to a bodily state in which the sympathetic and parasympathetic systems, which are responsible for fight-or-flight and rest-and-relaxation responses, respectively, and which are both constantly active, are balanced. However, the use of LF/HF is not universally accepted, because of the contested meaning of LF measures. A significant body of research uses LFHF measures, allowing researchers to benchmark their results against "normal" ranges of LFHF reported in other samples. For example, LFHF measures between 1.5 and 2 would generally be considered "normal" values (Task Force of the European Society of Cardiology and the North American Society of Pacing and Electrophysiology, 1996). While values outside of the normal range may indicate a strong physiological response, the possibility of artifactual outliers in the data should be considered. For example, one may discard data with LFHF <0 or LFHF >20, as such measures appear to be likely due to measurement error or artifact of the estimation technique used (this exclusion rule was used in Fooken & Schaffner, 2016; Fooken, 2017; Fooken et al., 2018, and typically eliminated somewhat <5% of observations at the tails). Another alternative to help "normalize" HRV data is to transform it with a (natural) logarithm, which has become conventional in some research areas.

Which Method Should you Use?

As outlined above, the choice of the best measurement approach is far from trivial. Resources to support this choice of method include Porges (2007), who provides an overview for measures using the time domain, publications by Camm et al. (1996), Task Force of the European Society of Cardiology and the North American Society of Pacing and Electrophysiology (1996), and Berntson et al. (1997). In the context of using HRV measures specifically in social science research, Appelhans and Luecken (2006) is very useful, providing a technical yet also intuitive understanding of what different measures can ultimately be used for. These publications can serve as a good starting point for understanding alternative HRV measures and determining which might best suit a particular research project. Massaro and Pecchia (2016), which includes further information about the practical choice of method, also provide insights on the choice of method and argue that using both frequency based and time based methods may be advisable in documenting the robustness of findings.

Getting a Good Recording

The following may serve as a simple checklist for generating high-quality HRV measurement in an experiment:

- Place electrode pads on the chest, as this placement will minimize artifactual measurement due to movement.
  - Sometimes, in case of men with large amounts of chest hair, recordings may be impaired. One solution is to request selected participants to shave. Otherwise, poor recording quality may need to be accepted. Also see the electrode placement instructions accompanying the heart rate monitoring device.
  - For women, researchers should be aware of personal modesty considerations and always allow for privacy in placing electrodes on the chest area. There can also be practical considerations, such as if the underwire in a bra puts pressure on the electrode, depending on its position. Allow the time and space to make necessary corrections to electrode placement.
- Prepare your participants!
  - In laboratory research, Parker has used these instructions to prepare participants before their testing session:

    "Please remember that during the session we will measure your heart rate. Because of this physiological measure, we would ask that you please abstain from alcohol and other drugs 24 h prior to your session, to please not eat two hours prior to the session, and finally to please not exercise on the day of the session. Your heart rate is measured via four leads attached to your chest area via disposable electrode stickers. The researcher will help you position these electrodes onto yourself, so you can then connect yourself to the heart rate monitor. For your comfort, we recommend you wear a loose-fitting shirt on the day."

- In the case of conducting lab-in-the-field studies, participants might need to connect or reconnect themselves. For this reason, a good induction, some training, and take-home instruction materials are important. It may also be desirable to provide subjects with researchers' contact details in case of trouble.
- Sufficient time should be allowed for set up and connection of the heart rate monitor. Participants who have not previously used a recording device will require at least 10–15 min of preparation and connection time. Longer time periods are required if participants use the device independently.
- Use good quality monitors!
  - Monitors that produce multiple-channel ECG trace reports (as illustrated in Fig. 1), requiring several electrodes to be attached are preferred to so-called IBI monitors that detect only the R-peak shown in Fig. 1. Recorders based on smartphone applications and wearables usually do not record data of sufficient quality for scientific purposes.
  - Devices that allow you to view the ECG trace in real time once a participant is connected are preferred. This real time monitoring allows the connection and placement of electrodes to be checked and time to be synchronized with other measurement tools (e.g., a participant's watch, when filling out an activity record or diary).

The Type of Device to Use

There are several types of monitors that can be used to record HRV. Some are very simple, nonintrusive or wearable, and potentially connectable to mobile phone applications. However, even most advanced wearables and apps only measure pulse rate or indications of HRV of low reliability. Moreover, these devices and apps rarely allow the researcher access to the raw data, and often automate data cleaning and other postcollection manipulation in ways that might not be suitable. On the other end of the spectrum are medical-grade recorders with a multitude of electrodes attached to a participant's chest and fixed to a nonportable stationary computer. For the purposes of social science research, we recommend selecting a middle ground between these extremes. One advantage of HRV is that it can be recorded in relatively flexible environments, such as in a classical computer laboratory, as well as in lab-in-the-field environments. Very simple tools, such as wristbands, are not precise enough for many scientific purposes. While these tools may provide general information, data collected over relatively short periods is not reliable enough. Therefore, measurement tools with electrodes attached to a participant's chest are more advisable.

HRV can be measured with so-called halter devices that use up to five electrodes. The term halter is usually used for devices that are easily portable (e.g., in the pocket or attached to a belt). Further electrodes usually impede wearability, and the halter nature of the device is much reduced. On the other hand, the more electrodes used (and thus, the more recording channels available), the better the data quality. Given the fact that in most social science research shorter time periods for HRV measurements tend to be more desirable, leading to the need for higher quality data reading, ECG-trace-producing devices with at least three electrodes are advisable. A fourth electrode may further allow to control for breathing patterns, although this point tends to be debated—some evidence suggests breathing pattern has no bearing on HF (e.g., Porges & Byrne, 1992), while other evidence suggests that it can influence LF (e.g., Beda, Simpson, Carvalho, & Carvalho, 2014). It should be kept in mind that devices with more electrodes may have been designed for use in a medical context, where measured individuals wear the device for some time in a nurse's or doctor's office while attached to a larger piece of nonmobile infrastructure. By contrast, in most social science research, participants will wear the electrodes under a shirt during a task or while completing their normal day to day activities.

The presence of a shirt squeezes cables together, which can reduce recording quality. The more cables, the larger the potential entanglement, meaning that more electrodes are not always better. This is particularly the case in contexts where participants may have a natural tendency to cross their arms over the chest, which can interfere with the recording. Similarly, highly synthetic shirts can interfere with the electrical signal recording of the device. For this reason, it is best to advise participants not to wear synthetic fabrics when participating in a study measuring HRV (if such restrictions are deemed acceptable). Ultimately, the device chosen will depend on available budgets, the nature of the research, envisaged participant sample sizes, and related factors. Researchers may also need to consider whether recording devices are suitable for the compliance requirements of a research study. For example, two-lead IBI monitors may be desirable in studies during which participants wear recorders for extended time periods, as the interference with daily activities for the participant, as well as the effort to re-apply the device over several days, are minimized.

THE NATURE OF HRV DATA

Not everything can be measured using HRV—for example, HRV is unlikely to capture the mental or emotional states accompanying decisions of very short duration. One may also wonder about the degree of within- and between-subject variability in HRV measures. Will the researcher be able to detect effects using between-subject measures? Are baseline measures useful in determining the individual-specific component of HRV, and what could these be? What determines the quality of the data, to what degree can data cleaning help, and how is it done? The following sections share our experiences on these issues.

Optimal Duration of Measurement Episodes

How long should an episode of HRV measurement be in order to provide useful data? For the computation of HRV, the typical minimum duration is referred to as the "window width" or "epoch". We will use the term "epoch" in this chapter. Importantly, an epoch is not the rate of sampling of the recording device, which is usually described in Hertz (Hz, where we recommend a sampling rate of 1000 Hz). Rather, an epoch is the duration for which one HRV measurement point will be determined (i.e., HRV at a given moment in time). Most frequency domain techniques have a computational lower bound on the epoch, essentially determined by the underlying logic of the frequencies. This technical lower bound is about 30 s (in data collected in some of the studies of Fooken & Schaffner, 2016; Fooken, 2017, it was 27 s). The epoch is usually set (by default in HRV estimation software) as 30 s, 1 min, or 2 min in duration. This decision is often partly based on how much data there is, or, in other words, the total duration of the recording session within one subject.

Importantly, one epoch should ideally not be what is connected to a given decision, task, or phase of a study that is of interest. See Fig. 2 for an illustration of the relation between epoch and the duration of other tasks of research interest, possible epoch lengths, and aggregation to the HRV variable of interest for a

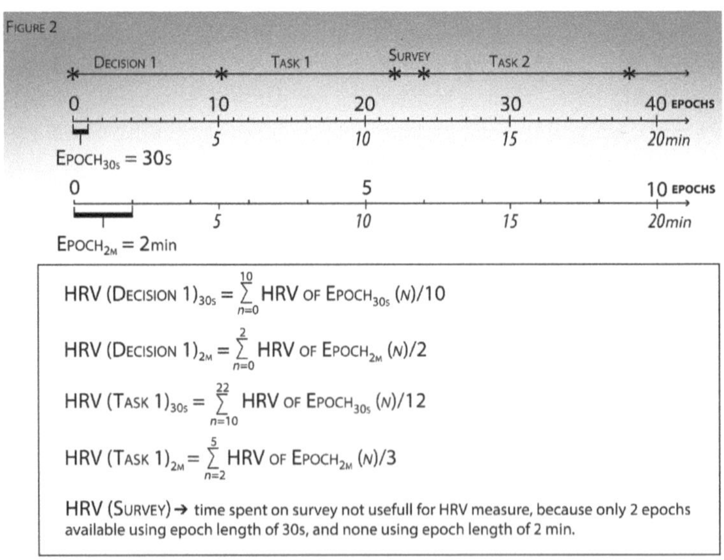

FIG. 2 The relation between epoch and the duration of other tasks of research interest, possible epoch lengths, and aggregation to the HRV variable of interest for a given research question.

given research question. A succession of several epochs is often chosen in connection with another variable of interest—for example, a decision or the time that an experimental participant works on a task. For example, if epochs are chosen to have a length of 30 s and a task is completed over a period of 6 min, then data from the 12 epochs that elapse during the task are averaged and aggregated into the HRV measure that is assigned to the task. If tasks or decisions are longer (e.g., 20 min), longer epochs are possible (e.g., 2 min instead of 30 s).

At least one epoch, and preferably more, is required per event of interest. If possible, the event of interest should be at least 5 min long. Several epochs are averaged over the duration of the event to one HRV measure per event. Hence, all of what happens during the event of interest (e.g., set of decisions taken, performance in a task) will be aggregated over multiple epochs into one event measure that is matched via synchronized time to the HRV measure. Ideally, during the duration of the event, nothing or not much else happens other than the phenomenon of interest.

For example, in Parker's lab-in-the field research (Greenaway, Parker, Hofmann, Newton, & Jimmieson, 2018; Parker et al., 2015, 2018), to match HRV data with surveys (e.g., experience sampling surveys, which are brief surveys that participants do at specific times in situ, reporting on their current experience), 2 min epochs were used and aggregated into time periods of 1 h or 3–4 h, and even 24 h, to correspond with the surveys. But more importantly, the time periods were designed to address in a targeted fashion the research questions of the specific study. In laboratory studies on work stress and coping (e.g., Parker et al., 2014), we have used 1 min epochs and aggregated these into time periods of 5 or 10 min, to correspond with trials, tasks, or surveys.

When measuring HRV, we advise researchers to design their study in a way such that participants are making decisions or doing tasks that span at least 5 min each. Data reliability increases with duration. Time periods shorter than 4 min (although we advise no shorter than 3 min) may be possible, but most likely will necessitate more data cleaning, an often error-prone process that raises the risk of limited replicability. While large effects can still be detected using shorter durations, we do not advise designing any data collection with this in mind from the outset, because if a small but potentially still significant and meaningful effect is present, researchers may not be able to make affirmative judgments about its existence or absence.

Another issue to consider when using relatively short time intervals is that the finer the measurement is meant to be, the more the issue of time synchronization becomes important. For example, in our laboratory research we used computer programs to present our tasks, decisions, and other manipulations to participants. Those programs recorded important timing information using time stamps. Recorded HRV will, in almost all cases, connect with other recording devices (e.g., a computer, if a person is filling out an online questionnaire) and matched based on these time stamps. The time set on the computer and on the HR monitoring device must be therefore be synchronized. Small software programs can then merge these two sets of data based on time.

Within- Versus Between-Individual Analysis

HRV data is subject to large variance, hampering inference, particularly in small samples. Small samples, in turn, are a likely scenario given the somewhat complicated process involved in HRV data collection. Whether within- or between-subject analysis is likely to be more fruitful depends on whether the variance observed in HRV data is mainly due to within-individual variability or differences between individuals. The unfortunate answer to this is that the variance in HRV measures tends to be large both within- and between-individuals. That is, there are level differences in HRV between different subjects as well as differences in how much HRV changes within subjects over time. For this reason, a research design that can account for both within- and between-subject analysis is advisable. For example, repeated measures on individuals can help to normalize individual-specific HRV values, which can then be used in cross-individual analysis.

Candidate activities for baseline measurements of HRV for a given subject include watching TV or videos, or periods of rest, sleep, or sustained physical activity. However, in our experience, constructing baselines sounds more promising than it is. Some individuals may have high HRV during their sleep and show significant indications of stress, but are not stressed during other activities, such as those investigated in the research project at hand. Watching videos or TV may be accompanied by large HRV activity that is not present during other activities. In a way, the "correct" baseline activity may be different for every participant. Furthermore, HRV in social science research will typically be gathered in relatively controlled environments, and changes in HRV during target decisions are best understood when compared with changes during other activities undertaken in this very same environment. However, even here some caution may be necessary. For example, if a "meditation" or "paced breathing" stage is used as a baseline activity in an experiment, even this may lead to different HRV reactions between individuals. Hence, such activities often do not serve as baseline activities very well. Reasons for this could be that some individuals are very relaxed during meditation, while others are emotionally stressed. Whether they are stressed or not during the meditation phase may be unrelated to what is investigated in the project's main research question. Most importantly, how the baseline and treatment manipulations of the study interact is unknown and unobservable to the researcher.

Therefore, it may be most advisable to find baseline measures within the framework of investigation (for example, using activities in the laboratory that mimic the target activity). Alternatively, researchers may consider creating a synthetic baseline. This is done by normalizing HRV measures at a given moment in time using the average HRV of that individual during the full duration of the study. This may be done by demeaning all measures and dividing this normalized value by the individual specific standard deviation, by using multilevel (regression) models, or by using models with individual fixed effects.

Because every individual reacts differently to stimuli, within-participant reactions in HRV can be very different. For this reason, it is advisable to normalize measures within individuals, and subsequently make between-individual comparison of those normalized measures. Useful between-subject design features include using different experimental treatment conditions, using a control condition, or exploiting gradually varying individual responses, such as reported stress level changes in response to questionnaires.

Readers interested in the issue of baselines in laboratory-based physiological research might find Jamieson (1999) useful. Field researchers should also be careful about the use of "baseline" measures, particularly when relying on very short measurement durations to indicate between-person differences (see Heathers, Brown, Coyne, & Friedman, 2015). The homepage of James Heathers (http://jamesheathers.com) also discusses a number of issues in the context of using HRV.

Data Cleaning

As with most data generated on human activity, there is no fully clean data generating process that transforms the truth of reality into a given measure with mathematically exact accuracy. The result of this is that social science data in general, and HRV data in particular, is not clean. The quality of the data depends on several factors and can be impacted by equipment and design choices. Even with high quality collection, data cleaning may be necessary. However, this does not mean that data cleaning is desired; ideally, it should be kept at a minimum.

A first step is visual inspection of the data and identification of very large outliers, which often indicate that a subject's recording is of poor quality. Outliers can be the result of signal misreadings. Checking for outliers is ideally done before HRV data is aggregated over the time period of interest (e.g., of 5 min or more, as described above), but for every epoch calculated (e.g., 30 s to 2 min, as described above). See also Fig. 2 for an illustration for possible epoch lengths used and the potential impact of deleting epoch-level data before aggregation to the HRV data point of interest.

There are two primary ways to correct errors in the data. One is to edit the data. That is, to remove erroneous beats that "look" like measurement artifacts, or to insert beats that the program appears to be failing to detect. Different software programs will allow you to do this in different ways. Another method is to delete "messy" data, for example when the QRS complex is not visible in the ECG trace or the heart rate peak cannot be identified. The shorter the epoch, the fewer data points are at risk of being dropped, which is generally desirable.

Furthermore, data should not be dropped based on visual inspection alone. For transparency and replicability, the criteria for dropping data should always follow general rules, and criteria should be standardized and symmetric. For example, when cutting off tails of the distribution of initial LFHF measurements, a rule might be to drop all observations of LFHF <0 and LFHF >20 if LFHF <0 for the lowest 5% of observations, and LFHF >20 for the top 5% of observations. Overall, while it may be necessary to edit or discard some data, a rule of thumb that has emerged in the literature (e.g., as included in Massaro & Pecchia, 2016) is that no >20% of the data should be eliminated and no >5% of the data should be edited. Furthermore, if 20% of the data is dropped, this should ideally be compensated for by samples that are 20% larger than the originally determined minimum sample size.

WHEN AND WHEN NOT TO USE HRV

There are a number of alternative physiological measures that also relate to mental and emotional states. Some of these alternatives may be better, cheaper, or more practical than HRV for a given project. For example, a researcher may consider using a brain scanner, skin conductance measurements, cortisol measurements, quantitative questionnaires, or qualitative interviews. Factors to consider include equipment cost, availability, and the time needed for data collection and processing.

Another factor relates to physical restrictions. A brain scanner can only be used in a highly controlled laboratory environment, and study participants typically cannot walk around with a brain scanner. In contrast, walking around while under observation is clearly possible with many HRV recording devices. Nevertheless, an HRV recording device is still more invasive than a pedometer or accelerometer (which are usually worn on the wrist), as it is physically attached to the subject via electrode pads and leads. Hence, HRV recording is feasible in some lab-in-the-field settings but can still be limiting. Furthermore, loss of a controlled environment can also create recording errors, including in the process of matching HRV with other data and outcome variables.

What Type of Studies?

The degree of intrusiveness of HRV measurement partly informs the type of research for which is it most suited. Halter devices are relatively unnoticeable for the individual wearing the device after a brief (2–3 min) period of adjustment. Hence, participants can perform most regular activities without any interference with the device. The device in turn records without much technical trouble during most activities, with some exceptions such as intense physical activity or movement. During the latter types of activities, measures may still be recorded, but are unlikely to be comparable to measures taken during the other activities. Perhaps the most interesting interpretations of HRV data are possible when measured individuals perform tasks involving relatively low physical activity, such as sitting down and making choices.

Bearing this in mind, there are two types of studies for which HRV measures may be particularly useful. One is laboratory studies, in which participants engage in sedentary activities and where little movement from the participants is required. HRV is not a barrier to interaction between participants, as is the case with brain scanners or even skin conductance measurements, because the recording device is attached in a way that does not interfere with regular activities. For example, HRV may be very useful in classical laboratory environments in which several participants interact or make simultaneous decisions in groups while facing similar conditions, as in Dulleck et al. (2016). With the use of brain scanners this would not be feasible, because multiple scanners cannot usually be placed in the small space of a laboratory. At the same time, HRV collects objective physiological information that cannot deliberately be controlled by participants, which may be an advantage, depending on the research question.

The second type of study for which HRV can be well suited is lab-in-the-field studies, where the boundaries of the laboratory are expanded. For example, Fooken (2017) used HRV measurements of more and less stressful mental activity during daily activities of participants (students studying versus taking an exam). The difference in mental engagement during studying and during the exam was used to quantify the size effect of HRV correlates during pro-social decisions in a classic laboratory (i.e, to answer a question about how an HRV increase of, say, 0.9 in the laboratory compares to the increase observed in the real world under the additional stress of an exam compared to studying). Fooken et al. (2018) measured the HRV of voters while they took their voting decisions in order to test theories about the emotional elements of voting. Parker et al. (2015) assessed how employees regulate their emotional reactions to stressful work events during the work day (both physiologically via HRV, and psychologically as reported by the participants). Capturing such measures in situ would hardly have been possible using more extensive measurement equipment to record mental or emotional stress levels, such as brain scanners or cortisol sampling.

However, HRV measures are still more difficult to handle than questionnaire-based measures. The time and involvement required from participants is substantial, falling well beyond what is required to simply respond to questions. Furthermore, HRV data alone will deliver very little understanding, and is best combined with other measurement tools.

The Cost of Using HRV Measures

In practice, a factor that often limits the choice of a data collection method is cost. When collecting HRV data, not only are there the fixed costs of acquiring equipment (e.g., HRV recording devices and software to process the generated data), but there are also nonnegligible variable costs.

Halter recording devices, recommended earlier due to their portability, are relatively affordable depending on the device selected. We have personally relied on 3- and 4-electrode ECG trace halter devices supplied by the company Schiller. Parker also has used 2-electrode R-wave detecting (also called inter-beat interval detecting) wearable devices supplied by the company Firstbeat. The cost of a single ECG trace recording device in 2017 was about EUR 3000 (USD 3600) and the cost of the software to generate the data of interest was about EUR 7000 (USD 8400). The cost of an IBI type recording device was about EUR 300 (USD 360) and software was EUR 700 (USD 850). Similar devices by other manufacturers of HRV recording equipment are priced comparably or slightly less—for example, the price of an alternative device, Faros 360, was about EUR 1500 (USD 1800), although its accompanying software package was slightly more expensive. Before purchasing equipment, researchers are advised to consider how they will use the device, how many parallel devices are needed for recording and data processing, and by how many researchers the devices will be used at different moments in time. Further features such as battery life, the ability to observe live feedback, the feasibility of time synchronization, and the ease of data storage and transfer functions should also be considered.

As a recording device can only be used by one person at a time, the number of devices required should correspond to the desired sample size of subjects in a given study - specifically, to how many participants the researcher wants to test simultaneously (e.g., groups of 5 or 20?)—plus at least one additional device for cases of technical malfunction. While the functionality of devices should always be checked on the day prior to a data collection session, recording failures or device dysfunction may still occur. A one-in-ten spare recording device rule appears reasonable. The reason is that sufficient numbers of participants are usually not easy to attain, as recruiting for HRV studies is more difficult than for other experimental or observational studies that do not involve HRV measurements. For example, the time, effort and possibly anticipated uneasiness associated with carrying a device may dissuade would-be subjects from participating. At the same time, it is particularly important for HRV data usability to have sufficient observations, because statistical power critically depends on the number of participants and obtaining clean data on them. For these reasons, we advise allowing for much more generous buffers when planning recruitment if using HRV devices than when running conventional experiments.

The *variable* costs of HRV recording include the costs of electrode pads needed to connect the recording device to a participant's chest and the administrative costs of data cleaning. In 2017, the cost of electrode pads was about EUR 125 (USD 150) for a box of 500 if these are for usage over a few hours up to a full day, and EUR 190 (USD 230) for a box of 500 pads that will last for longer recordings. Electrodes generally come in small bags of 25 but are usually purchased in larger quantities. Bulk purchasing is usually cheaper and sometimes electrodes are only available in bulk, but the pads have a relatively short expiry period, and an open pack should be used within 3 days. Using old or expired packs is not recommended, because the recording quality suffers. The reason for this is that electrodes work by using a wet conductor liquid that connects the skin and the metal receptor; the more the liquid dries, the less it conducts and consequently the recorded data becomes of lower quality. Closed packs are usually good for up to 1 or 2 years (but check the expiry date), which may seem long but is a relatively short time within the context of an HRV research agenda. Electrode pads sold at reasonable prices usually need to be ordered somewhat in advance. About 1 month should be allowed for this, in addition to time required by an institution to make payments to a supplier. Hence, time management as well as cost management is necessary.

The most significant variable costs in HRV measurement involve the administration of the process of data collection, as well as data cleaning and coding, work usually performed by one or several research assistants due to the high amount of relatively repetitive tasks.

To help participants attach a device, explain its basic functionalities, describe what kind of actions are best to avoid, and answer participants' questions, 10 min per participant are easily invested. Furthermore, as the electrodes are often attached in private (with or without assistance of the research assistant, depending on the participant's comfort), the research assistant may need to wait until the participant has comfortably attached the electrodes. If researchers want to double-check that the device has been correctly attached, checking by a research assistant (ideally not the involved researcher) of the same gender is recommended. However, in our experience, participants usually attach the pads and the device correctly when adequate time and examples that provide sufficient and clear instructions are given to them. Hence, having same-gender research assistants may not be the most crucial concern. For lab-in-the-field research where participants may need to connect and reconnect themselves, pre-study induction/training (or a video demonstration) is advisable, as well as other instructions/materials (e.g., a FAQ sheet and the researchers' contact details). It is also advisable to have further research assistants available when handling large groups of individuals at once (and consider research assistant training beforehand), because others may have to wait until all participants are ready, which can take a long time if everyone is in the same queue.

The time required for setting up can be variable and the total time required to get a participant ready can be reduced by providing the required support to participants. For example, a study recording HRV of voters arriving at a voting location used numerous research assistants and designated spaces for applying the electrodes, and ensured experienced researchers were available to provide further explanations if required (Fooken et al., 2018). In a study on work stress (Parker et al., 2015), participants wore the monitors over one working week, and to enable them to connect and reconnect themselves during the time period of the study they undertook a one-hour study induction where they were trained in how to use the monitors and were allowed to ask questions. This is helpful because participants in such studies can be curious about what is being measured or may simply be reassured by the presence of a person available for questions. Because HRV measurement requires high involvement and commitment by participants, all steps of should be taken to make it as easy as possible for participants. Finally, because the recording device may not be noticeable to a participant after a few minutes of wearing it, researchers should be aware that participants may accidentally walk away and forget to return the monitor. In ongoing lab-in-the-field research of Parker et al. (2015, 2018) where participants take the monitors home with them, a reply-paid postbag has been supplied to help with the return of monitors. This has never been a problem in our experience, but the promise of tailored individual feedback on the HRV recording has served as an incentive both to participate and to return the monitor.

Further costs may arise when providing incentives to participants. These can be direct monetary incentives (payments to participants), but often also nonmonetary incentives, such as feedback about the recording. Without any incentive it may be very difficult to recruit participants. Providing feedback can be very time intensive, particularly if a formal report on heart rate activity is provided. If prepared by a research assistant, a report on a single subject may require 1 h of preparation plus up to an additional hour for meeting with the subject in person to provide feedback. Training research assistants for such tasks can also be highly time consuming. Significant time costs also arise when research assistants are given data cleaning tasks.

Necessary Sample Sizes

Different disciplines within the social sciences have differing standards as to what is considered a sufficiently large sample. We therefore recommend considering sample sizes that take account of the nature of the HRV data and the fact that it displays large variance both within- and between-participants. In the presence of larger variance, larger samples are usually required to identify effects, unless differences between conditions or treatments, or relevant covarying explanatory variables, have a very large effect on the outcome (which can be the case for HRV). The problem of large variance can only be partly mitigated by using longer measurement periods of HRV, because HRV and changes in HRV in response to a stimulus can differ across days within individuals. Repeatedly measuring the same individual can introduce more noise, which reduces the effect of having larger samples. Some of the problem of large variance can also be mitigated by using multilevel modeling techniques (as per Parker et al., 2015, 2018). Although designs that blend within- and between-participant analysis are generally desirable, within-participant designs can be highly affected by attrition (i.e., participants not taking part in all parts of the study), which requires dropping part of the data. Researchers may therefore consider sample size not only between, but also within participants.

Timelines

How long in total does it take to design, collect, clean, and analyze data from a research project that uses HRV? People work at differing speeds. However, particularly when students are contemplating using HRV, some caution is advisable. It is usually not feasible to apply HRV measurement in a Honours or Masters research project (i.e., student research projects of 1 year duration), unless the supervisors have extended knowledge and experience using HRV and have a research team around them with sufficient funds to support the project. It takes time to understand what HRV can and cannot measure very well, and to get an overview of the relevant literature in the target field of social science, and in physiology. This is difficult to achieve in less than half a year. Add to this the time required to design a research project, and collect the data, and it quickly becomes infeasible for many students to use HRV in their project and still graduate on time. Even for PhD students well supported by their supervisors and institutions, there are almost always practical limitations in place, from the number of available recording devices, to the availability of participants in research, for which several months need to be budgeted in. The study by Fooken (2017) collected data over the course of 3 years, mainly due to limits to the number of eligible participants. Moreover, in the lab-in-field study by Parker et al. (2015), it took 1 year for useable data to be collected from 72 participants, each of whom wore a heart rate monitor for a 1-week period while reporting daily via surveys on their work stressors. In contrast, in the lab study of Parker et al. (2014), data collection was completed over 3 months, with 110 participants run in groups of three to five and about 90 min spent in the lab by each group.

After data collection, data cleaning can take one to several months. Only at this point does the scope of a classical postgraduate research project start, i.e., the analysis of the data and the description of results. However, in a practical sense, by this point an HRV researcher is already easily in year two of the research project. The process is additionally slowed by the scarcity of senior researchers who have already worked with HRV data. For these reasons, using HRV is recommended only for longer-term research projects that are well resourced.

SUMMARY

We have shared four sets of experience-based insights in this chapter.

First, we pointed out that HRV data is a complicated construct, and that understanding it requires becoming familiar with at least part of the central literature discussing this type of physiological measurement. We also discussed different measurements (HF, RSA, RMSSD, LFHF, and others) that are available, and noted that there is no overall consensus on which measure is the uncontested best one. We use HF and LFHF, estimated using frequency-domain methods, in our studies and have found these to be the most convincing indicators. However, there are arguments for different measures and these should be considered before making a choice.

Second, we reviewed a number of practical considerations to do with HRV data collection and cleaning. These include advisable durations of HRV measurement, synchronization with variables of interest related to the research question, and use of within- versus between-participant variation. We also included a short checklist and other advice regarding how to get a good recording and minimize measurement error, as well as advice on equipment and experimental design choices, and how collected data can subsequently be cleaned.

Third, we discussed when HRV data might be preferable to other data. We argued that using HRV may be most promising in laboratory studies with a larger number of participants studied at the same time, for which other, more extensive, recording tools such as brain scanners are not usable. HRV may also be a useful tool for lab-in-the-field studies, as HRV measurements do not (or only minimally) interfere with daily activities. When comparing HRV to other recording tools, costs are another important practical issue that we discussed. We also discussed the issue that required sample sizes are larger due to the relatively large variance in HRV measurements.

Finally, we discussed the time necessary to carry out a research project using HRV. While we argue that HRV studies tend to be too extensive for research projects carried out in the context of Honours or Masters programs without intensive support from experienced researchers, establishing a research agenda over the course of 2–3 years appears feasible. However, throughout all steps of the research, time-intensive work needs to be budgeted for, including fully understanding the available measures, acquiring recording devices, data collection, data cleaning, and fitting one's own research into the debate in the field.

References

Appelhans, B. M., & Luecken, L. J. (2006). Heart rate variability as an index of regulated emotional responding. *Review of General Psychology*, *10*(3), 229.

Beda, A., Simpson, D. M., Carvalho, N. C., & Carvalho, A. R. S. (2014). Low-frequency heart rate variability is related to the breath-to-breath variability in the respiratory pattern. *Psychophysiology*, *51*(2), 197–205.

Berntson, G. G., Thomas Bigger, J., Eckberg, D. L., Grossman, P., Kaufmann, P. G., Malik, M., et al. (1997). Heart rate variability: Origins, methods, and interpretive caveats. *Psychophysiology*, *34*(6), 623–648.

Berntson, G. G., Norman, G. J., Hawkley, L. C., & Cacioppo, J. T. (2008). Cardiac autonomic balance vs. cardiac regulatory capacity. *Psychophysiology*, *45*(4), 643–652.

Camm, A. J., Malik, M., Bigger, J. T., Breithardt, G., Cerutti, S., Cohen, R. J., et al. (1996). Heart rate variability. Standards of measurement, physiological interpretation, and clinical use. *European Heart Journal*, *17*(3), 354–381.

Dulleck, U., Fooken, J., Newton, C., Ristl, A., Schaffner, M., & Torgler, B. (2016). Tax compliance and psychic costs: Behavioral experimental evidence using a physiological marker. *Journal of Public Economics*, *134*, 9–18.

Fooken, J. (2017). Heart rate variability indicates emotional value during pro-social economic laboratory decisions with large external validity. *Scientific Reports, 7.*

Fooken, J., Morton, R., & Torgler, B. (2018). *Physiological responses when making emotional votes* (Mimeo).

Fooken, J., & Schaffner, M. (2016). The role of psychological and physiological factors in decision making under risk and in a dilemma. *Frontiers in Behavioral Neuroscience, 10*, 2.

Geisler, F. C., Vennewald, N., Kubiak, T., & Weber, H. (2010). The impact of heart rate variability on subjective well-being is mediated by emotion regulation. *Personality and Individual Differences, 49*(7), 723–728.

Greenaway, K., Parker, S. L., Hofmann, W., Newton, C., & Jimmieson, N. L. (2018). *Bodily awareness promotes emotion awareness and emotion regulation* (Mimeo).

Heathers, J. A., Brown, N. J., Coyne, J. C., & Friedman, H. L. (2015). The elusory upward spiral: A reanalysis of Kok et al. (2013). *Psychological Science, 26*(7), 1140–1143.

Hoover, A., Singh, A., Fishel-Brown, S., & Muth, E. (2012). Real-time detection of workload changes using heart rate variability. *Biomedical Signal Processing and Control, 7*(4), 333–341.

Jamieson, J. (1999). Dealing with baseline differences: Two principles and two dilemmas. *International Journal of Psychophysiology, 31*(2), 155–161.

Jorna, P. G. (1992). Spectral analysis of heart rate and psychological state: A review of its validity as a workload index. *Biological Psychology, 34*(2–3), 237–257.

Massaro, S., & Pecchia, L. (2016). Heart rate variability (HRV) analysis: A methodology for organizational neuroscience. *Organizational Research Methods.* https://doi.org/10.1177/1094428116681072.

Parker, S. L., Sonnentag, S., Jimmieson, N. L., & Newton, C. E. (2018). *A calm body and calm mind are both important for relaxing after work and feeling energized the next work day.* (Mimeo).

Parker, S. L., Jimmieson, N. L., & Newton, C. J. (2015). Do specific work events trigger emotion regulation? A diary study on heart rate variability. Included in L. Venz & D. Unger symposium "I feel good but why?" In *Proceedings of the 75th annual meeting of the Academy of Management, 7–11 August, Vancouver, Canada.*

Parker, S. L., Laurie, K. R., Newton, C. J., & Jimmieson, N. L. (2014). Regulatory focus moderates the relationship between task control and physiological and psychological markers of stress: A work simulation study. *International Journal of Psychophysiology, 94*(3), 390–398.

Porges, S. W. (2007). The polyvagal perspective. *Biological Psychology, 74*(2), 116–143.

Porges, S. W., & Byrne, E. A. (1992). Research methods for measurement of heart rate and respiration. *Biological Psychology, 34*(2–3), 93–130.

Segerstrom, S. C., & Nes, L. S. (2007). Heart rate variability reflects self-regulatory strength, effort, and fatigue. *Psychological Science, 18*(3), 275–281.

Task Force of the European Society of Cardiology and the North American Society of Pacing and Electrophysiology (1996). Heart rate variability standards of measurement, physiological interpretation, and clinical use. *Circulation, 93*, 1043–1065.

Tarvainen, M. P., Niskanen, J. P., Lipponen, J. A., Ranta-Aho, P. O., & Karjalainen, P. A. (2014). Kubios HRV—heart rate variability analysis software. *Computer Methods and Programs in Biomedicine, 113*(1), 210–220.

Thayer, J. F., Åhs, F., Fredrikson, M., Sollers, J. J., III, & Wager, T. D. (2012). A meta-analysis of heart rate variability and neuroimaging studies: Implications for heart rate variability as a marker of stress and health. *Neuroscience & Biobehavioral Reviews, 36*(2), 747–756.

Torgler, B. (2018). Opportunities and challenges of portable biological, social, and behavioral sensing systems for the social sciences. In G. Foster (Ed.), *Biophysical measurement in experimental social science research.* Cambridge: Academic Press.

Zahn, D., Adams, J., Krohn, J., Wenzel, M., Mann, C. G., Gomille, L. K., et al. (2016). Heart rate variability and self-control—A meta-analysis. *Biological Psychology, 115*, 9–26.

Index

Note: Page numbers followed by *f* indicate figures and *t* indicate tables.

H

I

J

K

L

M

N

O

P

Q

R

FSC
www.fsc.org
MIX
Papier | Fördert
gute Waldnutzung
FSC® C083411

Kolibri 360 GmbH
Ferdinand-Jühlke-Straße 7
99095 Erfurt, Deutschland
produktsicherheit@kolibri360.de